VIOLENT VICTORS

PRINCETON STUDIES IN INTERNATIONAL HISTORY AND POLITICS

Tanisha M. Fazal, G. John Ikenberry, William C. Wohlforth, and Keren Yarhi-Milo, Series Editors

For a full list of titles in the series, go to https://press.princeton.edu/series/princeton-studies-in-international-history-and-politics

Violent Victors: Why Bloodstained Parties Win Postwar Elections, Sarah Zukerman Daly

An Unwritten Future: Realism and Uncertainty in World Politics, Jonathan Kirshner

Undesirable Immigrants: Why Racism Persists in International Migration, Andrew S. Rosenberg

Human Rights for Pragmatists: Social Power in Modern Times, Jack Snyder

Seeking the Bomb: Strategies of Nuclear Proliferation, Vipin Narang

The Spectre of War: International Communism and the Origins of World War II, Jonathan Haslam

Active Defense: China's Military Strategy since 1949, M. Taylor Fravel

Strategic Instincts: The Adaptive Advantages of Cognitive Biases in International Politics, Dominic D. P. Johnson

Divided Armies: Inequality and Battlefield Performance in Modern War, Jason Lyall

After Victory: Institutions, Strategic Restraint, and the Rebuilding of Order after Major Wars, New Edition, G. John Ikenberry

Cult of the Irrelevant: The Waning Influence of Social Science on National Security, Michael C. Desch

Secret Wars: Covert Conflict in International Politics, Austin Carson

Who Fights for Reputation: The Psychology of Leaders in International Conflict, Keren Yarhi-Milo

Aftershocks: Great Powers and Domestic Reforms in the Twentieth Century, Seva Gunitsky

Why Wilson Matters: The Origin of American Liberal Internationalism and Its Crisis Today, Tony Smith

Powerplay: The Origins of the American Alliance System in Asia, Victor D. Cha

Economic Interdependence and War, Dale C. Copeland

Knowing the Adversary: Leaders, Intelligence, and Assessment of Intentions in International Relations, Keren Yarhi-Milo

Nuclear Strategy in the Modern Era: Regional Powers and International Conflict, Vipin Narang

Violent Victors

WHY BLOODSTAINED PARTIES WIN
POSTWAR ELECTIONS

SARAH ZUKERMAN DALY

PRINCETON UNIVERSITY PRESS

PRINCETON & OXFORD

Published by Princeton University Press
41 William Street, Princeton, New Jersey 08540
99 Banbury Road, Oxford OX2 6JX

press.princeton.edu

All Rights Reserved
ISBN: 978-0-691-23132-7
ISBN (pbk.): 978-0-691-23133-4
ISBN (e-book): 978-0-691-23134-1

British Library Cataloging-in-Publication Data is available

Editorial: Bridget Flannery-McCoy and Alena Chekanov
Production Editorial: Jenny Wolkowicki
Cover design: Katie Osborne
Production: Lauren Reese
Publicity: Kate Hensley and Charlotte Coyne
Copyeditor: Joseph Dahm

This book has been composed in Arno Pro

10 9 8 7 6 5 4 3 2 1

To Weston, Sebastian, Alice, and Louise

CONTENTS

Illustrations   ix

Acknowledgments   xiii

Abbreviations   xvii

1	Introduction	1
2	Political Stage, Actors, and Audience	15
3	Violent-Victors Theory of Political Behavior after War	25
4	Postwar Voters and Survey Experiments	63
5	Military Draw in El Salvador	110
6	Government Victory in Guatemala	158
7	Rebel Victory in Nicaragua	194
8	Political Life after War Globally, 1970–2015	210
9	Implications for Postwar Peace, Justice, Democracy, and Governance	240
10	Conclusion	253

Appendix   263

Notes   277

References   331

Index   369

ILLUSTRATIONS

Figures

2.1. A Continuum of War Outcomes   23

3.1. Claim to the Security Issue: A Gulliver among the Lilliputians   35

4.1. Government Belligerent Party Strategies: Experimental Design   79

4.2. Rebel Belligerent Party Strategies: Experimental Design   80

4.3. Combat Boots: Army versus Rebel   81

4.4. Effect of Government Belligerent Party Strategies on Probability of Being Deemed More Competent on Prospective Security   83

4.5. Probability of Being Preferred on Security for Selected Government Belligerent Candidate Profiles   85

4.6. Effect of Government Belligerent Party Strategies on Probability of Receiving Credit for War Termination   86

4.7. Probability of Being Elected for Selected Government Belligerent Candidate Profiles   87

4.8. Probability of Being Elected for Selected Rebel Belligerent Candidate Profiles   87

5.1. Campaign Ad: ARENA Saving El Salvador from Communism   125

5.2. Campaign Ad: ARENA's Hand Alone, Signing the Peace Accords   126

5.3. ARENA Campaign Plan: Targeting of Undecided Voters   129

5.4. ARENA: Potential "Restrained Sovereign" Presidential Slogans   130

5.5. "We Will Fight Crime Since We Have the Experience"   133

5.6. "That the Crimes Began When We Demobilized Is Pure Coincidence" 134

5.7. "We Will Eliminate the Criminals and Organized Crime. . . . Careful, We Will Be Left with No Base" 134

5.8. ARENA Maps of FMLN Violence: Undermining FMLN's Security Competence 135

5.9. "I Commit Not to Destroy All That I Have Promised" 136

5.10. FMLN's Cartoon Campaign Ads 138

5.11. FMLN Slogan, "First, the People" 140

5.12. Findings of Truth Commission and Public Perception of Relative Blame 145

6.1. FRG Logo: "Security, Welfare, Justice" 168

6.2. Text Analysis of FRG versus PAN Security Platforms 171

6.3. FRG Vote Share across Ideological Spectrum 183

6.4. Wartime Government Atrocities and FRG Postwar Vote Share at the Municipal Level 184

8.1. Frequency of War Outcomes in the CWSP Dataset 217

8.2. War Outcomes and Rebel Vote Shares in Founding Elections 222

8.3. War Outcomes and Government Belligerent Vote Shares in Founding Elections 223

8.4. War Outcomes and Electoral Performance in Cleaner and Less Clean Elections 224

8.5. Subnational Wartime Victimization by Rebels and Postwar Rebel Successor Party Vote Share 226

8.6. Subnational Wartime Victimization by Government and Postwar Government Successor Party Vote Share 227

8.7. Subnational War Outcomes and Belligerent Successor Party Vote Share 228

8.8. Proportion of Security Voters around the World 230

8.9. Marginal Effect of Being a Security Voter on Voting for the Militarily Winning Belligerent Party 230

8.10. War Outcomes and Vote Shares in Founding Elections following Ethnic versus Nonethnic Conflicts 232

8.11. War Outcomes and Vote Shares in Founding Elections with Clientelistic and Programmatic Linkages 238

9.1. Effect of Paramilitary Politician Win on Thefts 250

9.2. Effect of Paramilitary Politician Win on Education Coverage 251

A4.1. Alternative Combinations of Party Strategy on Perceived Competence on Security 265

A4.2. Santismo's Rule of Law versus Uribismo's Law and Order 266

A8.1. Wartime Victimization and Successor Party Vote Share 268

A9.1. Validating the Regression Discontinuity Design: McCrary Test 276

Tables

3.1. Rationale of Tactical Immoderation: Parties' Strategic Interaction 42

3.2. Equilibrium Party Strategies after Large-Scale Violence in War 57

4.1. Survey Sample of Victims and Nonvictims 68

4.2. Offsetting Experiment Results 73

4.3. Offsetting Experiment: Heterogenous Results 75

4.4. Order Effects of Mitigation and Contrition Narratives on Probability of Being Elected 77

4.5. Parties' Optimal and Actual Strategies and Their Electoral Implications in 2018 92

4.6. Determinants of Vote Choice, 2018 Presidential Election 102

4.7. Secret versus Open Ballot Results 105

4.8. Information and Judgments about Atrocities 108

5.1. ARENA Messaging Objectives 123

5.2. Determinants of Vote Choice, El Salvador 1994 150

6.1. Hand Coding of Security Platforms, Belligerent FRG versus Nonbelligerent PAN 172

6.2. Determinants of Vote Choice, Guatemala 1999 189

8.1. Correlates of Civil War Successor Party Success Around the World 220

9.1. Empirical Cases of Postconflict War and Peace   244

9.2. Effects of Founding Election Results on Postwar Justice and Democracy   246

9.3. Difference in Means: Security and Public Goods Outcomes   248

9.4. RD Estimates: Security Outcomes   249

9.5. RD Estimates: Public Goods Outcomes and Spending   249

A4.1. Descriptive Statistics of Survey Sample   263

A4.2. Offsetting Experiment: All Outcomes   264

A4.3. Results of Hand Coding of Security Platforms   266

A5.1. Party Manifesto Project Variables: Right-Left Party Positions   267

A8.1. Summary Statistics, Civil War Successor Party Dataset   268

A8.2. Correlates of Civil War Successor Party Success, Robustness Checks   269

A8.3. Alternative Explanations and Endogeneity   270

A8.4. Sources of Data on Subnational Violence, War Outcomes, and Postwar Elections   271

A8.5. World Values Survey and Founding Election Dates   273

A9.1. Correlates of Remilitarization after Postwar Elections   274

A9.2. Validating the RD Design: Continuity Tests, Lagged Outcomes   276

ACKNOWLEDGMENTS

THE SEED FOR THIS PROJECT was planted in an undergraduate course at Stanford University in which I learned about the politics of human rights. We studied the tragic coup and brutality that brought Pinochet to power in Chile and consolidated his dictatorial rule. I came to anticipate that all Chileans would reject this dictator who stole the lives and imprisoned over forty thousand of their copatriots. Shortly thereafter, I moved to Santiago, where I lived with an extraordinary Chilean family. To my surprise, my Chilean family supported Pinochet and joined the ranks of approximately 40 percent of Chileans who were pro-Pinochet at this time, *after* the transition to democratization, *after* the threat of coercion against the political opposition had waned. I went to visit the places where Pinochet forces had tortured and then disappeared innocent civilians. I heard the stories of victims. I could not reconcile these two realities.

Between 2006 and 2009, while living in Colombia, I was similarly perplexed by the reality I confronted. Despite being targeted by arbitrary massacres, rapes, and homicides, victimized populations I lived among in Antioquia, Córdoba, and Chocó tolerated and even endorsed the violent nonstate actor who had unleashed this ruthlessness. I have spent the years since trying to solve this puzzle.

Many people have aided my journey to understand patterns of posttransition support for political actors who inflicted mass violence. I am deeply indebted to Virginia Page Fortna for advising that what might have been a kernel of my first book become a full-fledged second book manuscript and to Jack Snyder for volleying my theory with the giants of political philosophy. To my extraordinary Columbia and external colleagues who workshopped the manuscript with such consideration: your mark is on the page. This includes Virginia Page Fortna, Timothy Frye, Anna Grzymala-Busse, John Huber, Susan Hyde, Robert Jervis, Kimuli Kasara, Noam Lupu, John Marshall, Gwyneth McClendon, Maria Victoria Murillo, Carlo Prato, Jack Snyder, Jeremy

Weinstein, and Keren Yarhi-Milo. Many others have provided invaluable feedback on parts of the project at different moments in time. I am very thankful to Deniz Aksoy, Sheri Berman, Nancy Bermeo, Johanna Birnir, Robert Blair, Taylor Boas, Ian Callison, Allison Carnegie, Daniel Corstange, Jon Elster, Gustavo Flores-Macías, Frances Hagopian, Caroline Hartzell, Alisha Holland, Lise Morjé Howard, Reyko Huang, John Ishiyama, Turkuler Isiksel, David Johnston, Morgan Kaplan, Robert Keohane, Elizabeth King, Melissa Lee, Steven Levitsky, Scott Mainwaring, Kimberly Marten, Roger Petersen, Stephanie Schwartz, Jacob Shapiro, Hillel Soifer, Elisabeth Jean Wood, and Deborah Yashar. Three research assistants were integral to the project: Pablo Argote Tironi, Jonathan Panter, and Oscar Pocasangre. I am also grateful to Juan Diego Duque, Julian Geréz, Olivia Grinberg, Minju Kwon, Ashley Litwin, Camilo Nieto Matíz, Taylor Miller, Jasmine Park, Valeria Restrepo, Manu Singh, Wenjun Sun, and Lucía Tiscornia. For facilitating my fieldwork, I sincerely thank Michael Allison, Gerson Arias, Regina Bateson, Alejandro Eder, Ana Milena López, James Loxton, Andrés Suster, Juan Pablo Trujillo, and Valeria Vaninni. To all the people who shared their stories, at times very painful stories, with me, I am awed by your generosity and hope my words honor your voices.

The book's theory and empirics also benefited from input from participants at the Princeton University Comparative Politics Colloquium and International Relations Colloquium; Berkeley Comparative Politics Colloquium; University of Chicago Program on International Security Policy Seminar and Workshop on the State, Violence, and Social Control; MIT Security Studies Program Seminar; UNC Lethal Aid and Human Security Workshop; George Washington University Institute for Security and Conflict Studies Workshop; Columbia University Junior Faculty Workshop; Yale University Order, Conflict, and Violence Seminar; Harvard University David Rockefeller Center for Latin American Studies Seminar; Washington University in St. Louis Conference on Political Violence and Terrorism; Notre Dame Comparative Politics Working Group; University of Washington International Security Colloquium; Princeton ESOC Labs; Folke Bernadotte Academy Research Workshop; Temple University Comparative Politics Colloquium, Institute for Latin American Studies Seminar; Politics After War Research Network Conference; and annual meetings of the International Studies Association, American Political Science Association, and Latin American Studies Association.

Supplements, additions, and corrections can be accessed through the book's web page within the Princeton University Press site, https://press .princeton.edu/isbn/9780691231341.

My great appreciation goes to Bridget Flannery-McCoy and three anonymous reviewers for providing me critical guidance and helping me transform my draft manuscript into a book. I express my gratitude to the editors for including this book in the Princeton Studies in International History and Politics series. I share my appreciation with the production team at Princeton University Press.

This project would not have been possible without the extraordinary support of the Carnegie Corporation of New York, which awarded me a two-year Andrew Carnegie award. The Princeton Program on Latin American Studies provided me a fellowship, fertile environment, rare ephemera collection, and feedback that greatly nurtured the book. A Folke Bernadotte Academy Research Grant provided critical support for my original survey, and the Minerva-US Institute of Peace, Peace and Security Early Career Scholar Award sponsored the creation of the database of paramilitary politics. I am grateful to the Arnold A. Saltzman Institute of War and Peace Studies and the Institute for Latin American Studies, my research homes.

Finally, to Bobby, Weston, Sebastian, Alice, and Louise, and to the rest of my family, for keeping me tethered during every stage of this process. The initial draft of this book was written in my daughter's first three weeks of life. Named after Barbara Cooney's Miss Rumphius, she is asked, "What will you do, little Alice, to make the world more beautiful?" If small glimmers of hope for human action may be gleaned from these pages, this will be her first contribution. This book is dedicated to my children.

ABBREVIATIONS

ANN New Nation Alliance / Alianza Nueva Nación

ANSESAL National Security Agency of El Salvador / Agencia Nacional de Seguridad Salvadoreña

ARENA Nationalist Republican Alliance / Alianza Republicana Nacionalista

CD Democratic Center / Centro Democrático

CDN Nicaraguan Democratic Coordinating Committee / Coordinadora Democrática Nicaragüense

CEDE Center for Studies on Economic Development / Centro de Estudios sobre Desarrollo Económico

CEH Commission for Historical Clarification / Comisión para el Escalarecimiento Histórico

CNDD-FDD National Council for the Defence of Democracy–Forces for the Defence of Democracy / Conseil National pour la Défense de la Démocratie–Forces pour la Défense de la Démocratie

CWSP Civil War Successor Party

DIA Authentic Integral Development / Desarrollo Integral Auténtico

EGP Guerrilla Army of the Poor / Ejército Guerrillero de los Pobres

ELN National Liberation Army / Ejército de Liberación Nacional

ERP People's Revolutionary Army / Ejército Revolucionario del Pueblo

FARC Revolutionary Armed Forces of Colombia / Fuerzas Armadas Revolucionarias de Colombia

FDN Nicaraguan Democratic Force / Fuerza Democrática Nicaragüense

FEVCOL Colombian Federation of Victims of the FARC / Federación Colombiana de Víctimas de las FARC

FMLN Farabundo Martí National Liberation Front / Frente Farabundo Martí para la Liberación Nacional

FPL Farabundo Martí Popular Liberation Forces / Fuerzas Populares de Liberación Farabundo Martí

FRELETIN Revolutionary Front for an Independent East Timor / Frente Revolucionária de Timor-Leste Independente

FRG Guatemalan Republican Front / Frente Republicano Guatemalteco

FRODEBU Front for Democracy in Burundi / Front pour la Démocratie au Burundi

FRUD Front for the Restoration of Unity and Democracy / Front pour la Restoration de l'Unité et de la Démocratie

FRUD-AD Front for the Restoration of Unity and Democracy–Ahmed Dini / Front pour la Restoration de l'Unité et de la Démocratie–Ahmed Dini

FSLN Sandinista National Liberation Front / Frente Sandinista de Liberación Nacional

HDZ Croatian Democratic Union / Hrvatska Demokratska Zajednica

IUDOP University Institute for Public Opinion / Instituto Universitario de Opinión Pública

LAPOP Latin American Public Opinion Project

LTTE Liberation Tigers of Tamil Eelam

MOE Electoral Observation Mission / Misión Observatorio Electoral

NSA nonstate actor

ORDEN Nationalist Democratic Organization / Organización Democrática Nacionalista

PACS Civil Self-Defense Patrols / Patrullas de Autodefenas Civil

PAN National Advancement Party / Partido de Avanzada Nacional

PCDN Democratic Conservative Party of Nicaragua / Partido
Conservador Demócrata de Nicaragua

PCN National Conciliation Party / Partido de Conciliación
Nacional

PCS Salvadoran Communist Party / Partido Comunista
Salvadoreño

PDC Christian Democratic Party / Partido Demócrata Cristiano

PLI Independent Liberal Party / Partido Liberal Independiente

PLN Nationalist Liberal Party / Partido Liberal Nacionalista

PMP Party Manifesto Project

PRTC Revolutionary Party of Central American Workers / Partido
Revolucionario de los Trabajadores Centroamericanos

REMHI Recovery of Historical Memory Project / Proyecto
Interdiocesano de Recuperación de la Memória Histórica

RN Armed Forces of National Resistance / Fuerzas Armadas de
Resistencia Nacional

RPF Rwandan Patriotic Front / Front Patriotique Rwandais

SWAPO South West Africa People's Organisation

TNA Tamil National Alliance

UCDP Uppsala Conflict Data Program

UNID Democratic Leftist Union / Unidad de Izquierda Democrática

UNO National Opposition Union / Unión Nacional Opositora

URNG Guatemalan National Revolutionary Unity / Unidad
Revolucionaria Nacional Guatemalteca

V-DEM Varieties of Democracy Project

WVS World Values Survey

VIOLENT VICTORS

1

Introduction

Puzzle: Why Do Bloodstained Parties Win Postwar Elections?

In Guatemala, Efraín Ríos Montt, a "merciless" and "born-again butcher,"[1] led the country's armed forces as they perpetrated 86,000 murders and 90 percent of the civil war's widespread atrocities.[2] After the war ended, Ríos Montt's party, the Guatemalan Republican Front (FRG), competed in the 1999 presidential and legislative elections that founded the country's postwar political order. U.S. expectations of the outcome are revealed in declassified U.S. diplomatic cables: "An [electoral] victory of Rios would prove very difficult given his reputation as a major human rights violator."[3] The Truth Commissions had publicized the facts of the brutality; a genocide case had been filed against Ríos Montt. And yet Ríos Montt's FRG party won in elections seen as "free and fair,"[4] defeating a competitive opposition party that was untainted by the bloody past. Ríos Montt himself became president of Congress. FRG won a majority in every province, even, astoundingly, in the indigenous zones that had suffered the most from Ríos Montt's scorched-earth tactics. "Witnesses to and even survivors of the massacres that had taken place under his administration"[5]—an estimated 47 percent of victims[6]—voted for the executioner-turned-democrat.[7]

Similarly in El Salvador in 1994, the ARENA party,[8] the "aboveground alter ego of the notorious 'death squad' networks,"[9] won free democratic elections,[10] besting the far less violent FMLN[11] rebel party and an opposition party unimplicated in the country's carnage.[12] Although the death squads had been responsible, with the armed forces, for 95 percent of the war's 70,000 political killings, ARENA secured the votes of 40 percent of victims, including 40 percent of displaced victims.[13] Votes for ARENA were collected even in areas most brutalized by state violence, in elections widely seen as "orderly, peaceful, and transparent . . . which permitted the popular will of the Salvadoran people to be expressed . . . without fear of violent incidents."[14]

In Colombia, the party of President Álvaro Uribe, who faced hundreds of investigations for ties to illegal paramilitaries, and a spree of extrajudicial killings labeled "one of the worst episodes of mass atrocity in the Western Hemisphere in recent decades,"[15] also won multiparty postwar democratic elections. After the paramilitary armies had demobilized, politicians linked to them won a third of the country's congressional seats and hundreds of local elected offices. Even in places terrorized by paramilitary massacres, assassinations, and disappearances,[16] where citizens historically had backed the guerrillas, 88 percent of the population deemed the presence of the paramilitaries positive and 41 percent viewed the ex-paramilitaries as protectors.[17] "Being a paramilitary victim or nonvictim [was] not a characteristic that [could] determine if the [paramilitary politicians would] win more or less support,"[18] in an environment in which "everyone [knew] . . . [which politicians had] paramilitary connections."[19]

How could this happen? Yet these cases are not aberrations. Around the world, after episodes of mass political violence in war, citizens choose who will govern their countries in posttransition elections that are critical to peace, justice, democracy, and governance. In these elections, astonishingly large numbers of citizens vote for political parties that have deep roots in the bloodstained organizations of the past, even those most guilty of heinous atrocities. These belligerent successors often outperform nonbelligerent parties and win clean elections; they attract votes not only from their core supporters but also from swing voters and even from the victims of their wartime violence.

The electoral successes of bloodstained parties cannot be understood with conventional explanations. Across postwar elections globally, parties that proved electorally successful were not those that had been more restrained in their wartime violence; the votes they won came not just from people who were their beneficiaries or at least not victims of their transgressions.[20] Instead, belligerents that committed high levels of wartime brutality and that won militarily performed well in the elections; they performed just as well as war victors that had refrained from extensive atrocities. Votes for belligerents' successor parties in regions that had been terrorized were comparable to votes in regions left unscathed by the belligerents' wartime campaigns. Victims themselves voted as often for their perpetrators as for parties unstained by war.

This cannot be explained by the fog of war, or that voters did not know what had happened during wartime. While this fog was still lifting, in many places elections followed widely publicized reports of truth commissions, so voters could well have known whom to blame for the violence before casting their votes. It also cannot be explained by an argument that these belligerent successor parties won only coerced votes[21] in nondemocratic elections, or only agreed to elections they believed they could win.[22] They also won abundant freely cast votes in postwar elections, widely seen as free and fair, and held in the aftermath of nearly every armed conflict.[23] Although alternative explanations based in well-established determinants of political behavior, such as economic voting, clientelism, and partisanship,[24] can account for partial patterns of the elections, they leave significant variation in political life after war unexplained.

This book illuminates that critical unexplained share of the vote delivered to bloodstained wartime belligerents by looking to the experiences, outcomes, and legacies of significant violence in war. Using the tools of political behavior, it joins an important body of international relations scholarship that leverages these tools to understand public opinion toward the use of force and to explain the electoral drivers and consequences of security in its international and domestic manifestations.[25]

The Argument in Brief: Violent Victors Secure the Future

Why do parties that have engaged in violent atrocities in civil war perform well in postwar democratic elections? How do parties guilty of violence against the civilian population seek that population's votes? Why would a victimized population elect its tormentors to govern it? This book develops a counterintuitive answer: these bloodstained parties, if victorious in war, successfully present themselves as the most credible providers of social peace.

War outcomes, then, can tell us what to expect of the electoral prospects of militarily belligerent successor parties. Belligerents' electoral opponents might seem to have an advantage: parties without roots in the violent organizations of the war can claim a cleaner human rights record and show themselves in a positive light compared to the successors of belligerent transgressors. Their civilian elites assert that they can oblige the government to control itself, and this claim is made more credible by their record of abiding by the rules designed to protect the population's civil liberties.[26]

The victorious or stalemated belligerent must counter the attention to its dismal human rights record that would raise doubt about its ability to control its use of coercive power against the population. A winner in war earns and may deploy a potent electoral weapon: credit for ceasing the wartime violence. To adroitly play the strategic game of postwar politics, it may leverage this weapon in order to alter how voters judge the past and predict the future.[27] Specifically, it may seek electoral rewards for not inflicting continued war against the population and for instead ending the population's suffering and giving it the security of peace. Such credit for war termination may lend it a cloak of immunity under which a bloodstained party's record of coercion becomes not an electoral liability but an asset, bolstering its reputation for competence on security. It can argue that its record uniquely positions it to provide sustained stability: that it alone is powerful enough to "overawe" others who might threaten disorder,[28] and thus that it alone can "enable the government to control the governed."[29] To counter valid suspicions that it could use its power to repeat its past offenses, it makes a show of purging rights abusers from its ranks, but not the strongman who exemplifies its security credentials. It also moderates programmatically and promises to serve and protect the broader electorate as its constituency.

Both the nonbelligerent and belligerent parties seek to harness the power of media to propagate their respective messages and persuade the citizenry of their claims to restrained protection, a valence issue for voters. These voters, battered by a "war of all against all," crave security—particularly those who are victims, direct and indirect, of the conflict's violence. They weigh which party they can trust to handle the tasks of securing their future. As the establishment of political order from war is decided through elections, these voters wrestle with the foundational questions of human collective life: who can seek to establish the "monopoly of the legitimate use of physical force"?[30] Who is best at wielding coercion to curb societal violence?

In this dilemma, I argue, voters are more persuaded by the victorious combatant party than by less violent belligerents that lost the war, or by nonbelligerents who are untainted by war.[31] They reward the war winner for the stability of peace, rather than punishing it for the atrocity of war. As a result, they deem the war winner better able than its less tainted rivals to preserve societal order going forward. A Madisonian variant of Hobbes wins out and core, swing, and even victim voters elect what I call "Restrained Leviathans" to govern them.[32]

The electoral performance of the heir to the militarily vanquished belligerent, meanwhile, is constrained by its inferior war outcome, and such a party generally makes a poor showing in the election: it is blamed for past violence, while it lacks credibility as a provider of future security. If, however, it apologizes for its transgressions and advances a nonmainstream, nonsecurity platform, it might earn a small foothold in postwar politics and a reputation that can help it in future elections.

I test this explanation for the electoral success of violent victors with a rich empirical design, combining extensive fieldwork; individual-level experimental data from an original survey in Colombia; party-level archival evidence from El Salvador, Guatemala, and Nicaragua; and cross-national evidence from data on all 205 belligerent parties around the world that transitioned from war between 1970 and 2015.

Implications for Peace, Democracy, Justice, and Governance

This book explains why people vote for the very political actors guilty of violence against the civilian population. It argues that war outcomes influence the results of founding postwar elections by guiding party strategy and voter behavior. The selection of bloodstained parties in these pivotal elections is highly consequential for fundamental questions of postwar peace and war recurrence, democracy and political development, justice and reconciliation, the rule of law, and public goods provision. In such postwar elections, voters tend to opt for an end to armed conflict, but at the price of justice, liberalism, and welfare.

War and Peace

The elections at the center of this book constitute a linchpin in theories of whether war resumes or peace consolidates. Scholars herald such elections as conducive to sustained conflict termination by establishing institutionalized channels for opposition, which tend to dampen subsequent violent conflicts and limit social unrest.[33] An open political system and access to political participation have been found to inoculate a society against a return to civil conflict,[34] and to bestow legitimacy upon the postwar political order. Allowing ballots should diminish any resort to bullets.[35]

At the same time, the advent of elections in postwar societies also brings risk.[36] There is concern, specifically, that, as Dawn Brancati and Jack Snyder warn, electoral "losers will refuse to accept the results peacefully"[37] and return to war.[38] This concern has motivated a robust body of scholarship aimed at determining how to harness the benefits of democracy for peace while mitigating democracy's perils; among the proposed tools are inclusive elections (with provisions for rebel participation),[39] delaying the elections,[40] deploying international election monitors,[41] and institutionalizing power sharing.[42]

The book departs from this pioneering scholarship by focusing not on such structural features of the pivotal founding elections but instead on their results. In so doing, it opens the black box of the elections themselves and illuminates the relationship between how well belligerents perform in the elections and the decision to remilitarize.

The book's argument implies that postwar elections, in and of themselves, are not likely to lead to a return to violence. Instead, such elections should be stabilizing if the balance of military power remains constant after war.[43] The prevalence of security voting gives war victors the upper hand in the elections, and these victorious belligerent parties emerge as the most capable of both suppressing their own violence and deterring their opponents—the losers—from remilitarizing. With an unaltered distribution of military power after war, there exists little reason for either the war winner or war loser to reinitiate violence; the election results reflect this underlying power balance, and a new war would be unlikely to yield a different outcome.[44] "Negative peace"[45] should thus hold. Such stability, in turn, facilitates economic recovery.[46]

However, if the balance of power instead inverts after war's end and if the electorate, using the heuristic of war outcomes to guide their votes, chooses the now weaker war winner, electoral results become misaligned with military power and the newly empowered war loser has electoral incentives to return to war. This is because the strong correlation between war outcomes and electoral performance in the first postwar political contest creates perverse incentives for belligerents: a return to war becomes beneficial rather than costly for a newly strengthened war loser.[47] This belligerent may reinitiate fighting to take advantage of the power change, hoping to try its hand at the polls again in the future from a position of a superior war outcome. The founding selection of bloodstained parties therefore has critical implications for whether war recurs or peace sustains.

Democracy

The war-to-peace transitions that are central to this book also strongly influence the prospects for democracy. Studies by Elisabeth Jean Wood, Virginia Page Fortna, and Reyko Huang tell when to anticipate democratization to emerge from war.[48] The work of Thomas Flores and Irfan Nooruddin, Caroline Hartzell and Matthew Hoddie, Aila Matanock, and Leonard Wantchekon underscores the fragility of such democratic elections where there is a history of violent conflict.[49]

This book's examination and explanation of why and how bloodstained parties perform well in postwar elections offer vital answers to questions of democratization. Adapting the logic of Dietrich Rueschemeyer, Evelyne Huber Stephens, and John Stephens, the book suggests that such election results, although perhaps surprising, may actually facilitate democratic stability because "those who have only to gain from democracy"—here, war-winning belligerent parties well positioned to succeed in elections—"will be its most reliable promoters and defenders."[50]

Many such parties born in the ashes of war prove durable, particularly if they are able to respond as voters' more diverse nonsecurity concerns proliferate and if the parties are able to cultivate political machines to mobilize voters and distribute patronage. War and revolutionary uprisings consolidated many of the world's strong parties.[51] Election to office in the founding elections may thereby transform these parties into stable democratic actors, cementing the political party system around them.[52] (Indeed, the book reveals significant path dependency for political development triggered by the critical juncture of the founding electoral contests). At the same time, like former autocrats following negotiated democratic transitions,[53] these belligerent participants, while often sustaining a minimalist version of democracy, tend not to advance a more liberal variant.[54] At times, they cause or allow later democratic backsliding.[55]

Justice

Postwar elections are the book's centerpiece. They reflect a critical tension between the goal of sustaining the termination of violence and the goal of holding the perpetrators of rights violations legally accountable. What is necessary electorally to avert instability and recurrent war may also protect human rights abusers. By enshrining amnesties, the elections may prevent countries from effectively closing the books on their nightmare pasts.[56]

This implication of the book joins the "peace-versus-justice" debate among scholars and practitioners of international transitional justice.[57] At the macro level, Martha Finnemore and Kathryn Sikkink advance a "logic of appropriateness," arguing that there is a moral and legal imperative to hold perpetrators swiftly to account criminally.[58] By this logic, security is the fruit of justice.[59] This "prosecute and punish" solution to what Samuel Huntington called the "torturer problem"[60] is echoed in micro-level studies of transitional justice across generations, which find, time after time, that descendants of victims seek political retribution against their perpetrators.[61]

On the other side of the debate, Monika Nalepa, Jack Snyder, and Leslie Vinjamuri advance a "logic of consequences," whereby possibilities for legal accountability are constrained as a practical matter by power balances, self-interest, and feasibility.[62] By this logic, justice is the fruit of security.[63] This accords with the realist tradition that identifies systems of norms and justice as the products of power politics and argues that great powers determine the standards of morality that best suit their interests. So, too, in the domestic arena, powerful political players lock in the legal regimes that best protect their own interests.[64]

The argument that peace and order constitute preconditions for justice, rather than the other way around, finds robust support in the micro-level literature on transitional justice in the immediate aftermath of war. Surveys conducted in diverse environments around the world show that victims do not primarily seek truth, punishment, and reparations; rather, they pursue security first, under which they can get on with their lives, disregard the past, and focus on other concerns such as power and jobs.[65]

In line with the latter approach, the implication of this book's argument is that, by voting perpetrators of atrocities into office, citizens reward rather than punish the past violence of the winning side. Armed with legitimate political power, the former abusers may engage in regressive justice and lock in their impunity, at least in the short to medium term. Their whitewashing of the violent past in their rhetoric and official historiography leaves a lasting scar by distorting national memory and the pursuit of truth. However, as peace consolidates, citizens gain breathing room from heightened insecurity and possibilities for justice may increase.[66]

Governance

The book's theory of "violent victors" has implications for governance, particularly social welfare and security provision. It suggests that the citizenry is likely to gain in the near term in the domain in which the militarily successful belligerent has a comparative advantage, competence, and expertise, and that is the security domain. However, because the belligerent successor party prioritizes law and order over other social and development expenditures, voters' electoral choices tend to lead to the sacrifice of social welfare. This is consistent with scholarship revealing how budget reallocation to defense cannibalizes spending on social services, degrading development outcomes.[67] It also aligns with research documenting the trade-off when ironfisted security policy has priority over alternative crime-reduction strategies, such as human capital enhancement, showing that, as a result, both rule of law and the provision of public goods degrade over time.[68]

In sum, the book's theory and findings about why and how violent victors win postwar elections have critical implications, previously understudied, for our understanding of war recurrence, democratization, justice, security, and welfare over both the short term and the long term.

Security and Political Behavior

This book uses the analytical tools of political behavior to answer important questions in international relations about war and peace. It also demonstrates the value of bringing security issues at the core of international relations more centrally into the study of political behavior.

By building a theory of the electoral consequences of use of force in war, drawing upon the toolbox of political behavior, I join scholars including Joshua Kertzer, Jon Pevehouse, Mike Tomz, Jessica Weeks, Keren Yarhi-Milo, and Thomas Zeitzoff, among others, who bring developments in domestic politics into the study of international relations and identify the significant electoral drivers and effects of security and defense policies.[69] A well-established literature illuminates the effects of war, belligerence, and casualties on domestic audiences and vote outcomes; it has focused predominantly on U.S. public opinion and electoral behavior surrounding America's international use of force.[70]

This book studies voter attitudes and behavior surrounding the use of force domestically in intrastate war. The importance of these attitudes and behavior to determining postwar political order has rendered elections a central focus of many international relations theories of conflict termination and recurrence, although, with few exceptions,[71] they leave the strategic interactions of parties and voters underexplored.[72] The study of political behavior helps shed new light on patterns of postwar peace and war.

The resulting argument is that war outcomes affect who will rule the country after civil conflict, through the process of parties vying to own the salient security issue and voters choosing candidates, based on security grounds. By identifying the political legacies of different forms of conflict termination, the book adds to scholarship on how wars end.[73] In emphasizing how military outcomes influence public reaction to belligerence and atrocity, the book accords with the work of Alexander Downes, Richard Eichenberg, Peter Feaver, Christopher Gelpi, and Jason Reifler, and Daryl Press, Scott Sagan, and Benjamin Valentino; they find that citizens respond positively to the use of force when it achieves decisive victory,[74] battlefield success,[75] or military utility.[76] In emphasizing party strategies, the book aligns with the work of Matthew Baum and Tim Groeling, Adam Berinsky, Elizabeth Saunders, and John Zaller on how political framing,[77] issue ownership,[78] and top-down elite cues[79] mediate mass opinion toward and voting on security issues. The book thereby brings the electoral consequences of use of force and military success in intrastate wars into dialogue with the significant scholarship on the domestic politics of belligerence in interstate war and intervention. It also motivates a research agenda that integrates the two, which I spell out in the book's conclusion.

Security Voting

By studying security with the repertoire of political behavior models, the book shows how these models can apply to noneconomic issues. In the canonical theory of democratic political behavior, voters "reward the [parties] for good times, punish [them] for bad."[80] Voters' choices are also based on their predictions about the parties' management of salient issues in the future.[81]

Theories of political behavior acknowledge that nonmaterial variables factor into vote choice.[82] Ferejohn (1986) writes, "If the incumbent administration has been successful in promoting economic growth and avoiding major wars, it will tend to be rewarded at the polls." Fiorina, Abrams, and Pope (2003) state that "election outcomes depend on the 'fundamentals,' especially peace and prosperity." Despite this acknowledgment of the importance of security, the literature's emphasis on material assessments has led most to refer to its canonical voting logic as "economic voting theory." This is largely because theories of electoral politics tend to concentrate on richer and more economically developed democracies, contexts that, in recent times, have not experienced widespread insecurity from full-scale international and civil wars, rampant crime, or brutal repression.

In lower- and middle-income democracies, economic voting is also manifested,[83] but insecurity is not rare, geographically or demographically isolated, or distant. In fact, one and a half billion people face the threat of violence as armed conflicts ravage large swaths of the developing world. State-based armed conflicts, the focus of this book, have taken place in 157 places globally since World War II and have stolen the lives of sixteen million people.[84] Over forty million people across the globe have become forcibly displaced or refugees of intrastate war and violence; millions more have suffered extortion, captivity, torture, and sexual violence. With attention to interstate wars, terrorism, and organized crime as well, it becomes clear that security issues may be highly salient for many voters globally and therefore likely influence their political behavior.[85]

This book shows that well-studied frameworks of party and voter behavior have significant explanatory power under such conditions: how parties script their programs, recruit their elites, target their voters, and campaign when security issues are paramount and how, under these conditions, voters make their electoral choices. In so doing, the book joins research on the effects of other forms of insecurity on political behavior, including terrorism,[86] high-casualty interstate wars,[87] crime,[88] military service,[89] and international interventions.[90]

Its conclusions align with studies that find that both victims and nonvictims facing threats of disorder tend to place less importance on civil liberties and prove more willing to accept repressive measures and ironfisted strongmen.[91] By shedding light on why victimized populations elect tormentor victors to office, the book contributes to the study of a broader phenomenon of political behavior: why people in democracies vote for "bad guys," people with known ties to violent criminals,[92] militias,[93] warlords,[94] and corruption.[95]

Road Map: How This Book Is Organized

The book is organized in ten chapters. The first part of the book presents the building blocks of the argument and shows how they are assembled into an explanation for why bloodstained parties win postwar elections. Chapter 2 sets the political stage for the theory chapter by defining the backdrop of postwar democratic elections; the cast of characters, comprising nonbelligerent parties and rebel and government belligerent successors under various war outcomes; and the audience, conflict-affected populations for whom security is a highly salient issue. Chapter 3 presents the book's theory of how war outcomes influence electoral performance through party strategies and voter behavior. It outlines how, against the backdrop of the war-to-peace transition, nonbelligerent,

war-winning, and war-losing parties devise their respective programs and platforms, reckon with the violent past, build and target their constituencies, and
retain and recruit (or expel) members of their elites. It delineates how voters
emerging from war evaluate parties' competencies and formulate their political
attitudes and behavior, and as a result elect civil war tormentors as they seek to
secure their future during the pivotal foundation of postwar political order.
Chapter 3 concludes by laying out the observable implications derived from
the theory and from alternative accounts and describing how each is evaluated
in the book's subsequent empirical chapters (4–9).

Chapter 4 tests the book's individual-voter-level hypotheses with experimental evidence from an original survey of fifteen hundred victims and nonvictims in Colombia. It evaluates whether war winners as candidates are able
to shift voters' references points so as to launder these candidates' violent pasts
and to cultivate a reputation for security, while losing belligerents cannot.
With a series of survey experiments, the chapter then evaluates the party strategy of what I call a Restrained Leviathan, comprising military and civilian
candidates, a platform convergent on the interests of the moderate voter, and
a focus on the security valence issue, and assesses whether such a strategy
does, as predicted, prove more successful for the militarily advantaged belligerent. I examine whether the political strategy of what I call the Tactical
Immoderate, comprising civilian candidates, an immoderate platform, and
nonsecurity valence priorities, proves more successful for the militarily disadvantaged belligerent. The original survey also enables me to experimentally
evaluate alternative mechanisms of voter coercion and voter ignorance. I use
the observational survey data to assess the robustness of security voting in
actual elections against other drivers of political behavior: economic voting,
clientelism, and partisanship.

The survey findings reveal what types of strategies would likely be optimal
for different types of parties. Based on more than two cumulative years of
fieldwork in Colombia; 350 interviews with victimizers and victims, campaign
strategists, and candidates; text analysis of party programs and more than half
a million Twitter posts from politicians' feeds; and review of daily press coverage and actual voting results, I examine the specifics of the political campaigns
in the 2018 Colombian elections to explore, briefly, whether the parties followed or diverged from these optimal strategies, why, and with which electoral
implications.

From the theory's voter-level underpinnings, Chapters 5 to 7 turn to its
party-level ones, examining them in the context of Central America, which

experienced the full range of war outcomes. Chapter 5 examines a military draw in El Salvador; Chapter 6, government victory in Guatemala; and Chapter 7, rebel victory in Nicaragua. To reconstruct how each party developed its strategy, I conducted in-depth interviews with former presidents, presidential candidates, campaign strategists, senators of all political colors, and military commanders. I collected and analyzed, both with natural language processing and with qualitative review, the parties' political platforms, speeches, campaign advertisements, and rhetoric from multiple archives of newspaper, radio, television, and campaign data. I identified the war background of the candidates of each (belligerent and nonbelligerent) party and reviewed declassified U.S. embassy cables on the electoral contests. Each chapter looks at the effects of the parties' strategies on public opinion and voting behavior, using survey data collected contemporaneously during the elections. I use these survey data, together with municipal-level election data, to evaluate alternative explanations based on victimization, coercion, ideology, and economic voting. In each of these three case studies, I consider the implications of the founding elections for peace, democracy, party stability, rule of law, and justice. While the survey evidence and case material of Chapters 4 to 7 support the theory's observable implications, they also confirm that the real world proves more complex than a few variables can describe.

Chapter 8 examines the phenomenon of violent actors who win votes on a global scale to understand the generalizability and limitations of the theory. It uses an original dataset, the Civil War Successor Party (CWSP) cross-national dataset, which encompasses the full universe of belligerents around the world that transitioned from civil war between 1970 and 2015. The dataset traces the postwar political trajectories of the civil war belligerents, identifies their successor parties, charts their electoral performance, and identifies their nonbelligerent opponents. It shows that, consistent with the theory of the rest of the book, parties with violent pasts tend to dominate the elections and that war outcomes are powerful predictors of belligerent party performance, irrespective of the belligerents' use of mass atrocities. If militarily winning, abusive belligerent parties perform well, even where elections are clean, free, and fair. The CWSP dataset also enables an evaluation of factors that might, in theory, confound the relationship between war outcomes and election results: incumbency status, popular support, mobilization capacity, provision of public goods, organizational cohesion, and financing.

Chapter 8 then turns from cross-national data to newly assembled subnational data on violence, war outcomes, and voting. It shows that successor parties' vote shares remain relatively constant whether the belligerents were responsible for all or none of the atrocities at the local level, but that these vote shares track with whether the belligerents militarily won or lost the war locally. The chapter concludes by investigating whether and how the logic works in contexts where the framework's assumptions hold more loosely: where ethnicity is a dominant cleavage, security is not highly salient, victimization is bounded geographically or demographically, electorates are bifurcated by secession, or politics are centered on patronage rather than programs.

Chapter 9 explores the implications of elections of bloodstained parties for war recurrence, transitional justice, democracy, and governance. To do so, it uses new global data that reveal not only whether a conflict resumed but also, through belligerent-level coding, *who* reinitiated the fighting. It shows that postwar elections increase the chance of renewed war if there is an inversion or reversal of the military balance of power after war, and if the war loser has performed poorly in the elections. If, instead, relative military power remains stable, civil war actors are unlikely to remilitarize if they lose the elections. The chapter then combines the book's CWSP cross-national data with information on amnesties and liberal democracy in an analysis that suggests the tragic (even if potentially temporary) trade-offs between peace and justice, and between peace and liberalism. To probe governance implications of the elections of violence-tied actors, the chapter analyzes an original database of 784 paramilitary mayors, based on over 42,000 pages of Colombian Supreme Court sentencing documents, to compare the administrations of paramilitary mayors who barely won with those who barely lost the elections along dimensions of security and public goods outcomes. It shows that the election of belligerent politicians generated a reduction in common crime but had pernicious effects on the provision of other public goods. The politicians' prioritization of security crowded out resources for social welfare.

The book concludes in Chapter 10 by specifying avenues for future research on political behavior and security, and beyond the temporal and geographic scope examined here. The book closes by touching on the policy implications for practitioners aiming to prevent atrocities and to promote peace, liberalism, and human rights after violence. It highlights how interventions aimed at buttressing the balance of power, reducing the urgency of security issues, bolstering nonbelligerent parties, and countering historical distortion may speed up the normalization of politics, dampening the perverse electoral potency of war outcomes, and amplifying opportunities for justice and democracy after war.

2

Political Stage, Actors, and Audience

THIS CHAPTER SETS the political stage for the theory: the arena, the set, the cast, and the audience. It establishes the theory's assumptions and underlying definitions and the boundaries of its applications. The plot of the theory then unfolds in the following chapter: how wars produce nonbelligerent and belligerent parties that, respectively, prosecute and launder the bloodstained past to generate a reputation for competence on security, and how they posture to own the salient valence issues, position themselves programmatically, target different sectors of the electorate, and recruit their political elite.

Postwar Environments

This book is about how parties that committed atrocities in civil war do well in postwar democratic elections. To answer this question, it employs the tools of political behavior, revealing the pathway by which war outcomes influence the behavior of political parties and voters and thus electoral outcomes after episodes of mass violence in civil war. The book follows the Uppsala Conflict Data Program (UCDP) and defines civil war as "a contested incompatibility that concerns government or territory where the use of armed force between two parties, of which at least one is the government of a state, results in at least 25 battle-related deaths."[1] The book studies conflicts that, according to the UCDP Armed Conflicts Dataset cumulative intensity variable, had in excess of one thousand battle-related deaths over the duration of the conflict. It does so given the project's theoretically driven questions: to focus on episodes of violence that were great enough to have had impacts on the population and to have generated political consequences, and for which scholarship on "normal" nonviolent political behavior might, therefore, not fully apply.[2]

The book studies political life after a meaningful termination of conflict at the dyadic level. This allows it to examine multiparty civil wars.[3] It defines war termination as the belligerents transitioning from violence, meaning they engaged in costly steps to terminate their violence, rather than merely paused from active fighting. In this sense, the book goes beyond the UCDP Conflict Termination Dataset v.2–2015 approach, which defines termination as an active year "followed by a year in which there are fewer than 25 battle-related deaths."[4] In many cases of conflict termination by this latter definition, the parties did not even briefly demilitarize; the cases just did not cross the reported death threshold in the given year. The book includes conflicts terminated along the full spectrum of outcomes, from government victory to rebel victory. This project's Civil War Successor Party (CWSP) dataset covers belligerents meeting these criteria that terminated their conflicts between 1970 and 2015.[5] A detailed online codebook provides transparency on the coding decisions and sources for each case.[6]

Voters

The book's framework makes several empirically justified assumptions about voters emerging from war. The model has the greatest explanatory power in environments in which these assumptions hold.

First, I assume that the postwar electorate comprises a population battered by war. I distinguish the segment of the population *directly* victimized by the government, militias, and rebels. These are individuals who experienced acts of violence against themselves or their loved ones, including assassination, forced disappearance, kidnapping, physical harm, torture, sexual violence, forced recruitment, displacement, and extortion.

I assume that a broader swath of the electorate has been affected only *indirectly* by the violence, meaning they or their families were not directly targeted by lethal or nonlethal violence, but they experienced consequences of the conflict. This broader segment of the population has, I argue, experienced the fear of war that pushes them to "satisfy safety concerns . . . [and] heightens [their] desire for security."[7] Its members, for example, avoided crossing frontlines, did not leave their homes at night, kept their children home from school, closed their businesses. They traveled with their phones predialed to their loved ones in case of a kidnapping.[8] They fled, not under orders, but out of prevention. In other words, they lived under the shadow of war even if they were not themselves its direct victims.

The framework's scope condition of two-sided armed conflict narrows the third segment of the population, that of unaffected nonvictims, because a constituency protected by one side often becomes the target of the other side. Those that benefit from the violence of one side may suffer, or fear suffering, at the hands of the other side.[9] Nonetheless, where violence is geographically bounded or selectively targeted, a population of nonvictims may remain unaffected by the war.

Second, I assume that war leaves what Charles Tilly (2003, 22) called an "uncommitted middle." Populations victimized by multiple sides or indirectly victimized, in particular, are often undecided in their postwar electoral allegiance and preferences. They are thus more persuadable by the political strategies of the parties of both the belligerents and nonbelligerents in war's aftermath. This "swing" electorate comes into play especially during the founding postwar elections. (The book's logic will have less explanatory power where party affiliation is frozen, racialized, or ethnicized; swing voters are absent; and electorates are bifurcated,[10] contexts I discuss in Chapter 8.)

Third, the framework assumes that security and recovery are issues that are critical to the population (Chapter 8 validates this empirically, with survey data from around the world). In particular, it assumes with Hobbes that the "final cause, end, or design of men (who naturally love liberty, and dominion over others) . . . [is] the foresight of their own preservation, and of a more contented life thereby; that is to say, of getting themselves out from that miserable condition of war."[11] Emerging from war, "people [are] desperate for peace."[12] The book assumes that this heightened concern for security is manifested in both a sociotropic form—a desire for an end to anarchy and the establishment of political stability and order, a prevention of the horrors of war recurring, and an absence of crime and violence[13]—and an egotropic form: a desire for personal safety and avoidance of bodily harm. The postwar citizen cares about how vote choice affects personal safety and the stability and reconstruction of the country.

The framework uses the stylized case in which security is highly salient across the population, but in practice, exposure to violence, salience of insecurity, and importance of economic recovery vary significantly across countries, regions within countries, and individuals; war terminations bring highly varied peace dividends. My theory has the greatest explanatory value in explaining the political behavior of those more exposed to wartime violence. In addition, voters' concerns include far more than security[14]—with other preferences over an n-dimensional policy space.[15] Usually a faltering or devastated economy with high unemployment, poverty, and wartime destruction is also high among voters' postwar concerns, so recovery is another salient valence issue. Issues of ethnic rights, health care, education, inequality, resource management, inflation, sovereignty, infrastructure, agrarian policy, and corruption may also command attention. Belligerents and nonbelligerents further draw on core ideological supporters motivated by a commitment to the wartime cleavage or to a partisan identity. Below, I relax the framework's assumptions to account for these myriad nonsecurity issues that concern voters and to examine the effects of variation in insecurity across populations.

In places in which security is not so salient because the length of time between war's end and the founding elections is extended and new threats do not emerge, or because war is isolated in specific regions of the country, the model will have less explanatory power on voting behavior: normal politics centered on economic voting, clientelism, and partisanship, and the like are more likely to dominate.

Belligerent and Nonbelligerent Parties

I adopt Sartori's definition of a political party as "any political group identified by an official label that presents at elections, and is capable of placing, through elections (free or non-free), candidates for public office."[16] I assume that there are two types of parties after war: belligerent parties and nonbelligerent parties. Belligerent parties are those that have blood on their hands to some (significant) degree. Nonbelligerent ones do not. Belligerent parties are those that fought either on the side of the government or with the rebels.

I define belligerent parties or civil war successor parties as the postwar parties representing the ideological and organizational characteristics of the wartime armed organizations.[17] A *government belligerent successor party* is defined as a political party, group, or organization that possessed authoritative control over the state's coercive apparatus during the conflict. In some cases, the government belligerent party is one that was active through the era of the conflict. In other cases, it is a postwar party that formally adopts the name, program, or mantle of the government's armed forces, or the party whose platform and membership are most closely associated with the government belligerent's side.

The *rebel* is defined as the armed opposition organization. A *rebel successor party* is the political party formed by or around the rebel belligerent. It may be a previously existing party that represented the rebels during the conflict. If no conflict-era rebel party existed, the rebel belligerent successor is the party that formally adopts the name, program, or mantle of the rebels, or is the party whose platform or membership is most closely associated with the rebels.

Nonbelligerent parties are conflict-era parties or organizations that did not have a coercive apparatus and did not participate in the armed conflict, or they are new parties that emerged after the war whose platforms and memberships do not represent the wartime armies. Such nonbelligerent parties may be, for example, nonethnic parties, where the conflict pitted violent ethnonationalist parties against each other.[18] They may be parties espousing peaceful self-determination in contexts of violent secessionism. They may represent opposition to authoritarian or democratic regimes, in wars with rebel movements aimed at state takeover. They may have served in governing coalitions, but without control of the coercive apparatus. They may be a new governing party that ended the war's brutalities and ushered in peace and that now, as electoral incumbents, seek reelection in founding postwar contests. Their defining feature is that they did not take part in the war as a belligerent. An empirical tendency is that they tend to be more moderate than belligerents, whose social bases were forged in the polarizing, radical-rewarding, and outbidding environment of war.[19]

Motivated by theoretical parsimony, in the theory I model the political arena as comprising only three parties—winning (or stalemated) belligerent, nonbelligerent, and losing belligerent. However, in the empirics I discuss multiple parties in each category and the implications for voter calculations.

I assume that parties are uncertain about voters' preferences when they propose their platforms and set their campaign agendas. I further assume that the parties do not move simultaneously but instead sequentially: first, the electoral incumbent party—whether nonbelligerent or successful belligerent—then the opposition party (again, whether nonbelligerent/successful belligerent), and last the militarily losing party.

Democratic Elections

The book focuses on democratic elections after war. It adopts Schumpeter's minimalist characterization of democracy: "The democratic method is that institutional arrangement for arriving at political decisions in which individuals acquire the power to decide by means of a competitive struggle for the people's vote."[20] Under this definition, countries in which there is "free competition for a free vote" are designated as democratic.[21] The book therefore excludes contexts in which no elections were held after war.[22] It also excludes cases of elections in one-party states.[23] While we know that electoral "choice-less choices"[24] are made under conditions of autocracy, sham democracy, and extreme repression,[25] this book aims to explain why there are voluntary votes for bloodstained parties, even in democratic elections with viable competition. Electoral intimidation, fraud, and coercion can no doubt account for some of the abundant votes for tormentors, but this book's emphasis is not on these less puzzling votes that are cast under coercion.[26] It is for this reason that the book focuses primarily on postwar and not wartime elections. In wartime elections, preferences and vote choice are formed under the shadow of the gun; participation may be restricted, and some violent parties (usually rebels) are banned.[27] Thus wartime elections often constitute "demonstration elections" that do not offer meaningful choices and from which it becomes challenging to infer voters' preferences. I nonetheless pay close attention to the countries' full political trajectories from wartime to postwar political contests.[28]

Electoral Institutions

The transition from war to peace can assume different forms. In some cases, war takes place under undemocratic conditions, and the end of war brings new democracies and elections.[29] In many of these cases, the institutions are endogenous to the war termination; a nascent political system takes hold after the war and new rules are written, oftentimes by the pen of the very wartime belligerents.[30] We know from the work of Seymour Lipset, Stein Rokkan, and Carles Boix that, during these critical junctures, powerful actors design the electoral system that best locks in their power and prevents new political entrants.[31] Accordingly, in these contexts, postwar electoral performance may reflect institutional choice rather than voter preferences, complicating the process of inference.

In many cases, however, postwar founding elections are not the country's first experience with elections. Regular elections may have been interrupted by war.[32] Or elections took place during war because democracy persisted throughout the conflict, or democratization took place amid armed conflict. In such cases, prewar (or wartime) constitutions may be sustained or resurrected after the war, and thus institutions governing the founding elections become exogenous to war outcomes.

The book's empirics center on the Latin American context because of the plausible exogeneity of the institutions there: the constitutions were unchanged by war, and the peace accords did not establish new electoral institutions that favored the wartime belligerents. Instead, the strong regional norm and institutional homogeneity of proportional representation (PR) systems with a strong presidency endured, and none of the cases adopted power-sharing arrangements.[33] (In Chapter 8, I explore the generalizability to other institutional environments.)

Party System

These institutions help structure the number and character of the postwar electoral contestants. Duverger's law and hypothesis tell us that the nature of the electoral rules and institutions can determine the party system: a simple-majority single-ballot system favors the two-party system, while proportional representation favors multipartyism.[34] Social cleavages may determine the actual number of parties, while the electoral system sets an upper limit on the number of parties through the effects of "strategic voting" and "strategic entry."[35] It follows that postwar elections taking place under proportional representation rules are, irrespective of the war outcome, more likely to involve multiple rebel and government belligerent parties and also multiple nonbelligerent parties. In contrast, a majoritarian party system is more likely to be influenced by the nature of the war outcome: an asymmetric military outcome (including rebel or government victory) is likely to present voters with parties that represent only the war-winner belligerent party and a single nonbelligerent party. Under majoritarianism, a symmetric war outcome (military draw) is likely to yield a two-party system, with one government belligerent party and one rebel belligerent party. This suggests that while the war-winner party is likely always to be a contender in national elections, whether the war-loser one will be involved may depend on the nature of the electoral rules.[36] A belligerent that is completely decimated will be less likely to enter the race; secession-seeking belligerents that operated only in specific regions of a country may enter only regional electoral contests postwar.

Selection

There are several sources of selection that might bias the picture I paint of postwar politics. (I address selection-based threats to inference in Chapter 8.) The book explores the full universe of cases of conflicts that terminated between 1970 and 2015 and that were followed by democratic elections. Of course, the electoral success of groups who chose not to end their fighting and that of former belligerents who did not run for office are unobservable. It may be that groups who believed they would perform dismally in founding elections chose not to disarm, or chose not to participate in elections.

Several pieces of empirical evidence moderate these selection concerns. Many groups that did run gained less than one percent of the vote. It is possible that these groups misestimated their electoral success, but it is hard to believe they could have done so by such large margins; this suggests that some unpopular groups do test their prospects at the polls. Additionally, only eight groups in this dataset formally boycotted the postwar elections. Elections took place in the vast majority of postconflict countries, and only seven groups were banned from running, indicating that electoral runs by successor parties were widespread; nearly every case of civil war that ended in the period 1970 to 2015 had participation by belligerents in the postwar elections. Moreover, the norm of democratic contestation has become so strong internationally[37] that it may have led belligerents to trade bullets for ballots, even when doing so may not have been a rational strategy in terms of the organizations' own survival.[38]

Founding Postwar Elections and Electoral Success

I define the *founding elections* as the first legislative, presidential, and regional elections following the termination of armed struggle.

This book is about electoral performance. I follow Lupu (2016) and define the outcome—*electoral success*—as receiving a plurality of the vote, winning the first round, or attracting no less than one-third of the winning vote share. The empirics on Latin America focus on presidential rather than legislative elections because presidential elections carry greater weight in determining policy and voter behavior in the region, and they have strong coattail effects on legislative elections.[39] The cross-national analysis explores performance in lower-house legislative elections, which take place in all political systems, and which present lower barriers to participation.

Military Outcomes

This book argues that war outcomes influence the electoral success of blood-stained parties and of those parties untainted by wartime violence through mechanisms of party and voter strategies.

| Government | Relative government | Military | Rebel |
| victory | victory | draw | victory |

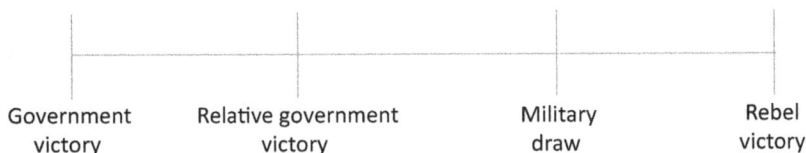

FIGURE 2.1. A Continuum of War Outcomes.

I define war outcomes along a spectrum ranging from outright government victory (rebel defeat) to outright rebel victory (government defeat). In the middle are indecisive outcomes in which neither side wins the war outright, which I classify into two outcomes on Figure 2.1's continuum.[40] In the left-hand middle category, the war ends with the government winning the war, although the rebels' organization remains viable. I call this outcome "relative government victory." In the right-hand middle category are belligerents who ended war at a draw or a "mutually hurting stalemate." These middle two categories might terminate in either (1) negotiated settlements that conclude the military behavior of the parties through negotiated surrender (in cases of military asymmetry) or robust peace agreement (in cases of a draw) or (2) sustained ceasefires, truces, armistices, or some other mode of freezing that results in a cessation of hostilities and termination of military operations, but does "not deal with the incompatibility" so as to resolve the underlying conflict. I use the terms "militarily advantaged," "stronger," "victorious," "winning," "successful," and "war-winner belligerents" interchangeably to refer to the categories of rebel victors, government victors, and relative government victors. I use the terms "militarily disadvantaged," "weaker," "vanquished," "losing," "unsuccessful," and "war-loser belligerents" to refer to the categories of defeated government (under rebel victory), defeated rebels (under government victory), and relative rebel losers (under relative government victory). For belligerents at a draw, I use the terms "draw," "stalemated," and "militarily successful" interchangeably.

What determines war outcomes, and do those determinants also influence postwar electoral success? I explore confounding conceptually here and empirically in Chapter 8. Many factors influence civil war outcomes, including underlying preferences, international intervention, external support, incumbency, resources, organizational capacity, ethnic diversity and geography, network structures, belligerent cohesion, interstate war, terrain, population size, access to arms, cross-border sanctuaries, per capita income, and inequality.[41] These factors could also influence postwar electoral performance.

The endogeneity problem is alleviated somewhat by the fact that these same factors do not consistently determine the second critical ingredient of the theory: the optimal political strategies of nonbelligerent and belligerent parties. Additionally, some factors that enhance advantageous war outcomes, such as mountainous terrain, jungle refuge, lack of roads, cross-border sanctuaries, access to arms, or illicit resources from drug trafficking, are unlikely to be applicable in the electoral arena, particularly in highly monitored elections. External funding for war often dries up in peacetime, offering little electoral benefit. Neither fragmented conglomerates nor singular, cohesive organizations appear consistently more successful, either militarily or electorally (e.g., IRA, FMLN).

A possible important threat to inference is contained in the idea that popular parties or belligerents win both wars and elections. As I discuss in Chapter 3, given the book's focus on voluntary votes, of course "popularity," defined as the populations' preferred party, wins elections, but this party is not necessarily representative of the population's underlying prewar preferences. Were these fixed preferences determinant of war outcomes, we would not observe the highly variable levels of relative military strength present in most wars over time. We also would not observe the fluid civilian side switching seen during nearly all wars.[42] The empirical frequency of elections of highly abusive belligerents that are not representative of the majority's preferences is also inconsistent with the observable implications of the argument based on underlying popular support.[43] The public-support argument has the greatest leverage in explaining the different parties' hardcore activists, but these are the least surprising of the voter populations. Such an argument, however, cannot explain the behavior of the many unaligned voters at the end of many wars. There are, of course, cases in which groups representing the underlying preferences of the population win the war and also go on to win the elections. In these cases, it is not possible to separate out the explanatory power of winning the war from that of prewar sentiments. My argument is that belligerents that win wars outright or fight them to effective stalemate will gain electoral support irrespective of their levels of atrocity against and degree of ideological alignment with the population.

This chapter set up the environment, model, and players of the violent-victors theory. In Chapter 3, I develop the book's theory of how bloodstained parties, if war winning, perform well electorally in postwar elections.

3

Violent-Victors Theory of Political
Behavior after War

THIS BOOK ASKS why parties that engaged in atrocious use of force in civil war perform well in postwar democratic elections and even gain support from some of those whom they terrorized. It answers that bloodstained parties, if successful in war, become deemed the most credible providers of future societal peace. The mechanics of how violent victors go about burnishing a reputation for competence on security and becoming victors of elections lie with party strategies and political behavior.[1]

This chapter introduces the book's framework of how the outcome of the war shapes how parties reckon with the ghosts from their past, script their programs, construct their constituencies, select their candidates, and propagate their messages to own the salient security issue and garner votes after large-scale violence in war.[2] It outlines how these party strategies, in turn, influence how voters affected and victimized by violence form their political attitudes and make their electoral selection. It shows how, intersected, the strategies of parties and voters emerging from civil war produce a generalizable pattern of votes for belligerent successor parties with significant implications for peace, democracy, justice, and governance. The chapter concludes by discussing the theory's observable implications and those of alternative accounts and presenting how the empirical chapters evaluate these implications.

Valence Politics

As laid out in Chapter 2, I borrow from Hobbes and assume that, battered by war, the postwar voter seeks to ease, first, "the fear of not otherwise preserving himself [from violence]."[3] Security is a valence issue: an issue on which, like prosperity, low crime, or minimal corruption, virtually all voters have the same goals or ideal end points, and voters judge parties based on their competencies in achieving these goals.[4] Of valence issues, Stokes (1963) writes, "If the condition is a future or potential one, the argument turns on which party, given possession of the government, is the more likely to bring it about."[5] The theory of party ownership defines an ability to "handle" an issue as "a reputation . . . produced by a history of attention, initiative, and innovation . . . which leads voters to believe that . . . [a given party] is more sincere and committed."[6] The crucial mechanism behind a valence advantage is credibility: "Candidates cannot simply appropriate any issue they please and claim it as their own. Instead, heresthetical maneuvers[7] work best when candidates are perceived as credible. . . . Party reputations, with their accumulated historical evidence, provide this credibility."[8] To decide who is most likely to provide the key valence issues in postwar environments—future societal peace and recovery—voters thus base their assessments on judgments of (1) how the parties have performed in the past—their reputations—and (2) how they are likely to perform in the future—their credibility.

I argue that winning the war, even if not outright, enables a belligerent to make the compelling case that it is able, even better than untainted nonbelligerent parties and less-violent, but war-losing, belligerent rivals, to preserve security and order going forward. For this to be rational, however, it is necessary to wrestle with two further puzzles: (1) why would a party that victimized the population have a reputation for competence on security rather than one for inflicting harm (and why would this reputation for security competence be superior to that of its opponents less tarnished or untarnished by violence)? And (2) how can a belligerent party, which committed atrocities against fellow citizens, convincingly promise that, once elected, it will preserve peace and restrain itself rather than turn its guns on the population and revictimize in the future (and, again, how can it render this promise more credible than that of its rivals that used less or no force against civilians)?

I argue that resolving these puzzles guides party strategies after war, which, in turn, influence voter strategies and ultimate electoral outcomes. In particular, solving these puzzles structures postwar party tactics for how to assign blame for the instigation and perpetration of wartime atrocities; how to formulate programs responsive to the myriad issues that arise during transitions—whether to emphasize valence, position, or nonpolicy politics;[9] whom to target electorally—their core, swing, or opposition voters—to maximize votes; and how to choose their party elite—whom to recruit, promote, demote, and put forth to represent the party on different public stages. For belligerent parties specifically, addressing these puzzles guides whether they deny, deflect, embrace, mitigate, or apologize for their past transgressions; retain or moderate their (usually radical) wartime platforms; prioritize a narrow or broad constituency; elevate or sideline the human rights abusers among them; and transform their war-waging organizational machines. How the parties settle these dilemmas then shapes how different classes of citizens cast their ballots.

Why Do Bloodstained Parties—if War Winners—Emerge with a Reputation for Competence on Security Superior to That of Less-Tainted Rivals?

I first discuss how distinctive parties—nonbelligerent and belligerent—seek to claim ownership of the salient prospective valence issues.

The Nonbelligerent Party's Claim to the Security Valence Issue: The Rule Abider

Unlike their belligerent rivals, nonbelligerent parties have clean human rights records and a reputation for not using violence against the population. Accordingly, in equilibrium, they may seek electoral rewards for this reputation. They may advocate for punishment at the polls of the belligerent adversaries on grounds that "truth and justice require . . . [a] moral duty to punish vicious crimes against humanity."[10] This push for retributive voting against the transgressors would coincide with the period when the fog of war is clearing and liberated civil society and international truth commissions reveal the extent and nature of the wartime violence and seek to hold victimizers to account. The nonbelligerent parties may further argue that votes for them would strengthen the rule of law and deter future violations of human rights, establish "the validity of the democratic system," and cement the "principle of accountability . . . essential to democracy," as Samuel Huntington wrote.[11] In other words, nonbelligerent parties can compete under a Hume-inspired banner declaring that peace and order are not possible without justice.[12]

The manifesto of the Green Party in Colombia, titled "Together for Democratic *Legality*,"[13] exemplifies this nonbelligerent case.[14] In it, the party rejected the belligerent's logic that "'the end justifies the means' . . . [that] in order to . . . win in conflict [and bring peace], anything goes." Instead, the party advanced, "Let us recognize first of all that each life is irreplaceable, that life is sacred. Let us . . . strengthen in Colombia the understanding, respect and compliance with the *rules*. The protection of life is the fundamental purpose of our security policy."[15] Nonbelligerent parties can argue credibly that they can provide such security within the bounds of the law while protecting the fundamental human rights of the citizenry.

On the design of government, James Madison wrote in the *Federalist No. 51*, "If men were angels, no government would be necessary. If angels were to govern men, neither external nor internal controls on government would be necessary. In framing a government which is to be administered by men over men, the great difficulty lies in this: You must first enable the government to control the governed; and in the next [second] place, oblige it to control itself."[16] Where non-belligerent parties may fall short on the first Madisonian claim—being strong enough to control the people—they make up for with their reputation on the second—being able to keep themselves in check, having not transgressed in the past. Given a country's recent experience with ruthless groups turning their guns against the population unchecked, this commitment to stick to the rules and institutional checks, and guarantee security enshrined in a rights-based regime, should give a nonbelligerent party a compelling claim to the security valence issue. Given that effective rule of law provides a strong solution to often widespread postwar criminality, nonbelligerents' commitment to justice, punishment, and deterrence should further bolster their claims to this issue.

In addition to a likely valence advantage on rule-based security, nonbelligerent parties will have spent the period of armed conflict engaged not in war making but (potentially) in gaining other competencies. They therefore may have credible claims to own a variety of valence issues, including, most importantly, economic recovery.

The Belligerent Party's Claim to the Security Valence Issue: The Restrained Leviathan

The militarily winning or stalemated belligerent party has a distinct claim to the security valence issue. It can argue that it is the party that is strong enough to establish postwar political order. Its past record of bringing an end to the war points to a competency advantage at keeping the militarily losing belligerent under control or the other stalemated one at bay. Its termination of war also signals that it can (at least temporarily) keep its own hands tied: these are the two requisites of peace. This belligerent can therefore make the case that it is best able to deter remilitarization and secure the future.

LAUNDERING ITS REPUTATION

To make this prospective case convincing, however, the former tormentor has to confront the challenge of how to foster a reputation for security rather than one for harm. The solution, I argue, lies with its ability to claim credit for peace and shift voters' frames of reference of the use of force,[17] thereby altering how they judge the violent past to predict a secure future. To demonstrate this logic of reference-dependent preferences in war-ravaged contexts, in Text Box A I adopt a simple formal model based on Grillo and Prato (2021) in which voters evaluate outcomes based not just on external standards but also on context-dependent factors that can be manipulated by parties.[18]

Box A. Model of Reference-Dependent Preferences on Past Atrocity

The conflict setting in this model comprises a unit mass of voters (V) indexed by i, and a party, which can be a nonbelligerent, winning/ stalemated belligerent, or losing belligerent type, Pt with $t \in [NB, W/S, L]$. In the model's first stage, the party (P) has two possible choices: go to war, and commit violence against civilians in the process $(h = 1)$, or abstain from war (and remain a nonbelligerent) $(h = 0)$. Subsequently, if the party opts to go to war, the belligerent then, in the second stage, chooses whether to escalate the conflict and double down on its violence $(d = 1)$, or to withdraw from the conflict and instead bring peace $(d = 0)$. In observing h, citizens have consistent beliefs: a reasonable expectation to fear the belligerent doubling down.[19] For simplicity, I construct each as a binary choice. U(h, d) is decreasing in both arguments, and thus, the assessment of the belligerent is $v = u(h, d) + \eta(u(h,d) - u)$, where η denotes the importance of the relative (psychological) payoff versus the absolute (material) payoff and $u_h = E\{u(h,d)|h\}$.[20] The utility function also includes ideology, economic considerations, expectations of clientelism. However, I focus on explaining variation explained by the experience of violence, and not accounted for by these well-established dimensions of political preferences and behavior.

If in the first stage, the party decides *not* to wage war and *not* to use violence against the population $(h = 0)$, then the assessment, v, equals zero. This, in effect, becomes the assessment of the nonbelligerent party; it is *neutral*.

If the party decides to wage war and inflict material pain and loss, and then to double down and continue to use violence $(h = 1, d = 1)$, the assessment equals both the material and also the psychological negative payoffs $(u(1,1) < u)$—disappointment[21]—and is *negative*, $v < 0$.

Continued on next page

However, if the party uses violence and then ushers in peace—as does the winning (or stalemated) belligerent ($h = 1, d = 0$)—then the assessment becomes *positive*, provided η is large enough: the material payoff (wartime suffering) is negative, but the psychological payoff (relief of peace) is positive. Moreover, because the military victor (or stalemated belligerent) is in a strong position to double down on violence, voters' relief that it opts not to do so is strong ($u = 1,1$ is lower), rendering the psychological payoff higher.

In contrast, for the losing belligerent, because of the negative material payoff caused by the wartime violence ($u(h, d)$), but the lack of a psychological payoff of credit for peace ($\eta(u(h, d) - u)$), voters' retrospective assessments of the losing belligerent remain *negative*: $v = u(h, d) + \eta(u(h, d) - u) = u(h, d) < 0$.

In sum, the model reveals that voters punish vanquished belligerents for their violence, but they do not punish winning belligerents for their violence; instead they reward them for terminating the war and providing the relief of peace. Nonbelligerents' records are assessed neutrally, and they achieve surprisingly little benefit from maintaining clean human rights records.

This model of voters' reference-dependent preferences illuminates why mitigation[22] emerges as the war-winner (and stalemated) parties' optimal strategy for laundering their violent past to render their wartime credentials an asset—a reputation for competence on security—rather than a liability.

War outcomes bestow upon the war winner (and even belligerent at a draw) an ability to shift voters' frames of reference, a corollary of being able to control the (de)escalation process. Violence-affected voters' reference point becomes not a world in which no war ever occurred, but one in which war continued. Compared to the bleak prospect of persistent war and victimization, peace and security appear far superior. The war victor receives credit for providing this peace and security, and this changes the voters' judgments.

If the war ends with a decisive military outcome, the victorious belligerent can argue that it deactivated the massive threat to the people by defeating the enemies: a government belligerent can declare that it vanquished the rebel danger, while a rebel belligerent can claim that it defeated the repressive regime. If the war ends indecisively, but asymmetrically, the winning belligerent can claim that it brought the adversaries to their knees, forcing their negotiated surrender, and opted to end its own armed struggle though it was in a solid and superior position to continue fighting. If war ends in military parity, both belligerents can equally seek credit for bringing peace.

The counterintuitive result is that, if a belligerent that uses excessive force can then, militarily winning, usher in peace rather than expand its violence, it may convince citizens to value it higher than if it had remained a nonbelligerent and not used force in the first place. Rather than becoming blamed for the suffering of war, the militarily advantaged belligerent becomes rewarded for the *relief* of peace. The words of a paramilitary victim essentialize this logic: "In general the community accept[ed] the [blood-soaked] ex-paramilitaries because they [were] happy that they [didn't] have to live in war and fear anymore."[23] Text Box B elaborates on this example to illustrate the offsetting mechanism.

Box B. Offsetting the Violent Past: An Example

Prior to the paramilitaries' dominance and then war termination in certain regions, the populations in those places had experienced periods of high-intensity violence during which people could not cross from one territory to the next without the risk of encountering active combat between powerful armed actors.[24] For example, in a community called Popular, "combat occurred day and night between . . . La Galera and La 38 . . . [armed actors who were] irreconcilable enemies because one was allied with the guerrillas and the other contracted by the paramilitaries. . . . Many students didn't go to class . . . [because] the [armed groups] were waiting and would kill based on mere suspicion." A resident explained, "If one is from Avenue 49 . . . and one crosses Avenue 50, death is automatic. . . . We can't even cross to take our sick and injured to the hospital."[25] This one feud caused more than 70 families to abandon their homes; especially at risk were those living on the second and third floors, where explosives tended to hit.[26]

In areas where the paramilitaries achieved local victory over the rebels before demilitarizing, violence levels dropped significantly.[27] Residents described how this was felt on the ground: they are "not killing each other block by block. . . . You can now go all the way to Zamora because the paramilitaries have already co-opted all of the communities [on the way]. . . . Now you hear fighting only far away."[28] In everyday terms, this "peace" meant inhabitants could venture out into the streets again, open their bakeries and markets, and attend social gatherings.[29] It meant that displaced people returned home; development, investment, and participatory politics returned to these areas, long abandoned and silenced by violence. An older woman in Popular described how, as the

Continued on next page

conflict diminished, her dance club and her group of female friends became her principal focus; she could return to the everyday concerns of civilian life.[30] In Manrique, a young man related with relief how he was finally able to complete high school; before, he could not leave his house.[31] "Our neighborhood has changed completely because now the people are free, you can have a party in your house *tranquilo*," said a civil society leader in the neighborhood Villa Hermosa.[32] A resident of Robledo recounted, "I see it this way . . . before, it was impossible for children to go outside to play . . . at any hour there could be an exchange of gunfire. . . . Further up the hill, narrow passages wind between the houses. Each nook guards a story of death and evokes memories of victims. Here fell so-and-so and further down, so-and-so."[33]

With local victory, this changed. As a result of the reduction in violence, citizens were happy that they could return to normal life again, and, in certain regions, they associated this return to normalcy with the paramilitaries, and with their allied politicians. A word association exercise asked a random sample of a thousand civilians, "What do you think of when you hear the word 'reintegration'?" The most frequent responses were "peace," "opportunity," and "tranquility."[34] In these localities, the paramilitaries became known as the "great pacifiers."[35] In Montería, for example, "there were many people who . . . simply knew that there were no longer robbers . . . that there were no longer bombs. . . . With this perception of security, that neither the state nor the guerrilla had generated for them [but that the paramilitaries had provided], . . . What they said was, 'well, here we are now better off.'"[36]

Militarily victorious in these regions, the paramilitaries and their political allies were credited with these security improvements. Moreover, as the sources of greatest violence themselves and at the peak of their power, their agreement to tie their hands and voluntary demilitarize *when they did not have to* further boosted assessments of them.[37] One paramilitary commander declared, "We had no problem continuing the war. None."[38] And yet, his brigade opted not to double down on its indiscriminate and brutal violence; instead, it terminated its violence. This decision resulted in tangible psychological relief and political support for the paramilitaries[39] and allowed them to "assume political power directly."[40] They won, on average, 21 percent of the vote where they were militarily victorious at the municipal level compared to, on average, 8 percent in municipalities in which they were defeated.[41]

This logic—psychological in nature—has an emotional corollary. Whereas violence elicits "the cognition that [the belligerent] has committed a bad action against one's self or group,"[42] which produces anger and a desire for revenge, security—relief from the negative emotion of fear[43]—(which stems from war termination) may moderate that cognition, as the belligerent has also committed a good action by reducing fear. This renders the cognition neutral or even positive, short-circuiting the revenge mechanism, a process I provide survey evidence for in Chapter 4.

Given these preferences, optimally, the war-winner (or stalemated) belligerent will seek to mitigate the past: to convince voters to consider not only the crimes committed (as the nonbelligerent argues) but also the mitigating circumstances surrounding those crimes, and to elevate its provision of security to the top of these extenuating factors. An example of mitigation from Colombia again is apt: in his confessions, one paramilitary founder wrote, "It was worth it to kill . . . some 200 civilian guerrillas and some hundred guerrillas in uniform. Come and see! This region is awaking from a lethargy. There is [now order,] employment, education, health, harmony."[44] The mitigation narrative builds upon the war winner's conflict-era propaganda that justified its struggle, but departs in its key plot point, which is the achievement of peace offsetting its violence.[45]

The posited reference-dependent preferences will be strongest and belligerent mitigation will prove most potent at reinforcing these preferences where the book's overall assumptions hold: the population has been directly or indirectly victimized, and it experiences security gains and relief from peace. Through mitigation, the victorious belligerent party may cleanse its record without renouncing its wartime credentials, which it may tout to contribute to voter perceptions of its competence and credibility on the highly salient security issues.

BURNISHING ITS SECURITY CREDENTIALS

These credentials, the war winner may argue, along Hobbesian lines, uniquely position it to provide social peace: in a society emerging from "anarchy,"[46] with imminent threat of backsliding into "war of all against all," it can advance that there is sufficient cause—fear of violent death—to "move . . . a man to become subject to another"; a Leviathan, in Hobbes's terms, is necessary. The winning belligerent may claim that, given its war outcome, it alone possesses the "power able to over-awe" and protect the population against all threats (including postwar crime) required of such a sovereign. To sling mud at its nonbelligerent opponents' rule-based security platform, it discredits them, claiming that, in Hobbes's words, "covenants, without the sword, are but words."[47]

At the same time, how can the winning belligerent claim this power to protect when it has taken the costly steps to meaningfully end its armed struggle? Reflecting this tension was the question asked by a nonbelligerent party in Mozambique: "Where does [the belligerent successor party's] strength lie? I do not have that strength. [It] should not have it too because [it] has demobilized [its] troops and we are now equal [in terms of an armed apparatus].... What is [its] strength? Is it just political?"[48] The belligerent's claim to the security valence issue must derive not only from a coercive structure but also from a wider variety of factors.[49]

One such factor is that even if the winning belligerent party purges or distances from its armed apparatus (discussed below), it may argue that, compared to other parties, it maintains the strongest relations and networks with the state's armed forces and can most easily deploy and control them. A second factor is that it can point to skills, training, knowledge, and expertise at running successful military operations, which effectively terminated the war, to signal that its past use of force got things done; it *worked*.[50] This would differentiate it from a losing belligerent, whose violence failed. A third factor in the victorious belligerent party's claim to the security valence issue is that its members' operations during the war, unrestrained and without regard for the law, displayed the party's capacity and willingness to achieve security by any means necessary.[51] It can thus make credible promises to prioritize security in its programs and resource allocation and to be tough on threats to safety and defense. Finally, the successful belligerent may highlight a symbolic advantage: the psychology of the strongman. It can convey an impression of raw power and activate people's visceral reactions to generals, caudillos, strongmen, revolutionaries, and warlords who display themselves publicly in fatigues, with assault weapons in hand, visibly powerful.[52] In the literature on American politics, Monika L. McDermott and Costas Panagopoulos document the powerful heuristic that a military background conveys to voters.[53] Jeremy M. Teigen similarly finds that, irrespective of party affiliation, voters evaluate candidates with military backgrounds as better able to handle defense and security issues.[54] Hobbes described this nonrational mode, by which a sovereign projects its aura of protection: a Leviathan must physically be "of greater stature and strength than the natural."[55] A 1868 *Harper's Weekly* campaign cartoon neatly portrays this "*psychological* edge" on security.[56] It depicts presidential candidate General Ulysses S. Grant, emerging victorious from the Civil War, as an "unflappable and powerful giant," Gulliver among the Lilliputians (Figure 3.1).[57]

SIGNALING RESTRAINT FROM FUTURE VICTIMIZATION

However, as James Madison illuminated in the *Federalist Papers* (as discussed above), evaluations of a party's credibility on future societal order hinge not only

THE MODERN GULLIVER AMONG THE LILLIPUTIANS.

FIGURE 3.1. Claim to the Security Issue: A Gulliver among the Lilliputians.
Source: "The Modern Gulliver among the Lilliputians," *Harper's Weekly*, September 12, 1868, 592.

on sufficient strength to "enable the government to control the governed," but also on *restraint* enough to "control itself."[58] A sovereign that is a "Leviathan," in Hobbes's term, may "do *whatsoever* [it] shall think necessary to be done . . . for the preserving of peace and security,"[59] sowing serious doubts about its intentions to limit its use of force. The successful belligerent party must therefore confront voter concerns and nonbelligerents' critiques: how can the combatant party, stained with the blood of its fellow citizens, convincingly promise that it will keep its side of the social contract and, once elected, restrain itself and use its competence on security not to revictimize, but to provide for the population's "peace and common defense"? For the belligerent party's core members, the answer is likely that the Leviathan would kill only out-group members, and not them. However, the phenomenon of voting for belligerent successors goes well beyond the votes of the belligerent's core group. The combatant successor must also convince broader swaths of the electorate, including the vulnerable opposition—its former victims—and the contested swing voters, not only that it will protect them from criminality and remilitarization by other actors, but also that it will protect them from itself.

This creates a fundamental tension. To make a credible case that the *Leviathan* will be not only strong but also *Restrained*, the belligerent party must engage in high-stakes actions such as prioritizing voters it previously harmed or, at best, ignored;[60] purging its ranks; distancing from or demobilizing its coercive structure; and recruiting a fresh-faced party elite.[61] However, where these actions are sufficiently costly to be credible, and to constrain the belligerent after it has won the elections, they also risk undermining the belligerent party's image of competence on security. Otherwise, the very thing that makes it credible on security (its military war outcome of strength) renders it not credible on restraint. A belligerent party's electoral strategy guides whether it solves this elemental Madisonian equation between strength and restraint.

OTHER VALENCE ADVANTAGES

All else equal, belligerents likely do not have similar claims to other valence issues such as the economy. To bring the economy to a halt or slow it down constitutes a key tactic of rebels in asymmetric war.[62] All military campaigns destroy economic infrastructure such as residences, roads, bridges, ports, refineries, and factories. Government belligerents divert funds from social services to defense, often with detrimental health and development effects.[63] Belligerents may nonetheless still claim a general managerial competency: that their military effectiveness signals their "efficacy, experience, and ability to 'get things done.'"[64] If the nonbelligerent parties (for exogenous reasons) make strong competency claims (about the economy, or in general), belligerent parties may argue instead that economic recovery cannot take place without political stabilization, upon which they claim a valence advantage. Hobbes, again, is apt: "In such condition [wherein men live without . . . security], there is no place for industry; because the fruit thereof is uncertain; and consequently no culture of the earth; no navigation, nor use of the commodities that may be imported by sea; no commodious building; no instruments of moving and removing such things as require much force; no knowledge of the face of the earth; no account of time; no arts; no letters; no society; and which is worst of all, continual fear and danger of violent death; and the life of man, solitary, poor, nasty, brutish, and short."[65] In sum, citizens must choose among multiple parties seeking to own the salient valence issues. Whereas the nonbelligerent may prove insufficiently strong to control the governed, it can be more readily trusted to control itself. In contrast, the belligerent party is strong enough to rule the people but may prove too strong to be restrained.[66] And if it can be restrained, it might lose its strength to rule. Citizens must evaluate these trade-offs. These tensions manifest in the respective parties' positional politics, electoral targeting, and candidate selection as well.

Programs and Positional Politics

Both belligerent and nonbelligerent parties must present citizens with programmatic appeals that are responsive to the issues confronting the country. I assume that belligerent parties tend to be less moderate than nonbelligerent contenders.[67] This means that, to succeed at competitive polls, belligerent parties often cannot rely on just their activist core members, but must appeal to a broader electorate. It further suggests that nonbelligerent parties have a positional advantage over belligerent ones. They more credibly represent the centrist voter and should therefore adopt a platform that coincides with the ideological position of the moderate voter, highlight this positional advantage, and electorally "target" this moderate (their core) voter.[68]

The winning belligerent party, meanwhile, could seek to parlay its claimed valence advantage on security into an ideological position that is closer to its more extreme ideal point. However, another effect pulls it in the opposite direction: to frame the election around valence, on which it may have an edge, the belligerent party likely pursues ideological convergence. Specifically, if it repositions itself along the left-right ideological spectrum and moderates, choosing a position closer to that of its nonbelligerent opponent, it deemphasizes the importance of their policy differences. "This increases the relative importance of valence. In effect, it causes the median voter to say 'Well, if the [parties] are so similar on policy, I'll vote for the one who is superior on valence.'"[69] Emphasizing the security valence issue helps, in particular, win the votes of nonideological voters for whom this issue is important.[70] It further enables the belligerent party to avoid "the problem of taking unpopular or non-credible stances on existing issues"[71] and thereby to sidestep, partially, the trade-off between its loyalists and the more moderate sectors of the electorate. In sum, where ex ante the nonbelligerent and successful belligerent parties have competing competencies on security—the former based on rule of law, the latter on law and order—the platforms of each should *trend* toward convergence on the programs preferred by moderate voters.[72] However, I predict that nonbelligerent parties will emphasize these positional issues, while belligerent ones will downplay them.

(It should be noted that, if my assumption of ex ante uncertainty about which party has valence advantages is not true [due to early and reliable polling, free and inclusive wartime elections, or previous founding elections, for example], we might observe the party that is, in fact, disadvantaged on the security valence issue, deciding to locate itself less centrally, to differentiate itself from the more competent party.)[73]

Electoral Targeting

My moderation postulation suggests that, to maximize its expected vote, the belligerent party will likely prioritize swing voters—those "indifferent on ideological grounds"—over core voters, those with "a strong preference for a particular party."[74] Importantly, electorally "targeting" the moderate voter facilitates the belligerent party's restraint message, by expanding the definition of the in-group subject to its future protection from its narrower wartime base to a wider national constituency that includes undecided and even opposition voters.

To attract these contested and unaffiliated voters requires that the belligerent modify its image. At the same time, to retain its roots in specific sectors of society and avoid appearing inauthentic, it cannot abandon its character. To resolve this dilemma, the belligerent party may seek to activate overarching identities,[75] and to shift from defining its voter base as a particular segment of the population to defining it as the broader electorate. Following wars that pit capitalism against communism, for example, this involves downplaying the belligerent's elitist or proletariat roots to appeal across classes; this is often done through appeals to nationalism. In ethnic contexts, it requires a more dramatic reframing within the "collective field of imaginable possibilities,"[76] often by activating a civic-nationalist identity while downplaying the ethno-nationalist ones.[77] The winning belligerent becomes a constructivist for electoral reasons, seeking to upgrade latent cross-cutting identity categories while downgrading wartime cleavages.[78] In this way, it protects its flanks while drawing in a larger voter base that comprises even its victims.

Prioritizing swing voters, however, creates potential vulnerabilities of mobilization[79] and coordination[80] for the belligerent party,[81] risking its ideological supporter turnout and threatening its cohesion. I propose that several features of these warring parties allay these risks. Combatant parties tend to possess strong brands and "ideational capital": they have a "*reputation* for standing for [certain] principles" in the eyes of their supporters.[82] In particular, civil wars create a higher cause that imbues ideologically committed activists with unconditional loyalty and renders them what Angelo Panebianco calls "believers."[83] A strong brand, in turn, facilitates mobilization: the flank will tend to turn out, at least and especially in the founding elections.[84] It also will not defect to prospective splinter parties. Adrienne LeBas shows that conflict creates "us-them" distinctions: "the hardened partisan boundaries generated by violent polarization effectively 'trap' potential defectors inside the organization."[85] Belligerents have military-style internal discipline and the ability to monitor and enforce their members' behavior. As Steven Levitsky and Lucan Way reveal, abandoning the party becomes seen as treason.[86] They argue such parties, built through a history of "sustained, violent, and ideologically driven conflict," are less likely to suffer schisms, mitigating the coordination risk.[87] Therefore, in the short term, belligerent parties can focus on swing voters to maximize votes and signal restraint. In future elections, however, this moderation may risk diluting their brand by reducing interparty differentiation,[88] dampening participation and enthusiasm of their stable partisan base, and undermining party cohesion, rendering splits possible.

Leadership Selection: Party Elite and Candidates

The violent-victors theory has implications for the primal party decision: that is, the selection of politicians.[89] In recruiting, training, and promoting their party elite, belligerent parties face particularly complicated questions about who the public face of the party should be, given that its most prominent members tend to be implicated in its worst human rights abuses. These parties have to decide whether to elevate or sideline these past perpetrators.

In the framework, winning or stalemated belligerent parties target swing voters; and valence issues are crucial in attracting the votes of these nonideological voters.[90] This means that, for national contests, such as those for the presidency, and for races in the most contested districts, successful belligerent parties should select high-valence candidates, that is, those who exhibit a high individual suitability for holding office.[91] For these parties, high valence entails the Madisonian balancing act between strength and restraint; it calls for a display of wartime credentials, as exhibited by military personnel, but also a display of credibility that, once in office, its coercive power will be controlled. The party's members endowed with strength, however, are often also murderers, while new faces cannot claim competence at keeping disorder at bay. To resolve this tension, the belligerent may run its larger-than-life strongman prominently—its victimizer record whitewashed through mitigation—but then, to signal restraint, purge the remaining rights abusers (or run these low-valence party members on closed legislative lists[92] and in core electoral districts deemed safe)[93] and, for the most competitive, swing districts, recruit and field fresh civilian candidates who do not appear to require restraining.[94]

Following the same logic, nonbelligerent parties may place their own high-valence candidates—which for these parties instead means the cleanest, most human rights abiding—in the top posts and swing districts, and send their lower-quality candidates (those tainted by other sins such as corruption, dishonesty, incompetence, and the like) to safe districts and closed lists.

One may question whether the belligerent party strategy of moderation, expanding constituencies, and paired party elite could work to convince the broader electorate of its restraint credentials. The parties assume that the *Restrained* Leviathan strategy will likely work on a low-motivation audience who are not paying much attention. But they also assume that it will work primarily on the reverse-motivation audience: realists and pragmatists who want to elect the belligerent candidates, even if bloodstained, to provide security, but who want to have plausible deniability for social desirability reasons. For this class of audience (many swing and conflict-affected nonvictim voters among it), the fig leaf helps. What is more, for the direct victim voters, for whom the trade-off between strength and restraint is most acute, tactics to signal future controls on coercion matter greatly; not all victims will be so convinced, but some may.

There may be further cause for believing the belligerent's restraint message, through backward induction. As raised in Chapter 1, violent-victors perform well in democratic elections and therefore may be anticipated to defend the political system that rewards them. At the same time, if the military power balance is anticipated to hold, there exists little reason to expect the belligerent parties to renege on peace.[95] These expectations bolster electorally favored belligerents' claims of restraint.[96] It is important to underscore here that I restrict the scope of the project to cases of meaningful conflict termination in which belligerents have undertaken costly steps to end their fighting (e.g., disarmament, demobilization, security sector reform, concessions, power sharing, permission for international intervention). I therefore make an empirically grounded assumption that belligerent successors are not lying in wait for an opportune moment to ambush vulnerable civilian prey, but rather, in transitioning from war, have committed themselves (in some significant way) to peace.

The Tactical Immoderate

What of the war-loser party, in contexts other than a military draw? If poor war outcomes are to limit this party's electoral success, and it is going to lose anyway, why would it bother reinventing itself or contesting elections at all? As motivated in Chapter 2, this militarily weaker party is, in fact, less likely to engage in strategic entry under majoritarian rules. However, under proportional representation, it likely enters, even with bounded and dimmer electoral prospects, seeking to win a minimum number of seats to gain a foothold in the political landscape and be in a position to shape policy.[97] A (counter)revolutionary or independence movement does so as a continuation of its armed struggle by other means. It also does so to honor the sacrifices made in pursuit of its cause.[98] Securing internal guarantees against its adversaries' defection on the peace terms may further motivate its electoral participation.[99]

War-Loser Party's Platform: Valence and Position

Conditional on deciding to enter the race, how does the losing belligerent script itself programmatically? I argue that even if it committed fewer or more discriminate atrocities during its wartime campaigns of violence, the war-loser does not emerge with a more credible reputation for providing security in the electorate's eyes. Lacking credit for bringing peace, it cannot manipulate voters' reference points to benefit from a change in public perceptions of the violence its forces committed. Therefore, voters hold net *negative* assessments of the war loser's past record (see Text Box A); they saddle it with blame for the human costs and physical destruction of the war and, despite it also possessing guns, strongmen, and battlefield expertise, deem it incompetent on stability and order.[100] At the same time, the war loser's likely more radical position, albeit effective with its activists, disadvantages it with the broader electorate.

Given these valence and positional liabilities, relative to the nonbelligerent and successful belligerent parties who move first, if the militarily losing party moderates and emphasizes security, it puts itself in direct contestation with these parties and is likely to perform poorly. Forming coalitions with former bitter enemies and untainted parties also is unlikely an option for this antisystem belligerent party.

As a less competent challenger, the more vanquished belligerent's optimal strategy (on electoral, not normative grounds) instead becomes to adopt and emphasize immoderate positions in order to differentiate its platform from the more competent parties and gain at least some votes.[101] Albeit vulnerable to "capture by an ... extremist wing,"[102] the party's immoderation results not only from the likely sincere ideological preferences of its leaders,[103] but also from the tactical interaction of valence and positional politics.[104]

Jon Eguia and Francesco Giovannoni present a compelling theory for why this is so.[105] They argue that where other parties—in this case, the militarily advantaged belligerent and nonbelligerent parties—"own" the mainstream ideas, the militarily disadvantaged party can cede this mainstream ground. This latter party may invest instead in a clearly distinguishable alternative

TABLE 3.1. Rationale of Tactical Immoderation: Parties' Strategic Interaction

		Nonbelligerent Party and War-Winning Belligerent Party	
		Security, moderate	Nonsecurity, immoderate
War-Losing Belligerent Party	Security, moderate	0, 1	$\propto$, 1 − $\propto$
	Nonsecurity, immoderate	**1 − $\propto$, $\propto$**	0, 1

policy and can develop quality proposals around this alternative that are pinned, not to lofty wartime ideals, but to grounded, contemporary realities.[106] This alternative program falls outside the mainstream: it is bounded and ideologically off-center. It emphasizes the issues for which the war-loser party's members fought and died, those on which it has the greatest credibility over rival opposition parties and the greatest commitment given its organizational history. But it offers a disarmed and democratic version of this platform.

Table 3.1 displays this logic of tactical immoderation driven by the interactive nature of party strategy in multiparty systems; what is optimal for one party depends on what the other parties do. In it, $\propto$ > 1/2 represents the probability that a security/moderate platform is the more responsive one; 1 − $\propto$ is the likelihood that a nonsecurity valence issue and a nonmainstream position is more responsive. Accordingly, since the other parties—nonbelligerent and successful belligerent—move first and have advantages that will lead them to win if the militarily losing belligerent proposes the same platform, the losing belligerent's equilibrium strategy (moving sequentially after the other parties) becomes programmatic divergence.[107]

Eguia and Giovannoni write, "Tactical extremism is a last-resort strategy. As long as voters continue to prefer the mainstream policy, it leads to electoral defeats. However, . . . if voters become disillusioned, and wish for an alternative, tactical extremism pays off: the party that had chosen tactical extremism enjoys the valence advantage in providing such an alternative." Eguia and Giovannoni predict that a substantially disadvantaged party is more likely to opt for tactical extremism under two conditions, both of which hold for a war losing party: "(1) its reputation for policy-specific competence in delivering standard, mainstream policies is poor [given its radical wartime platform and its security and recovery valence disadvantages] and (2) voters' confidence in mainstream policy prescriptions is not too high, and this confidence is at least somewhat likely to dissolve in the future," given the great uncertainty and contestation surrounding the future direction of the country after war. "By going extreme," they write, "the party condemns itself to an immediate electoral defeat in hopes of a future electoral gain that may not materialize."[108] It is in this sense that the militarily disadvantaged belligerent's immoderation is tactical.

However, even to compete electorally on a tactical, immoderate program, in equilibrium, this vanquished belligerent's successor party must establish its commitment to working within the nonviolent system. This is especially important given the war-winner party's narrative, which casts the losing combatant as the instigator and chief victimizer of the war, and the most likely future threat. To establish this commitment, the military loser may show contrition; it can acknowledge the violence, express remorse, apologize for the harm caused, and renounce the brutal aspects of its past.[109] During the armed struggle, it justified its violent means with reference to the movement's ultimate goals, such as revolution or counterrevolution, secession or territorial integrity. However, as it slipped militarily, those ends became elusive. By "denouncing former misdoings and crimes,"[110] it can repent not only for the direct violence its forces committed, but also for causing the war and suffering in general, even if the accusations against it are disproportionate to its actual responsibility. Victors write history, and it is thus a "victor's justice" that the more vanquished side must accept.[111] Through this effort to reckon with the traumas and scars of the past, the losing belligerent regenerates in the eyes of voters.[112] The imperative to prove its contrite and pacifist intentions also drives the disadvantaged belligerent's strategy with respect to selecting its party elite, an issue to which I now turn.

War-Loser Party's Elite and Candidate Selection

The war loser's prominent party members are bloodstained (as those of war winners), but they lack security and recovery valence advantages. Losing belligerents therefore ideally will sideline their human-rights abusers completely and run only civilian candidates, particularly where transitional justice regimes are reporting. To retain their military elite would be to contradict their expressions of contrition and would raise doubts about their commitment to peaceful political contestation. However, their commanders, who are important to the party brand and to core supporters, usually do not wish to sideline themselves; also, the losing belligerent's elite pool may not run very deep. Accordingly, this strategy—running only civilian candidates—proves among the most difficult to adopt.

In sum, given the dilemmas of programmatic, elite, and constituency transformations, the *Restrained Leviathan* strategy becomes optimal for the militarily winning or stalemated successor; the *Rule Abider* the nonbelligerent party's
optimal approach; and the *Tactical Immoderate* the losing successor's most
favorable playbook.

Political Persuasion and Communication

A core underlying theme of the book is the use of persuasion, or rhetoric in
William Riker's terminology.[113] To amplify their narratives of the war[114] and
competencies in confronting the country's insecure future, belligerent and
nonbelligerent parties employ media arsenals, representatives and supporters
that can credibly disseminate their messages.[115] Through rhetoric, framing,
and marketing, they seek to capture and channel the power of propaganda to
mediate or exaggerate the relationship between past atrocities and political
reaction, and to alter perceptions of issue ownership, thus controlling the
"marketplace of ideas,"[116] and swaying citizens' political attitudes and behavior
in their favor.[117]

Against early accounts, which assumed that past records, policy positions,
and competencies of all major parties are equally well known,[118] in many elections across the world, parties do not compete on a level playing field in terms
of media;[119] the material, institutional, and reputational resources political
actors possess to propagate their messages are unevenly distributed.[120] Gaining control of the state apparatus usually affords disproportionate leverage in
political communication. This means that whatever party is the de facto incumbent administration entering the founding election tends to have a media
advantage: an ability to magnify the political information available to voters
and skew it in that party's favor, disadvantaging its rivals.[121]

Rebel victors often take control of state radio and television as they conquer
the country and the government falls.[122] Government parties—belligerent or
nonbelligerent—that are in positions of *electoral* incumbency[123] control the
state's apparatus, including its media access. Parties in the opposition tend
to lack this informational leverage, especially where the mass media are concentrated in state hands. War-losing belligerents can sometimes control their
own radio channels and newspapers. However, since armed conflict also
involves a war of propaganda, these media are usually clandestine, with
limited coverage and circulation, and they often become military targets.[124]
This means that the vanquished belligerent is further disadvantaged in

disseminating its narrative of the violent past, and in propagating its political platform for the future.

This logic suggests that the informational environment may shape the balance of rhetorical combat between the parties. In campaigns following a military draw, in particular, stalemated belligerent parties have the same optimal strategies and symmetrical electoral prospects. They are predicted to gain equal credit for ending the war through ceasefire, truce, or accords, and equal ownership of the security issue. However, their ultimate performance rests on the effectiveness of their strategies, which, in turn, likely depends on the effectiveness of their persuasion. Communication imbalances may therefore matter more following such a war outcome; while the warring parties at a draw are anticipated to split the security vote, unbalanced propaganda control may render this split unequal.

Voters

I turn now to the voters on whom electoral results pivot. How do war outcomes, and the party strategies they suggest, influence voters' images of the parties? Do the proposed strategies have their intended consequences on citizens' perceptions, preferences, and electoral behavior and therefore are optimal as predicted?

Voters respond to the "consummately political"[125] memory work of assigning guilt and innocence for the past "wrongdoings and sufferings."[126] They respond to programmatic and nonpolicy appeals, the party elite, heuristic cues, and political communications. They judge, based on parties' past performance and liabilities, whether the parties have the competencies, experience, and expertise necessary to achieve campaign promises to address salient issues. In particular, they decide whether the parties can implement the peace, protect them from contemporary and future insecurity, and resurrect the economy. Casting ballots on the basis of expectations about the parties' likely future behavior once in office—prospective voting—becomes especially important during the highly uncertain transition from war to peace.

I have proposed that both the nonbelligerent and militarily successful belligerent parties have credible claims to the salient issues—the nonbelligerent a Rule Abider claim, the belligerent a Restrained Leviathan one—and that their political platforms tend to converge on the moderate voter. In theory, the claims are both valid, so, in practice, which do voters deem most credible on securing social peace and achieving recovery going forward? Observers, scholars, and the parties themselves do not know the answer to this question, and all may very often get this wrong.

I argue that, on security grounds, citizens vote not for the untainted non-belligerent's rule of law and credible self-control. Instead, during the highly volatile trajectory from war, voters—particularly "those who suffered the war in their own flesh [and] who most understand the need for peace"[127]—experience stability and, in the pivotal moment of electing postwar order, prefer a Restrained Leviathan with its offering of ironfisted security.

If the militarily successful belligerent adopts political strategies that burnish its credentials, its military record becomes a political asset rather than a liability among security voters (those most exposed to violence), swing voters for whom valence is important, and even among some of the belligerent's own victim voters. These voters prove likely to view the belligerent as more competent than the nonbelligerent on security, contemporary and future; to estimate stability as a precondition for economic crisis management and recovery; and to forgo justice to achieve order, at least temporarily. They may accept as sufficient the belligerent's efforts at reform and its signals of restraint. Together with its core voters, these security, swing, and some victim voters provide the more victorious belligerent, militarily, a significant base of support to run effectively in the founding elections, as defined in Chapter 2. (If at stalemate, the belligerent successors instead divide these security and swing votes; relative to a winning belligerent, voters perceive those at a draw as less competent on security, but, assuming comparable propaganda control, deem the stalemated parties as equally able to secure the country's future.)[128]

Meanwhile, the nonbelligerent party, with a Rule Abider strategy, proves likely to win its core voters, but to lose these nonideological and security voters in the founding election. Its record and promises are assessed neutrally, and it achieves surprisingly little electoral benefit from maintaining a clean human rights record. And, if the war-loser party adopts its respective, optimal playbook—Tactical Immoderation—it is likely to lose valence voters but attract at least a marginal, ideologically bounded constituency and win credibility on nonmainstream policies for future elections.

Playing the Wrong Hand: Off-Equilibrium Paths

I have made the case that, emerging from mass violence in civil conflict, war outcomes guide the optimal strategies for parties to appeal to victimized voters and succeed politically in founding elections. I find that most parties select the optimal strategies most of the time. However, sometimes parties play the wrong hand.

At times, militarily advantaged or stalemated belligerents, rather than mitigating the violent past, renounce their past and seek not to restore their party image but to gut renovate it. Instead of running combinations of civilian and military elite, owning the security issue and adopting programmatic moderation, they field only fresh-faced civilian candidates with no security credentials, "trespass" on other parties' valence issues,[129] and advance non-middle-of-the-road platforms. Alternatively, these successful belligerents might, at times, embrace an objective, non-spun version of their past, run only commanders, and prioritize the policies preferred by their radical activists. Nonbelligerent parties might, at times, focus on "forgiving and forgetting" or campaign on strong-arm security, field low-valence candidates, or advocate noncentrist policies. Rather than expressing contrition, more vanquished belligerents might instead choose to glorify their historical justification, deny their own wrongdoings, maintain an outright extremist program, or elevate the victimizers among them.[130] These, however, are all likely doomed electoral strategies.

Why, given the electoral imperatives that winning or stalemated belligerents run as Restrained Leviathans, that losing ones run as Tactical Immoderates, and that nonbelligerents run as Rule Abiders, would they fail to do so and undermine their electoral prospects? Why do they not choose more successful strategies? What can we discern about the types of parties that prove best able to strategize effectively to maximize their electoral performance?

There are cases that are off the equilibrium path because the party leaders, despite access to the optimal strategy, make mistakes, for idiosyncratic, usually personal reasons. I do not theorize about these. There are other cases in which the parties play the wrong hand because features of their circumstances make the equilibrium paths unavailable to them. Whereas the former are off equilibrium because of choice, the latter are so because of structure or organization. Given that electoral playbooks are decided in strategic interaction, the optimal one may become unavailable because another party has claimed the strategy. Moreover, one party adopting a nondominant strategy renders other parties more likely to do so. In such cases, I consider the first party's move a choice, the subsequent parties' moves structural.[131]

The organizational conditions for strategic erring often stem from what Kenneth Greene calls "birth defects" related to a party's origins. These defects tend to persist and shape the party's behavior after transitions in ways that are detrimental to its electoral prospects.[132] For belligerent parties in particular, effectively navigating the political obstacle course requires flexibility from the inertia of a constraining institutional machine or powerful diehard ideologues. It requires that these parties, while carrying the mantle of the belligerent, retain the nimbleness to shift programmatically, have sufficient pools of party leaders to restructure internally, be able to expel their tarnished elites and incorporate fresh, shiny faces, and prove willing to defy their own core constituents in order to reform.[133] It demands that they be not blinded by the bubble of militancy, but instead able to gauge the temperature of public opinion accurately. Those born as "niche parties," for example—hermetic, inward-looking organizations—tend to be beholden to rigid orthodox loyalists and inflexible structures that hinder political maneuver,[134] whereas centralization and organization around a strong, charismatic leader can facilitate flexibility.[135]

While structural conditions may limit the strategy choice set, they might also expand it. In environments in which viable nonbelligerent parties do not exist, due to the nascence or incompleteness of democracy (largely excluded from the scope of the study), military war outcomes alone might guide electoral outcomes: then, the advantaged belligerent will not have to engage in strategy to attract votes and any strategy might be successful.

Before turning to the founding elections' implications for peace, justice, and political development, I pause to consider alternative accounts of the electoral performance of belligerent successor parties.

Alternative Explanations

This electoral performance, I argue, cannot wholly be explained by conventional explanations emerging from literatures on violence, political behavior, and transitional justice. A first intuitive, alternative explanation for post–civil war party success might be that those parties that prove electorally successful were (more) restrained in their violence during war and that the votes they win come from beneficiaries of that violence rather than from its victims.[136] If this were the case, we would observe belligerent parties achieving greater electoral success following conflicts and in regions in which they carried out only limited violence, and winning votes primarily from nonvictims of their transgressions.

This is not, however, what history shows. Cross-national evidence in this book reveals that parties with roots in organizations that controlled their use of violence performed no better in postwar elections than those derived from belligerents that committed indiscriminate atrocities. Subnational data from eighteen conflicts globally show that terrorized regions voted for the successor parties in proportions similar to regions unscathed by the belligerents' wartime campaigns. And individual survey evidence across Latin America suggests that victims themselves proved equally likely to vote for their perpetrators as for parties unstained by war. An information experiment embedded in a survey in Colombia and in-depth interviews with victims across the case studies indicate that these patterns are not reflective of a fog of war: voters not knowing whom the perpetrators were. The book argues instead that military war outcomes produce asymmetry in the attribution of blame for the violence—whom the victimized populations will punish, and why—and therefore, voting does not correlate with the intensity of the crimes committed.

A second alternative explanation would argue that voters who support politicians with bloodied pasts do so not out of affinity but out of (fear of) coercion, rendering their electoral behavior unsurprising.[137] This logic is subtly distinct and risks observational equivalence with that of the book. While doing so is challenging, I seek to disentangle the two logics. This book studies postwar democratic elections, delineated as specified in Chapter 2; it excludes manifestly unfree and unfair elections. Were intimidation driving votes even in the contexts studied in this book, the success of civil war successor parties would likely correlate with their use of electoral violence and fraud; belligerent parties would disproportionately win the votes of the most vulnerable, those casting their ballots under fear of retribution; belligerent parties would not necessarily gain office over time as the memory of coercion faded, and they would receive voters' ballots, but not their attitudinal support. Additionally, those fearing war recurrence would be particularly likely to cast their votes for the belligerent parties and these parties would win on strength; signals of restraint would not matter. Accordingly, war winners would be unlikely to engage in the (at times costly) strategies proposed by the book's model (such as purging the organization, moderating, targeting swing voters, and risking core voters). Finally, nonbelligerent parties would likely fare dismally, ceding to belligerent parties not only undecided segments of the electorate, but also their ideological supporters.

Using municipal data on intimidation and votes, sensitive questioning experiments, observational survey evidence, and cross-national evidence of electoral violence, I find that citizens vote for the belligerent parties even without (fear of) "guns to their heads." I show that citizens worried about war recurrence are no more likely to elect belligerent parties than those that express little concern over a resumption of armed hostilities. I further demonstrate that it is not that citizens in these elections have only bad alternatives to vote for; voters could choose parties of nonbelligerents who are not awash in their citizens' blood,[138] and even viable and untainted opposition parties led by Nobel Peace Prize winners. These nonbelligerent parties often perform well (albeit more rarely win), and they retain their core voters. Finally, using examples of parties that adopted off-equilibrium strategies, I show that war-winner parties did not perform well irrespective of strategy. I do not deny the existence of votes cast out of fear or coercion in postwar elections, but seek to explain the voluntary votes for bloodstained parties.

A third possible alternative answer to the book's puzzle centers on underlying political preferences: popular belligerents—even if bloodstained—win wars, while unpopular belligerents lose wars.[139] Popular parties then win elections while unpopular ones lose elections. Popularity may therefore constitute a key and omitted variable. Were this argument correct, underlying prewar allegiances should explain war outcomes. Instead, however, evidence reveals that military outcomes change significantly over the course of wars, rendering fixed prewar levels of support a poor predictor of war outcomes, and allegiances prove fluid and endogenous.[140] A variant on the popular support argument is a selection one whereby blood-soaked belligerents that can build popularity over the course of the war prove more likely, in turn, to succeed militarily and electorally. If popular support—whether prewar or endogenous to war—were driving votes for tormentors, these abusive belligerents who perform well in the elections likely would be representative of the majority's ideological preferences or ethnic demography, but often they are not. The "underlying preferences" account offers little to explain the existence or behavior of the large numbers of contested and swing voters at the end of many wars, which often prove decisive in the founding elections. I dispute the underlying allegiances account because it fails to differentiate popularity of different kinds or at different times. I argue that the causality may in fact be at least partially reversed: militarily winning belligerents are popular because they bring security.[141] Moreover, given the book's focus on voluntary votes, it risks tautology to argue that popular support dictates votes. Instead, we must explain *why* citizens prefer the belligerent parties. I argue that it is not necessarily because they are aligned with the voters' underlying (prewar) ideologies, but because they are deemed best able to secure the voters' futures.

A fourth viable alternative framework centers on organizational strengths, such as party machines, cohesion, finances, and a reputation for general competence—and posits that brutal belligerents may just be better at organizing, which is why they perform well in elections as well as in wars.[142] This explanation has greater leverage in accounting for variation in the success of different belligerent parties than in explaining belligerents' performance relative to nonbelligerent parties. I concur that these organizational assets help overcome mobilization and coordination challenges that emerge, in particular, for more victorious belligerents as their postwar programs trend toward moderation. These assets also have important bearing on the parties' durability over time. However, the evidence suggests that these organizational assets do not correlate significantly with electoral performance in the founding political contests after war.

Several additional alternatives merit careful consideration, including economic voting,[143] partisan issue ownership,[144] and incumbency.[145] Few countries emerge from war into positive economic conditions; most are in crisis. In theory, in these contexts, there are therefore relatively few positive retrospective economic votes to give to incumbent parties; prospective economic voting becomes linked to security voting as recovery presupposes stability; and bread-and-butter issues are often on hold until basic security is established.[146] I show, however, the significant marginal effect of security voting even when controlling for this well-established material determinant of vote choice. Where the belligerents fall on the ideological spectrum might determine whether they are deemed competent on security; the right "owns" security.[147] My argument departs from this partisanship explanation to argue instead that any successor to a wartime belligerent can, depending on its war outcome, own this issue. In my framework, the electoral tactics and successes of rebel victors largely mirror those of government victors, undermining explanations centered on prewar incumbency and the asset control that the state apparatus affords. This is because victorious rebels tend to gain de facto state control when the previous governments fall. However, I find that media control does matter, and to the extent that it rests in state hands, incumbency also matters. Alternative explanations can account for an important share of the postwar vote but leave significant variation in electoral outcomes unexplained. Each stage of the book's empirical development seeks to evaluate the book's framework against these strong alternatives.

Peace or War Recurrence

The political dynamics discussed thus far are those present in the lead-up to the founding elections after mass violence in war. Now, I elaborate upon the implications for what happens after these elections: When do the predicted polling results prove stabilizing, and when do they instead create a revolving door back to war? What happens to the belligerent parties over time if the transition to peace becomes solidified: what effect do these elected blood-stained parties have on democracy, justice, and governance?

If the military balance of power after war remains stable,[148] there exists little reason for either the winning or losing belligerent to reinitiate hostilities; because their "mutual expectations about the consequences of [future] fighting . . . remain the same, the bargain struck between the belligerents should persist since neither side expects that a resumption of conflict would result in a better deal" and thus a different future election result.[149] The winning belligerent enjoys both the motivation and the capacity to sustain order. Peace should thus hold.[150]

However, if the power balance becomes inverted, with the electoral loser militarily favored,[151] the fact that voters tend to use war outcomes as the heuristic guiding their security voting[152] can create a perilous tension: the war winner is no longer more powerful than the war loser and yet nonetheless wins the election. In this case, the loser will remilitarize. Because military success in war yields a unique electoral dividend, a return to war becomes ex ante beneficial for the war and election loser. The war loser, now militarily advantaged, will decide to remilitarize in order to win the next war and enter future elections from a position of victory. Thus whether war recurs or peace sustains depends on stability in the balance of power and the election outcomes.[153]

Belligerent Successor Parties over Time

If peace holds, the belligerent party—benefitting from elections—is likely to maintain democracy but block its deepening, and also obstruct transitional justice. Given this backdrop, how do the successor parties fare over time, and with what prospects for political development, regime type, and legal accountability? Huntington argues that strong parties are often a "product of intense political struggle" to "overthrow the existing system, to control the existing system, or to enter the existing system."[154] However, many other parties that "emerg[e] as a product of war"[155] dissolve over time, despite extraordinary achievements in the first one or two elections. What permits success of the belligerent parties in the founding election might not be the same as what facilitates their electoral durability. To continue to win, as voters' preferences change and party politics normalizes, requires party machines able to respond to citizens' diversifying concerns, to boost economic growth, to mobilize voters, and to manage clientelism.[156] Ironically, the parties best able to weather the political transition—those that are rooted in militarily successful belligerent organizations headed by dominant charismatic leaders with security valence, but otherwise elusive, programs—may be precisely those with a less developed political machine to buy votes, rally activists, and respond to nonsecurity concerns, particularly the economy.[157] Politicians who mobilize support based on personalistic appeals are often reluctant to invest in party structures that might limit their power and autonomy.[158] Where the belligerent parties can develop such political organizations and prove responsive on other issues, their electoral success should prove more durable over time. Where they cannot, their political clout is likely to evaporate after several rounds of elections.[159]

The power of the belligerent successors' security brand may diminish because, as the transition becomes cemented, citizens' concerns become more multifaceted, the justification for a strongman declines, and thus the potency of the Leviathan strategy erodes. This is consistent with the short time horizon observed around security-crisis-induced "rally-'round-the-flag" effects, which generate quick boosts in executive approval that fade over time.[160] Gratitude for peace is short-lived.[161] Indeed, the book's model predicts that voters elect the party best able to keep the peace; through its early success, the belligerent party therefore could put itself out of business.

But even if security concerns do not become less salient—perhaps because crime spikes, or power later shifts and the strengthened belligerent remilitarizes—the security brand becomes vulnerable to two trends over the medium term. Once in government, voters judge the belligerent successor not only on its record of bringing wartime violence to an end, which is receding into the past, but on the immediate record: whether it is succeeding or failing to combat insecurity and tackle other issues.[162] Given the challenge of crime reduction in environments ripe for illicit activity (including postconflict ones),[163] the militarily advantaged belligerent may perform well in the short term in the domain in which it has a comparative advantage, competence, and expertise—security—but over time it may still fail more often that it succeeds. Tough-on-crime approaches tend to erode public safety over the long term,[164] and prioritizing security over other public goods often crowds out social development expenditures with detrimental welfare consequences.[165] Lack of education spending, in particular—shown an important antidote to crime—reduces public safety over the long term.[166] When ironfisted policies generate few results over time, a belligerent's claim to the security issue may fade. Voters might hold it accountable and begin to see nonbelligerents as potentially more competent on security and be willing to experiment instead with rule-based security.[167] The belligerent successor parties must then find a new dimension on which to run.

The eroding potency of the security brand does not portend its extinction, however; rather, it often lies dormant, able to be resurrected during future spells of insecurity. If the country confronts another uncertain transition, or an upsurge in crime or risk of war, the belligerent parties have incentives to revive public memories of fear and violence. Through "issue priming"[168] and "agenda manipulation,"[169] the belligerent parties again may plant the idea that the issue they own—security—is the criterion by which the electorate makes its vote choice and thereby set this "choice as a decision to be made in terms of problems facing the country that [the belligerent party is] better able to 'handle' than [its] opponent[s]."[170] This transforms the nature of these future campaigns.[171] Thomas Hammond and Brian Humes explain, "Instead of the candidates trying to figure out what positions to take, then, [these] political campaigns are turned into contests about what the issue dimensions of the campaign will be."[172] Belligerent parties have greater incentives to keep security threats alive through their rhetoric, but may also, perversely, feel compelled to do so, by fomenting low-level insecurity.[173]

Second, over time, the reference points modeled earlier may shift back (see Text Box A). I posit that voters' selection of belligerent parties will impede a comprehensive transitional justice process in the short to medium term. As peace consolidates, the mitigating effect of security on the attribution of blame is, however, likely to decline; demands for more complete transitional justice are likely to expand. Perpetrators may thus be unable to evade blame forever. There is thus promise that, over time, progress toward legal accountability may become possible.[174]

Observable Implications and Research Design

The book's violent-victors theory has observable implications for the relationship between how wars end and party performance in the founding postwar elections. It also has observable implications for what strategies parties will adopt and why, and how voters will respond and for what reasons. Finally, it suggests implications for how these pivotal, founding election results influence postwar peace, justice, democracy, and governance.

These observable implications require testing at different levels of analysis and with a variety of methodologies. An ideal research design would randomize wartime violence, war outcomes, and party strategies. Of course, this would be ethically unthinkable. I integrate different methods to evaluate each of the observable implications of my argument against alternatives, using "each method for what it is especially good at."[175] My resulting research design comprises voter-level experimental evidence and observational survey data; rich case studies of party strategizing and behavior based on archival research, in-depth interviews, databases of candidates, and text analysis of party programs, propaganda, and social media; and analyses of cross-national and subnational data on violence, war outcomes, and electoral results.

I lay out each set of observable implications of my theory and my research design for testing the implications. In-depth methodological details follow in the relevant sections of the book.

War Outcomes and Postwar Election Results

The key claim of the book is that violent victors of wars go on to become victors of postwar democratic elections. If this claim is correct, we should expect war outcomes to be powerful predictors of belligerent successor party performance. We should further anticipate that this relationship between how the war ends and the elections unfold would hold irrespective of the belligerents' extent of mass atrocities, and that abusive belligerent parties should perform well, even where elections are clean, free, and fair. These implications likely should be reflected at the subnational level as well; belligerent parties should perform better electorally where they won the war locally, and geographic patterns of atrocity should have little bearing on regional election results.

To evaluate this first set of implications, I use an original cross-national dataset of the full universe of belligerents around the world that transitioned from civil war between 1970 and 2015. This is the first dataset to study postwar electoral outcomes of both the rebel side and the government side of the conflict, and to identify the vote share for parties without a violent past. On average, government belligerent parties gained 40.8 percent of the vote, while rebel parties won, on average, 25.6 percent of the vote. Meanwhile, parties without a violent past gained, on average, 43.6 percent of the vote share, suggesting that parties with violent pasts (rebel and government) tended to dominate the elections, claiming the remaining 56.4 percent of the vote. Electoral success, however, varied dramatically from case to case. To evaluate the theory's subnational implications, for eighteen conflicts globally, I collected data on atrocities, military outcomes, and postwar voting, disaggregated by belligerent, at the smallest subnational political unit.

Party Strategies

The book argues that war outcomes characterize parties as winning-belligerent, losing-belligerent, and nonbelligerent and these characterizations drive the parties' postwar electoral strategies (which, in turn, influence voter behavior and thus postwar electoral outcomes). These strategies include what valence issues to emphasize; how to ideologically position and with what programmatic specificity; how to reckon with the bloodstained past; whether to play to militant and mobilized core supporters, or instead seek to shift the votes of uncertain swing constituencies; how to select party elite and whether to sideline or promote rights abusers; and how to propagate and prime campaign messages. The book predicts that, in equilibrium, winning belligerent parties will adopt a Restrained Leviathan strategy, nonbelligerent parties a Rule Abider strategy, and losing belligerent parties a Tactical Immoderate strategy. It further anticipates that the parties will engage these strategies for the reasons outlined throughout this theory chapter. The skeletal components of each party strategy are spelled out in Table 3.2.

To evaluate the book's observable implications for party strategizing and strategies, I use the comparative settings of El Salvador, Guatemala, and Nicaragua.[176] I selected these Central American cases for several reasons. One, and most important, they exhibited nearly the full range of the model's independent variable of who won the war—a draw in El Salvador, government victory in Guatemala, and rebel victory in Nicaragua—and thus provided insight into how war outcomes might structure and constrain the belligerent and nonbelligerent parties' electoral strategies. While varying in who won the war, all three cases are similar in a history of authoritarianism, repression, poverty, and inequality—the general causes of the conflicts—war duration, geopolitics, and external intervention, providing a tightly controlled, small-n comparison. Two, Latin America provides institutional continuity and homogeneity, such that the electoral systems may be treated as exogenous rather than a product of the war outcomes. Three, the cases fit the scope conditions of the theory:

TABLE 3.2. Equilibrium Party Strategies after Large-Scale Violence in War

	War Winner or Stalemated Successor Party	Nonbelligerent Party	War Loser Successor Party
Strategy	Restrained Leviathan	Rule Abider	Tactical Immoderate
Valence	Security (iron fist)	–Security (rule-based) –Other valence	Nonsecurity
Violent past	Mitigation	Punishment	Contrition
Position	Moderate (vague)	Moderate (specific)	Immoderate
Electoral targets	Swing voters	Moderate voters	Immoderate voters
Candidates	–Key strongman + civilians –Purge rights abusers or hide in closed lists	Cleanest civilians	Only civilians

they were postwar and held democratic elections with meaningful alternatives[177] (with critical caveats in the Nicaraguan case, which render it a shadow case only, but one critical to the research design given its war outcome of rebel victory). The three cases also exhibited the conditions under which the framework should perform best: widespread impact and victimization by armed conflict, a prevalence of unaligned voters, high security salience, a single electorate, and (relatively) programmatic as opposed to clientelistic politics.[178] (I use cross-national data and skim qualitative evidence globally to explore the theory's generalizability to cases in which these conditions hold more loosely.)[179] Four, the cases provide insights into alternative explanations. In the Salvadoran and Guatemalan cases, wartime violence and underlying voter preferences were highly asymmetric, offering a sharp test of the logics of retributive voting to punish atrocities and prewar popular support. In these two cases, truth commissions issued their reports before the founding elections, so voters could have known the "facts" of the violence before casting their votes; this reduces the chance that voter ignorance drove party strategies and political behavior. Whereas in El Salvador the government belligerent was the electoral incumbent, in Nicaragua the rebel belligerent had become the de facto incumbent in the lead-up to the elections, and in Guatemala a nonbelligerent party was the electoral incumbent. This variation enables me to disentangle the effects of incumbency. Finally, in Guatemala and El Salvador, the right-wing belligerents sought to win on the security issue, while in Nicaragua, the left-wing belligerent did; this provided a test of the partisan underpinnings of issue ownership.

The goal of these cases was to test the party-level hypotheses, which center on process (the underpinnings of party strategizing), outcomes (the parties' platforms, rhetoric, propaganda, electoral targets, and candidate lists), and performance. The ideal tests of my theory would require access to internal party debates in which party members discussed the key party challenges of the book. I was able to peek into these debates through records maintained in party archives held privately by the parties' campaign strategists or publicly in museums or archives. However, for the most part, these black-box deliberations were not observable. Contemporaneous interviews with party elites and election observers could shed some light on what might have taken place behind closed doors. These included journalistic and diplomatic renderings. I therefore collected historical interviews with candidates, news coverage of the campaigns, and declassified U.S. embassy cables. To complement the historical interviews, I conducted my own in-depth interviews with former presidents, presidential candidates, campaign strategists, senators, and military commanders. These sought to reconstruct the party discussions about strategies to take credit for conflict termination, narrate the bloodstained history, exploit media to control the marketplace of ideas, activate or deactivate security, economic, or ideological voting, prove their party's competence on different valence issues, moderate or radicalize party manifestos, target different types of voters, and sideline or elevate those responsible for the worst atrocities. However, these interviews were ex post and subject to social desirability bias. While I sought to corroborate what they told me from other sources, I cannot know if they were telling the truth.

I therefore turned to what the parties ran on, what they spoke about, and whom they fielded as candidates. I collected and analyzed, both with natural language processing and with qualitative review, their political platforms, speeches, campaign advertisements, and rhetoric from multiple archives of newspaper, radio, television, and campaign data. I also catalogued their party lists, looking in particular at their candidates' wartime liabilities. To explore whether the parties succeeded or failed at political framing, I analyzed survey data collected during the elections to infer, observationally, the effects of the party strategies on public opinion and voting behavior and to evaluate alternative explanations.

Voter Strategies

The theory has implications for how voters respond to the war-outcome-dictated party strategies. It suggests that voters—particularly security, swing, and even some victim voters—should reward winning belligerents for peace, rather than blame them for violence. These voters should further deem winning belligerents who adopt a Restrained Leviathan strategy as more competent on security and more electable than winning belligerents who adopt non-equilibrium strategies. This security issue ownership, in turn, is predicted to boost the war winners' electoral performance.

In contrast, the theory anticipates that voters should hold losing belligerents responsible for the war's atrocities and deem them noncompetent on security. Ideologically more extreme voters should prefer losing belligerents who campaign with a Tactical Immoderate strategy over those who run on alternative strategies. This strategy should enable losing belligerents to carve out a small, circumscribed electoral foothold in the political arena.

Finally, voters should neither blame nonbelligerent parties for the wartime violence nor credit them with peace; accordingly, they should see nonbelligerents neutrally: as neither competent nor incompetent on security, though they may attribute other valence advantages to these parties untainted by war. While security, swing, and some victim voters are likely to support the winning belligerent party over the nonbelligerent one, with a Rule Abider strategy, nonbelligerents should earn the votes of their usually ideologically centrist core voters.

To test these observable implications for voter attitudes and behavior, I use an original survey from Colombia and observational data from Central America as noted above. The peace process between the government and the FARC rebels[180] in 2016 in Colombia provided a unique opportunity to realize a survey whose immediacy would minimize problems of recall, and whose design would facilitate the estimation of causal effects. At the time of this writing, Colombia was the only country in the world emerging tentatively from war and experiencing elections. The survey yielded the fine-grained data to permit inferences about what are fundamentally individual-level cognitive processes: the voter-level mechanisms of the theory linking war outcomes and party strategies with postwar election results. My sample included 1,510 citizens in Colombia across thirty-eight municipalities, with a rare overrepresentation in the sample of 855 direct victims of the conflict and 645 nonvictims, some of whom were nonetheless affected adversely by the conflict.

The survey presented respondents with hypothetical scenarios of episodes of violence that varied by perpetrator—government or rebel—and varied by whether or not peace and security were provided. The design then collected evidence on the effects of these treatments on public opinion toward the use of force to assess whether militarily winning belligerents are able to use credit for peace to shift voters' references points, while losing belligerents cannot. Using an information treatment, I evaluate whether, as hypothesized, mitigating the violent past proves electorally expedient and therefore rational for a successful belligerent, while contrition proves optimal for an unsuccessful one. With two double vignette conjoint experiments,[181] I estimate whether a Restrained Leviathan party strategy proves more successful for the war winner, whereas the Tactical Immoderate strategy proves preferable for the war loser. With observational survey data, I test whether voters support strongman security over rule-based security.

The original survey also enables me to evaluate alternative mechanisms of voter coercion through list experiments and a randomized secret ballot, and of voter ignorance through an information experiment. I use the survey data to model vote choice and the relative share of that choice explained by security voting, relative to the myriad other factors known to influence voters' decisions.

I briefly pivot from voters back to parties in this context to explore whether, in Colombia's 2018 electoral campaigns, parties followed the equilibrium strategies suggested by the survey results, or instead diverged from them, why, and with which electoral implications. To do so, I rely on hundreds of interviews and text analysis of party platforms and Twitter feeds.

Implications of Elections for Peace, Democracy, Justice, and Governance

The theory has implications for the postwar elections' impact on peace, justice, democracy, and governance. I use diverse sources of data and methods to evaluate these implications as well.

WAR AND PEACE

The project anticipates that the risk of postwar remilitarization should increase if there is a power shift and the newly militarily stronger party (the war loser) loses the election to the now-weaker war winner. To test this observable implication, I return to the book's original cross-national dataset. I merge the dataset with existing data on changes/stability in the distribution of power and present newly assembled data on which belligerent reinitiated war. I use the Central American cases and several abbreviated case studies to illustrate the strategic logic.

JUSTICE

The book's framework anticipates that the electoral selection of bloodstained parties will imply regressive transitional justice over the short term but that, as peace consolidates, opportunities for legal accountability may materialize. To evaluate this observable implication, I use information on the tormentor parties' vote share from the cross-national Civil War Successor Party dataset, which I overlap with evidence on postwar amnesties. I also explore in the book's case studies how the elections of belligerents influenced patterns of transitional justice over the long term.

DEMOCRACY

The book's theory would expect war-winner parties to champion the democratic rules that elected them, at least in the short term, but to hinder further development of the democratic regime. While the equilibrium strategies implied by the book (e.g., moderation, sidelining rights abusers, and stretching constituencies) may help transform the belligerent successor parties into more democratic actors, their long-term success ultimately depends on their uncertain ability to mobilize a party machine and address voter concerns as politics normalize from violence. Merging the CWSP cross-national dataset on belligerent successor parties' electoral performance with data from the Varieties of Democracy project on liberal democracy, I probe these implications of the book's argument. I further trace, in a cursory fashion, the political trajectories of the case study parties over time.

GOVERNANCE

Finally, the book's argument has implications for how belligerent parties govern if they win the elections. In particular, it implies that they will perform well on the provision of public safety and poorly on the provision of other public goods. One of the challenges in studying the governance implications of the commonplace election of bloodstained parties is endogeneity bias: because the election of these parties is nonrandomly assigned, a variety of factors might influence the likelihoods both of belligerents winning the elections and of belligerents governing in a specific fashion. An original database of 784 paramilitary-tied mayors, based on over 42,000 pages of Colombian Supreme Court sentencing documents, provided a sufficient sample size to use a regression discontinuity (RD) design and compare the administrations of paramilitary candidates who barely won with those who barely lost the elections. I therefore briefly leverage this opportunity for causal leverage on the effects of belligerents' election on governance outcomes.

Through this multilayered research strategy, employing diverse qualitative and quantitative data at different levels of analysis, and combining my personal observations with the testimonies of protagonists themselves, I am able to chart the electoral performance and political roles played by civil war belligerents and victimized voters in the aftermath of war and to shed some light on questions of great importance to the populations living through transitions from armed struggle to peace.

Conclusion

The book's violent-victors theory explains how parties that committed mass atrocities in civil war do well in postwar democratic elections. It proposes that belligerent status and war outcomes guide parties' strategies for capturing the prospective vote: how parties script programmatically in terms of valence and position, define their constituencies, select their party elite, and persuade voters of their messaging. In equilibrium, nonbelligerents run as Rule Abiders, successful belligerents as Restrained Leviathans, and losing belligerents as Tactical Immoderates. Security, swing, and even some victim voters elect war-winner parties for their offer of law and order over nonbelligerents' rule-of-law alternative. Given the salience of the security valence issue, these bloodstained parties become electorally bolstered. Nonbelligerents, meanwhile, win only their core voters; losing belligerents carve out a delimited place in the postwar political landscape. These pivotal elections tend to keep the peace, but at significant costs to the citizenry who sacrifices legal accountability, social welfare, and liberalism.

4

Postwar Voters and Survey Experiments

THE VIOLENT-VICTORS THEORY links war outcomes with democratic outcomes through a strategic interplay between parties and voters. On the one hand, it posits that parties rationally choose their strategies by anticipating the likely effect of those strategies on voter behavior. On the other hand, said Sandra Ramírez, widow of FARC's founding commander, the success of the belligerent party "depends a lot on us, on how we convey the message."[1] Through their campaign choices, parties shape voters' attitudes and preferences. The parties also engage in strategic interaction with each other.

In my framework, these interplays generate equilibrium strategies for parties of different war experience and military success to position themselves for the future. This chapter evaluates the plausibility of these equilibrium strategies and specifically tests the book's individual-voter-level hypotheses. The book posits that war outcomes shift voters' reference points such that voters disproportionately blame the weaker belligerents for the past violence, and they credit and reward the stronger belligerents for termination of that violence. As a result, the book proposes that mitigation of the record of atrocity draws electoral support for the latter and contrition does so for the former. It further argues that, compared to alternative strategies, a *Restrained Leviathan* one attracts more votes for the military winner, and a *Tactical Immoderate* strategy does so for the military loser. In the model, individuals expect that the war victor party will be the most competent to maintain security going forward; this wins it the ballots of security voters, swing voters, and even some victim voters.

The book's case studies (Chapters 5–7) show that the proposed logic guides the derivation of party strategies and that, in equilibrium, parties tend to adopt these strategies. I argue that these strategies are rational; they track with and reflect citizens' perceptions, preferences, and electoral behavior. But we cannot know from a study of aggregate relationships whether the individual-level mechanisms are at work. Studies of political legacies of violence share the presumption of a direct translation of objective attribution of violence into ballot-box choices, and most studies of electoral behavior advance alternative, nonsecurity determinants of vote choice. If these studies are correct, there is reason to doubt the book's hypothesis of asymmetric attribution of blame based on war outcomes, and the explanatory power of its model of prospective security voting. We therefore need to test directly whether belligerent parties' tactics for addressing their bloodstained inheritance, positioning themselves programmatically, selecting their candidates, and generating their valence appeals really have the proposed consequences on war-ravaged voters at the individual level, leading such victimized populations to vote for tormentors.

In order to test the effects of the theoretical party strategies on individual voters, I embedded experiments in a survey of 859 victims and 642 nonvictims in Colombia. The experiments manipulated exposure to security provision as an offset to a record of violence, and exposed respondents to mitigation and contrition narratives. The survey also randomly assigned voters to different party strategies that suggested either the Restrained Leviathan or the Tactical Immoderate approach. Testing these propositions observationally proved problematic. By randomly assigning respondents to these treatment and control groups, the experiments made the treatments exogenous to observed outcomes, which allowed the identification of causal relationships.

Colombia provided a fertile case in which to investigate the dynamics of postwar party and voter strategies. In this case, according to Congresswoman Juanita Goebertus, "We don't have a good and a bad, we don't have someone who is clearly the most responsible [for atrocities]. There is responsibility all over."[2] Whereas the rebels were deemed accountable for the vast majority of kidnappings, mine placements, and child recruitment, the paramilitaries were found guilty of over 60 percent of the massacres, assassinations, and disappearances;[3] the army was responsible for a particularly vicious, systematic, and large-scale pattern of extrajudicial killings known as "false positives," in which soldiers abducted innocent, marginalized civilians, "killed them, placed weapons on their lifeless bodies, and then reported them as enemy combatants killed in action."[4] Over 80 percent of Colombia's more than nine million victims were civilians.

The theory posits significant evolution of political life after the founding elections, over time. Therefore, it was important to capture the dynamics as close in time as possible to peace accords and first postwar political contests. At the time of this writing, Colombia alone was emerging tentatively from war and experiencing elections. After the November 2016 peace accords with the FARC, Colombia held legislative and presidential elections in spring 2018 and local elections in October 2019.[5] As part of the final peace accord, FARC transitioned into a political party, known as Fuerza Alternativa Revolucionaria del Común (FARC).[6] During this period, the transitional justice regime was reporting its findings, the belligerent and nonbelligerent parties were active in framing the revelations of this regime; and party strategies varied significantly. Therefore, voters had some prior beliefs about the parties' violent pasts, but these priors varied and were potentially malleable. This afforded me the opportunity to field a survey during a live war-to-peace transition to evaluate the theory's individual-level hypotheses in real time. The context also lent itself to testing alternative explanations with polling data.

Using survey experiments and observational data, I find support for the effect on postwar voters of winning and losing belligerent party strategies for reckoning with the violent past, scripting their programs, and selecting their party elite. These data further cast doubt on alternative logics of fog of war or voter coercion and suggest an important role for security voting, even when considering other determinants of vote choice including economic voting, clientelism, and partisanship. The survey experiments imply optimal playbooks for parties—of varying war outcomes—seeking to maximize their share of the vote in founding elections. I pause on Colombia's 2018 elections to show the correlations between the on- and off-equilibrium strategies and electoral performance. Here, I rely on hundreds of in-depth interviews, text analysis of party programs and Twitter posts, and existing polling data. This chapter tests the micro voter-level underpinnings of the book's violent-victors theory, which link war outcomes, party strategies, and election results. Chapters 5 to 7 then test the book's party-level hypotheses in other contexts.

A Survey in Colombia

In 2020, I fielded a face-to-face survey of a random sample of 1,510 victims and nonvictims across Colombia. I had previously conducted fieldwork in Colombia over two cumulative years, across all of its regions, and I had experience enumerating challenging surveys in and out of prisons, and with vulnerable populations there. This background was crucial for the design and realization of the survey. Additional methodological details appear in the appendix; several considerations guiding the sampling strategy are spelled out here. The survey sought to reveal the attitudes and behavior of the population with which this book is concerned, and specifically two segments: conflict-affected victims and nonvictims.

Included in the scope of the book are postconflict societies that *experienced* the war and therefore exhibited political legacies of this experience. A presumption in this book, therefore, is that security and desire for peace are salient. In Chapter 8, I demonstrate the breadth of the validity of this assumption but also specify the implications of relaxing it. Chapter 2 previewed that discussion, arguing that, to the extent that security is not salient and victimization is isolated, my theory would have less explanatory power over political life than other theories of political behavior. Given these considerations, to test the individual implications of the book's theory, it was important to assess populations that were *conflict-affected*: those who were direct victims of the violence (disappearance, kidnapping, torture, rape, etc.), and those who were affected but not its direct victims (such as those whose daily lives were upended by the violence, who lacked even the most basic sense of safety, or who were otherwise adversely impacted by the war). I also wished to shed light on the populations that might plausibly be said to have been unaffected and unvictimized by more than fifty years of armed conflict.[7]

To approximate this heterogeneity in victim status, I engaged in a multistage stratified random sampling design. The sampling frame included all Colombian municipalities. Given Colombia's marked regional diversity, to ensure representative samples within each region, the design was first stratified by the main geographical regions of Colombia.[8] Each stratum was further substratified by size of municipality—large, intermediate, or basic—based on the categorization by Colombia's National Planning Department. The design was then stratified by the extent to which the municipalities were war-affected and by the identity of the perpetrators of the violence in each. To do so, I followed Colombia's classification of conflict-affected regions and stratified on the municipalities most victimized by the war. These comprised places that ranked very high or high on an index composed of armed actions, homicides, kidnappings, antipersonnel mines, and forced displacement.[9] The average percentage of registered victims across Colombia's less conflict-affected municipalities was 20 percent, whereas in the most conflict-affected this number was 78 percent. This made locating victims and conflict-affected nonvictims much more likely[10] and, given improvements in security in Colombia over the preceding decades, better approximated the postwar environments on which the book's theory centers. The sampling design then stratified on the perpetrator of the violence: rebel, state, paramilitary, or multiple belligerents based on data from CEDE and Daly (2012, 2016). Across municipalities, the samples included both victims and nonvictims. Given the high level of war-induced internal displacement in Colombia (15.7 percent of the population), this strategy elevated the likelihood of gaining samples of direct victims, conflict-affected nonvictims, and displaced victims of all wartime belligerents, and also gaining a sample of unaffected nonvictims (a relative term, as explained above).

Within these homogeneity strata, as the primary sampling unit, I randomly selected thirty-eight municipalities, the smallest uniform administrative unit in Colombia. The secondary sampling units were the clusters, blocks, or populated centers selected within rural and urban strata and proportionate to the population size, based on the national census. The tertiary sampling units were the households within each cluster, achieving an average of ten surveys. From a random start, interviewers walked in a randomly determined direction and selected households by interval sampling (every third household). Adult citizens within each household were then chosen by most recent birthday. Quotas were set for numbers of victims and nonvictims; victim status was determined using a filter question taken from the Colombian National Comptroller's Victim Survey, which asked whether the individual was a victim of any of the following acts related to the internal armed conflict: assassination or forced disappearance (of the respondent's spouse, partner, parents, or children), kidnapping, personal harm, torture, sexual violence, forced recruitment of minors, displacement, extortion, death threats. The survey instrument verified that common crime was not primarily responsible for these acts of violence. In the case of refusals or failure to contact the selected adult after two attempts, the household was replaced with the adjacent household and the interval sampling recommenced from that household. Table 4.1 displays the breakdown of the sample.

Colombia has a 95 percent literacy rate. However, given the remoteness of and conflict impact on many of the places sampled, enumerators were trained to administer the survey to both literate and illiterate respondents. All of the experiments and many of the questions involved visual aids to assist in comprehension and response. The experiments were also read twice, the second time with the enumerator walking the respondent through the visual aid.[11] Given the sensitivity of the topics, enumerators highly trained in working with vulnerable populations conducted the survey face-to-face.

TABLE 4.1. Survey Sample of Victims and Nonvictims

Region	Most Conflict-Affected		Not Most Conflict-Affected		Total		
	Victims	Nonvictims	Victims	Nonvictims	Total Victims	Total Nonvictims	Total
Bogotá			21	100	21	100	121
Caribe	140	65	45	50	185	115	300
Centro Oriente	86	50	43	31	129	81	210
Centro Sur	106	14	10	15	116	29	145
Eje Cafetero	175	61	20	51	195	112	307
Llano	42	20	21	19	63	39	102
Pacífico	131	120	19	55	150	175	325
Total	680	323	158	221	859	642	1,510

Survey Experiments

I embedded three experiments in the survey that tested important individual-level implications of the book's violent-victors theory. I included two additional experiments that evaluated alternative explanations. The varied nature of the experiments, mixing conjoint with vignette, information, and list experiments, proved to work well during piloting.[12] For motivations of statistical power, the experiments focus on the strategy choice set of winning and losing belligerent parties, and on voters' responses to these parties' different strategies.

The war between the Colombian government and FARC ended with peace accords. Despite significant concessions, these were not accords between armies at a military draw; rather, the Colombian armed forces terminated the conflict as the relatively "winning" belligerent but did not win outright; the FARC rebels were the relatively "losing" belligerent, sustaining a sizeable but diminished and degraded force.[13] Whereas in the 1990s the FARC insurgency had grown in strength and lethality, posing a significant threat to the national government, an immense U.S. counternarcotics and counterinsurgency aid package in 2000, Plan Colombia,[14] enabled President Uribe to wield his "military, much improved by U.S. hardware, training and intelligence cooperation in pursuit of unconditional victory against the . . . FARC. For the first time in four decades of conflict, Uribe [had] beefed up and deployed the coercive institutions of the Colombian state to improve the government's position on the battlefield."[15] By the end of Uribe's two terms as president, in 2010, the tides of war had turned, the FARC threat had largely been neutralized in the country's populated regions—those in which the vast majority of its voters were concentrated—and the severely weakened rebels had retreated to the country's jungle peripheries.[16]

While there is variation in perceptions of the war outcome in Colombia, which I exploit experimentally, the belligerent parties themselves, along with the nonbelligerent parties and voters, showed some consensus on the characterization of the FARC as militarily weaker than the government, but unlikely to be defeated decisively. This (relative) defeat led to the FARC's decision to declare a unilateral ceasefire and enter into and agree to peace negotiations.[17]

I largely divorce the survey experiments from the actual 2018 founding electoral campaigns. I particularly do so for the government belligerent side because (as discussed below after the survey analyses) multiple parties, in theory, could have claimed the mantle of the government belligerent party. Nearly half of the population also saw one of the nonbelligerent parties (a party led by an ex–M19 rebel combatant) as essentially the same as the FARC. This ambiguity points to the challenges of coding successor parties, particularly in multiparty democracies with civilian oversight of the military, but it also presents an opportunity to compare and contrast the effectiveness of on- and off-equilibrium strategies: a task addressed below. Given these considerations, to ensure the cleanest tests in the survey, I presented the government belligerent candidates simply as hypothetical ones affiliated with the military rather than tied to a particular party, and the rebel belligerent candidates as those affiliated with the FARC.

While Colombia presented a productive environment for this survey, it exhibited several limitations that may have attenuated the findings. In particular, two of the model's assumptions were stretched, albeit in a contradictory fashion. On the one hand, conflict with the second most powerful rebel army, National Liberation Army (ELN), continued, so the elections were not "postwar" at the country level, but only at the dyadic or conflict level. For theoretical and also safety reasons, in the sampling phase we planned to exclude municipalities of active conflict to which enumerators could not safely travel due to ELN presence.[18] On the other hand, while conflict with the ELN continued, it was at very low intensity, and the government had demobilized the paramilitaries[19] (although with uneven success) and severely weakened the FARC by 2010. Therefore, at the time of the survey's enumeration in 2020, Colombia exhibited many of the dynamics that the theory predicts would be manifest only over time, in the elections subsequent to the founding postwar ones. In particular, as anticipated by the theory, security, particularly that related to the armed conflict, had become less salient; politics had become more multivalent; demands for transitional justice had increased; and the effectiveness of the security brand had eroded and, if to play a deterministic role in the elections, would require issue priming. Despite these challenges, Uribe's handpicked candidate, Iván Duque, won the 2018 election, ushering in what I consider a government of the militarily winning belligerent party. However, for reasons that are largely uncorrelated with my theory's variables, the inexperienced Duque proved a poor executive.[20] Additionally, in the course of the survey's enumeration, when 996 of the 1,500 planned surveys had been completed, the COVID-19 global pandemic hit Colombia. As a result, the book's survey took place amid assessments of the already-elected belligerent successor, Duque, rather than assessments primarily of the war, violence, and peace accords. My argument hypothesizes that these evaluations of the successor party's social, economic, and public health record once in office will likely diverge from those dominating the campaign for the founding postwar elections.

Despite these myriad challenges, the case offers the opportunity to evaluate the theory's individual-level hypotheses with a textured mixture of experimental and observational methods.

Shifting Frames of Reference of the Violent Past

The first experiment is a vignette. It tests whether provision of security offsets the use of atrocities by more victorious belligerents, but not by more defeated belligerents, and thereby enables the former, but not the latter, to foster a reputation for competence on stability.

Mitigation Experiment

Respondents were presented with four hypothetical scenarios of atrocity that varied by belligerent perpetrator—*army* or *rebel*—and varied by whether or not *security* was provided. Treatment assignment probabilities were equal across conditions. Respondents in each scenario were given a visual aid with the script of the randomly assigned version of the vignette. The enumerator read out loud, "Now I would like to tell you about someone named Jorge." In a first version, respondents were then provided with the following *rebel–no security* phrase:

Jorge served in the FARC. During the conflict, he participated in the assassination of three people.

A second version changed the hypothetical perpetrator from the belligerent that was losing militarily, the rebels, to the winning belligerent, the army (*army–no security*):

Jorge served in the army. During the conflict, he participated in the assassination of three people.

A third version added the mitigation treatment to the rebel version (*rebel-security*):

Jorge served in the FARC. During the conflict, he participated in the assassination of three people. He has been widely renowned for having improved security and order, and reduced violence in the municipality.

A final version added the mitigation treatment to the army version (*army-security*):

Jorge served in the army. During the conflict, he participated in the assassination of three people. He has been widely renowned for having improved security and order, and reduced violence in the municipality.

To measure judgments of the violence, I consulted the psychology literature on emotions.[21] Following the vignette script, respondents were asked to rank, on a scale of 0 to 7, how justified they believed the assassinations were. They were also asked how angry they felt at Jorge (0 to 4), if they believed Jorge should spend time in jail for the assassinations and, if they answered in the affirmative, to how many years they would sentence him.[22]

My theory of altered reference points and mitigation suggests that respondents in the army–security mitigation condition (version 4, above) should be less likely than those in the army–no security mitigation condition (the second version above) to exhibit anger and desires to punish the perpetrators for their violence. Respondents presented with the rebel conditions should exhibit little to no difference between the security mitigation (version 3) and no security mitigation (version 1) conditions, instead desiring unconditional punishment of the losing belligerent for its violence. The model predicts that, all else equal, levels of respondent anger and blame at the losing belligerent will exceed those against the winning belligerent (that is, respondents exposed to rebel versions 1 and 3 will exhibit greater anger at "Jorge" than those receiving the army versions 2 and 4). It should be noted that, in the rebel–security mitigation condition (third version), the treatment attributes credit for security provision to the losing belligerent, which, according to my theory, voters do not do in practice. Therefore, the design may attenuate differences between the army and rebel treatments.

I use regression techniques to estimate average treatment effects (ATEs). I first pool the *army–no security* and *army–security*, and pool the *rebel–no security* and the *rebel–security* conditions, and calculate the ATE of the army treatments relative to the rebel treatments. I then calculate the ATE of *army–no security* relative to *army–security*, and *rebel–security* relative to *rebel–no security*. I estimate regression models that adjust for the following basic demographic covariates: education, age, sex, region, and socioeconomic status.[23] Reflecting the individual-level randomization, I use heteroskedastic robust standard errors throughout.

RESULTS

Table 4.2 shows the ATEs of the belligerent and security provision treatments on the offsetting of judgments of violence and desires for retribution. Models 1 and 4 report the ATEs between the army and the rebel pooled conditions. In models 2 and 5, I show the ATEs between the army–no security and army–security conditions. Models 3 and 6 capture the ATEs between the rebel–security and rebel–no security treatments. I present results for the outcomes most aligned with the theory: the extent to which the violence was deemed justified and the desire for punishment. The other outcomes—reported in the appendix—exhibit consistent findings.

As shown in Table 4.2, respondents who were presented with the army conditions were, relative to the rebel conditions, on average significantly more likely to view the excessive use of force as justified and less likely to impose a prison sentence. This suggests that winning belligerents' provision of security can alter and mitigate citizens' judgments of the atrocities committed in a way not as strongly available to the losing belligerent. The difference between the *army–no security* and *army–security* treatments is statistically significant, suggesting that offsetting had a positive effect on assessments of the violent past. Respondents' priors may have attenuated this result if they imputed preexisting beliefs about the army's credit for security into the *army–no security* treatment, a possibility I explore statistically.[24] Overall, these results are largely consistent with the empirical implications of the theory. However, the data

TABLE 4.2. Offsetting Experiment Results

Variable	(1) Violence Justified	(2) Army Violence Justified	(3) Rebel Violence Justified	(4) Jail	(5) Jail Army	(6) Jail Rebels
Army belligerent (relative to rebel belligerent)	0.27** (0.11)			-0.08*** (0.02)		
Security provision (relative to no security provision)		0.31** (0.15)	0.35** (0.14)		-0.05* (0.85)	-0.03 (0.2)
Constant	2.64*** (0.37)	3.16*** (0.52)	1.92*** (0.52)	0.91 (0.01)	0.85*** (0.20)	0.92*** (0.16)
Observations	1,503	764	739	1,436	727	709

Note: All models use OLS regression with robust standard errors and include age, education, socioeconomic level, and gender covariates. Models 1 and 4 show the ATEs of the pooled army treatments relative to the pooled rebel treatments. Models 2 and 5 calculate the ATEs of the army–security treatment relative to the army–no security treatment. Models 3 and 6 display the ATEs of the rebel–security treatment relative to the rebel–no security treatment.

*p<.1. **p<.05. ***p<.01.

reveal a mitigating effect of security provision on judgment of violence, though not on desire for punishment, even for the losing rebel belligerent; this result was unanticipated by the theory and may be explained by the setup of the experiment, as described above, in which the relatively defeated belligerent, the rebels, was credited with security improvements, an experimental scenario that, the book argues, is unlikely to manifest empirically.[25] At the same time, this may validate the counterfactual: that, had the rebels fared better in war and thus gained citizen credit for security provision—an outcome that the observational survey data confirm did not happen in practice—they might, too, have been able to launder their reputation in the public eye.[26]

HETEROGENOUS TREATMENT EFFECTS

The theory anticipates heterogeneous effects. In particular, my model implies that victims and those nonvictims who were affected by conflict will be more swayed by the winning belligerent's mitigation than nonaffected nonvictims who did not experience the relief of peace (they compare peace to their refer-ence point of never having lived conflict, and therefore their reference point remains unaltered).[27] To measure level of conflict impacts, respondents were asked questions similar to the National Comptroller's direct victimization ones, but this time they were asked whether their *community* had been affected by each type of violence related to the internal armed conflict.

The results in Table 4.3 are consistent with these expectations.[28] Conflict affected individuals drive the offsetting effects observed in Table 4.2. Victim status (models 1 and 3) increased the mitigating impact of security on attribu-tion of blame and on retributive attitudes. Presented with the *army–security* condition, victims were far more likely than nonvictims to view the violence as justified and to feel that jail time was unnecessary.

This experiment tested the micro-level logic of shifting voters' reference points of the brutal past with the provision of security. The next experiment explores which *party* strategies, as a result, are likely to be more electorally expedient.

Narratives Experiment

The book's violent-victors theory posits that, given that a winning belligerent's establishment of peace will have an offsetting effect on the attribution of blame for its wartime violence, a strategy of mitigation will have a more positive

TABLE 4.3. Offsetting Experiment: Heterogenous Results

Variable	(1) Army Violence Justified (Victim Sample)	(2) Army Violence Justified (Nonvictim Sample)	(3) Jail Army (Victim Sample)	(4) Jail Army (Nonvictim Sample)
Security provision (relative to no security provision)	0.44** (0.20)	0.13 (0.23)	−0.08** 0.04	−0.00 0.04
Constant	1.25*** (0.14)	1.47*** (0.17)	0.78 (0.03)	0.82 (0.03)
Observations	437	330	409	318

Note: All models use OLS regression with robust standard errors and include age, education, socioeconomic level, and gender covariates.

$**p < .05. ***p < .01.$

effect on its electoral support than a contrition strategy, on average, enabling the party to foster a reputation for competence on security rather than one for inflicting harm.

The book argues that opposite tendencies are likely to hold for the belligerents who did not come out ahead militarily: for the losing belligerent, a strategy of mitigation will, on average, have a more negative effect on electoral support than will a contrition strategy.

To probe these hypotheses, respondents were exposed to two sets of randomly ordered candidate narratives about the past violence, first by a pair of winning belligerent (ex-government military) candidates and then by a pair of losing belligerent (ex-rebel) candidates. For each pair, respondents were asked for which candidate they would vote and to rank how much they supported each of the candidates. To construct the narratives of the bloodied history, I consulted politicians' propaganda, official statements, and Twitter posts, and engaged in personal interviews with parties that had adopted the divergent strategies in their electoral campaigns. The facts derive from the National Center for Historical Memory reports.

The final text included the preamble, "Now I am going to present you with the statements of two military/FARC candidates about the violence in Colombia and then I will ask you several questions." To guard against order effects, the sequence in which the statements were read was randomized.

The *military mitigation* script read,

> The violence in Colombia is the result of the offensives of the FARC terrorists. They were responsible for the vast majority of the kidnappings and forced recruitment of children. The victims of these atrocities deserve justice. The military bravely fought to defend the country against narcoterrorism, finally defeating it.

The *military contrition* version read,

> The army committed errors, which have brought Colombians great pain and suffering. It apologizes to the country for this violence. It renounces its past atrocities. Now, it argues, it is not the time for the hatreds of the past.

The randomly ordered statements by rebel candidates about the torturous past were as follows. The *rebel mitigation* script read,

> The state's bombardment of Marquetalia began the armed conflict in Colombia. The paramilitaries and the state were responsible for the vast majority of massacres and disappearances. The victims of these atrocities deserve justice. The guerrillas fought to defend the poor from the exploitation of capitalism.

The *rebel contrition* script read,

> The FARC admits that it caused a war that brought nothing but suffering. It begs forgiveness for the tears and pain that its five decades of fighting have inflicted upon Colombians. It renounces its violent past. Now it hopes to put an end to vengeance.

ANALYSIS AND RESULTS

The survey data reveal that 46.1 percent of respondents preferred the army candidate that engaged in *mitigation*; 53.9 percent preferred the candidate that engaged in *contrition* (see Table 4.4). This is a weaker preference for mitigation than I would have anticipated, one that could be explained by the length of time that had passed since the height of the conflict and the resulting increase in desires for transitional justice. However, a strong preference for the rebel candidates to break with the rebels' violent past rather than embrace that past is, as anticipated, observed in the survey data. Only 35.6 percent preferred for

TABLE 4.4. Order Effects of Mitigation and Contrition Narratives on Probability of Being Elected

	First Military Mitigation	First Military Contrition	Total
Prefer military mitigation candidate (%)	40.1	52.5	46.1
Prefer military contrition candidate (%)	59.9	47.6	53.9
Total (%)	100	100	100
	First FARC Mitigation	First FARC Contrition	
Prefer FARC mitigation candidate (%)	30.8	40.6	35.6
Prefer FARC contrition candidate (%)	69.2	59.4	64.4
Total (%)	100	100	100

the FARC to adopt mitigation; 64.4 percent preferred for it to instead adopt contrition. Comparing support for the FARC and for the army candidates on a 0–7 scale shows a larger gap, consistent with the theory's logic: whereas a contrite-FARC candidate scored only 15 percent lower than a contrite-army candidate, a mitigating-FARC one scored 32 percent lower than its mitigating-army counterpart.

The randomized ordering of the narratives reduces concern over order effects, which were strongly observed. At the same time, these substantial order effects may shed light on whether it makes a difference who controls the narrative and, in particular, whether it matters that a side is able to tell its story first: a persuasion effect. In the experiment, if respondents received the mitigation narrative first, they were significantly more likely to choose the candidates who promised contrition for their violent predecessor's role in the war, particularly if their predecessor was the FARC. Receiving the contrition version first had a much weaker order effect (Table 4.4). Below, I consider whether and how this dynamic may have played out on the ground in the 2018 campaign in which parties varied not only in their strategies, but also in their first-mover advantages and media access.

In sum, using a vignette experiment and exposing respondents to different narratives, I find that the winning belligerent's provision of security can mitigate citizens' (and especially conflict-affected nonvictims' and victims') condemnation of the atrocities committed in a way not as strongly available to the losing belligerent. I then probe whether a strategy of offsetting the violent past proves electorally expedient and therefore rational for a winning belligerent, while a contrition strategy proves optimal for a weaker belligerent. I find suggestive evidence that this is the case.

Restrained Leviathan vs. Tactical Immoderate Experiment

In a second set of survey experiments, I evaluate how party strategies of valence, position, and party elite mediate the relationship between successful war outcomes and electoral performance by influencing voters' perceptions of parties' security competence. In particular, I assess whether a Restrained Leviathan strategy—pairing a military strongman with civilian candidates, adopting a platform convergent on the wishes of the moderate voter, and focusing on security valence—raises perceptions of credibility on security and proves electorally preferable for the winning belligerent. I also evaluate whether a Tactical Immoderate strategy—only civilian candidates, an immoderate platform, and non–security valence priorities—proves preferable for the losing belligerent. To do so, I use two forced-choice double conjoint experiments.

The experiments put respondents in the real-world position of voters, asking them to choose between two hypothetical belligerent candidates running for Congress. Respondents were presented with information regarding randomized attributes of the two candidates. They were then asked which one of the two profiles they perceived better able to provide future security and public order. They were also asked, posttreatment, which they credited with peace and for which they would be more likely to vote.[29] This approach enables the estimation of the causal effects of multiple treatment components and assesses several causal hypotheses simultaneously. It also allows me to disentangle the effects of theoretically and observationally correlated attributes and has the potential to reduce social desirability concerns because it offers respondents the confidentiality of several potential justifications for a decision.[30] It further performs well relative to real-world behavioral benchmarks.[31]

Respondents were given four pieces of randomized information about each candidate. To maximize statistical power, each treatment had only two possible values. Given the complexity of the conjoint experiment and the particular challenges of implementing it in low-education contexts, the script was read aloud to respondents and was also complemented with pictogram flip

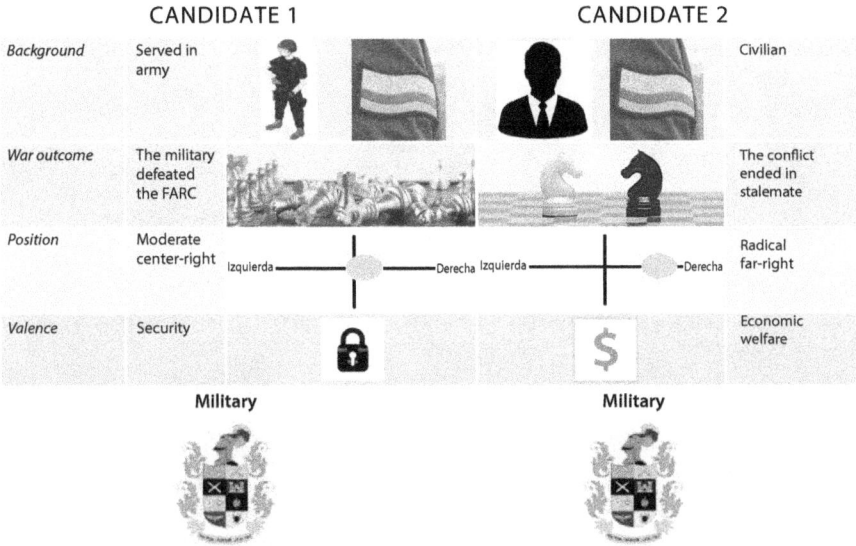

FIGURE 4.1. Government Belligerent Party Strategies: Experimental Design.

booklets. Candidates with randomized attributes appeared as text on the enumerators' tablet screens and instructed the enumerators which two randomly selected profiles to show respondents. The enumerators then located the two randomly selected profiles in a flip book and showed respondents the images of the two candidates side by side.[32] A script read aloud by the enumerator described, in vignette form, the characteristics of each candidate. The enumerator then read the vignette a second time, indicating to the respondent the corresponding images of each attribute of each candidate in the pictogram booklet.

The experiment was repeated twice. The first time, the respondent was instructed to compare candidates from the militarily winning side, that is, the government side, signaled in the text and, in the pictogram, with the emblem of the Colombian armed forces (Figure 4.1). A second, parallel experiment asked respondents to choose between two hypothetical candidates from the losing, rebel side, signaled with the emblem of the FARC political party (Figure 4.2).[33]

The first attribute probed the selection of party elite. Respondents were assigned (with equal probability) either a candidate with a military background or one having a civilian record. Corresponding to the candidate

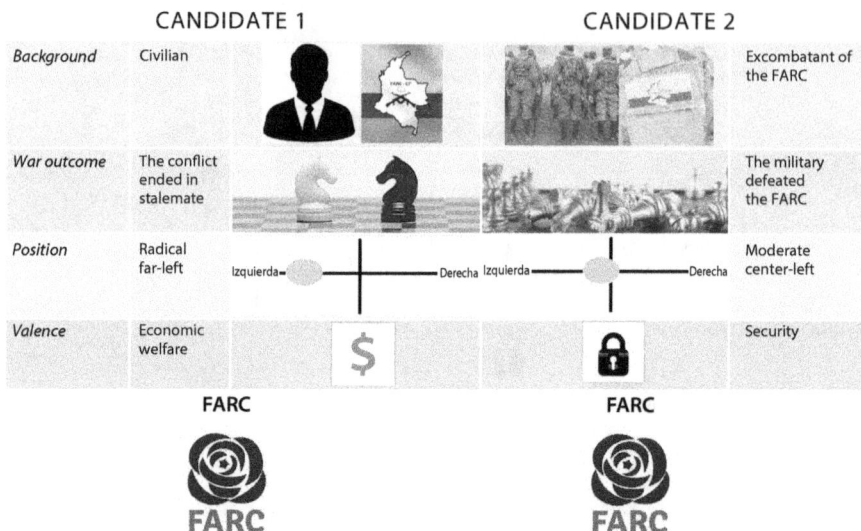

FIGURE 4.2. Rebel Belligerent Party Strategies: Experimental Design.

descriptions were images of members of the armed forces / guerrillas in fatigues, or a civilian in a suit, to evoke combatant versus noncombatant experience and expertise and also to evoke visceral responses to a military uniform as opposed to civilian garb. My participant observations in Colombia revealed that combatants' signature boot types and arm bands strongly signaled to citizens the belligerent's affiliation: government or rebel. The images of the army versus guerrilla combatants therefore featured their respective combat boots and armbands (Figure 4.3).[34]

The second attribute varied positional placement by randomizing the candidates as running on a moderate or immoderate platform, of a right- or left-wing nature, depending on the belligerent: government (right wing) or FARC (left wing). The corresponding images showed an ideological left-right spectrum with the position indicated with a circle.

Third, the experiments assessed the impact of prioritizing different valence issues by manipulating whether the candidates promised to improve security (padlock image) or instead promised to bolster social welfare (peso symbol).

Each of these treatments assesses the valence, position, and candidate concepts of party strategies mediating the relationship between war outcomes and electoral performance. Given that all of the attributes varied and their effects

FIGURE 4.3. Combat Boots: Army versus Rebel.
Sources: "Denuncian en Fiscalía venezolana existencia de 'casas seguras' para guerrilla," *EJE21*, June 2, 2021, https://www.eje21.com.co/2021/06/denuncian-en-fiscalia-venezolana-existencia -de-casas-seguras-para-guerrilla/; "FARC solo entregaron el 4 % de bienes inventariados para reparar a víctimas," *Panam Post*, February 15, 2021, https://panampost.com/efe-panampost /2021/02/15/farc-bienes-reparar-victimas/.

were measured on the same scale, the design allows an assessment of the relative importance of the respective strategies.

War outcomes were baked into the belligerent profiles in the Restrained Leviathan and Tactical Immoderate experiments. At the same time, I wished to assess whether how parties talked about these outcomes mattered and in particular whether they could manipulate this structural feature of the model. Accordingly, I randomly assigned to respondents either a candidate who argued that the Colombian armed forces were outright victorious over the rebels or a candidate who claimed that the conflict had ended in a military draw; these were described in the script and also illustrated with images of a chess board at victory or at stalemate.[35] My fieldwork confirmed that government defeat would be an unrealistic category. Manipulation checks showed that participants imputed relative victory for the government and relative defeat for the rebels, irrespective of the experimental treatments, suggesting that public perceptions of war outcomes are difficult for political parties to manipulate.

One set of the government profiles (see Figure 4.1) read,

The first candidate served in the army, which he argues militarily defeated the FARC. He is running on a moderate, center-right platform, and promises to improve security in the municipality.

The second candidate is a civilian with ties to the army, which he argues brought the FARC to a military draw. He is running on an immoderate far-right platform and promises to improve economic welfare in the municipality.

The framework anticipates that, relative to a Tactical Immoderate strategy, a Restrained Leviathan strategy is likely to have a positive effect on perceptions of the winning belligerent's competence on security, particularly among swing, security, and victimized voters. This security issue ownership, in turn, is predicted to boost electoral performance. The opposite is likely to hold for the militarily losing belligerent party. These expectations can be formulated as specific hypotheses for the treatment arms of the conjoint experiments.

Conjoint Experiment 1: Winning Belligerent (Government Armed Forces)

H_{1w}: *Party Elite*—Fielding a military candidate is likely to have a positive effect on perceptions of security competence and electoral support for the winning (government) belligerent, relative to fielding a civilian candidate.

H_{2w}: *Position*—Moderation is likely to increase perceptions of security competence and electoral support for the winning (government) belligerent, relative to immoderation.

H_{3w}: *Valence*—Running on the security valence issue is likely to increase perceptions of security competence and electoral support for the winning (government) belligerent, relative to running on the welfare valence issue.

Conjoint Experiment 2: Losing Belligerent (FARC Rebels)

H_{1l}: *Party Elite*—Fielding a military candidate is likely to have a negative effect on electoral support for the losing (rebel) belligerent, relative to fielding a civilian candidate.

H_{2l}: *Position*—Moderation is likely to decrease electoral support for the losing (rebel) belligerent, relative to immoderation.

H_{3l}: *Valence*—Running on the security valence issue is likely to decrease electoral support for the losing (rebel) belligerent, relative to running on the economic welfare valence issue.

Results

My primary interest is in estimating the average marginal component effect (AMCE), that is, the average marginal effect of an attribute compared to the reference category, averaged over the joint distribution of the remaining

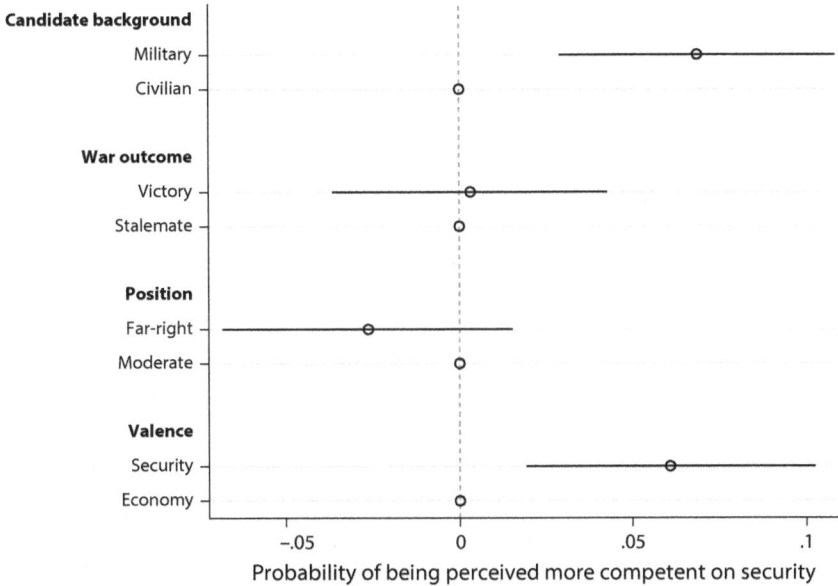

FIGURE 4.4. Effect of Government Belligerent Party Strategies on Probability of Being Deemed More Competent on Prospective Security.

Note: This plot shows estimates of the effects of the randomly assigned candidate attribute values on the probability of being deemed the more competent on security issues. Estimates are based on an OLS model with standard errors clustered by respondent; bars represent 95 percent confidence intervals. The points without horizontal bars denote the attribute value that is the reference category for each attribute.

attributes included in the conjoint. Since the attributes were randomized independently, I am able to estimate the AMCEs for all included attributes simultaneously through a simple linear regression, adopting the statistical approach of Hainmueller, Hopkins, and Yamamoto (2014). The dependent variable is coded 1 for the candidate profile that the respondent indicated he or she would select, of the pair (on securing the future, credit for peace, and in an election), and 0 for the candidate that he or she did not choose. The independent variables are dummy variables for each attribute. I cluster standard errors by respondent, following standard practice in the analysis of conjoint experiments. As a robustness check, and for the sake of efficiency, I also estimate covariate-adjusted regressions, using the same covariates described above.

Figure 4.4 shows how each attribute affects the likelihood of a candidate being deemed prospectively more competent on security. The figure displays both the AMCEs (points) and the 95 percent confidence intervals.[36] For the winning belligerent (the government), citizens appear to prefer candidates who have a military background (7 percentage points, $p = .001$ in two-sided test) over those with a civilian profile. This result is more pronounced among swing,[37] security,[38] and victimized voters.[39]

The next set of results involves programmatic position. I find that voters are more likely to deem candidates from the winning side competent on security if they run on a moderate as opposed to an immoderate platform (3 percentage points, $p = .22$), suggesting the logic of prompting voters to evaluate, "Well, if the [parties] are so similar on policy, I'll vote for the one who is superior on valence."[40] However, the coefficient is not significant by conventional standards for the whole sample, only for the theoretically key sample of swing voters (4 percentage points, $p = .054$).

Security and economic valence issues prove salient for voters. I find a positive effect of running on the security valence issue relative to a promise to improve economic welfare (6 percentage points, $p = .004$ in two-sided test). This rises to 8 percentage points among swing and victimized voters ($p = .000$). This may seem obvious; however, it underscores that a party's competence on security issues is rooted, in part, in its prioritization and programmatic emphasis. Moreover, while the framework does not force voters to choose between security and welfare, belligerent party strategists often argue explicitly (and persuasively) that security is a necessary precondition for and generator of economic well-being.[41]

The final set of results sheds light on the impact of war outcomes. On security, voters appear indifferent between winning belligerents who claim decisive and indecisive war results. On credit for peace, however, military victory is positively associated, as shown below. This may reflect a variable that is more resistant to manipulation; war outcomes are structural features of the model rather than elements of party strategy as in the experimental setup.

Importantly, the combined impact of the factors I analyze is substantial. Figure 4.5 charts the average probability of particular types of Colombian government belligerent candidates being chosen on security grounds. The figure shows that the probability of selection of a Restrained Leviathan is 64 percent, compared to 52 percent for a Tactical Immoderate. Figure A4.1, panels A–E, shows that no other interaction of the four components is significant, bolstering the claim that this specific combination has a unique effect.

The theory predicts that the relative war winner who runs on this Restrained Leviathan strategy—fields a strongman candidate, shows positional moderation, and prioritizes the security valence issue—will benefit from

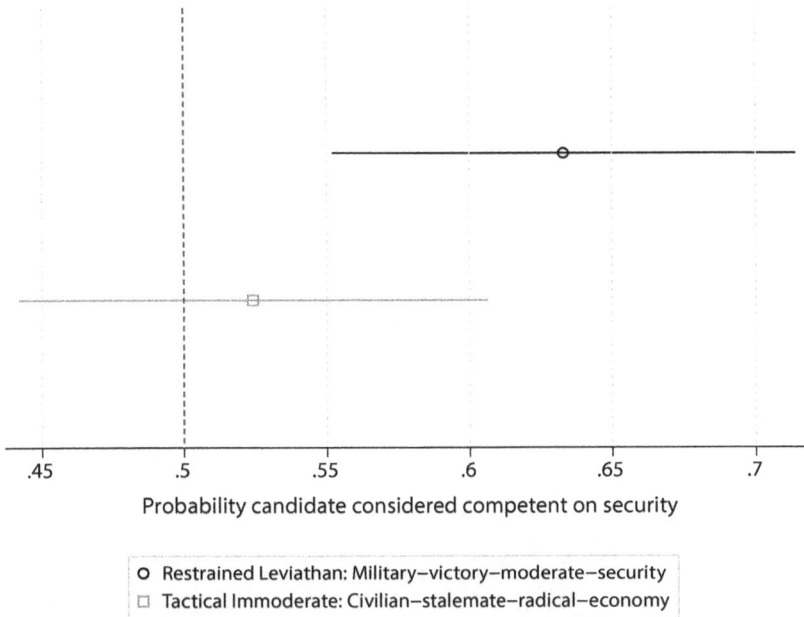

FIGURE 4.5. Probability of Being Preferred on Security for Selected Government Belligerent Candidate Profiles.
Note: The plot shows the average probability of being preferred for Congress on security grounds. The estimates are shown for profiles indicated in the legend. Bars represent 95 percent confidence intervals.

attribution with peace and, through security voting, improve their electoral prospects. Do the war outcomes and party elite, positional, and valence strategies influence outcomes through this proposed causal process? The survey measures the outcome variable and intervening variables with the same experimental treatment. Respondents were asked, posttreatment, which candidate they perceived to deserve more credit for reducing violence and bringing peace to Colombia and also for which candidate they would vote.[42] A finding that militarily winning influences credit for peace and that a Restrained Leviathan strategy also influences electability would help bolster evidence that security voting underpins the effect of war outcomes on political behavior. Figures 4.6 and 4.7 suggest such results.[43]

This was not true for the weaker, rebel belligerent; instead, as anticipated by the theory, the Restrained Leviathan strategy proves successful only for the winning belligerent. As described above, the second conjoint experiment

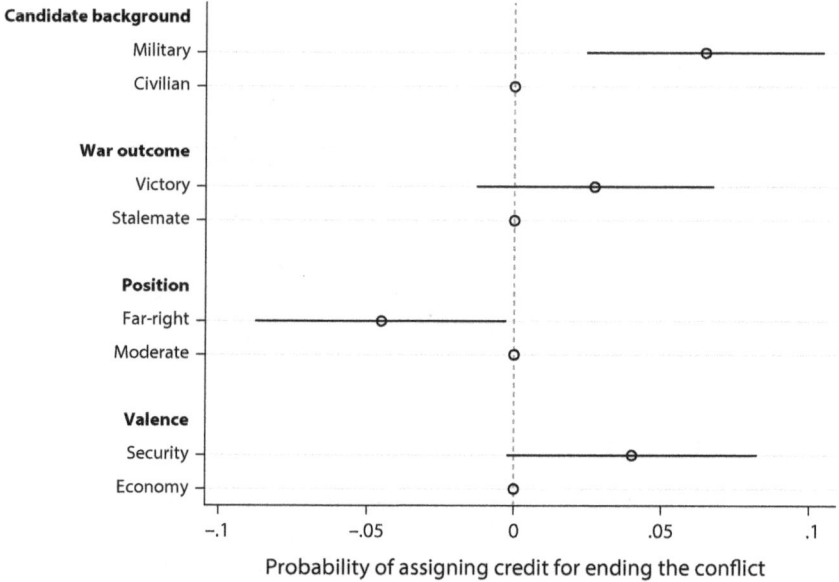

FIGURE 4.6. Effect of Government Belligerent Party Strategies on Probability of Receiving Credit for War Termination.

Note: Estimates are based on an OLS model with standard errors clustered by respondent; bars represent 95 percent confidence intervals. The points without horizontal bars denote the attribute value that is the reference category for each attribute.

repeated the design with two randomly assigned rebel candidate profiles. Figure 4.2 shows the profiles with the attributes translated into English. One set of the rebel profiles read,

> The first candidate is a civilian with ties to the FARC. He argues that the conflict ended in a military draw. He is running on an immoderate far-left platform and promises to improve economic welfare in the municipality.

> The second candidate served as a combatant of the FARC who concedes that the army militarily defeated the FARC. He is running on a moderate, center-left platform and promises to improve security in the municipality.

The analysis of the war-losing rebel profiles reveals that, combined, the average probability of electing a Tactical Immoderate candidate is greater from that of electing a Restrained Leviathan (Figure 4.8). This effect is largely driven by a strong voter preference for civilian over ex-combatant candidates

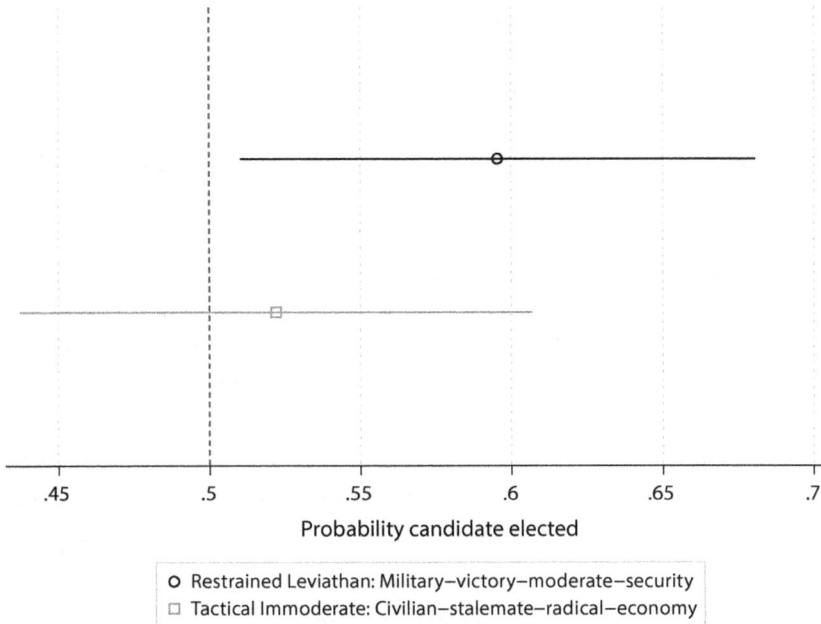

FIGURE 4.7. Probability of Being Elected for Selected Government Belligerent Candidate Profiles.
Note: The plot shows the average probability of being preferred for electoral selection for Congress. The estimates are shown for profiles indicated in the legend. Bars represent 95 percent confidence intervals.

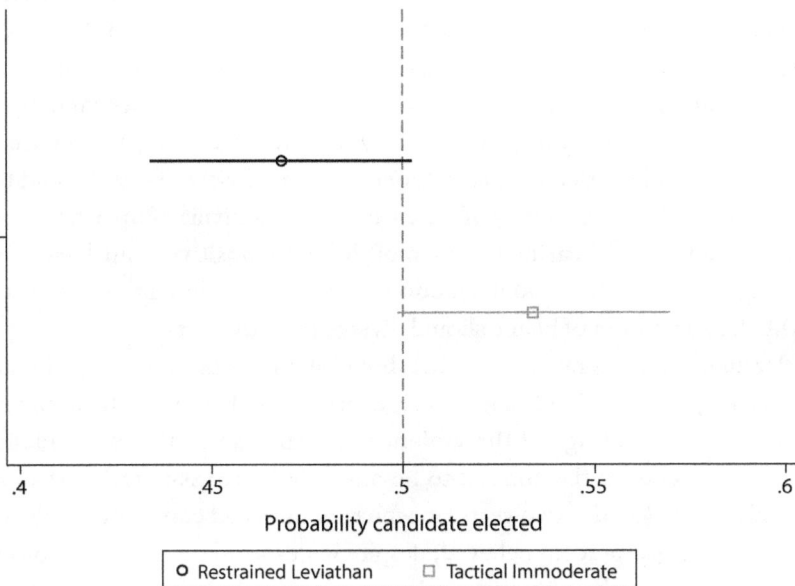

FIGURE 4.8. Probability of Being Elected for Selected Rebel Belligerent Candidate Profiles.
Note: The plot shows the average probability of being preferred for electoral selection for Congress. The estimates are shown for profiles indicated in the legend. Bars represent 95 percent confidence intervals.

(7.7 percentage points, $p = .012$). The analysis reveals a negative but insignificant AMCE for ideological position: voters prefer moderate to radical rebel candidates. This may reflect the preferences of the majority of the population, which is more moderate than the FARC, but would never vote for FARC (on a 1–10 confidence scale, 67 percent responded 1—that they had very little confidence in the rebels—and 13 percent responded 2).[44] This result might also reflect the fact that respondents had been exposed to FARC's actual political campaign, as discussed below, and disliked its outright radicalism. Among those leftist voters FARC was actually courting and able to attract, immoderation proved more expedient. Meanwhile, the data indicate a null effect of valence issues on rebel candidate election. However, in terms of candidate support rather than election choice, FARC politicians running on promises of economic welfare significantly outperformed those running on the security valence issue.

Observational Data

The experiments included in the original survey seek to evaluate the individual-level implications of the book's theory. Additional observational data could probe the plausibility of these implications further.

The book's model predicts that voters—both nonvictims and victims—will blame the losing belligerent disproportionately for the violence. The transitional justice process revealed that the rebels, paramilitaries, and state forces all perpetrated heinous crimes against humanity in Colombia. I use the observational survey data to analyze whether citizens' subjective understandings of the wartime violence correlated with the objective facts of that violence. If they did, I would anticipate that respondents would view the FARC and the paramilitaries as equally guilty of violence against the civilian population, with the armed forces—bearing the stain of the "false positive" murders—also sharing culpability. If the book's model of reference-dependent preferences is right, the attribution of blame should diverge from the facts.

Despite social desirability bias that should attenuate these findings, the survey data suggest that significant minorities of the population held highly asymmetric understandings of the violence committed. Of the respondents, 25 percent believed the conflict to be one-sided terrorism, rather than an armed conflict (of fifty-two years) in which all sides had committed violence. A staggering 35.4 percent believed, despite widespread public revelations to the contrary, that there were no "false positives"—the military's systematic practice of extrajudicial killings of innocent civilians falsely claimed as rebels[45]—only "false victims" (nonvictims ostensibly deceptively claiming to be victims) as segments of the military claimed.[46] Additionally, twice as many respondents believed that the armed forces' excessive violence was justified than believed rebels' excessive violence was justified in the context of their respective armed struggles and 26 percent agreed with amnestying the government belligerent for gross human rights abuses, whereas only 13 percent believed that the rebel belligerent should be amnestied for such abuses. Although the paramilitaries and the rebels carried out equal levels of wartime atrocities, twice as many respondents believed the rebels had had less respect for human rights than had the paramilitaries.

This asymmetric attribution of blame was manifest in the largest confederation of victims in Colombia, a group of 260 organizations in twenty-eight departments representing more than 215,000 victims. Its members included victims of the guerrillas, of the paramilitaries, and of the state. However, the organization decided to call itself the Colombian Federation of Victims of the FARC (FEVCOL).[47] In other words, even state and paramilitary victims were treated as victims of the FARC. FEVCOL's founder, herself a victim equally of the guerrillas *and* of the paramilitaries and the narcotraffickers, sought revenge only against what she called the "greatest perpetrator," the FARC.[48] Below, I provide evidence that this asymmetric assignment of blame cannot be explained by ignorance about the violence committed: a fog of war.

Assessments of Security Competence

The observational survey data also shed light on security voting. The theory suggests that security voters will prefer ironfisted security over rights-based security. The survey revealed strong support for law and order over rule of law. However, this preference manifests itself across the entire sample in roughly equal proportions, whether or not security was the most salient issue for the voters. In all, 90 percent supported the militarization of policing; 87 percent wished for greater ironfisted handling on security threats including criminals and rebels; 54.1 percent believed it was justifiable or very justifiable to violate human rights in order to quash the guerrillas, political violence, or terrorism. In contrast, only 28 percent deemed such violations justifiable in order to achieve accelerated economic growth.

Finally, the survey sought, observationally, to reveal whether, as the framework claims, there was a coupling of security competence in voters' minds— that is, whether competence in preventing war recurrence and fighting political violence was equated with competence in handling common crime, which would bolster a Leviathan story over a coercion story. If instead the coercion story is correct and the belligerent holds the electorate hostage in a protection racket—vote for me or I will remilitarize and harm you—the belligerent would not be considered a credible protector against all security threats, including ordinary crime. To evaluate this, the survey asked respondents about each party's and each candidate's competence on these different dimensions of security. I evaluate whether the indicators correlate in a statistically significant fashion. Consistent with my theory, the data indicate a strong correlation (on average .74) between perceptions of a candidate's competence on fighting political violence and that on combating crime.

All in all, the survey results provide suggestive evidence that adopting a Restrained Leviathan strategy to promise to secure the future is likely an optimal strategy for successors to (relatively) winning belligerents, and Tactical Immoderation the optimal strategy for successors to losing belligerents.[49] Given these findings, we should expect that the parties competing in the 2018 Colombian elections after conflict termination with the FARC would have considered the implications of their electoral strategies on voting behavior and each may therefore have followed the playbook described as optimal for its party. Further, if they did, they would likely have performed well electorally. If they instead had diverged from this optimal playbook, they would have performed more poorly. I pause on these 2018 electoral campaigns to consider these observable implications. Moving from the controlled hypothetical scenarios to the messy richness of actual political behavior reduces the model's explanatory leverage. Although it can account for additional variation beyond existing theories, there remain facets of the case relegated to the model's error term. Moreover, coding successor parties in Colombia, a country with electoral democracy persisting in spite of war, proves challenging, but also presents an opportunity to compare real-world strategies, presented here in stylized facts. I then return to the original survey data to analyze observational and experimental evidence for whether alternative explanations can better account for the voting dynamics revealed thus far.

Colombia's 2018 Elections

After Juan Manuel Santos was elected in 2010, there emerged a split in Álvaro Uribe's successor party. For idiosyncratic reasons, centered primarily on Santos's ambitions, convictions, and focus on his personal legacy,[50] upon his election

Santos purged and jailed the Uribistas in his government, thus initiating a political war between himself and his former patron.[51] This meant that, by 2018, two government belligerent successor forces existed: that of Uribe and that of Santos. Both had access to the legacy of the 2002–2010 Colombian government's successes in counterinsurgency against the guerrillas and the achievement of peace with the paramilitaries.[52] Santos had, further, negotiated peace with Colombia's most virulent rebel organization, FARC, in 2016. Both Uribe's and Santos's successors in 2018 therefore could have run on the state's favorable war outcome; they could run as "relative government victors."

In 2018, Colombia's party system was fragmented and its parties weak, used opportunistically by personalistic candidates.[53] Santismo and Uribismo, as Santos and Uribe's political forces came to be known, faced the nonbelligerent Sergio Fajardo and his Polo/Verde coalition.[54] They also faced two parties on the left: Colombia Humana (a nonbelligerent party, although it was led by a former M19 guerrilla member) and the rebel successor party, FARC. This renders the designation of the party types challenging and potentially controversial, but it also provides fertile ground to contrast and compare on- and off-equilibrium strategies. To build on the survey findings, I focus on the strategies of the belligerent successors.

As the electoral incumbent, and as the party best positioned to harness both private and state media, Santismo was the first mover.[55] Against both what the survey experiment results would advise and what the book's theory would predict, Santismo chose what I consider an off-equilibrium strategy for a relative military victor; it ran as a contrite Rule Abider. Uribismo responded to Santismo's move with what my argument would deem the optimal strategy for a relative military victor: Restrained Leviathan. The nonbelligerent coalition behind Sergio Fajardo pursued what I would deem the most favorable strategy: an abuse-punishing Rule Abider,[56] while the more defeated belligerent, FARC, opted for a nonequilibrium path of abuse-mitigating Radicalism. The candidacy of former M19 combatant-turned-democrat Gustavo Petro and his Colombia Humana movement is one that defies the book's categorization, as I explain below. For the purposes of counterfactual reasoning, I contrast Petro's party strategy—contrite Tactical Immoderation—with that of the FARC. Table 4.5 demonstrates the theory's predicted optimal party strategies, substantiated by the survey, the strategies actually adopted in 2018, and the electoral consequences of the actual strategies. As my model anticipates, equilibrium strategies paid off electorally; off-equilibrium ones did not. The goal of this section is to build on the original survey and show, qualitatively, a

TABLE 4.5. Parties' Optimal and Actual Strategies and Their Electoral Implications in 2018

Party	Predicted Equilibrium Strategy	Actual Strategy Adopted	Electoral Performance
Winning Belligerent (Santismo)	Restrained Leviathan *Violent past*: Mitigation *Position*: Moderate *Valence*: Hardline security *Candidates*: Key strong- man and civilians	Rule Abider *Violent past*: Contrition *Position*: Moderate *Valence*: Rule-based security *Candidates*: Civilians	Poor
Winning Belligerent (Uribismo)	Restrained Leviathan *Violent past*: Mitigation *Position*: Moderate *Valence*: Hardline security *Candidates*: Key strong- man and civilians	Restrained Leviathan *Violent past*: Mitigation *Position*: Moderate *Valence*: Hardline security *Candidates*: Key strongman and civilians	Good
Losing Belligerent (FARC)	Tactical Immoderate *Violent past*: Contrition *Position*: Immoderate *Valence*: Nonsecurity *Candidates*: Civilians	Radicalism *Violent past*: Mitigation *Position*: Radical *Valence*: Rule-based security *Candidates*: Military	Poor
Gustavo Petro	N/A	Tactical Immoderate *Violent past*: Contrition *Position*: Immoderate *Valence*: Nonsecurity *Candidates*: Civilian (/military)	Good

correlation between party strategy and voter behavior that mediated the relationship between war outcomes and electoral performance in Colombia. The goal is not to test the theory's party-level hypotheses, for which it is necessary to probe the calculated logic that informed the party derivation of strategy; for this, see Chapters 5 to 7 in the Central American context.

Santismo: Off-Equilibrium Strategy of Contrite Rule Abider

The theory expects that parties that inherit the reputation, experience, competencies, and endowments of belligerents that end war militarily winning should be more likely to run on that military victory, spin their side's violence, campaign on hardline security, moderate, and field a strongman paired with a civilian for electoral gain. Uribe's successor Santos, and his own successors in turn, had access to such endowments. As Santos self-reflected, "I am a war hero; I [was] the commander of the armed forces . . . that shifted the balance of power."[57] However, Santos and his successors instead decided to undermine the government's relative victory, apologize for the violence, prioritize rule-based security, and field civilians without security credentials, to the party's electoral detriment. The survey experiment on narratives suggests that there existed no first-mover advantage for adopting such a strategy.

In his inauguration speech in 2010, Santos stated that the FARC was defeated militarily and that he would achieve FARC's unilateral surrender.[58] But, rather than tout this military outcome of a government win, in the peace accord, the Santista government granted significant concessions. On the eve of the plebiscite in 2016, Santos caved to the FARC and rhetorically conceded to them military "stalemate with the state."[59]

Rather than mitigate the government's past violence, Santistas employed the language of reconciliation, acceptance of responsibility, and forgiveness of the guerrillas, in part to muster support for the peace accord referendum.[60] While normatively desirable, this was not electorally optimal. As Santos himself describes, "I changed from being a hawk to becoming a dove," a strategy that he understood would "cost [him] political capital."[61] Santistas opted to treat all parties to the conflict—rebels, paramilitaries, and military—as equally responsible for the war's violence—and to subject them all to the same form of justice: the Integral System for Truth, Justice, Reparation, and no Repetition.[62] For this, they drew criticism that they were betraying the armed forces.[63] Transitional justice was a key tenet of the peace accords to which Santistas pinned their legacy, and so they coupled this policy of justice with one of contrition. In public apologies, for both the state's atrocities[64] and those of the paramilitaries,[65] Santos declared, "in the name of the state, I asked for forgiveness."[66]

Santos had two quasi successors,[67] Humberto de la Calle and Germán Vargas Lleras, both sagacious veteran political figures, but with no security credentials per se; no connections with the military, police, or defense sector; no expertise on security policy; and no backing from any strongman. Vargas Lleras put little emphasis on security, running instead on patronage.[68] De la Calle's relatively anemic security plan constituted a rule-based approach, advocating crime prevention, demilitarizing security, arms control, peaceful coexistence, and nonviolent conflict resolution.[69] This approach—although optimal for a nonbelligerent party—did not seek to give voters confidence that de la Calle possessed the "power able to over-awe"[70] necessary to leverage the government's winning military outcome.

Uribismo: Equilibrium Strategy of Restrained Leviathan

Uribismo was the opposition in 2018. After Santos's "betrayal," Uribe decided to form a new electoral vehicle called Centro Democrático (CD).[71] The Uribista CD party adopted what this book predicts to be an equilibrium strategy for a war winner.[72] It ran on this military victory, which it claimed was outright. In CD's propaganda, the tune of Uribe's success at securing Colombia played on repeat, accompanied by the evocative imagery of the military uniform.[73]

Despite a broad consensus internationally and domestically that Colombia had, for five decades, experienced a *civil war*—two-sided armed struggle with violence committed by both sides—Uribistas opted to declare that *no* "armed conflict" or "war" had taken place in Colombia. Instead, they insisted that Colombian violence was one-sided rebel terror.[74] The version of history proffered by Uribistas meant, in their words, that "violence of the state and paramilitaries is the *consequence* of the violence of the guerrillas" and therefore merits exoneration. With this argument, Uribistas sought to make the case that "victims of the paramilitaries and of the state [were], in fact, victims of the guerrillas too" and that the losing rebels, lacking credit for security improvements, were ultimately responsible for *all* violence, pain, and suffering, direct and indirect.[75]

Uribistas sought vindication for the armed forces' violence, claiming exculpation by their military success and thereby cleansing their reputation for security provision. But, they wanted FARC to be punished for its atrocious transgressions and to underscore FARC's incompetence on security. The CD party inundated the population with statistics of FARC cruelty: Pro-CD ads exclaimed: "6,800 raped women. In impunity?" "200 municipalities destroyed. In impunity?" "To immunity for terrorists, I say no!" "The FARC recruited children, they raped children, and they violated the towns where the very poorest lived."[76] "To reward kidnappers, I say no!"

To propagate this spun story of the past, Uribistas promised to appoint a "conflict-denier" to head the National Center for Historical Memory and to change the leadership of the National Library, National Archive, and National Museum.[77] The Colombian electoral campaign became "awash in fake news, cynical misrepresentation of facts and shameless fear-mongering."[78] Indeed, in an interview with *La República*, Uribista plebiscite campaign manager Juan Carlos Vélez admitted to the use of misinformation to manipulate public opinion and ultimately the vote.

Uribistas articulated the CD party manifesto around a hard "security, justice and order line."[79] Security was claimed CD's "DNA."[80] Its presidential candidate Iván Duque asserted, "#Security is the most important of the public goods."[81] Uribista Senator María Fernanda Cabal declared, "Only when we overcome insecurity can we worry about health and education."[82]

To burnish its reputation for security competence, Uribistas pointed to its past record of war winning. Their script began with "one of the most tragic dates in the history of Colombia": 2000. "In this year, the dispute . . . had reached a climax in terms of violence. There were 30,000 deaths in one year. It was a country in *anarchy*, completely out of control. There were 3,000 kidnappings. And a brutal economic crisis, derived precisely from the insecurity. What we needed was a candidate who would return hope, a *credible* candidate, a *strong* candidate, an *authority*."[83] A sovereign.

Next, in interviews, Uribista party members would rattle off statistics about the record of security improvements and psychological relief that came with turning the tides of the war: "The government fought the violent [actors], and achieved a 45 *percent* reduction in violent deaths. There were 230 municipalities which had had no mayors because of violent threats. The mayors could return. There were more than 300 municipalities without a single policeman. The policemen could return. . . . President Uribe became a star in Colombia because people felt hope again. In 2000, everyone [had] felt desolate, everyone wanted to flee the country, everyone was afraid, people could not leave their homes."[84]

Between 2002 and 2010, under the leadership of Uribe, the script concluded,

> The economic indicators grew impressively, just by providing security to the people. [Uribe's defining] "Democratic Security Policy" transformed the life of Colombia. . . . Why? Because it took as its premise that the primal responsibility of the state . . . is to *protect* the lives of its citizens. Under Uribe, the army began to reach places long inaccessible, began to recapture territories, began to *win* confrontations against the guerrillas. This enabled people to return to work. And when people return to work in the countryside, private businesses flourish again. For example, in Bogotá, we were

trapped, if you went down the road to los Llanos, the guerrillas would kidnap you. If you went to Tolima, the same. On each route out of Bogotá was laid a famous guerrilla trap: "la pesca milagrosa." Uribe liberated Colombia with his plan "Live Colombia, Travel It," which secured the country's main thoroughfares with troops, helicopters, and tanks. . . . Hope returned.[85]

In this narrative, Uribista credit for security provision mitigates government violence and provides the Uribistas a reputation for competence on prospective security.

However, because security was declining in relevance by 2018, CD needed to prime this issue[86] on which it perceived itself to have the advantage. To do so, it targeted the electorate with a daily barrage of images, tweets, and news of the coming anarchy[87]—FARC dissidents, ELN guerrillas, rising drug cultivation, and a refugee crisis from the implosion of neighboring Venezuela—and offered an iron-fist remedy.[88]

Comparing the security agendas of Uribismo to Santismo confirms that Santismo was much more likely to emphasize rule-of-law security, whereas Uribismo was significantly more likely to emphasize law-and-order security (see Table A4.1 and Figure A4.2).

Programmatically, Uribismo moderated (albeit remaining to the right of Santismo). According to party members, the name Centro Democrático sought to convey "center as the balance between the left and the right . . . the balance between all of the social tensions."[89] CD used the color aquamarine to signal the blue hue of the Conservative Party but implying, by the softening of this color, convergence and ideological flexibility.[90] And CD opted to appeal to voters non-ideologically, targeting them "irrespective of our personal beliefs and positions."[91]

As the face of the party, to signal strength, CD maintained caudillo Uribe: seen "almost as a god" for securing the country. At the same time, "the false positives [extrajudicial killing scandal] . . . and the paramilitaries started to stain [Uribe] really badly."[92] Uribe's favorability ratings had fallen from a high of 75 percent in 2010 to 53 percent in 2018, as the mitigating effect of security on the attribution of blame eroded. Accordingly, "Uribe needed someone with no past."[93] "Along came Duque,"[94] seen as "a young, fresh person who had not been touched" by the scandals.[95] "With [strongman] Uribe behind him . . . he could win."[96] The Uribista party symbol was "a firm hand, big heart":[97] a Restrained Leviathan.

FARC: Off-Equilibrium Strategy of Abuse-Mitigating Radicalism

The theory predicts that successor parties to war-loser belligerents will be more likely to adopt a strategy of contrite, *Tactical Immoderation*. FARC, however, defied these predictions and instead rationalized its own violence, ran on a radical revolutionary program, targeted the votes only of its hard-core members, and fielded bloodstained candidates in 2018. FARC adopted these strategies, in part, because of its "organizational birth defects":[98] inertia imposed by an antiquated "Leninist institution constrain[ing] reform";[99] an orthodox leadership without its "finger on the pulse of public opinion";[100] and insufficient pools of party leaders to restructure internally.[101] The imperatives of party differentiation likely further caused FARC to diverge from an optimal strategy.

To reckon with its violent past, FARC adopted mitigation. FARC commander Pastor Alape insisted, "The largest responsibility for the human rights violations is the Colombian state, followed by the paramilitaries . . . followed by the insurgency. That is the order." To back these assertions, he rattled off FARC's version of the facts (a version at odds with the transitional justice regime findings): "80% of the victims are victims of the state and the paramilitaries; 20% are of the guerrillas and other organizations." His comrade went farther, asserting, "The one responsible for *all* the violence is the state."[102]

While blaming its rival belligerents, FARC sought to spin its own violence as "committed for vulnerable groups . . . to protect them."[103] FARC commander Sandra Ramírez summarized, "They say that we are rapists, that we are narcotraffickers, that we raped women . . . but we are in the right. We know how the conflict began. . . . We fought because [the state] drove us to fight, not because we chose to. . . . Where is the proof that we really did all the atrocious acts of which they accuse us? . . . Except for the acts that were committed in the course of conflict, but these were very different. If we took a town over, and, in so doing, caused collateral damage, it was a product of the conflict."[104] According to government peace negotiator Juanita Goebertus, rather than contrition, there was "a lot of arrogance on the [FARC's] side. A lot of that [arrogance] was punished by potential voters . . . for not acknowledging enough responsibility. The more that they were to recognize [their serious crimes], the greater chance they would have had of convincing other sectors of the electorate to vote for them."[105] Instead, throughout the transition, FARC appeared blind and deaf to signs that its bellicose language extolling the glories of its armed struggle was not working with a broader base of leftist voters.[106]

For its elite, combatant Alape summarized, "we decided that those in charge during the conflict would be the [FARC] representatives in Congress and we decided that our presidential candidate would be our commander-in-chief, Timo":[107] a "radical hardliner"[108] facing thirty arrest warrants for illegal recruitment, terrorism, homicide, kidnapping, and drug trafficking.[109] The rebel party's rivals demanded, "FARC should find candidates not guilty of crimes against humanity to serve in politics."[110]

A minority within FARC advocated for breaking with the past: "We have to . . . carry the burden of all our mistakes in the war and [changing FARC] will allow us to permanently show that we do. It is necessary to enter politics as a new force, to refresh our image, to display our commitment to the [democratic] process."[111] Instead, the status-quo side countered and won: "We cannot renounce our past, our principles, our founders."[112] The party maintained the FARC acronym, modifying it in form but not in substance: the Revolutionary Armed Forces of Colombia became Common Alternative Revolutionary Force. With the words "force" and "revolutionary" still in its name, FARC signaled neither a nonviolent commitment to the system, nor a tactical pullback from its outright radicalism.[113] According to one of its commanders, "The [ultra-left revolutionary] political platform . . . remains the same. Our fundamental political proposal remains the same as when we launched it with weapons. . . . As a party, we have considered neither abandoning . . . these ideals, nor trying to modify these proposals in any way just because we are now participating in some elections."[114] With this radical program, FARC narrowly promised only "solutions for the problems of [its] combatants"[115]—its electoral core—rather than targeting a broader set of ideologically adjacent voters.

In adopting such off-equilibrium tactics during its founding political campaign, FARC retained a filthy record in the public eye. Polls showed that only 4 percent of the population had a favorable view of FARC's blood-soaked presidential candidate.[116] And 80 percent did not believe the guerrilla party's pacifist intentions, anticipating it to renege on the peace accords.[117]

Gustavo Petro

The success of M19 rebel-turned-democrat Gustavo Petro hints at how FARC might have fared had it adopted alternative electoral strategies. In 2018, Petro ran for president on a nonbelligerent party ticket, Colombia Humana, but, according to my survey, nearly half of the population saw him as indistinguishable from the FARC, a fallacy that the opposition exploited.

Petro advanced a tactically immoderate platform, seeking to own nonmainstream policies for future elections. According to his campaign manager, Petro "promised a new postconflict Colombia, playing into changes in the Colombian electorate [and targeting the ideologically leftist voter]: millennial, urban, progressive. He presented a modern, future version of a progressive platform. Petro spoke [not of war and peace, but] of global warming, of treating women well, of modern socialism."[118] As a candidate, Petro had a mixed history. He had a distant wartime past as a M19 rebel combatant, but a much longer and more recent civilian trajectory in government, including as mayor of Bogotá.[119] His party ran only civilians.

That Petro effectively adopted what the book calls the Tactical Immoderate approach, and that there existed little appetite within his movement to run in coalition with the FARC, may have taken these strategies out of FARC's repertoire; Petro's success came at the expense of the FARC.[120] Petro's candidacy nonetheless hints at counterfactual strategies with which FARC might have performed better, as seen in the survey experiments.

Equilibrium versus Nonequilibrium Party Strategies and Electoral Performance

Instead, FARC's candidate was driven from the 2018 presidential race,[121] and its party gained a mere 50,000 votes, less than 1 percent of the Senate and lower house vote shares.[122] FARC failed even in its "bastion," the municipality of San Vicente del Caguán.[123] In contrast, Petro performed well electorally, advancing to the second round of the presidential elections, an unprecedented feat for the political left in Colombia.

Similarly, on the government side, whereas "everyone thought [Santista candidate] de la Calle would be a huge success when he launched" his campaign[124] and [Santista] Vargas Lleras seemed "on a glide path to the runoff,"[125] both slipped, in part, I argue, because they adopted nonequilibrium strategies and their rival Uribista candidate adopted equilibrium ones described above.[126] These strategies correlated with the candidates' respective security issue ownership and electoral performance.

I asked Santos's chief of staff, Alfonso Prada, to draw a pie chart depicting how he believed that citizens assigned blame and credit for war and peace. He illustrated Santistas and the FARC with equal shares of blame for the violence, and gave Uribistas 100 percent of the credit for security gains.[127] The Uribista candidate Duque polled only 2 to 8 percentage points better than his closest competitor on health, education, unemployment, corruption, pensions, taxes, and the environment. However, on security he polled 20 percentage points higher, and on peace 15 percentage points higher.[128] Nearly twice as many voters viewed Duque as competent on security compared to his closest rival (46 percent versus 26 percent). Meanwhile, of the Santista candidates, de la Calle was deemed by only 3 percent of the population to be most competent on security, and Vargas Lleras by only 13 percent. Despite the declining salience of security in Colombia, 27 percent of the population said security would decide their vote, surpassing issues of unemployment, the economy, or health.[129] The 2018 Latin American Public Opinion Project (LAPOP) survey found that 34 percent of the population perceived security issues to be the most important ones facing the country.

Duque won 39 percent of the vote in the first presidential round and 54 percent in the second round. CD won the largest share of seats in the Senate (19) and the second largest share in the House (32). Santista candidate Humberto de la Calle received 2 percent of valid votes and Vargas Lleras polled only 7 percent. Thus, after eight years in government, Santos ended up with no successor in the second round of voting.[130] Of course, we cannot prove the counterfactual that Santos's successors would have performed better if they had run on the electorally optimal (albeit not necessarily normatively preferable) Restrained Leviathan strategy. However, the survey experiments suggest that they might have done better, particularly among swing, security, and conflict-affected voters, who proved consequential and tipped the balance in 2018. According to Fajardo's campaign strategist, "You had left and right leaning, but all became swing voters."[131] These voters went with Duque. According to Santos's finance minister, Mauricio Cárdenas, "Duque won the median voter."[132] Santista candidate de la Calle observed, "Many, many swing voters swung away from [us] . . . to [Uribe's] CD because they believed it could bring greater stability. . . . As the authority figure [what the book's theory calls a Restrained Leviathan], Centro Democrático [could] attract voters from all sectors . . . including from victims."[133] In my survey, security voters proved twice as likely as other voters to select Duque in the first round.

Alternative Explanations

My survey instrument allows me to test several alternative explanations: (1) that voting was driven mostly by other factors and the explanatory power of security voting was insignificant; (2) that people voted for a belligerent successor because they were coerced to or because they feared coercion; or (3) that people voted for a belligerent successor over nonbelligerents because they did not know about the victimization and, had they known, they would have voted differently.

Other Determinants of Voting: Economics, Ideology, and Clientelism

If my framework is correct, the data should reveal a significant marginal effect of security voting when controlling for the myriad other factors known to influence vote choice, such as economic issues, perceptions of overall party competence, partisanship, and clientelism, and individual-level factors including age, gender, education, and socioeconomic status.

To tease out the relative impact of security voting, I adapt the question wording and methodology of Calvo and Murillo (2019). In particular, I compare respondents' evaluations of each party's security competence[134] with indicators of their evaluations of each party's economic competence,[135] ideological distance from their own views,[136] and distributive expectations.[137] I use a design with respondent-specific controls—age, gender, education, and socioeconomic level—and alternative-specific variables, which vary by choice (each party). This model thereby estimates the marginal effect of perceptions of Uribista CD security competence on vote choice for the Uribista candidate relative to that of these other well-established determinants of vote choice, and then compares this effect to a vote choice model for each of the other contenders in the election in which the alternative-specific variables are coded for the contenders' respective parties.[138] In Table 4.6, models 1–5, I use a linear probability model:

$$\text{Vote} = \beta_0 + \beta_1(\text{Security}) + \beta_2(\text{Economic})$$
$$+ \beta_3(\text{Clientelism}) + \beta_4(\text{Ideological distance})$$
$$+ \beta'(\text{Demographics}) + \epsilon$$

Comparing the coefficients in columns 1 with those in columns 2–5, the results show that voters for Uribista Duque valued competence on security much more than did other voters. For Duque, a one-unit increase in perceptions of Uribistas' competence on security increased Duque's vote share by 15.6 percentage points, whereas, for all other candidates, the effect of security competence on vote choice hovered between one and five percentage points. What is more, the effect of security voting on vote choice for Uribistas is robust to the inclusion of perceptions of competence on the economy,

TABLE 4.6. Determinants of Vote Choice, 2018 Presidential Election

	(1)	(2)	(3)	(4)	(5)
		Vote Santista			
	Vote Uribista (CD: Duque)	Vote Santista (CR: Vargas Lleras)	Vote CH (Petro)	Vote Santista (PL: de la Calle)	Vote AV (Fajardo)
Competence on security	0.156***	0.029***	0.034**	0.016***	0.058***
	(0.013)	(0.006)	(0.015)	(0.005)	(0.009)
Competence on economy	0.024*	−0.000	0.037**	0.002	−0.003
	(0.014)	(0.006)	(0.015)	(0.005)	(0.009)
Clientelism	0.014***	−0.003	0.021***	−0.000	−0.006
	(0.005)	(0.003)	(0.004)	(0.002)	(0.004)
Ideological distance	−0.001**	−0.000**	−0.001**	0.000	0.007*
	(0.001)	(0.000)	(0.000)	(0.000)	(0.004)
Constant	0.000	−0.072*	−0.187**	0.008	−0.130**
	(0.091)	(0.041)	(0.080)	(0.032)	(0.062)
Obs.	1,155	1,110	1,114	1,131	1,119

Note: Models 1–5 use a linear probability model. CD = Centro Democrático; CR = Cambio Radical; CH = Colombia Humana; PL = Partido Liberal; AV = Partido Alianza Verde. Explanatory variables are party-specific. Results include respondent-specific variables: age, gender, education, and socioeconomic level.

*p < .05. **p < .01. ***p < .001.

distributive expectations, ideological distance and partisanship (which also captures wartime popular support and identities), the effects of which are more similar across the candidates.

Coercion

The observable implication of my theory—that belligerents who are military winners will perform well in founding elections irrespective of their past atrocities because they can own the security valence issue—risks observational equivalence with a logic that is subtly distinct, although often treated as synonymous: that these belligerents will perform well in the elections because they are well positioned to coerce and elicit fear in the population and thereby control their vote. Whereas Colombia is a long-standing electoral democracy, it is also one intertwined with violence. During the war, belligerents used elections to identify people's partisan identity in order to target them with violence.[139] Given the stronger counterinsurgency, it also is possible that past transgressions caused respondents to be influenced by social desirability bias and to overstate support for parties tied to the counterinsurgency.[140] Accordingly, this coercion explanation is highly credible in this context.[141] I echo Mia Couto and argue that in democratic elections "in times of terror, we [at times] *choose* monsters to protect us."[142] It is worth unpacking the implications of the coercion logic further.

VULNERABLE POPULATION

First, if the coercion logic is correct, we would anticipate observing significantly enhanced support for belligerent successor parties by individuals who report voting out of fear. I compare the vote choice of those who self-reported voting freely with those who stated that they voted with a lot of fear or who had been pressured with threats to vote for or against a candidate or party or not to vote. Eight percent stated that, in general, when they vote, they do so with a great deal of fear; these voters were only moderately more likely to abstain than those who declared that they were not voting out of fear (35 percent compared to 30 percent). Of those who acknowledged voting out of fear, 34 percent supported the Uribistas, a share equal to those who did not vote out of fear, suggesting that fearful voters were not more likely to support the Uribista candidate. That Santismo and Uribismo could both claim the mantle of the belligerent party, but only the latter succeeded electorally, further undermines this claim. Additionally, that Uribismo gained only 39.1 percent of the vote in the first round—in other words, 60.9 percent voted against Duque—suggests that people were willing and able to cast their vote against what I classify to be a winning belligerent successor in a democracy. The Misión Observatorio Electoral declared the 2018 elections the cleanest in Colombia, with negligible coercion.[143]

SECRET VERSUS OPEN BALLOT

Second, if the coercion logic is correct, we would anticipate finding depressed support for belligerent parties when voters believe their vote to be secret (rendering retribution unlikely), relative to when their vote choice could be known, which would leave them vulnerable to retribution. To probe this implication, I randomly assigned half of the respondents in my survey to a secret ballot for one of the vote choice questions, while the other half were assigned to an open ballot in which the enumerator recorded their vote choice.

The secret ballot was introduced to respondents with the following instructions: "For which of the parties which appear on the Tablet did you vote in the first round of the last presidential elections of 2018? Please do NOT tell me your response." The enumerator then passed the respondents the tablet that showed the randomly ordered parties and their logos[144] and instructed the respondents to indicate their vote choice and to press enter. The next screen asked the respondent to verify the vote choice response and to go back to correct it if it was entered erroneously; otherwise to press "next," which brought the respondent to a page from which it was not possible to go back to the vote choice screen. This sealed the confidentiality of their vote choice from the enumerator. Codes available only to the research team in the United States could link the anonymized respondents with their secret vote choices. The respondent then returned the tablet to the enumerator. Follow-up questioning during piloting exhibited confidence in the confidentiality of the question. Similar techniques used in Daly, Paler, and Samii (2020) reveal the effectiveness of using self-administered survey modules to elicit honest answers to sensitive questions. The survey experiment revealed an insignificant difference in the vote share in the secret ballot treatment compared to the control group of an open ballot (Table 4.7).

ANONYMOUS VERSUS DIRECT QUESTIONS

In a similar vein, a third observable implication of the coercion logic is that voters should express less support for the belligerents when they believe their response to be anonymous compared to when it is openly recorded. This may

TABLE 4.7. Secret versus Open Ballot Results

Candidates	Secret (%)	Not Secret (%)	Total (%)
Duque	32.1	31.9	32.0
Vargas Lleras	2.0	2.6	2.3
De la Calle	2.0	1.6	1.8
Petro	14.8	15.3	15.0
Fajardo	7.6	7.1	7.4
Didn't vote/Null	41.4	41.6	41.5
Total	100.0	100.0	100.0

be especially the case for attitudes about the military as Aila Matanock and Miguel García-Sánchez show.[145] To evaluate this, I randomized the question format.[146] Respondents were randomly assigned either to receive a list count version of the question, which created anonymity, or to answer each of the four items in the list directly through open questions.

Enumerators read the following script: "Colombians have distinct visions about what postconflict governance should look like. For example, they have different opinions about the system of government, the political parties, etc." Subjects receiving the *direct* question format then answered yes/no to each item individually, following the prompt: "Next, I will read you several alternatives and I would like for you to tell me whether these are outcomes you would accept or not. Would the following be acceptable for Colombia? Yes or no?"

Alternatives	Responses
1. Democracy with a strong Congress?	Yes/No
2. A system with more political parties?	Yes/No
3. Centro Democrático in control of the government?	Yes/No
4. Less defense spending?	Yes/No

Subjects receiving the list question format instead were asked to give a single *count* of yes answers to the items, following the prompt:[147] "Next, I will read you several alternatives. When I'm finished, I would like for you to tell me how MANY of the options you would find acceptable for Colombia. Do NOT tell me which ones you agree with, just tell me how many. I'll read the list twice. Please keep count mentally and then tell me with how many you agree."

The list mirrors the direct question. If coercion and fear were driving vote choice, we would anticipate that the averages elicited with the sensitive-question list technique would be significantly lower than the levels expressed in the direct, open questions. If, instead, fear were not influencing vote choice, the list would exhibit a mean similar to the open answers.

The results are largely consistent with the latter prediction. The average of the sensitive questioning list treatment was 1.95 compared with 1.98 for the direct question one, a statistically insignificant difference.

FEAR OF WAR RECURRENCE

Finally, I turn from fear of retribution at a micro or egotropic level to fear of retribution at a macro or sociotropic level: that stronger groups can credibly promise to return to war if the electoral results run against them, whereas weaker groups cannot, suggesting that citizens are voting not out of a sense of relief and security, but out of a sense of fear that these groups will spoil the peace.[148] If this version of the coercion logic is correct, we might expect to find among CD voters a stronger belief that "had Centro Democrático not won the 2018 elections, the army would have reinitiated hostilities against the FARC." This question was posed to respondents in the survey. The data reveal that CD voters were no more likely to have feared war recurrence than were citizens who supported the other parties. As described earlier, public opinion polls suggest that 80 percent of the population believed that the FARC would resume hostilities[149]—and yet, there also is no evidence that this belief drove citizens to vote for the FARC to prevent this outcome.

In sum, the evidence casts doubt on, but does not definitively disprove, an explanation centered on manifest coercion, anxiety over retribution, or fear of a return to war. Violence and fear certainly existed in Colombia during the transition; indeed, they sustained the salience of security. Disentangling the mechanisms underpinning voter support in such contexts is particularly challenging, and future analyses should continue to seek means of doing so.

Ignorance and Fog of War

The third alternative explanation that the survey data enable me to assess in this context is whether victimized populations elected parties with violent linkages because they did not know the nature of the violence against civilians. In more extreme terms, the fog of war, analogous to the view of the public as "lemmings"[150] hindered the attribution of blame, and voters were hoodwinked by the parties' strategies. In the Colombian case, the logic would be that voters were marinated only in the version of history of the relative belligerent winner—the (Uribista) government—according to which the FARC was disproportionately responsible for the war. If this theory is correct, learning the facts (in this case, those about paramilitary and state violence) should change the attribution process. My argument instead makes the case that people do know the broad brushstrokes of the facts, but that the attribution of blame is messy and does not track objectively with those facts. If I am right, learning the facts should not change the processing of blame. To evaluate these implications, in the survey, I randomized whether respondents were given complete or partial (but truthful) information[151] about the Colombian Center for Historical Memory's investigations of paramilitary and rebel violence.[152] Each respondent was randomly assigned a version with statistics either about *both* rebel and paramilitary violence (version 1), or about only rebel violence (version 2, likely reflecting respondents' pretreatment priors). While the enumerator read the statistics, respondents were provided a visual aid to follow along. Respondents were then asked whom they believed abused the Colombian population more: the rebels, the paramilitaries, or both equally.[153]

Version 1:

Centro de Memoria Histórica found that the rebels and paramilitaries were responsible for:		
	Paramilitaries	*Rebels*
Massacres	60%	21%
Mines	1%	98%
Assassinations	64%	23%
Kidnappings	12%	86%
Disappearances	62%	25%
Child Recruitment	23%	72%

Version 2:

Centro de Memoria Histórica found that the rebels were responsible for:	
	Rebels
Mines	98%
Kidnappings	86%
Child Recruitment	72%

I use regression techniques to estimate the average treatment effects (ATE) of the full information version 1 relative to the baseline rebel-only version (2).

TABLE 4.8. Information and Judgments about Atrocities

	Attribution of Blame		
	(1) Rebels	(2) Paramilitaries	(3) Equal
Information treatment: Rebel and paramilitary violence	−0.002 (0.027)	0.026 (0.020)	−0.028 (0.031)
Constant	0.251*** (0.019)	0.084*** (0.014)	0.633*** (0.022)
Obs.	1,002	1,002	1,002
R^2	.001	.008	.002

Note: Omitted category: Only rebel violence.

***$p < .001$.

The analysis, presented in Table 4.8, shows that informing respondents about the perpetrators' true and symmetrical responsibility for the violence had no effect on attribution of blame relative to the condition of only guerrilla violence. While the full information condition might have encouraged respondents to focus on the rebel column, in this experimental setting, respondents continued to believe the guerrillas to be more responsible for excessive use of force even after the disclosures.

This experiment casts some doubt on the notion that the reason people voted for belligerent successors was that they did not know about the victimization and that, had they known, they would have assigned blame and voted differently.

Conclusion

This chapter tested the individual-level implications of the book's model with original experimental and observational survey data. It employed novel experiments to randomize the provision of hypothetical security and measure its mitigating effect on the attribution of blame for atrocities. It found support for the ability of winning belligerents to shift voters' reference points, mitigate their culpability, and cleanse their reputations for security competence. The survey data also provided evidence for the electoral rationality of losing belligerents' adopting a narrative of contrition. A second set of experiments randomized three dimensions of party strategies—valence, position, and candidate selection—to test which variants worked better with the electorate.

Whereas more victorious belligerents benefited from a Restrained Leviathan strategy—moderation, security valence, strongman candidates—for more vanquished ones, a Tactical Immoderate strategy proved more electorally expedient. The chapter then turned to the real-world application of these strategies and their electoral implications, exploiting the multiparty nature of Colombia's system. It showed that strategies derived by the book's theory as optimal for parties of varying war outcomes correlated with positive electoral performance; those off-equilibrium doomed the parties' electoral prospects. Next, the analysis compared the relative weight of security voting to other determinants of vote choice and found that, even when controlling for well-established other guiders of elections, including ideology, economic voting, and clientelism, there remained an important share of the variation in vote choice explained by security voting. Sensitive question techniques sought to reveal whether the victimized population may have elected belligerent successors due to coercion, fear of retribution, or fear of war recurrence, and an information experiment aimed to discover whether the victimized population elected bloodstained parties because of ignorance about the atrocities. Both yielded null results, casting some doubt on the alternative explanations centered on the shadow of the gun and the fog of war.

This chapter sought to approximate the theory's party strategies so as to experimentally manipulate them. However, given real, practical, and ethical considerations, there were limitations to the ability to do so. This was a society reeling from the effects of fifty-two years of war, engaged in an already delicate and, at times, fraught process of writing Colombia's violent history and determining the optimal way to secure its future. The sanctity of this process was to be respected. In addition to the limitation of experimental and observational survey methods for testing the individual-level implications of my theory, Colombia is unique in many ways. I therefore next exported the theory to the Central American context. There, I sought to uncover the parties' strategizing and output, and to understand whether war-winner, war-loser, stalemated, and nonbelligerent parties adopted the hypothesized strategies and did so for the reasons and considerations that the theory posits. The book's next three chapters turn from the mechanism of postwar voters to that of parties.

5

Military Draw in El Salvador

Introduction: Party Strategy in Central America

The violent-victors theory posits that war outcomes influence founding post-war election results (and in particular, the puzzling success of bloodstained successors) through party strategies and voter choices. Chapter 4 leveraged a rare opportunity to embed experiments in an original survey in order to test the voter-level mechanisms of the book's theory. To evaluate its party-level mechanisms, Chapters 5 to 7 now turn to Central America. This region offers rich variation with respect to war outcomes: El Salvador's war ended in a military draw, Guatemala's in government victory, and Nicaragua's in rebel victory.[1]

The three chapters evaluate whether, given their war experience and outcomes, these countries' postwar parties chose what the theory predicts to be equilibrium or off-equilibrium strategies, but the chapters also trace the decision-making *processes* by which the respective parties arrived at their strategies. As a secondary objective, I document the postwar voters' attitudinal and behavioral responses to these strategies, the ultimate election results, the implications of these election results for peace and justice, and the trajectories of political life after the founding elections.

Each chapter in the trio first sets the stage: it paints the historical picture of the civil conflict that raged in each of the three Central American countries, the atrocities that the belligerents inflicted on the civilian population, and the military outcome of the war. It pauses to discuss the determinants of the war outcome and potential variables omitted from the analysis that might account for both war outcomes and subsequent electoral performance. The chapters introduce the relevant players in each country—the voters and the belligerent and nonbelligerent parties—and the evidence that the elections meet the book's scope conditions: they were founding, postwar, (minimally) demo-cratic elections that took place under plausibly exogenous institutional rules. Each chapter describes the sources of data on which I rely to approximate the internal party deliberations and strategies. These varied and rich sources in-clude personal interviews with the key protagonists; archives of party meet-ings and memoranda; party manifestos, propaganda, and campaign ephemera; local newspaper coverage; election observation reports; and declassified U.S. government cables.

Each of the three case study chapters then examines the parties' maneuver-ing to position themselves prospectively vis-à-vis the electorate. Here, I use confidential party memoranda as a window into the closed-door deliberations about how the parties decided on their strategies. Each chapter documents the political jousting within each party over what narrative of the violent past to present and how to attribute blame for that past. I scoured archives of the par-ties' internal records for information about whether nonbelligerent parties considered electoral punishment versus forgiveness of the wartime belliger-ents' atrocities, and whether belligerent parties debated denying, scapegoat-ing, concealing, apologizing, distancing, ignoring, or justifying their own participation in the wartime violence. I sought evidence showing why the par-ties opted for these approaches that they did.

A particular challenge arises when seeking a lens into belligerent parties' strategies for laundering their violent and, at times, atrocious pasts. While these strategies may constitute intentional manipulation of voter perceptions, they might instead simply reflect the perpetrators' own self-justifications and their true beliefs about what transpired. In other words, these parties may aim to *mitigate* their past violence in voters' eyes not because of a master plan to spin public opinion, but because they themselves *believe* that the past violence is offset by their achievement of war termination. If this is the case, we may not observe party deliberations leading to a decision to mitigate. Despite these empirical challenges, I look for evidence that the belligerent parties acknowl-edged the electoral importance, incumbrances, and benefits of the backdrop—that the broader electorate, affected by conflict, was concerned about peace and security—and I document the parties' considerations of how to transform their bloodstained liabilities into an asset: a reputation for competence on security. Given the relatively limited number of texts dealing with the violent past and their disparities, and the importance of assessing the sentiments the parties attached to the texts, I engaged in careful hand coding of the docu-ments rather than supervised text analysis. I used intercoder reliability tests;

research assistants who coded the texts were blind to my hypotheses and theory.

On ideological position, I look for evidence of deliberations about whether to moderate or radicalize, whether to be specific or vague in their policy proposals, and what positional issues to prioritize. The framework anticipates that war experience and outcomes would inform these deliberations. It expects that the belligerent parties would have debated the risks and rewards of playing to their militant and mobilized core supporters, or instead seeking to shift the votes of uncertain swing constituencies in their favor. It anticipates that, in particular, belligerents who had won the war (or achieved a draw), assured of a mobilized base and cohesion born of that war, would decide to prioritize a broader constituency in order to signal restraint, whereas those belligerents who lost the war would opt to focus on their core and safer ideologically adjacent voters.

To reveal the party *output*—the parties' strategies of valence and programmatic positions—I rely on computer-assisted natural language processing and hand coding of the parties' programs. I gained access to the parties' manifestos from the parties' own archives or national archives, and prepared the text corpus for machine processing.[2] I then analyzed the text using a dictionary and a structural topic model. Through the use of a dictionary approach, I first sought to reveal what share of each party platform was devoted to specific valence topics. To do so, I calculated the proportion of words in the manifestos dedicated to security, the economy, and social welfare topics. Second, I pooled the different parts of the manifestos dedicated to security and adopted an unsupervised machine learning approach.[3] I identified the subset of the manifestos that dealt with security-related issues. These tended to be demarcated sections of the programs under headings related to security, law and order, rule of law, defense, and so on, or separate security platforms. Within the security text corpus, I identified common topics in the programs, incorporating the metadata on political party affiliation (with parties defined as nonbelligerent, winning belligerent, losing belligerent). I estimated the difference in mean prevalence of security topic clusters across political parties of varying war outcomes.

Third, I used unstructured text analysis to understand, within five security topic clusters,[4] how the different parties were talking about security. I analyzed the maximum contrast in words between the parties for each topic and complemented the analyses with snippets of the input text to provide context. The smaller number of security texts also lent itself to hand coding and analysis, allowing for a more nuanced reading. I therefore engaged several coders to hand code the texts and to enhance intercoder reliability.

In the fourth step, I turned from valence to position on a left-right ideological spectrum to determine whether the platforms of the parties of interest in this book moderated and converged, or not.[5] Unfortunately, none of the parties on which this book focuses were included in existing manifesto databases. I therefore used the Party Manifesto Project (PMP) to train a machine learning algorithm on Spanish-language manifestos already coded by the PMP.[6] These included manifestos from countries across Latin America that are comparable to those that I analyze. I used Multinomial Naive Bayes to build the classifier, which identifies whether statements in the corpus reflect right or left-wing positions.[7] The classifier's accuracy score was 0.7958, which means its predictions were correct in 79.58 percent of the cases.[8] I used this classifier to code the platforms of the parties of interest in this book on a left-right ideological spectrum, with an eye toward identifying party positional convergence/moderation versus divergence/immoderation.[9]

The theory has observable implications for the parties' selection of their elite. To evaluate these implications, I extracted information about what qualities the parties sought in candidates for different offices and how they decided where to field distinct types of candidates. I looked, in particular, for what characteristics the parties believed to constitute highly competitive candidates: those with security competence, those able to signal restraint, or those with other credentials and how this varied by parties of different war outcomes. I also evaluated the parties' output, by engaging in quantitative analysis of the parties' lists. Finally, I used the diverse sources of party evidence to shine light on the parties' marketing strategies: how they planned to disseminate and propagate their messages.

After discussing party strategies with respect to valence, position, electoral targets, party elite, and campaigning, each chapter turns to how the conflict-affected voters formed their attitudes and cast their ballots based on nationally representative surveys conducted during the founding elections.[10] The surveys provide an array of relevant measures, including whom the populations credited with peace, whom they blamed for violence, and whom they deemed most competent on security, human rights, and recovery. The survey data demonstrate the correlations between party and voter strategies. They suggest a rationality to the parties' strategy decisions through backward induction, anticipating voters reactions. They also indicate the potential influence of party strategies on voter preferences. Combining the behavior of parties and voters, this section of each case study reveals the ultimate results of the founding elections, indicating, in particular, the success of the country's bloodstained parties. Each of the three chapters then carefully considers whether the book's violent-victors theory can better account for patterns of postwar party and voter behavior, and electoral outcomes, than can explanations centered on popular support, electoral coercion, organizational assets, or incumbency. The cases provide strong support for the theory, but also illustrate interesting and important nuances beyond it.

Each chapter concludes with the implications of the postwar elections for peace and justice; it outlines the dynamics over time as other concerns began to rival security. Here, I look for evidence of whether belligerent successor parties' durability over multiple electoral cycles correlated with their access to party machines and mobilization capacities, and whether they sought to activate new dimensions to political competition or to resuscitate the security brand. Combined, these chapters bring to life the war outcome-dictated process of party strategizing after mass violence.

Setting the Stage: El Salvador's War

Civil war ravaged El Salvador from 1979 to 1992. The war's participants locate its roots in La Matanza of 1932, the communist peasant uprising led by Farabundo Martí that was brutally suppressed with the killing of at least ten thousand suspected campesino participants.[11] A long series of military dictatorships followed. In the 1960s, diverse sectors of society began to mobilize. Liberation theology took hold among the population. It preached that peasants should not simply accept their fate on earth and hope for a better afterlife, but should instead seek to change their destiny on earth: to organize and mobilize to redress their economic, social, and political grievances.[12] These escalating grievances centered on rural landlessness (which grew from 12 percent in 1961 to 41 percent in 1975), increasing urban unemployment, proliferating shantytowns, and deteriorating living conditions.[13]

At the same time, the Cuban Revolution sparked a resurgence of the Communist Party. With the United States and Soviet Union locked in the Cold War, the latter and Cuba funneled resources to communist movements across Latin America.[14] The United States sought to counter this threat in its geopolitical backyard by funding conservative labor movements and seeking to redirect mobilization away from the political left.[15] The resulting popular mobilization in the 1960s and early 1970s remained segmented across the political spectrum and peaceful.[16] A minority within the Communist Party believed that armed mobilization would be necessary to foment change, but the vast majority believed that the electoral route provided the most effective means of advancing revolutionary progress.[17]

In 1974, fraudulent elections began to shift this balance within the Communist Party, undermining perceptions that a peaceful route to political change was feasible, and the armed left grew. In that year, the main opponent to the military regime, the Christian Democratic Party (PDC), won the election, but it was then stolen by the military regime's National Conciliation Party (PCN) through outright fraud.[18] Mass protests pressured the government for reform, but the state responded instead with indiscriminate repression.[19] It did so through its security forces, large-scale, organized death squads,[20] and militias numbering a hundred thousand.[21] Under this repression, the divided, relatively apolitical, nonviolent social movement turned into a united, revolutionary, and violent one, the leftist Farabundo Martí National Liberation Front (FMLN) guerrillas.[22] Indiscriminate state terror drove recruits into the arms of the rebels and generated widespread grievances that translated into popular support and resources for high-risk insurgency.[23]

As violence began to escalate in the late 1970s, reformist junior officers within the military carried out a coup. Allying with the civilian center and left to form the Revolutionary Governing Junta, they promised major reforms and to dissolve the militias,[24] the death squads, and the Agencia Nacional de Seguridad Salvadoreña.[25] The reformist military faction defied the economic elite that it had always served.[26] These reformists also "betrayed" conservatives and hardliners within the military who sought to "maintain the status-quo." In the minds of these conservatives, the reformists' alliance with the left—which they perceived as allied, in turn, with Cuba and the Soviet Union—meant essentially granting permission for outside communist forces to invade El Salvador by proxy force.[27] In response to this defiance and disloyalty, the elite and conservative military officers devised their own tools to protect their now insecure interests. They augmented existing private security forces, militias, and death squads under new guises; began a dirty war against the guerrillas and all potentially "subversive" sectors of society; and launched their own political party called ARENA.

These steps intensified the violence, as the reformist government had now lost any monopoly on the means of force. Its policies aimed at addressing popular grievances to try to reduce the appeal of insurgency were thwarted at every turn by the oligarch–death squad alliance in a "protection racket."[28] As a result, by early 1980, the war became high in intensity and began to touch the entire country. The United States wielded significant influence over El Salvador and decided to make its massive levels of military aid conditional on reform, aimed at defusing the ticking bomb of social mobilization.[29] "The [resulting, demonstration] election of a civilian-led government [sought to] improve the regime's international image, deflect pressure for a negotiated settlement, and convince [U.S.] congressional skeptics that the country was progressing toward democracy."[30] José Napoleón Duarte's Christian Democrats fit the bill, taking the government's reins in appearance, though not in practice.[31]

Given the tiny size of the country and the large-scale injections of arms and funds from the superpowers, violence was felt everywhere in El Salvador. Violence plagued rural areas, and the guerrillas "brought the war home to the wealthy neighborhoods of [the capital city of] San Salvador."[32] Each hamlet experienced a "microcosm of the wider civil war" between progovernment and rebel forces.[33]

Balance of Atrocities

The Salvadoran armed conflict took the lives of at least 70,000 in a country of just 4.6 million, and it left over one million refugees.[34] Seligson and McElhinny (1996) estimate that one out of every sixty-six Salvadorans died in the war. The 1993 report of the UN Commission on the Truth for El Salvador, publicized in the national media before the elections, revealed the highly asymmetrical nature of the atrocities. The FMLN rebels had "assassinated opposition mayors, forcibly recruited civilians to fight on its behalf, kidnapped wealthy businessmen for ransom, and engaged in widespread acts of economic terrorism."[35] The government's atrocities, however, far outnumbered those of the FMLN. The UN Commission estimated that the government side was responsible for 95 percent of the political killings, the rebels only 5 percent.[36] In 1980 alone, some twelve thousand people were killed, most "either captured and executed by the death squads or killed in wholesale massacres carried out by government forces."[37] Many massacres were huge; some killed over one thousand individuals.[38] State-sponsored forces abducted, tortured, and murdered victims and left the bodies "in designated locations that became so commonplace that they inspired a neologism: 'body dumps.'"[39] These forces engaged in "mountains of death threats and, [in their] war of extermination,"[40] left mutilated limbs and severed heads at bus stops where morning commuters would find them. They launched campaigns of mass suppression of unarmed unionists, teachers, students, peasants, and clergy, that included the call to "Be a Patriot! Kill a Priest!"[41] Accordingly, as FMLN presidential candidate Rubén Zamora explains, "Everyone felt *affected* by the conflict, everyone feels they were victims."[42] And given the widespread nature of the atrocities and the reporting of the Truth Commission, according to the ARENA government peace negotiator David Escobar Galindo, the fog of war had lifted: "It's not as if people didn't know what had happened. Everyone knew."[43]

War Outcome

The war ultimately ended in a draw, but the military balance changed dramatically over the course of the conflict. The FMLN was relatively weak during the 1970s. However, during the 1980s, significant external transfers of funding and arms, combined with domestic support provoked by the state repression, increased the FMLN's military strength, and it became a formidable force. Against this, the Salvadoran government became "increasingly dependent on U.S. assistance for its survival."[44] By 1992, the FMLN was locked in a stalemate with the Salvadoran military.[45] The Salvadoran state was unlikely to be able to "defeat the insurgents militarily"[46] and military victory was "similarly out of the [FMLN's] own reach."[47] The war outcome resulted, in large part, because each side was sponsored by a Cold War superpower, producing a "dynamic equilibrium."[48] This sponsorship fell with the Berlin Wall in 1989; the dynamic of military advances and retreats became frozen at this specific moment in time, leaving the belligerents at a draw, and with few prospects for significant changes in the balance of power. According to contemporaneous polling, this stalemate was widely recognized; only 12 percent of the population believed that the FMLN was losing militarily, and just 4 percent thought the government was losing militarily (IUDOP 1991).[49]

The civil war finally terminated in a comprehensive negotiated settlement, the Chapultepec Accords, in 1992. El Salvador therefore constitutes the testing site for the theory's observable implications in the case of a war outcome of a draw. The theory anticipates that the stalemated belligerent successor parties from the rebel and government sides would enjoy equal credit for peace and equal ownership of the security issue, and therefore would mirror one another, in that both would adopt a *Restrained Leviathan* strategy. To the extent that the government controlled the media, the model predicts an incumbency advantage in propagating the messaging of this strategy.

Verifying the Scope Conditions: Postwar Democratic Elections

Following the peace accords, the FMLN-Salvadoran government conflict entered a postconflict phase, the first scope condition of the theory. The FMLN disarmed and demobilized as of December 15, 1992.[50] The armed forces were reduced by 50 percent, and the National Guard, Treasury Police, paramilitary forces, civil defense units, Intelligence Agency, and National Police were dissolved.[51] A new national civilian police force was created.

Two years later, in 1994, founding elections were held.[52] The elections were "deemed to be free and fair."[53] The international community spent more than twenty million dollars and deployed three thousand observers in support of these elections. The International Foundation for Electoral Systems reported that the voting process was conducted in an "orderly, peaceful, and transparent fashion which permitted the popular will of the Salvadoran people to be expressed . . . without fear of violent incidents."[54] Even the FMLN presidential candidate, Rubén Zamora, defended the elections, stating, "There were no irregularities."[55] The results were "accepted by contenders and observers alike."[56]

The presidential elections were decided by absolute majority in a two-round system, the legislative elections by closed-list proportional representation.[57] These institutional rules followed the constitution enacted in 1983, which largely resurrected that of 1962. The electoral institutions therefore were not endogenous to the war outcome.

Characterizing the Voters

In the lead-up to the founding postwar elections of 1994, citizens' main concerns were implementation of the peace accords and preservation of the recovery in terms of security and the economy. At the same time, while political violence had dropped precipitously by 1994, the homicide rate in El Salvador reached 138 per hundred thousand inhabitants, two and a half times the rate at the height of the war.[58] In this founding election year, nearly 40 percent of the population across all socioeconomic groups and 48 percent of unaligned voters cited violence-related issues as the main problems facing the country.[59] The category of "unaligned" included 62 percent of the Salvadoran electorate.[60] The remaining population pointed to other economic issues including poverty and inflation. The dominant cleavage in El Salvador was class; the population was distributed across the left-right ideological spectrum, but leaned more to the political left (60 percent) than to the right (40 percent).[61]

Introducing the Parties: The Nonbelligerent

In the founding election, government and rebel belligerent successor parties faced a party without roots in the violent organizations of the past: Duarte's centrist opposition, the PDC.[62] For mostly idiosyncratic reasons, orthogonal to the book's theory, PDC played only a minor role in the 1994 election. The chapter therefore focuses on the election's main contenders, but pauses here to consider this nonbelligerent party.

The PDC had served as the longtime opposition to military rule and repression. Its underpinnings were centrist and pacific, representing the alternative to political violence.[63] Accordingly, the population did not associate the PDC party with the government belligerent's excessive violence. My interviewees across the political spectrum confirmed that, in the population's eyes, PDC did not have blood on its hands.

At the same time, PDC was not entirely untainted by the war. Under intense pressure from the United States, the right-wing elite and conservative military faction allowed Duarte to lead the Junta (1980–1982) and—after the United States essentially reversed the 1984 election results—allowed him to hold the presidency from 1985 to 1989.[64] PDC's nonbelligerent credentials were somewhat tarnished by this time in government. In particular, while in office, it could not and did not control the military, stop the repression, or prosecute the perpetrators. In the execution of the war, it operated as a civilian puppet; the military and death squads preserved their own institutional autonomy and overall direction of the war efforts.[65] Therefore, PDC was not held responsible for the violence, but it was not entirely exonerated.

To maximize its vote share, PDC generally followed the optimal strategy of nonbelligerent parties predicted by the theory. It advanced a reformist agenda from the center, sought to activate vengeful voting against the belligerent parties, and promised rule of law. For example, it argued that "the war is a sad and unfortunate reality that persists even though the national conscience rejects all violence and deems totally illegitimate the pursuit of power by force."[66] It warned that the "death and total war is precisely what the [belligerent parties] promise the country" in the future.[67] In contrast to the belligerent parties, in its political platform, PDC promised prospective rule-based security: "To strengthen the rule of law, such that there is respect for the Constitution and all other laws, generating certainty that the [laws] will be carried out by efficient and rigorous courts. This is the foundation of *legal security*. We will guarantee legal security, personal security, and collective security."[68] Despite the adoption of this equilibrium strategy, PDC proved noncompetitive in the 1994 election for largely exogenous reasons. It was weighed down by a corruption scandal relating to earthquake relief spending. A leadership struggle and bitter split[69] stemming from its charismatic leader's terminal illness left the party "adrift."[70] Accordingly, "PDC found itself increasingly squeezed out as the FMLN and ARENA moderated their platforms."[71] Given the PDC's relative electoral irrelevance,[72] it is on the two belligerent parties—the FMLN and ARENA, the main electoral competitors in 1994—that the chapter focuses.

Civil War Belligerent Successor Parties

The rebel successor party campaigned under its wartime banner, as the FMLN. It ran on its own in the legislative election, but for the presidency, it allied with Democratic Convergence, comprising the Popular Social Christian Movement and the National Revolutionary Movement.[73] Democratic Convergence had appeared in a joint delegation with the FMLN at the first peace negotiations in September 1989. According to Salvador Samayoa, the FMLN signer of the 1992 peace deal, the population perceived the movements as largely indistinguishable.[74]

Two parties competed for the mantle of government successor party. PCN was the official party of the military with which it had contested noncompetitive elections under authoritarianism for decades.[75] It persisted into the democratic era. ARENA, meanwhile, "was the 'aboveground alter ego' of El Salvador's notorious 'death squad' networks"[76] and "rooted in the security and paramilitary apparatus of the pre-1979 military regime."[77] In 1981, the elites and conservative factions of the military had established this new "extreme right-wing party." At the same time, these "founders were also engaged in another activity: the formation, in cooperation with the army, of paramilitary death squads."[78] For its name, the party adopted the word "nationalist" to signal its posture against any invading forces, particularly communism, which it considered a "parasitic force" fomented abroad. It also chose the word "republican" to emphasize its pro-status-quo flavor.[79] ARENA's founder and strongman, Roberto D'Aubuisson, was former deputy director of intelligence of the military regime who had lost his position in a palace coup.[80] He became the "father of the death squads,"[81] and was heralded by the "grandfather of the death squads," General José Alberto Medrano, as one of his "three murderers."[82] ARENA was formed on the backbone of the mass-based ORDEN militias,

which D'Aubuisson "retrofit . . . for his own purposes"[83] to be the "organizational core of the new party."[84] The PCN survived ARENA's formation,
but ARENA drew heavily from its ranks, stripped it of much of its personnel,
robbed it of its constituency, hollowed its organizational capacity; it thus
largely supplanted the PCN.[85] ARENA entered the founding elections as the
electoral incumbent, having won the last wartime "demonstration" elections
of 1989. I treat ARENA and the PCN both as government successor players,
but focus the chapter on the more significant of these, ARENA, the player with
the incumbent, first-mover advantage. I return to PCN's strategic response at
the end of the chapter.

The chapter traces how FMLN and ARENA each positioned itself to activate security voting in its own favor. The theory predicts that, having reached
a draw, equally militarily successful, both parties would have adopted a Restrained Leviathan strategy, and that this strategy would play equally well with
voters. ARENA, as the electoral incumbent, would potentially prove better
able to disseminate its messaging, an advantage with the electorate.

Data Sources

To evaluate these implications, this chapter draws upon rich and varied
sources. In addition to my own personal interviews with the parties' chief
protagonists, I collected newspaper, radio, television, and campaign data from
multiple archives, including those of the Salvadoran newspaper *El Diario de
Hoy*; the Salvadoran National Museum of Anthropology archive of *La Prensa
Gráfica*; the archives of Sebastián Alejos, 1994 campaign manager for the
FMLN; the archives of ARENA's campaign strategist Manuel Meléndez; the
archives of the Centro de Información, Documentación y Apoyo a la Investigación; the Museo de la Palabra e Imagen archives of historical interviews with
candidates, FMLN radio transcripts and political propaganda; and the Salva-
doran Archivos Perdidos del Conflicto ("Lost Archives of the Conflict"),
which include 250 hours of broadcast material.[86] I consulted the U.S. Digital
National Security Archives, "El Salvador: War, Peace, and Human Rights
1980–1994." The chapter's survey evidence derives from the Latin American
Public Opinion Project (LAPOP), Instituto Universitario de Opinión Pública
(IUDOP) of the Universidad Centroamericana "José Simeón Cañas," and
Consultoría Interdisciplinaria en Desarrollo S.A. / Gallup, conducted for the
United States Information Agency.

ARENA's Strategy to Campaign to Secure the Future

If the book's argument is correct, both ARENA and FMLN—at military stalemate—should have run on promises of security (deemed credible through mitigation of their violent pasts), moderated their platforms, targeted the broader electorate, and paired their strongmen with civilian elite. I first examine how ARENA decided with what valence issues, policy positions, electoral targets, and candidates to campaign to secure the future.

Programmatic Strategy

Internal deliberations on ARENA's formulation of valence priorities and ideological positions in the lead-up to the 1994 election are not available. Archived party documents on ARENA's communication and campaign strategy do summarize what ARENA decided to prioritize, but not why it selected these priorities. I first consulted these documents and then sought to infer the logic of the party's valence and positional choices from its output: its propaganda and manifesto.

ARENA's communication strategy memos reveal objectives for each week in the seventeen-week campaign season of 1994 and the key messages and advertisements that it would use to achieve those objectives. After messaging to introduce ARENA candidates, and before that aimed at particular segments of the electorate, weeks 4 to 12 focused on the goals shown in Table 5.1. As can be seen in Table 5.1, ARENA planned to cover the gamut of standard campaign issues, but this strategizing suggests where the party perceived its strengths—its credit for peace and prospective security—and where it saw its weakness: its ideological position. I first discuss valence and then return to position below.

Valence Strategy: Owning the Security Issue

ARENA pinned its programmatic strategy on the valence issues captured in its slogan: "Consolidate Peace, Progress, and Liberty, for All." To win these issues required not only that the population be motivated to vote on these issues (I discuss issue-priming below), but also that it would perceive ARENA to be the party most competent to implement them. At a draw in war, ARENA's actual competence on peace and security was relative, and FMLN, in theory, was its equal. What is more, FMLN had been much less brutal in war,

TABLE 5.1. ARENA Messaging Objectives

Week	Objective
4	To establish the need to continue constructing what we began on the solid foundation of peace.
5	We established peace; on this solid foundation of peace and economic stability, we will continue to construct the country that we all want: with justice, liberty, and a better quality of life for each Salvadoran.
6	Present the government plan: a national program of education for peace and democracy.
7	Message of peace and family unity.
8	Announce plan to strengthen the rule of law and public security and flesh out in detail the principal points of ARENA's government plan for security and rule of law. [Note: the only handwritten note in the margins of the document directs the communications team: "change this from 5 minutes and add 1.5 to 2 minutes more."]
9	Announce economic development plan.
10	Lay out the principal points of the plan for social development.
11	Present our solutions to specific problems of housing and basic services.
12	Present our solutions to specific problems of generation of employment. [The footnote reads, "Use messages full of optimism and abundant hope that we will consolidate all the good that has been done [peace]: will move forward on the path to . . . constructing a country that everyone wants."]

so its promises not to victimize the population in the future were significantly more credible than were those of ARENA, whose partisans, as described above, had perpetrated 95 percent of the atrocities in a conflict that had affected most of the country. With the end of fighting, revelations of the abuses, nonbelligerents' accusations, and multiple credible accounts of the violence, ARENA could not deny the past.[87] According to ARENA negotiator Escobar Galindo, "The truth commission was accepted and was seen as neutral by all because it was done by foreigners" and citizens knew and understood the asymmetry in the atrocities. ARENA also could not fully sidestep the past. Following the military stalemate, as Escobar Galindo explained, with "neither victor nor vanquished . . . both sides [were] involved in the narrative."[88] A potential strategy of mutual amnesia would have created a prisoner's dilemma: it could work only if both rebel and government actors complied. While there seem to have been efforts to create such an agreed narrative, as indicated by the blanket amnesties, levels of trust between the bitter adversaries were too low and electoral incentives to shirk any such agreement too high to sustain this equilibrium. ARENA could have admitted to the violence and expressed contrition. But, given its side's responsibility for most of the atrocities, this strategy would have been highly risky and, critically, it needed to burnish its wartime credentials to contribute to voter perceptions of its competence on salient issues of security. ARENA faced an uphill battle in its campaign to convince the electorate of its superior claims to be a Restrained Leviathan. Indeed, observers "were initially skeptical about ARENA's prospects. In the U.S. Embassy, for example, the consensus was reportedly that '[ARENA's leader, Major Roberto D'Aubuisson, is] just a right-wing extremist. He can't get any support.'"[89]

While the party archives do not reveal ARENA's deliberations on *how* it would seek to own the security valence issue it prioritized, my interviews suggest that, to generate confidence in its ability to realize its platform, ARENA decided to point to the past as portending the future. It sought to use its credit for peace to dispel the ghosts of its violent past, rewriting history to shift voters' frames of reference such that, for them, ARENA emerged with a salvaged reputation for future protection rather than one for harm.

Former FMLN commander and 1999 presidential candidate Facundo Guardado explained, "In 1994, the election was all about the rewriting of what each side had done during the war. . . . It was a 'war' over the causes of the war . . . and who were the constructors of peace. . . . It was two big rewritings" of history.[90]

ARENA aimed to use its ultimate achievement of order to offset the government's past use of violence: a net positive "balance."[91] ARENA members expressed, "Before ARENA's political struggle, there was chaos, demagogy, deception, [and] disrespect for life and all values." ARENA fought "to see our country in peace, progress and freedom."[92] Figure 5.1 displays an illustrative campaign ad showing ARENA saving El Salvador from violent communism.[93]

Another key ARENA advertisement showed *only* ARENA's hand signing the peace accords, with a graph in the background depicting the economic growth that followed from the establishment of security (Figure 5.2).[94] Pro-ARENA propaganda advanced that, by putting an end to "communist aggression," ARENA had brought "normalization of life," with "hundreds of new schools . . . being built across the country," the return of investment, and recovery. According to ARENA president Cristiani, "The national feeling in 1994 was that the war was over, all this violence and destruction and all that was over . . . and all of a sudden, now we have peace, there's prosperity and everybody's free to run around. . . . We [ARENA] promised peace, prosperity and liberty, and we came through."[95] In other words, ARENA sought for voters not

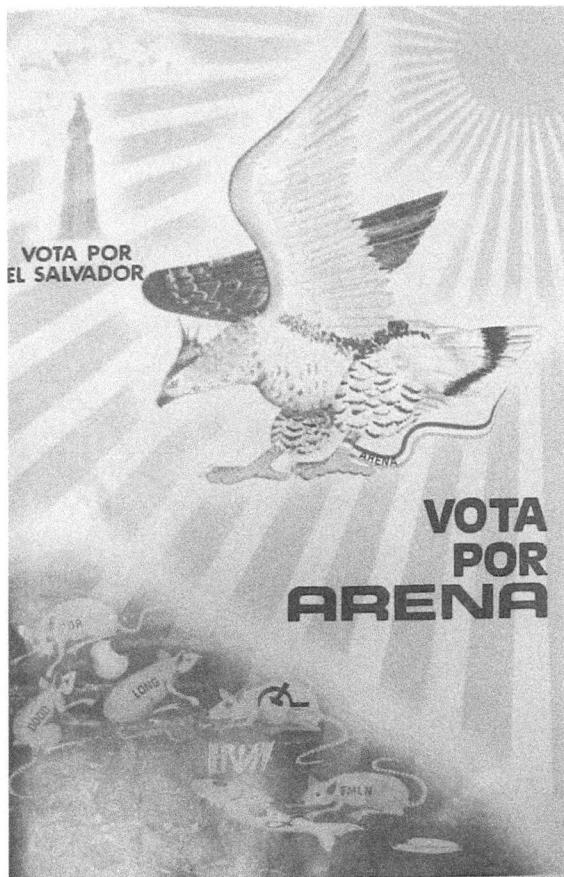

FIGURE 5.1. Campaign Ad: ARENA Saving El Salvador from Communism.
Source: ARENA propaganda, Universidad Centroamericana José Simeón Cañas archives.

to compare its story of wartime violence followed by peace with a reference point in which no violence had ever occurred, but instead to compare it to one in which the violence continued.

Compared to this bleak prospect, ARENA's advertisements could claim that it had ended the population's suffering, "achieved the . . . coveted peace . . . that all Salvadorans yearn for" and, as such, proved its ability to secure the population's future. Its security platform began, "We achieved peace and so now we commit to achieve societal peace, so that we [may] live in a climate of security."

Its communication team strategized how to further bolster its sovereign credentials among voters by underscoring that security would be its top policy

FIGURE 5.2. Campaign Ad: ARENA's Hand Alone, Signing the Peace Accords.
Source: *Diario de Hoy*, March 9, 1994, ad by ARENA.

priority: "ARENA will guarantee the implementation of the peace accords, continue with peace, reconstruct the country."[96] Its platform promised, "We will decisively combat crime, increase the number of well trained and equipped civil national police," and provide the police "with all the resources necessary."[97] Moreover, given its ties to the coercive state apparatus, it argued, ARENA was uniquely qualified to control this apparatus.

Finally, at the core of ARENA's claims to competence on security issues was the image of its strongman, ARENA's violent founder.[98] Wallpapering its offices and universally displayed on its party propaganda were images of the by then deceased Robert D'Aubuisson,[99] who embodied ARENA's militarily successful belligerent origins, provided ARENA the credit for war termination, and thereby established ARENA's credentials on security going forward. Massive banners at campaign events declared, "Thank you, Major D'Aubuisson."

At the same time, ARENA's heroic strongman suffered serious liabilities. He was, according to a former U.S. ambassador, a "pathological killer."[100] More generally, ARENA recognized that it needed to convince that it would use its competence on security to protect rather than to harm in the future. Doing so informed its positional strategy, electoral targeting, and candidate selection.

Positional Strategy

ARENA was born as an elite party of the "extreme [repressive] right." It seemed to recognize that this was a positional disadvantage in now-free elections in a country of poor citizens who had been tormented by state terror, the vast majority (58 percent) of whom placed themselves ideologically to the center or to the left.[101] During the 1980s, ARENA had softened its virulent anticommunism and its opposition to economic reforms, in particular land reform.[102] It increasingly focused on "neoliberal philosophies" and "embraced democratic procedures."[103] However, in the lead-up to the founding elections, it continued to constitute "the political vehicle for the oligarchy" and thus to oppose economic redistribution.[104] On this position ARENA could not compromise without enraging its core.

Party memos indicate that ARENA sought to rectify its positional disadvantage by emphasizing valence issues over ideological position and repositioning itself, at least rhetorically, on the ideological spectrum. It opted to exhibit programmatic vagueness and moderation on economic and social positional issues.[105] For example, issues of free market economics, structural adjustment, and opposition to redistribution did not appear anywhere in the campaign materials to which I gained access except in a single sentence on attracting investment through free trade with El Salvador's most important commercial partners.[106] I compare ARENA's programmatic positioning systematically with that of the FMLN below.

Consistent with the theory's predictions, ARENA's decisions on valence and position meant that ARENA targeted swing over core voters, and sought to make security a main dimension on which voters decided how to vote. I next discuss this electoral targeting and issue priming.

Electoral Targeting: The Moderate Voter

Party documents and interviews show ARENA regularly analyzing the electorate and deliberating which voters and localities to target.[107] They reveal that these deliberations yielded a focus on undecided voters. According to former Salvadoran president Cristiani, swing voters—composing a staggering 62 percent of the Salvadoran electorate—were the key to ARENA's 1994 campaign.[108] Of these nonideological voters, 48 percent stated that security was the most salient issue facing the country.[109]

ARENA's memorandum on its campaign communication strategy highlights this targeting plan. Weeks 2 and 3 of its campaign messaging put the focus on projecting "the message of the candidate to specific sectors." These were specified as swing sectors: peasants, workers, artisans in week 2; teachers, small businesses, youth, and working women in week 3. After programmatic messaging in weeks 4 to 15, the campaign planned in week 16 to blast the population with "adhesion testimonials," focusing on attracting undecided voters to ARENA. The plan was that the person to deliver the message of adhesion would be a campesino. In week 17, the singular stated objective again was "winning the undecided voters," and the person to deliver the closing message of the campaign to undecided voters "would be a worker" (Figure 5.3). The elite, oligarchs, business sector, armed forces, former militia—ARENA's core— appear nowhere in ARENA's communication strategy. Its focus did not appear to be on its loyal core. Personal interviews suggest there was little fear among ARENA party strategists that targeting the swing voters would result in depressed participation by its partisans, their defection (particularly to the PCN), or splintering, in what were called the "Elections of the Century."[110] ARENA had a strong brand to sustain its activists and a robust mobilization capacity among former ORDEN militia members.[111] Elizabeth Jean Wood observes that ARENA was "capable of managing internal tensions without significant schisms . . . [and was] broadly united."[112] Its moderate voter strategy, ARENA believed, was thus relatively insulated from mobilization and coordination risks.

To target swing voters, ARENA deliberated stretching its perceived "ingroup," expanding outward from the oligarchy and military to represent the whole of El Salvador. Its internal party records proposed a series of potential slogans for the party that explicitly emphasized nationalism as an overarching identity and unity.[113] "To create the El Salvador that we *all* want. . . . [To elect] the president such that we, *united*, continue improving."[114] Another: "we, the

```
SEMANA #17 / 28  - 3 DE MARZO

OBJETIVO:GANAR VOTANTES INDECISOS

XVI-MENSAJE DE CIERRE

        17.1-MENSAJE  DE FINAL DE CAMPAÑA DR. ACS*¬* 5  MIN CON
             REDUCCION A 1 MIN,TV Y RADIO- PRENSA PAGINA.
        17.2-PROGRAMA ESPECIAL DE LA GRAN MARCHA DE LA VICTORIA./5
             MIN CON RED A 1 MIN. PRENSA PAGINA
        17.3-INDECISOS *¬⁷
        17.4-CANCION DE CAMPAÑA #9
        17.5-CANCION POPULAR #9
        17.6-(6) SPOTS BATERIA
        17.7-PROGRAMA CIERRE CAMPAÑA ALCALDE/ 5 MIN CON REDUCCION A
             1 MIN TV Y RADIO.


¬⁷-NUESTRO PERSONAJE SERIA UN OBRERO.
```

FIGURE 5.3. ARENA Campaign Plan: Targeting of Undecided Voters.
Source: ARENA, "Estrategia de Comunicaciones, Campaña '94." Archive maintained by ARENA party campaign strategist Manuel Meléndez.

nationalists, representing *the Salvadoran people."* ARENA called itself "the Nationalist Brothers: The party of the majorities,"[115] emphasizing that "the doors of ARENA are always open to all citizens who love liberty, peace, and democracy."[116] Indeed, ARENA explicitly structured itself organizationally as a "sector party" to be able to gain access to swing voters.[117]

Issue Priming

ARENA strategized ways to downplay its specific positions and to emphasize valence issues. However, it also needed the electorate, particularly swing voters, to make vote choices along valence lines. Its strategic planning memos suggest that ARENA sought to use issue priming, to control the dimension upon which citizens' prospective votes would be made. In particular, one memo states that, by planning the campaign messages in advance, "Let's force others to talk about what we are talking about. Let us lead the opposition to our issues [peace, security, and recovery] and not have the opposition lead us to theirs." Through the media, ARENA implored people to cast their ballots on security grounds, to use "the only legitimate weapon"—the vote—"to construct a homeland . . . with security and with stability."[118] ARENA-sponsored newspaper articles similarly urged citizens to "contribute with their vote [to ARENA] so that [peace will consolidate and] this tragedy will never be repeated, that no one ever takes up arms" again.[119]

trust
future united
build new people country
get better
continue
everybody

FIGURE 5.4. ARENA: Potential
"Restrained Sovereign" Presidential
Slogans.
Source: Based on ARENA internal
document, "Puntos de Copy Para
Posicionar al Dr. Calderón Sol Como
El Presidente En Quien Todos Confi-
amos," June 1993.

Candidates

Party archives suggest that ARENA recognized that it had to locate high-valence candidates who would embody the qualities not just of strength, but also restraint. How did ARENA strategize to select its political elite in light of this priority? Internal documents indicate the qualities that ARENA believed were advantageous in its political elites. In a memo strategizing how to position and sell its presidential candidate, the words could describe a controlled sovereign: ARENA needed a candidate of an "iron will," "a President who . . . has never betrayed the Salvadoran people,"[120] a man possessing "unquestionable moral, Christian, and civil principles." In its political communication strategy, ARENA instructed its party operatives on how it would seek to frame its presidential candidate: "We have to highlight all the qualities that make him the only candidate to *trust*. . . . We have to put together the biography around all the attributes that make a person trustworthy." Figure 5.4 maps the most frequent words that appear in its potential presidential slogans with the size and boldness of the words indicating their relative frequency.

To further signal that the government would not victimize again, as the face of the party, ARENA claimed, "The most important thing that [mythical Major Roberto D'Aubuisson did was] convey the leadership[121] of our party to a man who understands the ideals of Freedom and Progress for our people": the fresh-faced businessman Armando Calderón Sol.[122] In other words, ARENA underscored that *strongman* D'Aubuisson endorsed and backed *restrainer* Calderón, who thereby inherited D'Aubuisson's security credentials, but not the blood on his hands. ARENA chose as Calderón's running mate one of the country's most prestigious lawyers: Enrique Borgo Bustamante who sought to signal ARENA's ability to be constrained by the country's institutions.[123]

For its legislative candidates, ARENA similarly opted not to put forward its human rights abusers, but instead to engage in costly actions designed to show its commitment to self-control. It sent generals' heads rolling, if only figuratively, and laundered its organization of abusers. The peace agreement called for a special ad hoc committee to examine the corps of army officers to determine "which ones were really bad from a human rights perspective . . . which had slaughtered people." President Cristiani describes it: "We thought the committee would come up with six to seven names. Everyone knew who they were though we did not want to say who they were. But this committee went way beyond and they came up with a list of 102 officers, starting with the Minister of Defense. Everyone was on the list. . . . I said, 'I'm not going to discharge 102 officers! There would be a coup here!'"[124] But Cristiani nonetheless did so: he "cleansed the military," forcing over one hundred to retire, and he abolished the paramilitary forces.[125] In in his own words, he thus sought to "separate" ARENA from the "repressive, old regime" and establish it as a party that "had nothing to do with the prior violence,"[126] a stronger attempt to break with the past than the theory would anticipate. President Cristiani "sort of got rid of the military when it became a liability. . . . The armed forces saw ARENA as selling them out, as traitors."[127]

ARENA did conceal a few military candidates on its closed legislative tickets,[128] but mostly, for its national and state committees, according to President Cristiani, ARENA recruited professionals and "new people." It did not want "old politicians."[129] According to ARENA's campaign strategist, ARENA investigated and then selected people who "did not have any problems."[130]

In sum, ARENA laundered its own reputation and backed its sovereign credentials in its program, elite choice, and voter targets. Given FMLN's congruent equilibrium strategies, ARENA simultaneously sought to undermine FMLN's efforts to do the same.

Undermining FMLN's Ownership of the Security Valence Issue

Accordingly to ARENA's campaign strategist, through intensive propaganda, ARENA sought to frame FMLN's military strength in the eyes of the broader electorate as signaling competence on victimization, and FMLN's prospective governance as likely to bring only further brutality, not protection. Internal ARENA party documents describe the derivation of this strategy:

> The [FMLN] opposition . . . offers us a very obvious attack strategy, but nobody has put it all together yet. [The FMLN has] committed a large

number of mistakes throughout its history. . . . [Violent] crimes and destruction of private property are its most salient ones. . . . The [election]
campaigns begin in November, the month of the [FMLN's large-scale mili-
tary] offensive [in 1989 against the capital city of San Salvador]. We cannot
allow the population to forget this [past atrocity] at the hour of voting. . . .
We [ARENA] cannot forget that the electoral law prohibits us from direct
attacks against candidates. We can show [our attack instead] as an Educational program that conveys the last ten years of our history . . . that re-
minds the population daily, who the [FMLN] people are who are now
asking for [their] vote. . . . Saying to the undecided voter, "before giving
your vote, think about the future without forgetting the past." . . . This could
be the ideal way to mount a good attack campaign.

ARENA crafted and executed this strategy to frame FMLN as future tormentors based on their past violence. These efforts had as their objective altering
the perceptions of *unaligned* voters, in particular. Such propaganda would have
been wasted on ARENA's core voters, but it played into the narratives these
voters held and therefore did not alienate them.

To reinforce this campaign messaging against its rival belligerent party,
ARENA party strategist Manuel Meléndez explained, "ARENA used testimonies from people affected by the war, by FMLN attacks." As an example, Meléndez cited the "ingenious" and "anonymous" advertisements that ARENA ran
frequently on television:

The camera focuses close-up on drawing paper and a small hand with a
crayon sketching a female figure. A child's voice-over says "this is mommy,"
and goes on to draw a second male figure identified as "daddy." The hand
then sketches a third smaller figure identified as "me." The drawing of "me"
has only one leg, and the small voice says that this is the result of a [FMLN]
terrorist mine. The child's soft voice tells viewers that the [FMLN] terrorists are hoping people will forget, but the child doesn't think mommy and
daddy will forget.[131]

ARENA planned other campaign ads, which underscored that the FMLN's
achievement of military success had come, not legitimately, but through the
blood of "slaughtered Salvadorans."[132] ARENA solicited the assistance of
right-leaning newspapers to run headlines, such as "Terror and Death: The
Real Face of the FMLN."[133] In March 1994, in a full-page newspaper spread,

ARENA declared, "No more guerrilla children! No more mutilated children! We want children studying! We want children eating!"[134] An article in *El Diario de Hoy* stated, "People have no doubt that, in the plans of the FMLN, the population has been the primary objective and target of its attacks. More than 70,000 dead—the vast majority of them civilians—was the balance [or tally] of the [FMLN's] onslaught against the defenseless population."[135]

In other words, ARENA's objective was to galvanize emotions of anger and indignation— "the noble, heroic people['s] ... [desires for] revenge"[136]—powerful tools of political struggle.[137] However, rather than acknowledging the government's own role in perpetrating 95 percent of the cited seventy thousand

FIGURE 5.5. "We Will Fight Crime Since We Have the Experience" *Source: La Prensa Gráfica,* January 6, 1994, ad by ARENA.

deaths, ARENA opted to advance a version of spun history in which the FMLN was responsible for *all* wartime violence.[138] It merits clarification that ARENA sought to play not with the facts of the violent acts and who perpetrated them, which were relatively known and agreed upon, but instead with the attribution of blame for the violence.[139]

It then used this version of the past to influence voters' perceptions of the FMLN's future security and restraint credentials. ARENA's 1994 internal documents state: "We have to position ... [the FMLN presidential candidate] as 'a Judas' who has betrayed his country."[140] In the national press, ARENA supporters questioned how the FMLN could select the most capable people to solve the nation's security problems when "it would reward them based on their length of time in the war," when it constituted an organization of "genocidal professionals."[141] ARENA formulated a series of ads (Figure 5.5) displaying the FMLN candidate dressed as a bandit with the caption, "We will [be able to] fight crime since we have the experience," implying experience as violent criminals. Another ad (Figure 5.6) displayed a guerrilla holding a civilian at gunpoint, "That the crimes began when we demobilized is pure coincidence." A third (Figure 5.7) showed the FMLN candidate promising, "We will eliminate the criminals and organized crime," as his running mate whispered in his ear: "Careful, we will be left with no base."

FIGURE 5.6. "That the Crimes Began When We Demobilized Is Pure Coincidence"
Source: ARENA, *Arenillas*: Una Publicación de ARENA, vol. 10 (San Salvador, El Salvador).

FIGURE 5.7. "We Will Eliminate the Criminals and Organized Crime. . . . Careful, We Will Be Left with No Base."
Source: ARENA, *Arenillas*: Una Publicación de ARENA, vol. 10 (San Salvador, El Salvador).

ARENA's propaganda sought to warn that a FMLN administration would rule prospectively as it had done during the war, according to ARENA: brutally.[142] It made comparisons in the press between a potential FMLN government and that of Stalin, Castro, Pol Pot, and Ceaușescu.[143] ARENA's campaign strategist boasts of ARENA's most successful series of advertisements aimed at painting a picture of what FMLN's governance would entail (see Figure 5.8). They featured maps of El Salvador showing the number of violent incidents in each region. The text read, "The terrorist [FMLN's] destruction of 2,698 towers and electrical structures impoverished people, ruined small businesses, and caused unemployment. Is that acting for the good of the people?" Another ad declared, "The destruction of 678 schools is the contribution of [FMLN] terrorism to the education of our children. Is this putting our children first?" A third ad announced, "The terrorists killed 12 mayors and destroyed 131 city halls. . . . Is to murder and destroy to act for the good of the people?"[144] Challenging how FMLN's security provision would translate into prospective economic recovery, ARENA ran an ad (Figure 5.9) with a caricature of FMLN's candidate, again in criminal garb, announcing, "I commit not to destroy all that I have promised." The background featured a bombed bridge.

According to President Cristiani, in the 1994 campaign "there was a lot of 'remember these [FMLN] guys. . . . They know how to destroy things, not to build things.'" Cristiani added that this campaign strategy worked for ARENA "because it was accompanied by 'We

FIGURE 5.8. ARENA Maps of FMLN Violence: Undermining FMLN's Security Competence.
Source: *El Diario de Hoy*, March 1, 1994, and *La Prensa Gráfica*, January 27, 1994, ads by ARENA.
Note: The texts read, "The terrorist [FMLN's] destruction of 2,698 towers and electrical structures impoverished people, ruined small businesses, and caused unemployment. Is that acting for the good of the people?" and "The destruction of 678 schools is the contribution of [FMLN] terrorism to the education of our children. Is this putting our children first?"

[ARENA] are going to solve your problems.'" "Areneros are known for building and not for destroying," read its marketing.

FMLN's Strategy to Campaign to Secure the Future

How did FMLN decide its valence issues, position, and candidates, and respond to ARENA's virulent attacks? As the electoral incumbent, ARENA was the first mover. Its media advantage also let it go on the offensive; FMLN fell to the defensive. Nonetheless, internal FMLN party documents reveal that, in its campaign for the founding elections, FMLN sought not just to gain a minor electoral foothold or position itself for competitiveness in future elections, but instead to "win the government, mayors, legislative assembly in 1994 . . . to take over state power."[145] If the book's argument is correct, to do so, FMLN—at a military draw—should have engaged in a *Restrained Leviathan* strategy congruent with that of ARENA, running on promises of security, mitigating its violent past, moderating its platform, targeting the broader electorate, and pairing its strongmen with civilian elite.

FIGURE 5.9. "I Commit Not to Destroy All That I Have Promised."
Source: La Prensa Gráfica, January 13, 1994, ad by ARENA.

Valence Strategy

Party archives illuminate the output but not the formulation of FMLN's valence priorities. FMLN's founding statutes list the consolidation of peace as its primary objective, followed by goals including strengthening civil society, boosting economic development, and reconstructing the country.[146] Its platform, like ARENA's, emphasized the "fight for the peace."[147] Personal interviews with FMLN's party strategists suggest that this platform was meant to be "based on the needs of the electorate: the electorate wanted peace, wanted employment, wanted to rebuild the country. . . . People were already glad that after 12 years of war, there was some tranquility, that you could go places where you couldn't walk before."[148] FMLN promised to cement that.

Owning the Security Valence Issue

To foster this reputation for competence on securing the future, FMLN sought to claim credit for the end of violence, according to its internal party documents. It argued that it had "fought a war to win peace" and thereby aimed to reframe its past in a positive light. Its 1992 memorandum on party communication strategized: "FMLN must present itself as the constructor of peace" and justify its violent struggle on the achievement of that peace: "The application of the agreements . . . [fulfills] the transformations achieved by 10 years of armed struggle."[149] FMLN saw its electoral fate as inextricably intertwined with the peace: "Implementation of the agreements is [our] fundamental axis, since the credibility of [the] FMLN [party] . . . depends on it."

According to my interviews and secondary materials, the sovereign claim to this issue proffered by FMLN stemmed from the effectiveness of its armed predecessor's fight to protect the population from and ultimately end the "sheer brutality of [government] repression."[150] FMLN also rooted its credibility on the security issue in its achievement of the demilitarization of the highly abusive coercive apparatus of the state and its participation in the newly formed apparatus (which incorporated a specified proportion of FMLN equal to the number of former military personnel).[151] With now strong ties to the new state's forces, FMLN could help control those forces from within. Its namesake, revolutionary Farabundo Martí, further embodied its security credentials, as did the commanders of its five constituent organizations. Posters of Farabundo Martí permeated party propaganda; its combatant leaders remained the public faces of the FMLN party, as I discuss further below.

However, again like ARENA, FMLN's security credentials were splattered in blood.[152] FMLN's internal party memos suggest that it conceded a resulting imperative to "overcome [citizens'] fears of . . . the monsters [it had been] painted to be."[153] It strategized to do so through its rhetoric, positional strategy, electoral targeting, and candidate selection.[154]

Much of FMLN's campaign material came to be "done with the fmln initials in lowercase letters [and] with cartoons to show a friendlier image" (e.g., Figure 5.10). Its campaign strategist, Sebastián Alejos, explained, "People on the outside, they [didn't] understand why [our party] graphic line [was] so soft for a force that derived from a political force of war . . . they didn't see fists on our posters. . . . But no. . . . It was important for us to make clear to the people that there was a break: that the weapons were surrendered and that they would never be returned,"[155] that FMLN would not use its military competencies to victimize, but instead to protect.

Positional Strategy

Personal interviews with FMLN's party strategists shed light on the more contentious internal deliberations that took place around ideological placement and moderation, which began with a debate over adapting the party's name and symbols:

> We designed a logo of a sun, with the logic of a new dawn, etc. . . . [but] the [commanders] said, no no no, the FMLN flag has too much blood spilled for it. . . . The team designed several [other] flags with . . . the star in the center to imply that the party was moderating, that it was no longer radical. . . . Of course, the idea of putting the star in the center was lost because, in the statutes, it said that it had to go on the left, but . . . the commanders . . . agreed to change [the logo] because they wanted to prove that they were not the same. . . . This was the most important change to the FMLN

FIGURE 5.10. FMLN's Cartoon Campaign Ads.
Source: FMLN Propaganda, Archive of FMLN party campaign strategist Sebastián Alejos.

because once you touched and changed the flag, it gave you authorization to enter into a logic of change of other dimensions [of the party].[156]

According to internal party documents, while the party still called itself leftist, this logic of change meant that FMLN had decided that "we need to fight . . . from the *center* not from the extremes."[157] The FMLN's 1992 refoundation statute described its ideological character as democratic, pluralist, and revolutionary, avoiding any mention of socialism or Marxism.[158] Internal debates indicate its potential pillars, none of which include revolutionary ideas.[159]

Writing contemporaneously, Héctor Dada argued that, in 1994, both parties—ARENA and FMLN—had similar electoral platforms.[160] I use the machine learning algorithm trained on Spanish-language platforms in the Party Manifesto Project to validate this claim. The classifier codes both parties' platforms on a left-right ideological spectrum ranging from −100 to 100. For ARENA, I was able to access only the employment, security, and education sections of its governance plan. The classifier labels 31 percent of ARENA's program "left" and 18 percent "right," thereby yielding a ri-le score of −13.7. It categorizes 32 percent of FMLN's program as "left" and 23 percent as "right," generating a ri-le score of −10.14 for the FMLN. It would be unlikely to find any convergence between these belligerent parties that were historically located at opposite ends of the ideological spectrum; finding it provides strong support for my valence-centered thesis. While this tendency toward convergence might have seemed disingenuous, as a party of parties[161] and thus an aggregation of different voices[162]—some moderate,[163] some radical[164]— FMLN provided a cacophony in which voters of different ideological leanings could hone in on the voice that most resonated with them. This rendered FMLN's move toward positional convergence more credible.[165]

Electoral Targeting: The Moderate Voter

Through moderation, FMLN opted to formulate "a programmatic approach that will be attractive to *new* sectors."[166] FMLN decided to seek explicitly to attract centrist voters to strengthen its electoral position and restraint message.[167] Shafik Handál explains how the key for the FMLN "was the campaign being able to connect with the whole population, [to] convince the *undecided*."[168] Its 1992 internal memorandum stated, "We must constitute a party that does not base its militancy on permanent inflexible [constituencies], but on flexible [ones] that allow the capture and repositioning of individuals and social organizations [in society]." In other words, FMLN decided to avoid remaining "limited to the [core] sectors in which [it had] traditionally had an influence" and to capture the votes of the "common citizen," the swing voter.[169] To target these voters, in its foundational party documents, FMLN decided to stretch from its traditional identity as a party of the Christian base communities, campesinos, and unionized workers, to become a party of "the interests of the *majority* and the *nation*."[170] "First the People" became its presidential slogan (Figure 5.11).[171]

As a confederation of five groups, which "maintained their own leadership and organizational structure throughout the war,"[172] FMLN appeared

POR LA SALUD Y LA EDUCACION

PRIMERO LA GENTE

El Dr. Rubén Zamora

FIGURE 5.11. FMLN Slogan, "First, the People."
Source: FMLN Party Archives, Museo de la Palabra e Imagen Archivo Histórico, San Salvador, El Salvador.

cognizant of the risks of the electoral targeting of the swing voter for coordination and mobilization. Its internal party memos warned, "One of the great challenges that the current conditions pose is whether we will be able to maintain unity. . . . The current situation is conducive to potential subdivisions."[173] Archives of FMLN's deliberations similarly indicate a recognition of the tension between the need to "adapt the party"—in order to target the moderate voter—and the risk of dampened mobilization caused by the "frustration and desertions of the militant base."[174] Nonetheless, in these debates, moderation seems to have won out. The adverse consequences of this played out in subsequent elections.[175]

Candidates

FMLN's strategy of elite recruitment also reflects the objective of generating confidence in the FMLN and its restraint message, according to an internal record.[176] Personal interviews confirmed,

> There were basically two strong positions [in the FMLN]. The first position was that we should . . . run only our own candidates, totally identified with the guerrilla movement . . . so that people would feel confident that they were voting for the FMLN leaders, the FMLN project. This position argued

that we cannot dilute the ideas of the FMLN. The second position was that the election was too early to have figures that had high protagonism in the war. . . . There was still so much fear in the potential voters that might vote for us, but who would feel more comfortable voting for a figure close to [but not in] the movement. . . . This second [position] argued we need a level of political opening to get us more votes. . . . And the second view won out.

The FMLN therefore decided to run as its presidential candidate not one of its commanders, but instead Rubén Zamora, who was a civilian and from outside the FMLN's ranks.[177] Even rival ARENA strategist Manuel Meléndez conceded that "as a candidate, Rubén Zamora helped calm down voters who would not have voted for a guerrilla at that time."[178] FMLN strategist Alejos explained, "The constant doubt about the FMLN was whether it had democratic [i.e., restraint] credentials or not. Rubén was really trying to present himself as moderate . . . and was trying to prove that we were not a war group" that might revictimize.[179]

The FMLN emphasized self-control in its candidate to highest office, but in its legislative lists, it emphasized strength, running commanders from each of its constituent military and political structures,[180] including two of its top commanders and fifteen of its core members.[181]

In sum, as my theory predicts, at a military draw, the belligerent successor parties in El Salvador pursued relatively similar strategies. However, whereas ARENA sought to both burnish its own reputation on security and tarnish that of FMLN, the FMLN made only its own case and provided little rebuttal to ARENA's rhetorical onslaught. While, in private, FMLN referred to ARENA as death squad members, in public, it neither launched a counternarrative offensive, nor sought to undermine ARENA's reputation for competence on security, despite this reputation resting on bloodstained laurels. This is puzzling behavior, given that the facts shown by the Truth Commission were on the FMLN's side. According to FMLN campaign strategist Alejos, "It was important for us [the FMLN] to face the accusation . . . that we were children-eaters." However, "if we answered saying that they [ARENA] were death squads, etc. [responsible for nearly all atrocities], it did not suit us."[182] FMLN presidential candidate Rubén Zamora explained this: "We could not point to ARENA's crimes because [the narrative of the war] was their territory."[183] Attacks against the ARENA party, "that they were associates of the death squads etc., . . . did not work."[184] This was because of ARENA's media advantage in disseminating its message.

Media and Persuasion

All else equal, ARENA and FMLN, at a military draw, faced convergent optimal strategies, as posited by the theory. However, in practice, all else did not prove equal. Instead, despite the rivals' equality of military war outcomes, ARENA alone had a powerful propaganda machine to amplify its messaging. ARENA had alliances with the oligarchy and controlled the state apparatus, including the media access thus afforded.[185] It also had greater resources to devote to campaign financing.[186] This broadcasting and financial advantage allowed ARENA to run a variety of ads and to run them often.[187] Moreover, the organization of former militias that underpinned ARENA had a wide geographic reach to transmit its narratives.[188] The ability to harness the media plays a role in the violent-victors theory, but not of the magnitude suggested by this case. I return in the conclusion to the implications of these empirics for the book's argument.

Internal FMLN party documents confirm FMLN's relative poverty in dissemination platforms: "We have a great disadvantage. . . . Our ideas are worth nothing if there are no ways to transmit them or if the inequality in communication is very large. . . . We cannot stay with methods of traditional protestors and with pamphlets." Strategy memos suggest that FMLN sought to address this imbalance: "Our biggest task is to fight against television monopolies. . . . We must create . . . new media companies in radio, television, newspapers, magazines . . . that compet[e] with the main newspapers of the right . . . [to] protect the historical [truths] . . . and [win the] battle over the story of [the violent] history."[189]

ARENA used its media advantage to launch a rhetorical onslaught and to preempt any FMLN counterattack.[190] Party memos document ARENA's communication strategy as "a tactic of hitting and retreating . . . only to hit on the other hand." According to its internal records, ARENA's campaign sought for its "educational program," which amplified ARENA's version of the past, to be "placed apart from our formal campaign," disseminated, and "sponsored by some democratic institution,"[191] in hopes that it would be accepted by the population not as spin but as fact.

As ARENA, FMLN also sought to propagate its spun narrative through neutral channels, assuming that this would increase its consumption as objective history: "The media outlets [we use] can no longer be party media or [our] official bodies. [They] have to be communication companies that have a democratic [credible] conception. . . . In the written press there is a large journalistic gap in the [political] center. We must fill this void."[192]

However, over time, the futility of these efforts and the ramifications of having limited media became clear.[193] Zamora described, "They, [ARENA], had more propaganda than we did . . . a powerful media apparatus. . . . The political lesson is: never lie, but also never say truths that are going to play into the other's hands. They committed most of the crimes, but it didn't matter. Because . . . they controlled all of the media, they could control the story."[194] In the postwar "marketplace of ideas,"[195] ARENA had the upper hand.[196] ARENA therefore won the "war" over the narrative of the war, and was able to shift perceptions in its favor.

Accordingly, whereas the framework anticipates that, stalemated and pursuing relatively similar strategies, ARENA and FMLN should have proven equally successful at selling themselves as competent on peace; they should have won equal shares of the security vote, split the undecided vote, and each gained access to some of its own victims' votes, contemporaneous survey evidence suggests otherwise. This was seemingly because ARENA was able to project its message farther, wider, and louder.

Voters

Credit for Peace

Factually speaking, both the government and rebels, then at a military draw, had achieved peace. According to my theory, voters should have given them both credit for war termination. But, despite this symmetry in war outcome, polls reveal that Salvadorans gave asymmetric credit to ARENA over the FMLN.[197] ARENA was viewed by a majority of the population as the party that "most favors the pursuit of peace." This did not mean the FMLN came up empty-handed: 38 percent of the population recognized that the FMLN "really wanted peace."[198] Nonetheless, across all sectors, achieving peace was deemed ARENA's great accomplishment.[199] As President Cristiani acknowledged, "When you look at it *objectively* [following a draw], it had to be *both* sides that wanted peace . . . but *politically* speaking . . . the population felt that the government, *this* government [ARENA] really brought peace."[200] FMLN commander Facundo Guardado confirmed this: in the public's perception, "it was ARENA [alone] that signed the peace."[201] In other words, the ARENA advertisement displaying only the hand of ARENA autographing the peace agreement came to be seen as reality; rather than giving both signatories equal credit, citizens doled it out in uneven measure. It should be noted that, while the government may, in theory, enjoy an advantage—it starts off the war with some presumption of legitimate use of violence whereas rebellion is by definition illegal—when blanket state repression is widely deemed the cause of war onset, this advantage is dimmed. It was therefore more likely the persuasion advantage rather than a government one driving the observed asymmetry of results.

Voters' Frame of Reference for the Wartime Violence

This disproportionate credit meant that ARENA had a greater ability than the FMLN to offset its violence in the eyes of the public. And the empirics suggest that ARENA played this mitigation card well; citizen perceptions aligned more with ARENA's narrative than with the FMLN's. Polls reveal that only 16 percent of the population had a negative view toward the armed forces, whereas at least 51 percent viewed the FMLN with some degree of hostility, and blamed it, rather than the government, for the war and economic destruction.[202] The rebels were also blamed for national economic conditions. In the 1991 LAPOP survey, 50 percent of the population blamed the war for limiting economic growth and causing low levels of employment, and more than twice as many people blamed the "guerrillas' destruction," rather than the government's public policies, for these economic woes.

Perhaps most remarkably, ARENA's "provision of peace" and its narrative seem to have worked to redirect blame for the wartime atrocities.[203] President Cristiani said, "It really depends on why the violence is done, how it is done, and violence by one side is not necessarily the same as violence by the other side."[204] The 1992–1993 Truth Commission found the state-sponsored forces responsible for 95 percent of the violence, and the rebels just 5 percent; the population generally accepted this as factual, but in attributing blame, 32 percent of the population believed the FMLN had shown *less* respect for human rights and had abused the Salvadoran population *more*, whereas only 17 percent believed that the government side had shown less respect for human rights and had been more abusive (see Figure 5.12).[205] This divergence between the objective accounting and the subjective understanding of the violence points to the effectiveness of a deliberate campaign to alter frames of

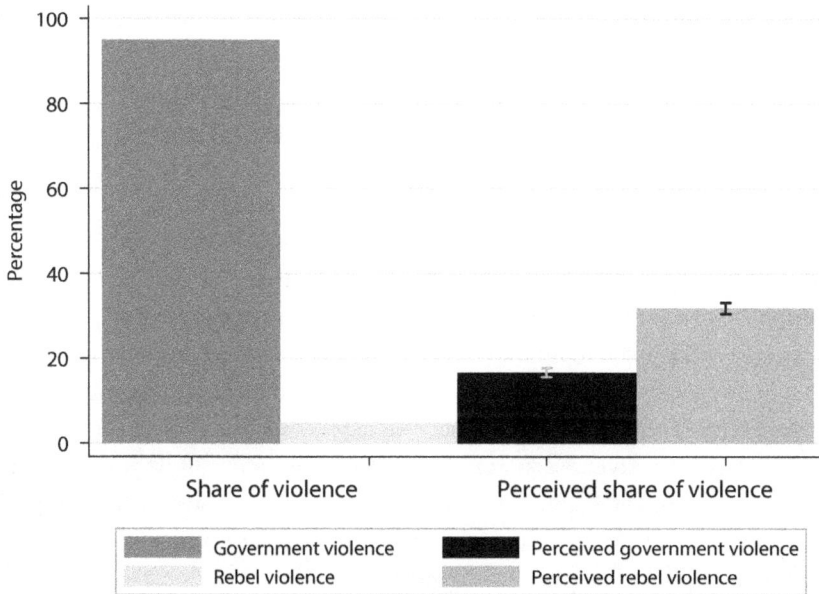

FIGURE 5.12. Findings of Truth Commission and Public Perception of Relative Blame.

reference, launder the government's reputation, and thereby tilt the prospective security vote in its favor.

Winning the Security, Swing, and Victimized Vote

In 1994, as noted earlier, nearly 40 percent of the population across all socioeconomic groups, and 48 percent of unaligned voters (who were 62 percent of the Salvadoran electorate) cited violence-related issues as the main problems facing the country.[206] The electorate seemed to value security credentials in their selection of an executive.[207] When asked in 1992 what characteristics the next Salvadoran president must have, respondents answered "watching over the population" and protecting it. Surprisingly, the data suggest that the population placed little weight on leaders being capable or democratic, helping the poor, or creating jobs.[208]

ARENA emerged better at convincing the population of its security competence at confronting different types of threats. According to Cristiani, "A sense of security . . . is one of the ingredients of feeling 'fine, not scared, I have a bright future' [in other words, prospective security voting]. The idea of a better future really helped ARENA."[209] An IUDOP survey asked respondents to elect between the parties on their capacities to address specific issues. ARENA emerged the winner on the ability to fight crime with 23.9 percent of the vote. FMLN gained 9.9 percent. Also, 24 percent voted for ARENA as most capable of implementing the peace accords, versus FMLN's 11.4 percent. Importantly, ARENA leveraged its security competencies to argue successfully not only that it would be best at providing security, but that it would not victimize again. ARENA emerged victorious even on grounds of best respecting and protecting human rights (21.8 percent), surpassing FMLN with 9 percent and *non*belligerent PDC by large margins; it received only 8.3 percent of this vote.[210] ARENA's success at achieving a reputation as a controlled sovereign is noted in the volume *Political Parties of the Americas*. It cites, as part of ARENA's "DNA," "a Hobbesian definition of the state that emphasized maintaining order."[211]

ARENA's effectiveness in convincing the population of its restraint and strength credentials enabled it to win the security vote. Survey data suggest that, of those voting on security lines, 41 percent preferred ARENA, while 27 percent preferred its rivals.[212] Support for ARENA was 8 percentage points higher, and intent to vote for ARENA was 15 points higher, among individuals who considered insecurity the most pressing national problem.[213]

ARENA appealed beyond, but did not lose, its core wartime constituencies; it managed to attract undecided voters, those concerned with the salient valence issues.[214] President Cristiani explained, "Because of the fact that we had brought about peace . . . the swing voters remained with ARENA."[215] Of swing voters, 49 percent said in a survey that, if they had to choose a party, they would choose ARENA; 12 percent said they would choose the left.[216] ARENA won 49 percent of the vote in disputed municipalities (65 percent of El Salvador) compared to FMLN's 16 percent.[217] Demonstrating the effectiveness of its moderate platform, centrists composed 53.5 percent of ARENA voters.[218] This generated for ARENA a multisector electoral coalition[219] "across regions and classes."[220]

Centrists constituted 24.9 percent of FMLN voters, indicating that its moderating, too, expanded its base of support beyond its hardcore constituencies.[221] FMLN won, for example, a majority of support in places in which it had had "no presence" during the war, such as the western part of El Salvador.[222]

FMLN nearly qualified for electoral success by this book's definition, attracting almost one-third of the winning vote share in the founding election and twenty-one of the eighty-four legislative seats,[223] but ARENA outperformed it. According to Cristiani, "The swing vote is what made ARENA win." ARENA won 49.3 percent of the presidential vote in the first round, 68.3 percent in the second round, and thirty-nine of the eighty-four legislative seats.[224] The theory can explain the electoral success of both the FMLN and ARENA, but cannot fully account for ARENA's outperformance, as I discuss below.

Winning Some Victims Votes

My theory predicts that, using a *Restrained Leviathan* strategy, abusive but stalemated belligerent successor parties should win even some of their victims' votes. I analyze municipal election results and categorize the atrocities (disappearances, homicides, kidnappings, torture, rapes) by perpetrator—government or rebel—using data from the Commission on the Truth for El Salvador.[225] Recall that the truth commission had widely publicized its findings (indeed a reported 86 percent of Salvadorans knew of them) and, according to government officials, they were seen as legitimate.[226]

Consistent with this implication of the theory, I find that the extent of atrocities committed by the government relative to those committed by the rebels did not track postwar electoral success. ARENA's vote share in a municipality remained constant whether the government was responsible for none of the atrocities there or 100 percent of them. I find similar results for the FMLN.[227]

I evaluate whether the belligerents won the votes of their victims or whether instead FMLN victims voted for ARENA, whereas government victims voted for the FMLN.[228] This is important to assess, given the massive displacement in El Salvador, which meant that the most victimized population might not have lived and voted where the violence had occurred.[229] I use the 1995 LAPOP survey, which asked respondents whether they had lost a family member or close relative as a result of the armed conflict. The question did not ask the identity of the perpetrator; however, given the proportions of victimization by the two belligerent sides, and given that the survey respondents were a representative sample of Salvadorans, we can assume that 95 percent of the surveyed victims were government victims and 5 percent were FMLN victims. I find that 40 percent of victims voted for ARENA, 24 percent for the FMLN. Moreover, 40 percent of individuals displaced by the conflict voted for the successor party to the government, the belligerent that was responsible for nearly all forced displacement in the conflict. This suggests that many victims, particularly victims of government violence, voted for their perpetrators' successor party. Consistent with this trend is anecdotal evidence from a nonrandom sample of personal interviews with government victims, who knew their perpetrator was linked to the armed forces or death squads but voted for ARENA anyway.[230]

Alternative Explanations

There exist several strong alternative explanations for FMLN's robust performance and ARENA's superior electoral success. These center on popular support, partisan issue ownership, incumbency, coercion, and organizational assets; I consider these next.

Popular Support

First, it may be that the founding postwar election was simply a byproduct of the same popular sentiments that also caused the draw between ARENA and FMLN at war's end. If we consider underlying sentiments to be those that prevailed prewar, this logic seems unconvincing. The government was widely disliked for its blanket repression, while the FMLN built upon mass popular mobilization. The extent of popular support and of military success did not correlate over time. Despite lacking popular support in the 1970s, the government was strong militarily; despite high levels of popular support in the 1970s, the rebels were weak militarily. If we instead consider underlying sentiments to be those that prevailed during and after the war and ask which party better represented the majority, the balance would also likely tilt to the FMLN, which was seen as the party of "the pueblo" (the people); ARENA as the party of the rich.[231] While I was speaking with members of the FMLN, people of all walks of life would come up and enthusiastically greet their *compañeros*. While I was meeting with ARENA figures, citizens kept their distance. The population's underlying appetite for the left becomes clear from polls and from the FMLN's upward political trajectory over time. The popular support thesis can help explain why the ARENA and FMLN belligerent successor parties won the votes of their core constituencies. However, it offers little analytic leverage on the electoral behavior of undecided, contested, and swing voters who proved pivotal in 1994.

Partisan or Incumbent Issue Ownership

A second alternative frame centers on partisan ownership of the security issue, arguing specifically that the right owns the security issue.[232] For later Salvadoran elections, for example, Holland (2013) argues that ARENA prioritized security to distract from redistribution issues. For the founding elections, this partisan-issue ownership argument would posit that ARENA sought and managed to win the security valence issue not because of the war outcome, but because of its positions on the ideological right, and that FMLN never had a chance on the security vote. The strongest evidence against this reasoning is found in Nicaragua where the political right, militarily vanquished, did *not* run on the security issue, whereas the political left, militarily victorious, did, and won. I explore this case in Chapter 7. Additionally, if partisanship were driving valence strategy and success, we should not have observed left-wing FMLN attempting this strategy, and we should have observed it pushing for redistribution. Instead, FMLN prioritized the peace valence issue and downplayed ideological issues. This partisan-issue ownership explanation is challenged to explain additional empirical facts of the case. If ARENA could win the security issue on ideology alone, why did it strategize to moderate and emphasize restraint? And why did it work so hard to undermine FMLN's security competence, if FMLN's left-wing ideology would have given it little chance on this issue? Finally, if this argument is correct, we would anticipate that political ideology might be an omitted variable explaining both security voting and vote choice for ARENA. The explanatory leverage of security voting should decrease or disappear if we include ideology in the model of vote choice, but the survey evidence does not support this (see Table 5.2).[233]

Where right-wing ideology did matter in El Salvador was in influencing media control, because this ideology gave ARENA strong links to the business elite. However, the Nicaraguan and Guatemalan cases show, in confirmation of the book's theory, that such media control had less to do with right-wing ideology and more to do with the war outcomes and electoral incumbency.

This discussion raises questions of whether ARENA performed well both in the war and in the elections because it was the incumbent, and whether its incumbent status dictated its strategies. Nicaragua and Guatemala again provide the strongest counterfactuals. In Nicaragua, the *rebel*

TABLE 5.2. Determinants of Vote Choice, El Salvador 1994

Variable	(1) Vote ARENA	(2) Vote ARENA	(3) Vote FMLN	(4) Vote FMLN
Security voting	0.13**	0.88**	−0.19***	−1.24***
	(0.06)	(0.39)	(0.05)	(0.42)
Economic voting	0.12**	0.76**	−0.19***	−1.17***
	(0.06)	(0.38)	(0.05)	(0.41)
Ideological voting	0.10***	0.60***	−0.11***	−0.85***
	(0.01)	(0.05)	(0.01)	(0.07)
Constant	−0.21**	−4.24***	1.09***	4.31***
	(0.09)	(0.62)	(0.08)	(0.70)
Model	OLS	Logit	OLS	Logit
Observations	658	658	658	658
R^2	.31		.41	

Note: Standard errors in parentheses. Security voting measures whether the respondents saw security as the most important issue facing the country. Economic voting measures whether they saw the economy as the most important issue facing the country. Ideological voting captures respondents' self-reported ideological placement on the left-right 1–10 spectrum. All the models include controls for gender, age, and socioeconomic status.

**$p < .05$. ***$p < .01$.

group won the war, adopted similar strategies to ARENA, and performed well in the elections; in Guatemala, the electoral incumbent adopted completely divergent strategies and underperformed the political opposition in the elections.

Coercion

A third explanation would argue that ARENA performed well because it was better at coercion. FMLN fought the government to a draw, however, and was therefore equally capable of coercion. A counterargument could be that because the belligerents had showed unequal levels of crimes of war, the citizenry feared ARENA more than the FMLN. In particular, it may have feared that a strong vote for the FMLN in their locality would have drawn targeted repression. The empirical evidence casts doubt on this argument and whether coercion drove the election results, for several reasons.

One, if ARENA could win the election through coercion or fear of coercion, why engage in costly actions? Why moderate its positions and electorally target swing voters, risking its core voters? Why purge the organ-ization and run new civilian candidates rather than military ones? In other words, if coercion and fear were the forces guiding electoral behavior, we should not have observed ARENA engaging in the strategies proposed by the book's model; it should have performed well irrespective of strategy. The electoral experience of the PCN, however (discussed below), suggests that this was not the case. Two, the elections in El Salvador were widely deemed to be free and fair, with voters able to cast their ballots voluntarily. Three, if coercion were driving the results, we would expect to see ARENA winning by a much larger margin and disproportionately winning the votes of the most vulnerable. However, 1995 LAPOP survey data reveal that only 1 percent of respondents said they did not vote in the 1994 election because of violence or lack of security, and 91 percent of the electorate reported never having been improperly influenced to vote for a specific party (although these public opinion data did not utilize sensitive question techniques and may be subject to bias). Additionally, victims (although more fearful of vio-lence) and nonvictims abstained in equal proportions from voting in the 1994 elections (33.22 percent and 33.47 percent, respectively). I examine subnational variation in blank and null votes, which might have been cast based on fear, and find no relationship between these votes and ARENA's electoral success at a local level.[234] Four, if coercion (or fear of coercion) drove ARENA's votes, then as the country moved away from war and ARE-NA's coercive threat eroded over time, its electoral success should have de-clined; instead, it remained relatively constant in the medium term. Finally, rather than using the threat of reprisals, intimidation, or remilitarization as a centerpiece of its campaign, ARENA sought to sell itself as the party of peace.

I turn now to implications of the founding elections for peace, justice, and politics over time.

Implications over Time

Peace

In 1994, Salvadorans voted in peace. During the founding political period be-tween the peace accord and elections, there was little shift in the relative bal-ance of power that had locked the FMLN in stalemate with the Salvadoran military.[235] Accordingly, the FMLN's plan, as revealed in its internal party memos, was to remain a peaceful alternative political force *even if* it narrowly lost the elections, as such a result would be congruent with its military strength.[236] FMLN members saw the rebels' competitive participation in national elections as a "significant victory even if we don't have a legislative majority."[237] "Whatever happens, we win," they declared.[238]

With the power balance unaltered, the FMLN did not expect a better military outcome, with correspondingly superior electoral prospects, were it to engage in renewed fighting.[239] Therefore, despite losing the election and retaining the organizational capacity to return to war in a powerful fashion, the FMLN did not remilitarize. Similarly, the government remained convinced that, were it to return to war, its military fate, and thus its electoral fate, would also remain unchanged.[240] Both thus decided to consolidate peace.

Justice, Crime, and Security Brand

While peace solidified, the belligerent parties' success in the election meant that security sector reform was inconclusive, and justice stalled for decades.[241] Blanket amnesties held unbroken until calls for transitional justice began decades later, in 2013. The national narrative scripted by ARENA proved surprisingly resistant to change, even after FMLN won the legislature and presidency.[242] This lack of reform and accountability, in turn, led El Salvador to suffer one of the world's highest rates of homicide.[243]

As a result of rampant crime, the salience of security did not fade, but instead persisted over time. Years after the war, over 60 percent of the population viewed insecurity to be the most salient issue.[244] As a result, in the second postwar election held in 1999, ARENA continued to evoke the government's successful record in war and converted it into a "mano dura" (iron fist) brand of fighting crime. The resulting policing policies did not work; crime surged further. In the third postwar election in 2004 therefore, ARENA ran on "super mano dura." This, too, failed. Eventually, no more adjectives could be put ahead of "mano dura"; ARENA had to recognize that, while insecurity was, perversely, electorally beneficial to it, its public safety policies were not working.[245] Even in 2019, ARENA sought to evoke its Restrained Leviathan brand, tweeting, "Governing El Salvador is not easy and only the party that achieved peace . . . can advance the country with moral authority."[246] But as Oscar Pocasangre skillfully demonstrates, by then, ARENA also adopted diversionary tactics to focus the electorate not on the country's seemingly insurmountable security concerns, but instead on nonsecurity issues.[247] At the same time, ARENA left its security brand intact, able to be revived by future political descendants of the wartime belligerents.[248]

Party System

As the effectiveness of the security brand faded, both ARENA and FMLN, born from war, nonetheless developed into strong parties, and the institution-alization of the Salvadoran democratic party system consolidated around them.[249] They did so by developing robust ground games to address voters' concerns and by doling out clientelistic and patronage benefits.[250] ARENA had "a committee in every single municipality . . . all on a grassroots basis."[251] It built upon the mass-based paramilitary and "para-political" ORDEN,[252] a group of "sympathizers, [albeit] not necessarily party operatives."[253] Accord-ing to an ARENA leader:

> We go and solve [people's] problems, that's how you get their votes . . . [ARENA] gives away T-shirts, glasses, aprons, caps that carry the logos and flags of the party. This helps to create the sense that the party is everyone. . . . Everyone seems to be supporting it so [voters say to them-selves] I'll support it [too]. . . . In some places where the party thinks it is going to lose, we have seen the candidates buy votes. . . . It is prohib-ited. But they hardly catch anybody . . . so people do it, but not as a policy.[254]

FMLN, meanwhile, evolved from a "professional electoral" party to a "mass bureaucratic" party as the orthodox wing won out over the moderate wing.[255] This meant that "activists' interactions with the party became increasingly impregnated by clientelism and allowed the FMLN consistently to field a large force for electoral campaigning and to defend the vote on election day."[256] It also strengthened FMLN's program "for the people," by bolstering its rec-ord of social and economic responsiveness, particularly at the local level.[257] Both ARENA and FMLN thus fared extremely well electorally over multiple election cycles.[258]

Before concluding this case study of El Salvador, I pause to consider the off-equilibrium case of the PCN and to discuss why ARENA proved adept at maneuvering the obstacle course of postwar political strategies whereas this other belligerent party did not.

Off-Equilibrium Case: PCN, the Other
Government Successor Party

As noted in the chapter's introduction, ARENA was not the only potential successor to the government side of the armed conflict. The PCN arguably had an even more credible case for carrying the mantle of the state belligerent: it was the official party of the Salvadoran army.[259] However, PCN opted for a divergent and suboptimal strategy for a successor party to a belligerent at a military draw. It embraced an unmitigated version of the armed forces' bloodied past.[260] It put forth a far-right platform. It defined its constituency narrowly as the orthodoxy tied to the "military regime,"[261] and it sought to regain the armed forces' power through elections.[262] It ran predominantly military candidates.[263] Its initial presidential candidate (later withdrawn) was the ultra-right-wing war criminal General Juan Rafael Bustillo, charged with offenses whose impact was still very raw in 1994, including the 1989 Salvadoran army's slaughter of six unarmed Jesuit priests on the UCA campus in San Salvador.[264] PCN then ran retired Colonel Roberto Escobar.[265] While it could offer voters the government's wartime credentials of strength, therefore, it offered scant promise of restraint.[266] As predicted by the theory, these strategies failed with voters at the postwar polls. PCN gained 5.4 percent of the first-round presidential vote, failing to advance to the second round. It earned only 6.2 percent of the legislative vote.

Why, given the electoral returns offered by the optimal Restrained Leviathan strategy, did PCN not adopt this strategy? And why, in contrast, did ARENA do so? Unlike the case of Colombia's Santistas explored in Chapter 4, the reasons for PCN's missteps rest more, I argue, with organizational flaws and strategic party interactions than with idiosyncratic mistakes.

Whereas ARENA was what Loxton (2014) calls an "inside out" party,[267] structured "very vertically"[268] around a charismatic leader with a constituency for reform, PCN, as a pure "insider," was burdened by its bulky institution. ARENA's founder, D'Aubuisson, had served in the military junta, but found himself outside when the reformists decided that the military would no longer be at the elite's beck and call. ARENA's main constituency became instead the extremely centralized Salvadoran elite, a group famously comprising a mere fourteen families, easily able to act collectively to generate either continuity or change. The work of Elisabeth Jean Wood illuminates how, as the conflict transformed the country's reliance on agriculture exports, this elite came to favor modernization, reform, democratization, liberalization, and war termination.[269] With a constituency external to the armed forces, D'Aubuisson acquired the mandate to defy the military elite and to distance ARENA from the worst of the past. With such prestige inside the party, as he steered a reformist course, others followed.[270] According to former president Cristiani, "D'Aubuisson backed the [transition] process and this calmed everyone else down. His leadership was very strong. Even the hardest core of the [ARENA] party would go along with anything the Major said."[271] This afforded ARENA agility in adopting the optimal strategy.[272]

In contrast, PCN had no alternative constituency, no nimble structure, and no charismatic and visionary leadership to facilitate its regeneration and transformation. It was born as "the instrument for guaranteeing the army's control of the executive and legislative branches."[273] Its ties and loyalty to a powerful but cumbersome institution—the military—hampered it. The armed forces worried about saving their skin, resisted security sector reform, and feared potential transitional justice. PCN's top personnel were incriminated, but did not wish to self-decapitate. PCN therefore dug in its heels, clung to the status quo, and reminisced about the glory days of the past. As a result, it remained the party most closely associated with the violent baggage of "military power," but with few of its laundered endowments.[274]

The second reason PCN failed to adopt optimal tactics, despite technically inheriting the same belligerent package as ARENA, might have had to do with its strategic interactions with ARENA. PCN may have recognized that ARENA, as the electoral incumbent and first mover, had achieved valence and positional advantages. Accordingly, PCN's optimal strategy might have shifted to immoderation, in order to pick up ARENA's ultra-right-wing flank as ARENA moderated. For this far-right electorate, embrace of the violent past and the offer of unrestrained security enforcement likely would have proven electorally expedient.

Given the lack of independence between cases, the PCN cannot be treated as a counterfactual to ARENA. However, the case does provide glimpses into how ARENA might have fared had it adopted a suboptimal strategy.

Conclusion

El Salvador emerged from war greatly victimized by mass violence. The perpetration of this violence was highly unequal, with the government almost twenty times worse offenders than the rebels. The fighting ended at a military draw.

The Salvadoran case offers support for the theory and for important nuances beyond it. It indicates that the parties recognized and considered the variables upon which the book's argument is based. They weighed how to appeal to the broader conflict-affected electorate, how to neutralize and redirect retributive voting, and how to mitigate their past atrocities. They struggled with dilemmas of strength versus restraint, their preferred extreme positions versus moderation, their militant base versus abundant undecided voters, their bloodstained strongmen versus fresh-faced civilians. Where they resolved these dilemmas by adopting the equilibrium strategies, they fared well: they won not only their core voters, but also security voters, swing voters, and even the votes of some of their victims.

However, the case also presents refinements of the framework. My theory would predict that equally military successful in war and largely convergent in electoral strategies, ARENA and FMLN would split the vote, but ARENA outperformed FMLN. It projected its messaging better, farther, wider, and louder. I find that this was because of media control, which, in this case, was tied to electoral incumbency and connections with the oligarchy that held a monopoly on the private media.

The theory does predict that parties will harness media to amplify their message, and that media control—often correlated with war outcomes and incumbency—may be uneven, with implications for the translation of the war outcomes into electoral performance. In this case, propaganda played an outsized role, which suggests a potential revision to the theory: media control might serve a particular and even dominant role following military draws when competing parties engage in similar strategies, and thus the party best able to project the strategy takes the advantage. In the Salvadoran case, where other assets were equalized by war outcome, media control was not, and this advantaged the incumbent. However, in cases in which media dominance is determined by other factors, it might not be the incumbent that benefits. I take this potential theoretical revision to Guatemala and Nicaragua, the case studies in the next two chapters, which I completed after the Salvadoran case.

The Salvadoran case focused on two belligerent parties; the nonbelligerent one played only a minor role. This could have been an outlier, or it could suggest an empirical regularity: that following a military draw, even under proportional representation rules that encourage a multiparty system, the main electoral competition might come to be between only the belligerent successor parties, while the nonbelligerents get squeezed out. The case of the Christian Democrats provides an additional potential qualification to the book's theory. It indicates that nonbelligerents who have participated in the wartime government, even if they did not control the coercive apparatus and were not complicit in the violence, may find their nonbelligerent status compromised in the public eye. The next chapter, on government victory in Guatemala, centers on the competition between a belligerent and a nonbelligerent party and suggests that the nonbelligerent contender(s) may have a greater role in contexts of asymmetric war outcomes. That the nonbelligerent was the incumbent, had greater media control, and was right-wing, yet lost the election to the belligerent successor in Guatemala, helps disentangle variables that, in the Salvadoran case, ran together.

6

Government Victory in Guatemala

THIS BOOK IS about the electoral consequences of how wars end. Chapter 5 exposed the politics of belligerent parties emerging from war equally successful militarily. With correspondingly comparable electoral prospects and a shared playbook, they sought to split the vote. In a virulent electoral campaign, the incumbent party, equipped with a far superior propaganda arsenal, outperformed the media-depraved rebel party. Chapter 6 travels north from El Salvador to Guatemala where the war ended not in stalemate, but instead in a (relative) government win. This war therefore left in its wake viable parties of all three prototypes: a militarily victorious successor party, a militarily vanquished one, and a nonbelligerent party.

The primary goal of this chapter is to study how a successful, but in this case winning, brutal belligerent maneuvered not against a rival belligerent successor as in El Salvador, but against a strong party without blood on its hands. And how this untainted party lost. The book's puzzle is therefore intensified in the Guatemalan case. As a secondary objective, the chapter traces the politics of a defeated, but extant rebel successor party, a type not seen in El Salvador. And finally, the chapter uses the Guatemalan case to evaluate alternative explanations implied by Chapter 5. Unlike in El Salvador, both the nonbelligerent and the successful belligerent parties in Guatemala were right-wing and therefore, by a partisan-ownership explanation, had equal claim to the security issue. The nonbelligerent was the electoral incumbent and therefore by an incumbency advantage theory—suggested in El Salvador—it should have outperformed the opposition, despite the latter's combatant origins. None of these implications of the alternative theories are borne out in the data. Whereas media control played a role in the Guatemalan case, its role was far more circumscribed than in El Salvador, suggesting that harnessing the media may matter most when the competitive parties face incentives to propagate convergent messages, as will be seen following a military draw.

Given the asymmetric war outcome in Guatemala, the theory would predict that, to own the most important issues, the militarily winning successor would likely pursue a Restrained Leviathan strategy common to successful belligerents (those populating the Salvadoran case) whereas the noncombatant party would instead seek electoral punishment of the belligerents for their violent past and to own the rule of law. The framework anticipates that, bested in war, the militarily defeated party would run an immoderate campaign. These strategies, if adopted, would guide particularly the vote choice of swing and security voters, who would help hand the branches of government to the war-winner belligerent party. In so doing, the framework anticipates that the voters would gain peace, but forgo justice. The chapter presents evidence largely consistent with these expectations.

Setting the Stage: Guatemala's War

Guatemala's long armed conflict began in the wake of its "Spring."[1] After right-wing dictator Jorge Ubico's brutal administration ended in 1944, President Juan José Arévalo and President Jacobo Árbenz began to engage in political opening and progressive reforms, only to see them abruptly reversed by a U.S.-orchestrated coup in 1954.[2] The coup slammed the peaceful doors of change shut, and convinced the left that only an armed strategy could reopen them.[3] The first guerrilla movement was mobilized by disenchanted and left-leaning young military officers, rising up against their conservative colleagues. It "never mustered much support in the countryside . . . and [its] urban terrorism, though spectacular, was ineffective."[4] The rebellion very quickly evaporated, but it inspired other leftist activists to try their hand at insurgency. This second generation of rebels—seeking to implant themselves in progovernment eastern Guatemala—also failed to get their armed organizations up and running. It was the third generation of leftist guerrillas, which mobilized in the mid-1970s in the predominantly indigenous Western Highlands, that succeeded in sparking a full-scale war. This war pitted the authoritarian state against four guerrilla armies, which, in 1982, merged into a confederation, the Guatemalan National Revolutionary Unity (URNG).[5] At this point, as Virginia Garrard-Burnett puts it, "The horrifying prospect of such a coalition—Indians and communists united!—posed such a lethal threat to the civil-military regime that it demanded immediate action."[6] President Romeo Lucas García reigned over that action; the military and death squads inflicted brutal and indiscriminate violence against the civilian population, resulting in the deaths of at least 35,000 citizens.[7] This government repression, however, did not curb guerrilla activity, which surged.

Then, on March 23, 1982, a "bloodless coup . . . brought into office an unusual military officer. . . . [Efraín] Ríos Montt quickly consolidated his position, dissolving the Junta after only seventy-eight days."[8] His top priority was "bringing the insurgency under control." To do so, he offered "Beans and Rifles," "Housing, Food and Work," and the "Plan of Assistance to Areas of Conflict." He expanded the Civil Self-Defense Patrols (PACs) to 400,000, relocated populations into "model villages," and offered over 2,000 guerrillas amnesty. These "carrots" were accompanied by a genocidal stick.[9]

Balance of Atrocities

During Ríos Montt's rule, the military launched actions against 4,000 villages, many of them demarcated by the military as "killing zones."[10] The military engaged in scorched-earth tactics: it burned homes, destroyed crops, murdered countless women, children, and even infants, and massacred whole village populations. It drove 1,200,000 noncombatants into internal or external exile. Approximately 86,000 people were killed during Ríos Montt's tenure.

Two truth commissions were established, the UN-sponsored Comisión para el Escalarecimiento Histórico (CEH)[11] and another sponsored by the Catholic archdiocese, Proyecto Interdiociano de Recuperación de la Memória Histórica (REMHI).[12] Both communicated their discoveries after the peace agreement of 1996, but before the founding postwar elections of 1999. CEH documented 626 massacres and REMHI 422. Both found blame for the violence, as in the Salvadoran case, starkly lopsided.[13] REMHI concluded that the state had committed 83 percent of the killings. CEH assigned blame to the state for just over 90 percent of the atrocities, which included murder, rape, forced abduction, torture, and the destruction of indigenous villages. Both projects "unequivocally lay responsibility at the feet of Ríos Montt."[14] Of the more than 200,000 deaths caused by Guatemala's thirty-six-year war, 43 percent occurred during Ríos Montt's time in office. Scholars labeled Ríos Montt's reign the "violent and bloody nadir" in a conflict characterized by innumerable monstrous moments. Ríos Montt's brutal campaign has been called the Mayan holocaust.[15] CEH declared it genocide under international law.[16]

Meanwhile, the "guerrilla atrocities . . . differed from those committed by the counterinsurgency in that they tended to be systematic and targeted, usually involving the killing of local officials, soldiers, and individual civilians singled out for 'revolutionary justice.'"[17] The UN-sponsored truth commission found the URNG's constituent rebel organizations responsible for only 7 percent of the war's human rights violations.[18]

War Outcomes

This brutal war ultimately ended in a government win. By 1984, the military had substantially weakened the guerrillas. In 1991, declassified U.S. cables revealed that Guatemalan "army officers today do not consider the guerrillas a threat or a serious problem to the stability of Guatemala . . . because they have all but defeated the insurgency on the battlefield."[19] Upon opening peace negotiations, the army asked, "Why do we have to negotiate with them if we [have] already won the war? . . . [if we have] the military strength to destroy the enemy?"[20] By late 1994, the U.S. Department of Defense estimated, the URNG had only "863 active combatants in the field,"[21] down from a high of 6,000 to 8,000 rebels in the early 1980s. According to such accounts, Guatemala's guerrillas suffered "virtual annihilation"[22] and a clear "strategic defeat."[23] These numbers, however, might have underestimated the rebels' strength; by other accounts, the URNG had experienced a moderate resurgence in the early 1990s. It posed a sufficient threat that the government, led by the nonbelligerent National Advancement Party (PAN), decided to terminate the conflict through negotiated settlement rather than unilateral surrender. After a decade-long peace process, the URNG and PAN signed the Agreement for a Firm and Lasting Peace in December 1996.[24]

This was thus a highly asymmetric outcome in favor of the state. While it was short of outright, decisive victory, completely vanquishing the losing belligerent side, the government won the war. The peace process brought about the disarmament and demobilization of 2,940 URNG combatants and 2,813 international and political rebel members.[25] The armed conflict terminated and the country entered a postwar period.

Verifying the Scope Conditions: Postwar Democratic Elections

In 1999, founding democratic, presidential, and legislative postwar elections were held. These constituted the first elections following the conclusion of the armed conflict and the first in which parties across the ideological spectrum participated. In the Report of its Electoral Observation Mission to Guatemala, the Organization of American States classified these elections as "free and fair."[26] Even nonbelligerents and the guerrillas themselves confirmed the democratic nature of the political contests. Of the elections, indigenous human rights activist (later awarded the Nobel Peace Prize) Rigoberta Menchú said, "All is calm." Former guerrilla commander Pablo Monsanto stated, "There is no military presence. . . . There is no pressure; all is calm. We can say that for the first time there is total freedom to express our will."[27]

The rules governing the elections may be considered to be independent of the war outcome. The president was elected by absolute majority in a two-round system, and the congressional elections were decided by proportional representation rules, introduced to Guatemala in 1946, with closed party lists, adopted in 1965.[28] In Guatemala, the "death of dictatorship," even if not the birth of a liberal democracy, had taken place during the war when a new constitution was inaugurated in 1985. This meant that the institutional arrangement, albeit not endogenous to the final war outcome, had involved the active participation of the military which, in 1985, held considerable sway over politics.[29] At the same time, these electoral rules mirror those present across Latin America and those that reigned in Guatemala prewar, suggesting that their adoption may have reflected regional norms more than military prerogatives. Additionally, nonbelligerent parties were able to win elections under the rules, indicating that those rules did not lock in the power only of belligerent successors.

Characterizing the Voters

Approximately 18 percent of the Guatemalan population had been direct victims of the violence. Counting their networks and those that witnessed the atrocities, a large proportion of the Guatemalan electorate was conflict-affected. While the most egregious wartime violence had been concentrated geographically in the Western Highlands, no place and no person was entirely unaffected by the conflict's reverberations.[30] For example, while nonindigenous in Guatemala City were largely spared the ruthlessness that the state unleashed against the Mayan population of the Western Highlands, they lived in fear of targeted guerrilla killings.

The end of Guatemala's thirty-six-year war brought a "moment of extraordinary promise and goodwill. Crowds of jubilant Guatemalans danced in the streets, and in a national poll, 77 percent of Guatemalans said they felt happy."[31] However, given that the leftist insurgency—effectively vanquished—had at that point largely wound down, the civil war had become rivaled in salience by other sources of insecurity, which began to soar in the 1990s. This is common to many postconflict environments.[32] In 1999, 34 percent of respondents cited lack of personal security due to violence, crime, and kidnapping as the most important issue facing Guatemala, a proportion equal to those most concerned about the economic crisis, poverty, unemployment, education, health care, and transport, combined.[33] Elevated levels of violence "deprived citizens of any sense of basic security in their daily lives."[34] Implementation of the peace accord and debate over its more than fifty reforms were also issues important to the electorate as the elections came on the tail of the referendum on packages of these reforms.[35] Insecurity especially concerned unaligned voters, who composed 89 percent of the electorate. Voters were also concerned about economic recovery. The dominant cleavages in Guatemala were class and ethnicity; the population distributed normally across the left-right ideological spectrum;[36] 38 percent of the population considered themselves indigenous, 62 percent Ladino.[37]

Introducing the Parties: The Nonbelligerent Party

In the founding postwar election in Guatemala, the National Advancement Party constituted a strong nonbelligerent contender without blood on its hands. Formed by "a group of technocrats and business people,"[38] it had had "little or no involvement in the past military governments."[39] This party also constituted the incumbent, having been elected to executive and legislative power in 1995.

Civil War Belligerent Successor Parties

Multiple political actors had sought to leverage the legacy of the government's war-winning coercive apparatus before the postwar founding elections of 1999, but only one was able to do so: General Ríos Montt's FRG (Guatemalan Republican Front). Ríos Montt had formed this new party in 1989 as his highly personalistic electoral vehicle; the FRG was "synonymous" with Ríos Montt.[40] The other would-be government successor parties had disappeared or were on life support by 1999.[41]

Meanwhile, the rebel successor party, URNG, was born out of the losing insurgent confederation. While the URNG had abstained from participation in elections during its armed struggle, opting not to legitimize the country's undemocratic political contests, it entered the political arena as a new party after the 1996 peace accords. Despite its defeat in war, it sought to navigate the transition and gain a foothold in Guatemala's postwar political order. To do so, it joined a leftist coalition, called the New Nation Alliance (ANN).[42]

Data Sources

This chapter portrays postwar politics in Guatemala based on materials from personal interviews and various archival sources. The first archive, called "Civil War, Society and Political Transition in Guatemala: The Guatemala News and Information Bureau Archive (1963–2000)," is held at Princeton University. It includes eleven thousand published and unpublished documents, pronouncements, press releases, flyers, news clippings, correspondence, and other types of ephemera and "gray materials." These sources document the civil war and peace and justice process from the perspectives of activist groups, government officers and politicians, journalists, international solidarity groups, and revolutionary organizations. From Princeton's Latin America physical ephemera collection, I also accessed FRG, URNG, and PAN party manifestos and propaganda for the 1999 elections. Of particular value was a Guatemalan civil society organization's pamphlet, which sought to inform citizens' vote choice. It documented the biographical profiles of all FRG, URNG, and PAN candidates, their work experience, political activities, unsavory antecedents, judicial cases against them, and their valence and policy emphases. From this resource, I created a candidate-level dataset, enabling analysis of which types of politicians—those with or without a violent past—each party fielded. Second, the Digital National Security Archives, "Death Squads, Guerrilla War, Covert Operations, and Genocide: Guatemala and the U.S. 1954–1999," contains 2,071 declassified primary source documents describing Guatemala's internal conditions. It holds decades of U.S. embassy cables and documents, such as a chilling "death squad diary" smuggled out of the archives of the Guatemalan military intelligence. These varied sources provided insight on the parties' strategizing and strategies. The chapter's survey evidence derives from LAPOP and Consultoría Interdisciplinaria en Desarrollo S.A. / Gallup polls conducted for the United States Information Agency.

The chapter traces how war experience and military outcomes influenced the electoral strategies of the parties—the nonbelligerent incumbent PAN, the brutal war-winner FRG, and the restrained but militarily defeated URNG. It is to this task that I turn next.

Winning the Prospective Vote:
Nonbelligerent PAN's Party Strategy

PAN, as the electoral incumbent, acted as the first mover in the 1999 campaign. As such, it influenced the calculus of the militarily dominant FRG, which in turn affected URNG's strategizing. I therefore discuss the parties sequentially.

Valence Strategy: Owning the Security Issue

As the incumbent, nonbelligerent PAN played the role of agenda setter. PAN recognized a valence advantage on security within legal bounds.[43] PAN therefore decided to present "itself as a force . . . capable of integrating into its discourse pressing issues of the moment such as the defense of human rights"[44] and to underscore to voters the difference between the choices on offer: FRG, a party that could not be constrained by institutions or the electorate, and PAN itself, which could. Its party program made this choice explicit. It read, "We are in a moment of defining the Guatemala that we want: one of the past or one of the future; one of conflict or one of solidarity and progress; one of impunity and abuses of human rights or one in which the State respects the law. . . . This is the decision to make. The next elections [between FRG and PAN] will decide this."[45]

PAN pinned its security competence to its own lack of past transgressions. Positioned in stark contrast to the bloodstained belligerent parties, PAN had only tenuous links to Guatemala's previous military regime. PAN's key leader, Álvaro Arzú, who served as President of Guatemala (1996–2000), had worked in the Guatemalan Tourism Agency during Lucas García's rule (1978–1982), but at that time belonged to a reformist and moderate movement (National Renewal Party). As James Loxton documents, when Arzú subsequently won the mayoral election of Guatemala City in 1982—a post he could not assume because of the coup—Ríos Montt offered to have the military install him as mayor.[46] He declined, a move that gave him and his party "political credit" as a nonbelligerent, and burnished their "democratic credentials."[47] The other PAN leaders were similarly untainted by the war: they were mostly "successful professionals who had had little or no involvement in the past military governments."[48] The PAN ruling party identified the electoral advantages of this clean human rights record.[49] Its strategists thus opted to seek to "turn human rights to their advantage, especially when they refer[red] to wartime crimes."[50]

While brandishing its own rule-of-law credentials, PAN sought to undermine voters' confidence in FRG's security competence by sounding the alarm that a FRG government would mean "a return to the past, with all of its burden of pain, bloodshed and death."[51] Building on the work of the Christian Democrats who had "persistently attacked the government's role in political violence,"[52] PAN's strategy became "to emphasiz[e] the links between FRG candidates and human rights violations."[53] The words of PAN's 1999 presidential candidate, Óscar Berger, encapsulated this strategy. Of the FRG, he said: "We can't allow those people who committed barbarities during the years when they governed the country, to return to lead the country again."[54] He called for voters to engage in electoral retribution against the FRG.

In addition to perceiving a potential rule-based security valence advantage, PAN also estimated that, having spent its wartime years engaging not in violence, but instead in developing other expertise, it might benefit from a reputation for general competence that could apply across multiple issue areas. In its program, it strategized how to play up this general valence and landed on a refrain: "We can get things done."[55] PAN's program pointed to its record of competency, highlighting, for example, how it had created a new civilian National Police force, enlarged universal primary education, extended public health to rural areas, and brought "services to all the Guatemalans ignored in the past."

Positional Strategy

According to archival records, PAN detected not only potential valence advantages, but also positional ones over FRG, a far-right party. On the ideological spectrum, PAN was considered the "moderate and responsible right,"[56] a "center-right"[57] or "modernizing right" party.[58] It maneuvered to emphasize this pragmatic nature, identifying "itself as a party of technocrats concerned with efficiency and good government, rather than with ideology and posturing."[59] PAN's published program, twice as long as FRG's, was replete with real proposals and explicit solutions.[60] Below, I engage in text analysis to systematically compare PAN's manifesto with that of FRG.

Electoral Targeting: The Moderate Voter

Positionally and in terms of valence, this programmatic approach suggested that PAN opted to prioritize moderate voters, a segment that overlapped to a large extent with its core voter pool of center-right supporters. While PAN's core was concentrated in the middle and upper classes, particularly in urban areas,[61] PAN did not bound its constituency. Its 1999 slogan became "A Guatemala that includes *everyone*, a Guatemala in which *all* can progress."[62]

Candidates

The book's theory posits that parties prove likely to field high-valence candidates, particularly for presidential contests and contested legislative races, in which unaligned voters comprise a larger share of the electorate. For PAN, high valence meant those with impeccable human rights records and overall competence. Internal deliberations on PAN's decision-making process surrounding its political elite are unfortunately not available, so I can infer motivations only from outcomes. As its presidential candidate, PAN ran Óscar Berger, a lawyer by training with origins in the business elite. Berger had a record of respect for human rights and of competence as mayor of Guatemala City.[63] Analysis of PAN's legislative slate reveals similar qualities among its other political elite. All of PAN's candidates had civilian backgrounds. Of those for whom unsavory antecedents were discovered—just 7.8 percent—their pasts involved harassment or violent confrontations. As shown below, the same was true of nearly twice as many (13.8 percent) of FRG's candidates.

In sum, as predicted by the book's theory, PAN adopted a *Rule Abider* strategy. It assumed that, targeted with this strategy, the electorate, particularly those voting on security, would opt for the party that had not previously turned guns against the civilian population. The book's theory predicts that the government belligerent successor party, FRG, militarily victorious, would perceive its own path to claiming ownership of the security issue.

War Winner FRG's Party Strategy

FRG assumed that the insecure electorate would want a Leviathan instead. Records of closed-door conversations on FRG's derivation of strategy do not, to my knowledge, exist. Publicly available sources, however, can shine some light on FRG's strategy; from the strategy, I seek to deduce strategizing.

Valence Strategy

The sources suggest that FRG focused programmatically on valence issues nearly exclusively; indeed, the three fingers in its logo stood for "security, welfare, justice" (Figure 6.1).[64]

As its core tenet, FRG opted for a "simple law-and-order message combined with a vaguely populist effervescence and inclusive economic discourse."[65] Ríos Montt himself described FRG's manifesto: "I don't propose an economic program, but rather an ethical and moral one. Our problem is disorder. We have to put order into our lives. We need law, order, and discipline."[66]

FIGURE 6.1. FRG Logo: "Security, Welfare, Justice." *Source*: Frente Republicano Guatemalteco, "Plan de Gobierno 2000–2004: Linamientos Generales" (1999).

Claiming Competence on Security

FRG perceived its credibility on future security[67] to lie directly with "memories of [Ríos Montt's] time in power as a kind of 'Pax riosmonttista.'"[68] Facing a rhetorical onslaught by PAN, a Truth Commission amplifying the testimony of witnesses to the military's carnage, a genocide trial against FRG leader Ríos Montt, and an imperative to reach noncore, unaligned voters, FRG recognized that, despite military victory, it could not sustain unaltered the narrative of the state's violence that justified the brutalities in ideological terms. This wartime propaganda—"caustically berat[ing] the guerrillas for wanton destruction"[69] while claiming that "state security forces heroically defended the fatherland"[70]—had played well with FRG's core and with a population enveloped in the disorientation of war, unable to attribute responsibility for the victimization accurately. However, confronted with greater public recognition of Ríos Montt's wartime role in crimes against humanity, FRG had to launder the asset upon which FRG could base its prospective electoral case: the Ríos Montt regime's military record.[71]

FRG therefore decided to seek to shift voters' frames of reference. In particular, it maneuvered to reframe voters' comparison of the mass slaughter under Ríos Montt, not to a world in which no slaughter had occurred, but instead to a world in which this unbearable violence had persisted. Before Ríos Montt's rule, according to the "master narrative of the nation"[72] woven by FRG, "a hostile ideology [and rebel force] seemed to, or in fact did, threaten [the state's] demise." By 1981, "at least a quarter of a million people in rural areas supported the guerrillas to some degree or another."[73] In response, Lucas García had instituted a "scorched earth strategy," but with scant results; entire villages were exterminated through "all-out 100 percent random slaughter."[74]

"In the cities, assassinations, death squad killings, and disappearances ... also became more common, marking a rapid downward spiral of capricious violence and death."[75] Before Ríos Montt took the reins of government, FRG reasoned, the military had been murderous but ineffective. Its atrocities therefore could not be offset by the provision of security and peace, because it had provided neither.

In contrast, under Ríos Montt, FRG argued that the country advanced from the "unpredictable, chaotic terror of a floundering dictatorship to Ríos Montt's more predictable textbook campaign."[76] This campaign ultimately delivered a decisive solution to the conflict: military victory, which pacified the country and ushered in an era of relative stability and ironfisted protection. FRG contended that, for not doubling down on the military's violence, but instead effectively ending it, it should be rewarded. Ríos Montt claimed, "I was called to put everything in order," and had made good on this.[77] Accordingly, Ríos Montt concluded, "it will be history"—meaning, specifically, the record of pacification—"that will judge what has been done in the past," meaning the record of atrocity.[78] While claiming exoneration for the government's violence, FRG did relatively little to redirect blame for the war toward the guerrillas. Militarily vanquished, URNG was not a worthy opponent. This stands in contrast to the Salvadoran case in which, at a military draw, both belligerent parties sought mitigation of the violent past, and each therefore faced incentives to undermine the mitigation efforts of its opponent.

Beyond defeat of the rebels and credit for peace, FRG perceived its credibility on prospective security[79] to further lie with its ties to the coercive apparatus,[80] and symbolic edge embodied in its strongman. "The figure [Ríos Montt] cut was instantly recognizable as the old-fashioned caudillo, the man on horseback who saves the nation. . . . The army uniform which Ríos Montt wore in campaign pictures is, for many Guatemalans, an icon of credible authority."[81] This endowed FRG with a unique "qualif[ication] to deal unflinchingly with criminals" as well.[82]

If the book's theory is correct, both the nonbelligerent PAN and the militarily victorious belligerent FRG would emphasize security issues. However, we should observe the former highlighting the second Madisonian requisite of a government laid out in the *Federalist Papers*—to be obliged to control itself—while FRG would emphasize the first Madisonian requisite: to be able to control the governed.[83] The empirical prediction is thus that the competing parties would diverge rhetorically during the campaign.

FRG versus PAN's Security Programs

To evaluate this implication, I engaged in computer-assisted text analysis of the PAN and FRG party manifestos. Having transformed the text corpus, I evaluated the proportion of the programs devoted to security issues. I find the nonbelligerent PAN and war-winner FRG nearly identical in their emphasis of security issues. Seventeen percent of PAN's program centered on security issues, compared to 14 percent for FRG. Consistent with the framework, PAN, more than FRG, emphasized other valence issues on which it had developed competencies: it devoted 30 percent more text to the economy than did the FRG.

While both PAN and FRG equally emphasized security issues, there was a marked difference in the way the two approached security. Topic modeling of the manifestos highlights that, whereas the parties were generally discussing similar subjects within the security theme, several topic clusters appear with frequencies that differ between the two parties.[84] For example, the topics of security and capacity were associated more with FRG than PAN, and the topic of peace building was associated more with PAN than FRG (though not to a statistically significant extent).

Within the same topics, PAN and FRG differed more markedly. Figure 6.2 shows the stemmed words associated with a topic, grouped by whether the topic was discussed by FRG (left-hand quadrant) or PAN (right-hand). The larger the words, the more frequently they appeared. The larger, further from the center, to the left or right, and darker in tone the words appear, the more strongly associated those words were with one party or the other. Figure 6.2 suggests that PAN's party manifesto and approach to security emphasized rule of law and reform with a focus on institutions and public services. FRG, on the other hand, showed much greater emphasis on strong-arm security: strengthening and modernizing the security apparatus, including procuring more arms and security personnel. Given the relatively small corpus of text, these findings are significant.

The small size of the text collection also lends itself to hand coding, which can better identify the different logics and sentiments around similar topics than can Structural Topic Models.[85] In a separate hand-coding process, two coders, blind to the theory, hypotheses, and party classifications, read each text independently and summarized the principal topics of each manifesto. They then coded them as advancing disarmament or rearmament, as

decentr

modern

profession

process

justic

law

secur   strengthen

intellig

provis

translat

public

citizen   crime

reform

peac

state

system   polici

improv   institut

FRG   PAN

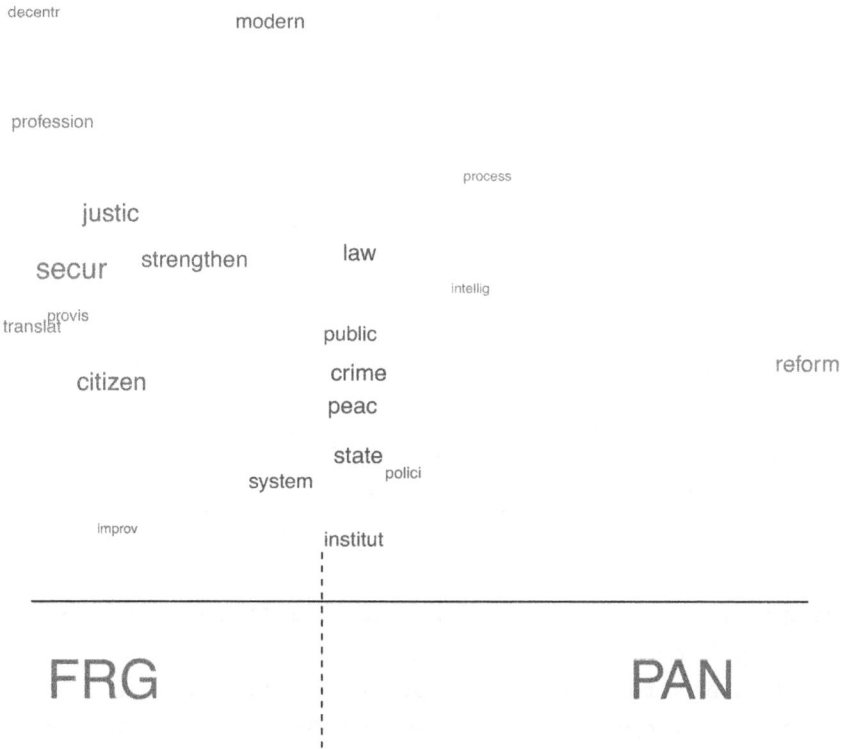

FIGURE 6.2. Text Analysis of FRG versus PAN Security Platforms.

emphasizing human rights (or not) and particularly freedom from coercion (or not), and as promoting a hard-on-crime or soft-on-crime approach. There was general consensus across coders. Where there was not, I present the coding that defied the book's predictions (that is, that coded nonbelligerent parties as favoring ironfisted security, or that coded winning belligerent parties as favoring rule-based security). Table 6.1 summarizes the hand coding results. Each cell reports the share of each party's manifesto that was coded as consistent with a particular theme. The results are generally consistent with the findings from the machine-learning analysis. The nonbelligerent, PAN, came out much more likely than FRG to be interpreted as advancing human rights, judicial reform, freedom from coercion, and peace; and more likely to promote prevention, rehabilitation and reducing penalties. As predicted, FRG was more likely to argue for a strong-arm approach. The hand coding yielded an unanticipated result showing that FRG was twice as likely to mention

TABLE 6.1. Hand Coding of Security Platforms, Belligerent FRG versus Nonbelligerent PAN

Topic	% of Words	
	FRG	PAN
Disarmament / decreasing military expenditures	22.1 (11.1)	9.8 (4.9)
Rearmament / strengthening military / increasing military expenditures	16.3 (2.3)	2.0 (5.0)
Emphasis on human and civil rights / judicial reform / freedom from coercion / peace processes	28.9 (14.7)	44.8 (6.9)
Soft on crime (prevention, rehabilitation, reducing penalties)	9.8 (2.8)	17.3 (8.7)
Hard on crime (strong government, strict law enforcement, tough actions against domestic crime, increasing support and resources for the police, importance of internal security)	26.7 (0.9)	17.3 (2.1)

disarmament compared to PAN. However, it was eight times more likely than nonbelligerent PAN to mention strengthening the military. Even though results from hand coding may present potentially high levels of variance and disagreement across coders, the analysis suggested certain themes as more likely to appear in the nonbelligerent manifestos or the belligerent ones respectively.

The text analysis suggests that each party paid lip service to its own areas of weakness: PAN mentioned strength and defense, while FRG "stress[ed] the need . . . for respect of human rights [and] pledg[ed] that a Ríos Montt government would put an end to the violations of human rights." However, the "dominance principle"[86] outweighed the logic of "riding the wave"[87] for both parties: PAN ran on rule-of-law, while FRG ran on law-and-order.

Issue Priming

FRG's Hobbesian claim to the security issue was most likely to play well electorally under conditions of "war of all against all."[88] Through issue priming, therefore, FRG sought to amplify perceptions of such conditions. In its propaganda, it warned that "the context is hectic, *anarchic*, uncertain," and that times are "like never seen in the history of the country before."[89] Its party manifesto proclaimed, "Currently, the people of Guatemala are going through a crisis of all orders . . . an alarming reality which could drive us to a situation of real economic and social disaster, whose political expression is also visible in terms of the ungovernability of the country."[90] Only a militarily strong sovereign like FRG, it argued, could save Guatemala. FRG's 1999 campaign invoked the debate over the Consulta Popular—the referendum on the peace accords—to stoke fears of a return to violence; fear of ceding the country to indigenous leaders, languages, culture, and customary law; and fear of Balkanization[91] and ethnic conflict between Maya and Ladinos.[92] Few wanted to relive the terror they had suffered during the civil war, so these alarmist messages of impending anarchy resonated.[93]

Positional Strategy

FRG acknowledged its positional disadvantage. It was closely associated with the military dictatorships, and historically positioned itself significantly more radical on the ideological spectrum than nonbelligerent PAN. This, it recognized, had to be remedied to seek votes from the broader population. FRG's leader Ríos Montt proved adept at such ideological flexibility. He was a chameleon and an evangelical, repeatedly being "born again": in the early 1970s, he was a democrat; in the early 1980s, a brutal counterinsurgent;[94] and in 1999, he decided to become a Leviathan. However, rather than emphasize moderation, FRG sought to downplay position entirely; it put forth a vague platform that could not be pinned anywhere on the ideological spectrum. Where it did highlight positional issues, they were uncontroversial, vacuous, and had little risk of alienating anyone. For example, FRG's program mentioned "tourism to generate new jobs, creation of technical careers, review of salaries."[95] It lacked any concrete plan to achieve these objectives.

To examine more systematically whether FRG moderated programmatically, I analyzed the party manifestos using text analysis. The classifier (described in the introduction to Chapter 5, which was trained on the Party Manifesto Project data) categorized 25 percent of the FRG's manifesto as "left" and 28 percent as "right," yielding a ri-le score of 3.37. The machine learning algorithm classified 21 percent of PAN's program as "left" and 30 percent as "right," yielding for PAN a moderate ri-le score, albeit further to the right, at 8.5. While both qualitative hand coding and computer-assisted text analysis are subject to advantages and disadvantages, together these analyses suggest that FRG moved significantly toward the center, converging positionally with nonbelligerent PAN.

Electoral Targeting: The Moderate Voter

Emphasizing an "iron fist" "law-and-order message" and avoiding any discussion of moderate or radical ideology,[96] FRG opted tactically not to prioritize its traditional supporters. These were "active and retired hard-line army officers, civilians who participated in the army patrols during the country's civil war, sectors of the oligarchy, fundamentalist churches and a conservative faction of Christian Democrats."[97] To reach the swing electorate, FRG opted to redefine its constituency not on partisan lines, but instead as one seeking "reconciliation . . . without ideological stain."[98] It coined the term, "Guatemalidad"[99]—Guatemalism—as its version of nationalism,[100] and promised to build a "multicultural nation"[101] to transcend wartime societal cleavages.[102] On its website, it defined itself as the party to represent "Catholics and Evangelicals . . . different ethnic groups, businessmen . . . and workers."[103] Taking a step further in its constituency stretching, FRG claimed, despite its far right-wing origins, that it was the "party of the poor";[104] it relentlessly attacked the PAN for being the "party of the rich."[105]

While FRG made its moderated, strongman case to the entire electorate, PAN offered fiery critiques against allowing brutal tormentors to govern.[106] The rebel successor alliance similarly warned that: "FRG offers human rights, but *has bullets prepared for the future.*"[107] Accordingly, FRG had to think hard about how to convince the electorate that it would use its security credentials for protection and not revictimization. In addition to influencing its rhetoric—which was mostly cheap talk—this calculus influenced FRG's recruitment of party elite, signals that were somewhat more costly.

Candidates

As FRG's strongman, Ríos Montt remained the public face of the party and the head of its congressional ticket, providing the party its security credentials. However, FRG sought to rebrand Ríos Montt as "honorable, honest," "responsible," and the "embodiment of . . . national integrity."[108] FRG went so far as to "promis[e] voters a 'more human' administration than that of the [nonbloodstained] PAN, keeping the militaristic, iron hand image . . . under wrap,"[109] a fig-leaf tactic aimed especially at unaligned voters. A constitutional provision that barred the candidacy of anyone ever involved in a coup rendered Ríos Montt ineligible to run for president.[110] As its candidate for executive office,

FRG picked Alfonso Portillo. Some have argued that, although Portillo was the candidate, Ríos Montt remained "the real power broker in the FRG, over and above President Portillo."[111] Party propaganda featured both candidates; supporters of the FRG wore "T-shirts that declare[d], 'Portillo to the presidency, Ríos Montt to power.'"[112]

While Ríos Montt provided the strength credentials,[113] Portillo was designed to be more than a puppet: potentially, he could effectively signal restraint to those most concerned about revictimization. As an ideological leftist, a former supporter of the Guerrilla Army of the Poor (EGP) rebels, and a defector from the Christian Democrats,[114] himself a victim of the conflict who had fled to Mexico in fear for his life,[115] Portillo signaled that FRG would not (re)victimize the former armed and unarmed political left. As a progressive, he also lent credence to FRG's positional and ideological breadth,[116] helping it expand its targeted constituency to the lower classes and progressive sectors.[117] The "peculiar alliance between a former leftist and an ex-general accused of massive human rights abuses" proved successful.[118]

FRG undertook a further costly signal of restraint by purging human rights abusers from its elite and stacking its legislative ticket with mostly civilian candidates[119] including evangelicals, businessmen, and former enemies, among them leftist guerrilla commander Pedro Palma Lau,[120] human rights ombudsman Ramiro de León Carpio, and newspaper columnist Miguel Angel Velásquez Bitzol, a vocal advocate of indigenous rights. Only 13 percent of its candidates had violent antecedents and these FRG sought to hide on its closed legislative lists. Party members purged from the lists, despite great loyalty to the FRG, included former police chief Pedro García Arredondo, one of the darkest figures from the years of repression under General Lucas García (1978–82), who was accused of rape, torture, kidnapping and disappearances during Montt's reign.[121] FRG also withdrew the congressional bid of Lucas Tecú, who had led a massacre of 99 mostly infants and young people in Baja Verapaz, yet sought to represent this very department in Congress. Fourteen other former army officers who sought to run for office on the FRG ticket were similarly denied candidacies.[122]

To characterize and analyze the different parties' candidate choices, I used materials from the political education campaign of the Guatemalan Kuchuj Voz Ciudadana. For the 1999 election, this NGO generated a nonpartisan pamphlet listing each candidate's party affiliation and past experience: military or civilian. Of the candidates for which information was available,[123] I find that, whereas PAN ran only civilians, as did the losing belligerent party, URNG, 14 percent of FRG candidates had a military background. This is consistent with the model's predictions.

War Loser Rebel URNG's Party Strategy

Neither the URNG nor its New Nation Alliance was a major player in the election. Vanquished in war, URNG's military fate limited its prospective electoral performance. Its military outcome also set constraints on its strategizing; Tactical Immoderation emerged its optimal course. URNG adopted this strategy, seemingly for reasons aligning with the theory. In so doing, URNG gained a place at the table of postwar politics, albeit a limited one.

Platform: Valence and Positional Strategy

To differentiate itself from parties more competent on security, who had first and second mover advantages, URNG emphasized nonsecurity issues. This is not to say that it did not lay out a plan for security and peace. It did, but it recognized its lack of credibility on these issues. The URNG guerrillas could claim credit for the accords, but not for the pacification. It had not *chosen* to end its violence, but had done so only when brought to its knees; its use of force was perceived to have failed. Accordingly, URNG lacked the key ingredient with which to launder its bloodied past and military record through mitigation.

To claw its way toward redemption and establish its nonviolent intentions, it therefore adopted an opposite tactic to that of the FRG: Contrition.[124] Faced with the Truth Commission findings, URNG did not respond with spin as FRG;[125] instead it "unconditionally sought forgiveness for atrocities it had committed and pledged to follow the [truth] commission's recommendations" for reconciliation and transitional justice.[126] Although it had committed 7 percent of abuses in the war, to reckon with the past, URNG strategized to engage in acceptance of responsibility, symbolic reparations and truth-telling.

Its programmatic focus was not on security, but instead on socioeconomic valence issues: "employment for all, social welfare and development."[127] For example, in its program, URNG pledged, among other things, free basic healthcare, seed money for enterprises run by women, and bilingual education.[128] Its slogans centered on these issues: "You cannot forget that the rumbling of the stomach is louder than the blast of the gun. . . . Guatemalans are still waiting for peace to reach their stomachs."[129] The party emblem showed *maís* (corn), a symbol of the indigenous people and of poverty reduction; URNG drew a persistent contrast with its rivals, who, it declared, "offer us bread for today and hunger for tomorrow."[130]

Given its far-left origins, URNG suffered a positional disadvantage relative to the moderate nonbelligerent and first-mover PAN. Accordingly, were it to advocate centrist policies, it would directly compete with PAN, and fail. Rather than positional convergence, URNG therefore bet on future elections, strategically gambling its prospects in the founding elections by cultivating a reputation for a detailed alternative platform that could attract voters in subsequent elections who were disillusioned with the mainstream. Analysis of its platform using the Party-Manifesto-Project-based classifier yields an immoderate (left-wing) ri-le score of −22.8. Contemporaneous analyses of its party strategy suggest that URNG sought to "maintain clear differences with the right-wing parties of the country . . . This differentiation [was] also maintained despite the fact that the once revolutionary left has moderated its programmatic approaches."[131] Its program, although less radical than its wartime goal of full-scale communist revolution, was strategized to be immoderate relative to the mainstream, and based on substantial reformation of the status quo. The policies were tangible and URNG's promises to realize them credible as they included those for which its members had struggled and sacrificed. Internal party memos outlined this approach:

> [URNG's program should be] based on the idea of a new Guatemala that should start from the construction of a multicultural and multilingual nation, from the demilitarization of the country. . . . In this direction, the URNG visualized nine [significant] changes: modernization of the agrarian structure; tax reform; labor reform . . . decentralization of power and transformation of urban-rural relations; education reform; reform of the public health and social security system; restructuring of public administration; viable and sustainable development policy; sovereign, active and progressive international policy.[132]

Electoral Targeting: The Immoderate Voter

Equipped with this revisionist programmatic strategy, a passionate speech by its presidential candidate Álvaro Colom described the party URNG sought to build as "of the poor, by the poor, and for the poor."[133] URNG decided largely to target core leftist voters and those adjacent ideologically. It did not seek to appeal to moderate, swing, right-wing, or security voters, nor did it seek specifically to win the ballots of the victims of the guerrilla armies. These it ceded to the PAN and FRG parties advantaged on security and position.

Candidates

Given that URNG was disproportionately blamed for the war, evidence suggests that its leaders realized that it could not run its military personnel for office. It therefore selected for its 1999 presidential candidate a civilian who boasted strong noncoercive credentials. Álvaro Colom was an industrial engineer, a moderate former government official, and the executive director of the government's National Fund for Peace.[134] Colom was "widely recognized as the country's most important democratic leader of the [preceding] 40 years."[135] URNG's vice presidential candidate was an indigenous Kaqchikel Presbyterian minister.[136] Other leading candidates included the leftist UNID and DIA secretary generals, and a Mayan URNG representative. All of its candidates were civilians; and although some had unsavory and violent antecedents, URNG proposed fewer such candidates than did FRG. The effectiveness of URNG's elite selection approach to quell fears about its commitment to peaceful political contestation reveals itself in the polls: of those who intended to vote for URNG's alliance, ANN, 17 percent said they would do so because it had a good presidential candidate. An additional 19 percent of people who planned to vote for the alliance would do so because they believed it had honest people, 17 percent because it had capable people.[137]

Media and Persuasion

In Guatemala, unlike in El Salvador, it was not the government belligerent party, but instead the *non*belligerent party that had an advantage in the persuasion of voters. As the electoral incumbent, PAN benefitted from "control of government and state-financed publicity."[138] PAN also had the closest ties to the country's business elite,[139] enjoying the support of its most important organization: the Coordinating Committee of Chambers of Agro, Commerce, Industry, and Finance.[140] PAN had the largest campaign budget[141] and outspent the other parties. The URNG had scant funds or dissemination tools, apart from its unpaid grassroots organizers.[142] FRG, meanwhile, benefitted from a singular ally: media owner Remigio Ángel González who poured a large sum of money into FRG's campaign and afforded it free airtime. FRG enjoyed the loyalty of some PAC militias that could help spread its political message. It also had a leader—Ríos

Montt—who proved masterful at manipulating "images and information" to create "new social constructions of 'reality'" through a hypnotic mixture of "religion, racism, security, nationalism, and capitalism."[143] Therefore, although PAN made a "millionaire investment" in its campaign,[144] both PAN and FRG enjoyed some material and political communication resources.

Voters

Did the PAN, FRG, and URNG's tactics for positioning themselves programmatically, narrating the bloodstained past, prioritizing voters, and choosing candidates have their intended consequences on citizens' perceptions, preferences and electoral behavior?

Credit for Peace

Whereas in El Salvador, the war party was also the peace party, in Guatemala, these diverged. It was the noncombatant party PAN, not FRG, that negotiated and signed Guatemala's peace accords. However, said Guatemalan scholar Ricardo Sáenz de Tejada, "Peace [was] not really attributed to [PAN's leader] Arzú."[145] While there was a "resounding affirmation of something called 'peace' . . . the peace *accords* [did] not figure strongly in the minds of the majority of the population," which voted *against* the accords in the referendum. However, "peace apparently [did figure strongly in the voting], at least in terms of the absence of war and increased security in the lives of people and their families."[146] The population gave FRG credit for bringing about this latter notion of peace. According to Sáenz de Tejada, in the Guatemalan historical memory, "peace is associated with the FRG. In 1981–1982, the massacres were crazy, out of control, but in March 1982, Ríos Montt managed to organize this violence. So, Ríos Montt is not seen as genocidal but as the peacemaker. People view him as the *pacifier*."[147] Using first-hand accounts, Virginia Garrard-Burnett 2010 exposes how, in zones of conflict, many people whom Ríos Montt's government policies affected directly, even those who had lost family or livelihood, nonetheless accepted that Ríos Montt offered some sort of coherent safety and order. "For many Guatemalans, [given their reference point,] the . . . general was an improvement." Through ethnography, David Stoll 1990 documents how Guatemalans described Ríos Montt's predecessor, Lucas García: "'A campesino seen was a campesino dead,' in contrast to Ríos Montt, whom they credited with saving their lives. 'If it hadn't been for Ríos Montt,

we all would have disappeared! Before, there were killers waiting on the corner; you couldn't even go out, because they would kill you. But Ríos Montt
took away all that.'" Ultimately, the population seems to have tolerated state
terror under Ríos Montt not because it was different, but because they believed that it "put an end to the violence."[148] They did not so perceive the
URNG.[149] Meanwhile, Guatemalans assessed PAN, on the one hand, as the
credible alternative to the "violence and corruption of the military" party,[150]
and, on the other hand, as relatively uncreditworthy for ending the ruthless
bloodshed and bringing security.[151] Polls show PAN leaders such as Arzú and
Berger enjoying neutral to positive favorability scores.[152]

Blame for Wartime Violence

Observers remarked upon the "highly selective nature of [voters'] memory."
Rather than blaming FRG for the genocidal violence, many sectors, especially
the indigenous (who were 83 percent of the victims),[153] "showered Ríos Montt
with encomiums, describing him as a visionary leader, a champion of law and
order, and a messenger of hope in the midst of despair."[154] "The General may
have violated human rights, but it was only in an effort to protect the . . .
people,"[155] defended one interviewee. Survey evidence shows that the population came to see the URNG rebels, not FRG, as more responsible for the
wartime violence.[156] FRG managed to launder its reputation for protection,
which it could employ to seek votes on prospective security grounds.

Preference for Belligerent's Ironfisted Security

During the period of uncertainty, as the country moved from conflict to postconflict and the population faced sky-rocketing insecurity and crime, polls
suggest that a majority of the citizenry (62 percent) defied the expectations of
international and domestic observers and even the parties themselves to favor
ironfisted security to rule-based security. The population viewed, on security
issues, the war winner, though blood-drenched, FRG as the most competent
contender, even over untainted PAN, and even though PAN was deemed to
have more competent leaders in general.[157]

Of the population, 70 percent responded that it was better "to live in an
orderly society even with limitations on some liberties than to respect all
rights and liberties even if this causes some disorder."[158] According to David
Stoll, Guatemalans reported, "We need a strongman to control us."[159] Even in

survey questions where social desirability would bias responses in favor of human rights, 43 percent expressed support for violating these rights, if it provided security, over never violating people's rights.[160]

It seems that Guatemala's voters viewed competence on security as linked to military experience and the military uniform. "De facto, the army is the country's most destructive institution, responsible for the murder of tens of thousands of citizens. De jure, it maintains peace and stability."[161] Whereas a civilian government was deemed by nearly all Guatemalans (90 percent) to be better able to solve problems of unemployment, worker rights, poverty, external debt, and inflation, a military government was deemed by 25 percent of the population as better able to resolve political violence, and by 31 percent of the population as better able to resolve crime.[162]

As a result, both FRG's Ríos Montt and Portillo came across as candidates *more* capable of dealing with insecurity.[163] "Since his days of leading military campaigns, Ríos Montt had successfully cultivated his appeal as a law-and-order candidate."[164] According to key peace negotiator, Héctor Rosada Granados, "In his election, the issue of Ríos Montt's massacres never came up."[165] Instead Ríos Montt, "a General responsible for carnage," paradoxically became perceived as a Hobbesian sovereign, "a symbol of national redemption. The uniform in his campaign picture held out the hope, however illusory, that he could overpower the most flagrant abusers of authority."[166]

Winning Security, Swing, and Victimized Votes

According to the model, the nonbelligerent party is likely to lose voters who care about security, such as swing voters, and war victims.[167] I analyze LAPOP 1999 survey data, which asked respondents their intended vote choice and the basis of that choice. Citizens who intended to make their electoral choice on security grounds were eight times more likely to vote for the FRG than if they planned to vote based on other issues. Of those who would base their electoral choice on the party best able to provide order and security (22 percent of the population), a staggering 85 percent would choose the FRG, in contrast to 42 percent of those who would base their vote choice on other issues. Of those who felt very safe, 45.6 percent intended to vote for FRG, while 60 percent of those who felt very insecure planned to vote for FRG.[168] Of those who would vote for FRG, 37 percent reported doing so because FRG would bring order or effectively fight crime. Of those who intended to vote for other parties, only 7 percent reported doing so because of a belief that they would bring order or fight crime. Only 2.78 percent of the voters surveyed planned to elect the war-loser rebel coalition on its ability to fight crime, and no one said they would do so because they thought it would bring order.[169]

Contrary to early predictions, Ríos Montt's electoral support was not limited to its core.[170] The importance of FRG's party strategy becomes clear in the number of voters it won during the campaign. (This further casts doubt on a wartime popular support argument, which I discuss below.)[171] "Both the PAN and the FRG started the campaign with similar levels of public support. In April 1999, . . . the two parties were supported by 29% and 21% of the electorate, respectively. By October, the FRG had increased its support level to 46%. After six months of campaigning, however, the PAN remained stuck at 29% support."[172]

Of Guatemalans, 88 percent did not have a party affiliation in 1999. FRG was poised to win 86 percent of voters who had cast votes for it in 1995, but also 35 percent of previous PAN voters and 50 percent of those who had not voted in the 1995 elections. Of the population, 59 percent seems to have swung to FRG. These were not ideological votes: only 12 percent reported intending to vote for FRG because they shared its political ideas.[173] Describing Ríos Montt, a U.S. state department cable had noted, "He cannot be accurately catalogued as right or left: he is a Latin American populist—demagogue to his detractors—with undeniable pull among the lower middle and working classes . . . [for whom] law and order issues have major significance."[174] FRG won across the right-left spectrum (the population as a whole also fell relatively evenly across this spectrum). (See Figure 6.3.)

These results surprised observers. U.S. embassy analysts had not expected Ríos Montt to win over large parts of the population: "He alienates the Catholic hierarchy and practicing Catholics. He is not trusted by businessmen. Some in rural areas fear a return of tough counterinsurgency in which killing subversives would be acceptable."[175] But FRG "was able to move beyond Ríos Montt's traditional base."[176] In the 1999 election, FRG performed well with Protestants and Catholics. It won votes across income levels.[177] It won in urban areas, but performed best in rural areas.

By winning security and unaligned voters, FRG gained 47.7 percent of the first-round presidential vote and 68.3 percent in the runoff in Guatemala's 1999 election. In the legislative elections, the FRG won 63 out of the 113 seats, and it won 153 of 331 municipalities.[178]

PAN's Rule Abider strategy largely paid off with its core voters, but not with security and unaligned voters.[179] PAN therefore skimmed the book's

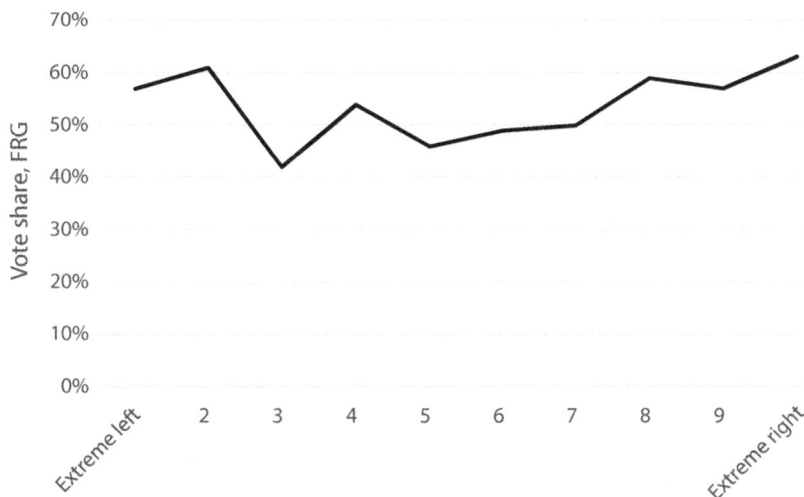

FIGURE 6.3. FRG Vote Share across Ideological Spectrum.

threshold of electoral success; it won 30.3 percent in the first round and 31.7 percent in the run-off. It won 37 legislative seats and 108 municipalities.

Meanwhile, URNG resurrected itself from its military defeat to win traction in the first postwar elections, although it fell well short of electoral success. With a strategy of Tactical Immoderation, its coalition ANN won 12.4 percent of the first-round presidential vote, 9 congressional seats (of 113), and 13 municipalities (of 331).[180] These votes were mainly from its activists and those positionally aligned: 20 percent of those intending to vote for URNG reported that it was because they shared its political ideas. It won votes only from the moderate to extreme left of the ideological scale, signaling that it was well defined as positionally off-center.[181]

Winning Some Victims' Votes

With its favorable electoral strategies, FRG managed to win even the votes of some of the government's civil war victims. I use fine-grained data to analyze the relationship between municipal-level violence from the CIIDH database[182] and voting from the Guatemalan Tribunal Supremo Electoral.[183] The analysis shows that FRG won a majority of the vote across municipalities, irrespective of whether the government was responsible for minimal or extreme levels of violence in the municipality during Ríos Montt's administration

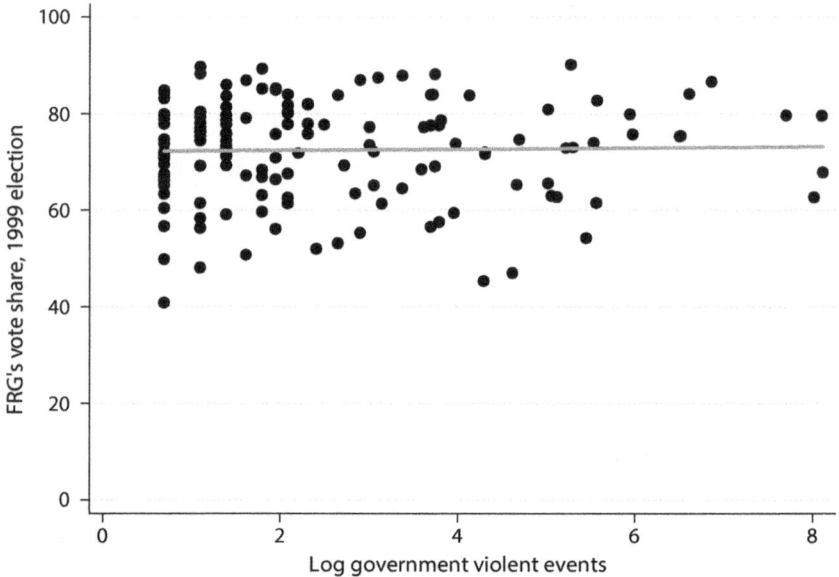

FIGURE 6.4. Wartime Government Atrocities and FRG Postwar Vote Share at the Municipal Level.

(Figure 6.4). It was therefore not only in regions that might have benefited from the government's transgressions that FRG performed well.[184]

I employ LAPOP 1999 survey data to address the challenge of studying victims' political behavior with voting data aggregated at the municipal level. Respondents are coded as victims or nonvictims of the conflict, based on their responses to the question, "During the armed conflict did you or any member of your family suffer any type of political violence such as kidnappings, murders, bombings or killings?" Given the time that had elapsed between the height of the hostilities and the survey, and the relatively robust response rate in the affirmative, it seems that, even without sensitive question techniques, this victimization question elicited truthful responses. LAPOP also asked respondents about intended vote choice. Among direct victims of the violence, of which approximately 90 percent would have been victims of the government given the representative national sample, 47 percent stated that they intended to vote for FRG. Only 36 percent of victims of the violence planned to vote for nonbelligerent PAN, which had only a peaceful record. Of the war's victims, 8 percent stated an intention to vote for the successor to the URNG rebels that used restrained violence during the war. Tellingly, 84 percent of victims who declared voting on security lines supported the FRG. It should be noted that the theory does not predict that victims will vote for blood-stained parties at a higher rate than nonvictims; rather the theory seeks to account for the particularly puzzling pattern that some (or any) victims voted for the FRG, and did so over the PAN. My own qualitative work and other scholars' deep ethnographic dives into Guatemala's war-torn regions align with these survey findings of victims of the war victor casting ballots for their tormentors.

Alternative Explanations

The evidentiary basis for the Guatemalan case study is consistent with the party and political behavior anticipated by the book's theory. The posited pathway to varied electoral performance and the steps of that pathway, however, might nonetheless be explained better by alternative frameworks, which I explore next.

Popular Support

As the Salvadoran case, an argument centered on underlying political preferences is challenged to explain the Guatemalan 1999 elections. Like its neighbor, Guatemala underscores how war outcomes may run independent of underlying popular support. The rebel forces' base of support gyrated from near zero in the 1970s to "over 360,000 (and possibly up to 500,000) supporters" in the early 1980s, falling back again to near zero by the early 1990s.[185] With allegiances thus fluid, wartime outcomes may have driven (a lack of) popular support for the rebels, rather than the other way around. Similarly, the government belligerent, despite representing the same ideological political platform throughout the conflict, was virtually a pariah under Lucas García's regime, but gained hero status under Ríos Montt. If underlying identities and partisanship were driving voting, we might anticipate superior performance by the more positionally credible center-right PAN, which explicitly stood for a defined program and which better represented the moderate right-wing voter, than by the far-right FRG opposition, which disingenuously whitewashed its positions. What is more, the analysis focuses specifically on the behavior of the nonideological voters, those without deep-rooted partisan bonds and preferences; such voters were numerous and decisive in the Guatemalan context. A popular support logic cannot account for their vote choice.

Partisan Issue Ownership

That both PAN and FRG were right-wing, and that FRG obscured its partisan identity to the point of nonrecognition, raise questions about a partisan explanation of security issue ownership. If the political right "owned" the security issue, we would anticipate voters perceiving PAN and FRG as equally competent on security, and security voters voting for them in equal measure. Additionally, if the right always favors strongarm security, we would not observe divergence in security strategies between the two right-wing parties, PAN and FRG. And, if the right always wins on the security issue, we would observe FRG's decision to run a progressive campaign causing damage to its ownership of the security issue. Instead, we observe its belligerent status overtaking partisan identity as a driver of voters' perceptions of issue competence. The facts on the ground diverge from the observable implications of a partisan issue ownership explanation to this case.

Incumbency

The body of evidence from Guatemala further casts doubt on the incumbency argument, and particularly on the variant centered on electoral incumbency: that the incumbent benefits from a variety of assets that might enable it to win both the war and the elections. In the Guatemalan case, the party that won the war was an opposition party at the time of the founding elections. Despite its incumbent status, PAN was unable to translate this advantage into an electoral win. Some have argued that the Guatemalan elections of 1999 therefore may be understood as demonstrating a strong anti-incumbency vote.[186] However, this argument tends to be made post facto, based on the known outcome of an incumbent loss. El Salvador provides a useful counterfactual: both Guatemala's PAN and El Salvador's ARENA were right-wing incumbents at the time of the founding elections, both successfully negotiated peace accords, both ruled over war-decimated economies in crisis and escalating crime, and both began to resurrect these economies with some competence, but could not forestall the new wave of insecurity. If the anti-incumbency argument is correct, then voting outcomes—based on the governing administrations' similarly uneven records—should have been similar. If we take into consideration the greatest difference between them—that ARENA was also bloodstained—we would expect that anti-incumbency voting in newly free elections would take down soiled ARENA sooner than clean PAN. Incumbency cannot explain both ARENA's win and PAN's loss. But belligerent status and war outcomes can. What is more, public opinion of PAN's handling of the country was mixed, but a majority believed the government of Arzú had done a good or very good job of combatting crime (57 percent), combatting corruption (52 percent), improving health (75 percent), improving education (84 percent), and complying with the peace accords (76 percent), suggesting that the political mood ahead of Guatemala's 1999 elections was not strongly anti-incumbent.[187]

Others have advanced an alternative (anti-)incumbency logic in this case: that FRG's win merely reflects the pattern in Guatemala that no incumbent party has won reelection since the first quasi-democratic elections of 1985. This pattern renders incumbency in Guatemala a likely liability rather than advantage. This empirical regularity, however, became clear only after 1999; during the time period with which this chapter is concerned, scholars consider Guatemala's parties to have been fairly consolidated: over the course of multiple electoral cycles, the same parties won a sizeable share of the vote. (This, of course, changed dramatically thereafter.)[188]

Organizational Assets

Organizational asset arguments face similar conundrums in this case. PAN had financial, organizational, and patronage advantages over the FRG and URNG. It had the largest campaign budget and state-financed publicity, and it was able to outspend the other parties.[189] Its control of government further enabled it to offer public works, including large-scale infrastructure projects[190] and patronage.[191] FRG had the mobilization resource of the PAC militias, but their loyalty was highly uneven[192] and PAN rivaled this asset with control of the state apparatus. These advantages did not translate into a superior electoral performance; an organizational endowment explanation leaves variation in political behavior unexplained.

Coercion

The Guatemalan armed forces under General Ríos Montt terrorized the population on a scale that undoubtedly sowed the seeds of lasting fear. This raises doubts about whether voters could have cast their ballots in line with their preferences. That Ríos Montt performed better in rural areas, in which the population was more vulnerable, underscores this concern. However, the OAS

Electoral Mission received only 108 complaints, and these were not concentrated where the FRG won; the OAS "was aware of no complaints that might have affected or hindered the normal conduct of voting."[193] FRG also did not seem to gain a disproportionate share of votes from those casting their ballots with trepidation. Of the population, 83 percent said they would vote in an election "with complete liberty"; the remaining 17 percent said they would vote with some degree of fear. The FRG won 51 percent of those in the former category; it won 54 percent of those who stated that they would vote in an election "with a great deal of fear," a statistically insignificant difference. FRG did not win outright in the first round. Instead, there was a large increase in votes for FRG in the second round, suggesting that voters were willing to cast their ballots for other parties initially, and then to shift to FRG; this outcome is inconsistent with a story of coercion. What is more, if fear were driving the election—either specific fear of direct retribution or a more diffuse fear of a return to violence—voters would not have elected nonbelligerent parties including PAN during the war when the belligerent parties' capacity for violence was even greater.

Ideology and Economic Voting

Finally, it could be that FRG's electoral success, particularly among security voters, can be explained by other determinants of vote choice, namely ideology or economic voting. To assess this possibility, I use LAPOP 1999 data on the basis of respondents' intended vote choice. I analyze whether the significant effect of security voting on vote choice for FRG remains when I control for these other drivers of political behavior. Consistent with the analyses above, Table 6.2, models 1 and 2 indicate a robust positive relationship between voting on security lines and choosing FRG whereas models 3 and 4 show a strong, negative relationship between those making their vote choice on security lines and opting to vote for PAN.[194] Partisanship ran shallow in Guatemala—the vast majority of voters did not subscribe to a party identification—and sharing political ideology with the FRG did not seem to influence vote choice for the belligerent successor; indeed, security voting is the strongest determinant of voting for this party.

A multitude of factors undoubtedly influenced the 1999 elections in Guatemala. However, the analysis provides strong support for the importance of war outcomes, and party strategy, in accounting for the electoral choice of swing and security voters, a bloc of voters that proved determinative.

TABLE 6.2. Determinants of Vote Choice, Guatemala 1999

Variables	(1) Vote FRG	(2) Vote FRG	(3) Vote PAN	(4) Vote PAN
Security voting	0.40***	2.18***	−0.34***	−2.25***
	(0.05)	(0.31)	(0.05)	(0.37)
Material voting	−0.04	−0.20	0.02	0.13
	(0.06)	(0.28)	(0.06)	(0.29)
Ideological voting	0.02	0.09	−0.12**	−0.58*
	(0.06)	(0.30)	(0.06)	(0.31)
Other	−0.07	−0.36	0.06	0.31
	(0.07)	(0.33)	(0.07)	(0.32)
Constant	0.58***	0.54	0.26	−1.18
	(0.18)	(0.88)	(0.17)	(0.93)
Model	OLS	Logit	OLS	Logit
Observations	592	592	592	592
R^2	.24		.19	

Note: Standard errors in parentheses. The independent variable is a five-category indicator explaining intended vote choice: *security* if the party's ability to establish order or resolve the problem of crime determined the respondent's vote choice; *material* if the party's ability to resolve the problem of poverty and cost of living determined vote choice; and *ideology* if the respondents indicated they would vote for the party because it "shared their political ideas." For the 10.9% of respondents who answered other reasons for their vote choice, a variable, *other*, is coded as 1. The omitted value of the categorical variable is leadership: voting for the party because it had a good presidential candidate, good legislative candidates, or honest or capable people. All models include controls for region, gender, age, education, religion, occupation, and ownership of goods.

*$p < .1$. **$p < .05$. ***$p < .01$.

These war outcomes and political strategies were not randomized and the counterfactuals are not observable. We cannot therefore establish what would have happened had the war ended in a different way or if the parties had adopted off-equilibrium strategies. The former is easier to imagine. Had the war outcome been different—for example, a military draw—URNG would have likely constituted a serious contender in the elections and, with an impressive war record, it could have sought to exonerate its own violent past and to claim the security valence issue. Such a dynamic would have forced FRG to work much harder to spin its bloody past and claim Leviathan status, and to undermine URNG's ability to do so. Media control would have likely mattered more. In a three-way race, the wartime belligerents might have squeezed out PAN, but more likely, if PAN remained the incumbent, the race might have been truly a multiparty one.

The counterfactual thought exercise becomes more difficult when it comes to party strategy. It seems highly plausible that, had FRG shown contrition—accepting responsibility for genocide—this would have played to PAN's strength, by increasing retributive voting against FRG. Had FRG mirrored PAN and run as a Rule Abider, selecting only untainted civilians, promising rule-based security, and retaining a right-wing position, it seems unlikely that it would have outperformed PAN. Similarly, if PAN had opted to ignore its rivals' bloodied past and to run as a Leviathan, cultivating a strongman as the face of its party, downplaying explicit positions, and advocating hard-line security, it is hard to imagine it overtaking FRG. And had incumbent PAN run as a Leviathan and opposition FRG, as the second mover seeking to differentiate itself, run as a Rule Abider, such a trading of strategies would likely have seemed inauthentic to voters, diluting the parties' brands to the point of non-recognition, and opening them to accusations of opportunistic selling out. Neither party had the past experience or reputation to back up these alternative strategies and render them convincing. That PAN did not have the organizational endowment to support a Leviathan strategy—it lacked a caudillo and, more importantly, lacked a history of "strength able to overawe"—helps explain why PAN did not pursue a Restrained Leviathan strategy, even though that is what ultimately proved electorally most successful. PAN did not opt for this strategy also because, consistent with the framework's assumption of ex ante uncertainty about which party has valence advantages, it did not predict that voters would, in fact, choose a genocidal party over a democratic one to provide societal peace.

Implications

This section turns, briefly, to consider the implications of Guatemala's founding election results for peace, justice, security, and political development.

Peace

The 1999 elections sealed Guatemala's transition from civil war. The war outcome of government victory had rendered the elections effectively a two-party competition between the war-winner party and the noncombatant incumbent party. Accordingly, as predicted by the theory, there existed little chance that the war-vanquished URNG could win the election, and thus little chance that the armed forces would have an incentive to return to violence in response to such a win. URNG, too, had little reason, after losing the elections, to remilitarize. With the balance of power between the belligerents stable after the accords, URNG had no real prospect of strengthening in a second round of fighting, in the hope of contesting future elections from a different war outcome. Had PAN won the election, a return to war also seems unlikely, as the government belligerent successor had already permitted PAN to win in the 1995 elections. The 1999 elections were therefore positioned to consolidate peace. FRG's victory nonetheless kept the military—potentially skittish at the concessions of the peace agreement—in their barracks and signaled to would-be detractors a return of an ironfisted commitment to order. The civil war terminated sustainably.

Transitional Justice, Violence, and the Security Brand

FRG's electoral success did not, however, bode well for transitional justice.[195] FRG confirmed amnesty for genocide and quashed security-sector reform in the short term. While in political office, Ríos Montt enjoyed parliamentary immunity, which shielded him from legal prosecution for human rights violations carried out during his dictatorship. Over time, however, as anticipated by the theory, the clamor for transitional justice grew louder and Ríos Montt found himself in legal jeopardy. By 2007, Spanish judge Santiago Pedraz issued an arrest warrant for Ríos Montt. In 2012, when the end of his legislative term also terminated his immunity, Guatemalan prosecutors brought a genocide case against him. He was convicted in 2013.[196]

This delay in justice, and the foreclosure of any attempt at reforming the coercive apparatus, fertilized a homicidal climate in Guatemala.[197] Guatemala, like El Salvador, suffered under one of the highest and most relentless violence rates in the world.[198] Once in office, "Ríos Montt and the FRG [thus] faced a backlash due to their total failure to curb Guatemala's violent crime epidemic."[199] This diluted FRG's security brand and FRG became unable to continue to leverage its winning belligerent inheritance.[200] This raises the prospect of a moral hazard problem for parties who do well when security is salient having an incentive to stir up insecurity in order to keep it salient. Other army candidates attempted to run on the brand, but tended to perform "very badly."[201] For example, in 2007, retired general Otto Pérez Molina resurrected the brand against the left-wing Álvaro Colom. His campaign met with "[television] ads and posters that . . . he was a murderer . . . [with] photos of [him] in the Ixchil area," notorious for the government's genocidal violence there. In

2011, this time facing Manuel Antonio Baldizón Méndez, Pérez Molina again sold himself "as a general of peace but also offer[ed] an iron fist."[202] This time, he succeeded, suggesting that the brand's effective revivification might depend on the type of opposition candidate it confronts.[203]

Party System

Finally, FRG's election may have portended the fragmentation of Guatemala's party system. In the 1990s, Guatemala's political system, despite its nascence, was dominated by parties achieving conventional standards of success and consolidation: over the course of multiple rounds of polling, the same parties won a significant proportion of the vote.[204] However, this changed in 2000. Born of political struggle, FRG and URNG could have established themselves as institutionalized parties by developing a ground game and responsive politics, as ARENA and FMLN did in El Salvador. Instead, over time, both failed to do so.[205] FRG, like ARENA, enjoyed support from civilian paramilitary groups (PACs) which, in 1983, numbered approximately 700,000 members, nearly 10 percent of the country's population.[206] However, unlike ARENA, FRG did not service this organizational network for party building. As a result, the militias' allegiances became far more fluid than in El Salvador, and they supported not just FRG, but "instead [parties across] the full ideological spectrum."[207] URNG similarly did little to cultivate its political organizers[208] and activate its base,[209] and both parties failed to develop clientelistic tentacles with which to ensnare voters in a lasting grip. As a result, FRG and URNG experienced waning success over time, and eventually disappeared from the political arena.[210] Guatemala came to constitute "a party non-system": an "inchoate party structure," a "case study in underinstitutionalization."[211] These longitudinal dynamics, and particularly why and how some parties founded by war effectively develop electoral machines whereas others do not, constitute a fruitful area for future inquiry.

Conclusion

The Guatemalan case presents a particularly puzzling and troubling case of citizens voting for political actors who had committed gross violations of human rights against the civilian population. Despite violence on the scale of genocide, Ríos Montt and his FRG party won the postwar elections and did so against a viable incumbent party without blood on its hands. The analysis suggests that this outcome cannot be explained by FRG coercing or threatening the electorate. Neither FRG's opposition status or right-wing origins, nor voters' preexisting allegiances, can account for FRG's electoral success. Instead, the data suggest that FRG performed well because the military victory of its combatant predecessor allowed it to claim credit for war termination and to gain a reputation for competence on security. Living through the transition, voters surprised the parties and observers alike by preferring belligerent security to the rule-abider variant on offer by the nonbelligerent party. Voting for a victimizer to provide societal peace nonetheless might have produced cognitive dissonance, at least, had FRG not managed to exonerate itself effectively by arguing that its violence brought an end to the country's violence and, as such, became justified, and had it not provided some reassurances—even if only in the form of a fig leaf of rhetoric and a laundered slate of candidates—that it would not turn its guns against the population again. Despite noncombatant PAN offering what, on its face, should have been a successful counter to FRG—that voters should use their ballots to punish human rights abusers and elect a party whose unbloodied past presaged a safe future—these appeals fell on deaf ears, particularly those of voters most desperate for security. These voters proved sufficiently numerous to swing the elections in FRG's favor. Once in office, FRG prevented a return to civil war and resurgence of political violence. However, it failed to tame crime and, as it did, FRG's security brand eroded and its logic of mitigating its horrific past with its provision of order became less convincing. Voters' frames of reference shifted back, and they again compared the past atrocities to a world in which no such atrocities had transpired. Ríos Montt could escape the dark shadows from his past no longer. He faced conviction for genocide and FRG lost electoral power.

The Guatemalan war ended in military victory for the government side. It is possible that there are underlying factors that allowed the government to win the war and also caused the government belligerent party, FRG, to perform well in the election. It merits testing whether there exists symmetry as the book's theory predicts; that is, whether rebel victory results in similar electoral success and whether rebel victors adopt strategies similar to those of government belligerent victors to promise to secure the future. The next chapter journeys to a shadow case of Nicaragua to undertake this test.

7

Rebel Victory in Nicaragua

THIS CHAPTER TRACES political life after the Nicaraguan civil war between the Somoza regime and the Sandinista rebels (1961–1979). The book argues that military war outcomes influence the strategies by which the parties of former combatants seek votes from war-ravaged populations; these strategies, in turn, guide whether victimized populations elect the successor parties to govern. Chapter 5 on El Salvador studied these dynamics in the case of a military draw, the Guatemala Chapter 6 in the case of government victory. This chapter examines the case where the rebels were victorious. The goals of this case study in the book, however, are circumscribed, due to important caveats to the case—it skirts the book's scope conditions—and data limitations—it lacks contemporaneous polling data. In general, the book models rebel victory as symmetrical to government victory. The preceding chapter tested the book's party-level hypotheses in the case of a military victory, so I do not seek to repeat those tests here. However, in the Guatemalan case, two factors covaried with war outcomes: government belligerent status and right-wing partisanship. This chapter uses evidence from Nicaragua to disentangle these variables, to verify that the dynamics of a rebel win largely mirror those of a government win, and to establish that neither the nature of the warring side as government or rebel, nor its partisan identity as right or left, can account better for belligerent parties' strategies and victimized populations' political behavior.

The book's theory anticipates that war outcomes will have far more impact than these other determinants of party strategy. In particular, it expects left-wing rebel victors to be likely to behave similarly to right-wing government victors: to run as Restrained Leviathans. Conversely, the framework expects that right-wing government belligerents, if defeated militarily, will be likely to behave similarly to vanquished parties of a left-wing, rebel flavor: they will adopt a strategy of Tactical Immoderation. This shadow case evaluates these

observable implications in the aftermath of the victory of the socialist Sandinista rebels, and the defeat of the conservative governing Somozas in 1979.

Backdrop of War and Peace

Nicaragua suffered a long, entrenched, and cruel dictatorship, which came
to power by coup in 1936. Despite a succession of farcical elections featuring
vote-buying, stuffed ballot boxes, and frequent rewriting of electoral laws, the
Somoza dynasty—Anastasio Somoza and his sons Luis and Anastasio—
effectively ruled Nicaragua until 1979. The dynasty's power derived from its
authoritarian political party, an alliance with the National Conservative
party, backing from the United States, and hegemonic military force concentrated in a personal army, the National Guard.[1] The Somozas governed
through repression of any perceived opposition and its suspected support
base. They were highly corrupt, plundering the nation's resources for their
private benefit.[2]

To confront this brutal and kleptocratic rule, an armed movement emerged
in 1961. The Sandinista National Liberation Front (FSLN) named itself after
Augusto Sandino, the anti-imperialist hero whom Somoza had murdered in
1934. Despite a potentially fertile environment for revolt, the Sandinista force
was all but expired by the end of the 1960s: "its military forays had been crushed
and most of its top leaders were jailed or in exile." Forced underground, it then
engaged in intensive organizing. After five years of training, it resurfaced with
a spectacular attack—the Casa de Chema Castillo raid[3]—in the aftermath of
which "recruits poured in, and soon the rebellion was on in earnest."[4]

Balance of Atrocities

Somoza responded to this uptick in armed dissidence with indiscriminate terror. His forces pulled young boys from their homes and left their dead bodies
in "vacant lots by the side of the highway or in garbage bins. Their arms [were]
broken; their eyes torn out; their tongues [were] cut."[5] As Somoza cracked
down on more and more sectors of society, his air force bombed towns,[6] and
his National Guard perpetrated brutal atrocities against nonviolent protests
and strikes. In response, these sectors politicized, radicalized, and joined a
united broad-based revolutionary coalition.[7] In the course of their armed insurgency, the Sandinistas too used violence and brutality.[8] Most accounts
characterize the violence against Somoza supporters as restrained in nature.

However, the records that could have verified the relative balance of atrocities were destroyed;[9] there was never a truth commission in Nicaragua as in the book's other case studies;[10] and the Sandinistas alone wrote the history, clouding any understanding of their side's responsibility for violence in a civil war that ultimately stole the lives of fifty thousand.[11] Nonetheless, it is fair to conclude that victimization and war outcomes generally covaried in Nicaragua, and thus this case cannot separate out and assess their independent effects. El Salvador and Guatemala have already provided sharp tests of the victimization logic, while Chapter 8's cross-national dataset evaluates the relationship between belligerents' wartime atrocities and their founding electoral performance across all postwar cases around the world between 1970 and 2015. This case study therefore omits a discussion of how the parties laundered their violent pasts.

War Outcome

In mass insurrection, FSLN, allied with a heterogenous front of Nicaraguans, overthrew the Somoza dictatorship in 1979.[12] The Sandinistas were the armed wing of the revolution, but the support base for overthrowing Somoza was much broader and balanced between belligerent and nonbelligerent factions.[13] The revolution ended with Somoza's negotiated exile to Miami. However, Interim President Francisco Urcuyo Maliaños reneged on this deal and announced his intention to remain in power. In response, the Sandinista rebels flooded from their rural strongholds to engage in an armed takeover of Nicaragua's cities, a spectacular show of force that brought Somoza's army to its knees. It also gave the FSLN the upper hand within the revolutionary junta.[14] In effect, while the mass insurrection had forced the ousting of Somoza, the Sandinista army was ultimately credited with bringing an end to the violence of the Nicaraguan civil war and an end to the dictatorship. Other sectors of society that had also supported the revolution could not bask in the revolutionary limelight. In 1979, the Sandinistas claimed rebel victory and the war ended.

Skirting the Scope Conditions: Postwar Democratic Elections

Following what the Sandinistas called the "War of Liberation," peace was short-lived and the nation experienced further violence, denying this case postwar status. The relative power of the belligerents shifted after the revolution, as large-scale U.S. military support propped up the vanquished government side of the conflict and gave it incentives to remilitarize. This second war pitted the Sandinista revolutionaries against the U.S.-backed counterrevolutionaries known as the Contras. The Contras began forming in 1981–1982 and comprised multiple factions including Somoza National Guard members who had fled into exile in Honduras after their leader's fall,[15] and later, the Anti-Sandinistas Popular Militia, the Democratic Revolutionary Alliance, and the autonomy-seeking Miskito indigenous groups.

According to historian Margarita Vannini, the Somoza National Guard reorganization was "very limited," and the Contra War became full-blown only after the elections in 1984.[16] At their peak in 1986, Contra troops maintained 15,000 to 22,000 members in arms, the Sandinistas 134,000.[17] Nonetheless, by the time of the 1984 elections, there was undoubtedly already another civil war brewing. The elections of 1984 thus constituted founding elections for the preceding civil war, ended in 1979, but did not constitute political life *after* war.

Despite this ongoing violence, the elections themselves were deemed peaceful, but there is debate over whether they were democratic. On the one hand, electoral observers, including the LASA electoral observation mission, concluded that "no party was prevented from carrying out an active campaign." Despite earlier political restrictions, the FSLN granted the opposition campaign funds, allowed it substantial TV and radio access, and permitted it to hold mass rallies.[18] LASA mission members documented, "The vote was truly a secret ballot, and was generally perceived as such by voters. We observed no evidence of irregularities in the voting or vote-counting process. . . . Most voters interviewed by our delegation and by foreign journalists did not feel coerced into going to the polls."[19] A retrospective poll conducted by the survey firm Doxa in 1996 found that only 5.1 percent of lower-class respondents—those most vulnerable to coercion—who voted for the Sandinistas' presidential candidate Daniel Ortega in 1984 responded that the 1984 elections had been unfair.[20] LASA concluded that "neither did the FSLN use its control of mass organizations . . . or police to create a generalized climate of fear and intimidation."[21] Over a thousand foreign and press observers monitored the election and described the election as "scrupulously conducted under procedures . . . that maximized secrecy of the ballot, prohibited pressure on or retaliation against voters and nonvoters alike, and effectively barred fraud."[22] Invalid votes composed only 6.1 percent of the total votes cast. Historian Margarita Vannini summarized, "The election was fair."[23] Nearly 94 percent of the estimated voting-age population registered to vote, and 75 percent cast ballots.[24]

On the other hand, while meeting a minimal procedural definition of democracy, most scholars would argue that the 1984 elections marked a shift from single-party rule to competitive authoritarianism rather than a shift to democracy.[25] The Varieties of Democracy (V-Dem) project shows a much lower electoral democracy score for Nicaragua 1985 (0.361) than it does for the other case studies in the book.[26] What is more, the United States played an outsized role in Nicaragua relative to the other cases; the United States heavily influenced party positions, pressured the FSLN with the Contra War, and successfully encouraged an important part of the Nicaraguan right-wing opposition to boycott the elections. Specifically, the Reagan administration drew up a plan in advance of the electoral season to have its Contra ally, the Nicaraguan Democratic Coordinating Committee (CDN),[27] withdraw late in the campaign alleging unfair electoral conditions, in order to delegitimize the elections.[28] The Contra party FDN handed out pamphlets declaring that "Sandinista Style Elections are worse than Somoza Style ones," with cartoons depicting the Sandinistas holding hostage the electorate, radio, newspapers, and television.[29] The U.S. government propagated, "The Sandinista elections on November 4 will offer no choice at all."[30] While observers of the election at the time, even those who criticized the conduct of the elections and the Sandinistas' heavy hand, did not advance the counterfactual that the electorate voted against their preferences and that, had they been given a more varied choice set, they would have voted differently,[31] given the withdrawal of important parties, it is challenging to interpret the electoral results as reflecting "sincere" voter preferences. Finally, most believe that the FSLN had little intention to give up power in the case of an unfavorable outcome,[32] having already usurped the power of the non-FSLN members of the initial post-1979 Junta de Gobierno and rejected negotiations with parties seen as sympathetic toward the Contras.[33] Given these critical caveats to the 1984 Nicaraguan political contests, and data limitations discussed next, the elections constitute a shadow rather than full test case of the book's theory. These caveats are a greater impediment to evaluating voter behavior and the electoral outcomes. However, they pose less of a challenge for the purposes of assessing how the war outcome of rebel victory influenced party behavior and to disentangle this effect from that of incumbency and ideology.

The Electoral Law of 1984 established the institutional arrangement governing these elections. The presidency would go to the party with a simple majority[34] and the legislative elections would be decided by proportional representation from the country's nine administrative districts, with a provision for seating the defeated presidential candidate of any party that won one-ninetieth (1.1 percent) of the national vote.[35] In this sense, the "electoral system benefited small parties, enhancing the Sandinistas' democratic credentials and broadening the base of representation."[36]

Characterizing the Voters

No public opinion polls exist that shed light on the nature of Nicaragua's electorate in 1984. Declassified diplomatic cables and secondary sources, however, suggest that, during the lead-up to the elections of 1984, citizens' main concerns were security, given the Contra counterrevolutionary mobilization; recovery, given the economic devastation of the war; and reform.[37] United in insurrection against Somoza, the mass movement that underpinned the revolution had developed fault lines, with some in favor of the Sandinistas and others against them.[38] Data are not available on the number of undecided voters in 1984, but experts argue that Nicaragua had an enduring bloc of swing voters or, as Vanessa Castro and Gary Prevost called them, the "mixed middle."[39] In 1990, polls would indicate that 30 to 50 percent were in this category.[40]

The Parties: Belligerent Successors and Nonbelligerents

The victorious Sandinistas (FSLN) in the 1979 revolution transformed themselves into a political party by the same name. Somoza's Partido Liberal Nacionalista (PLN) constituted the successor to the government belligerent, the National Guard. Militarily defeated outright, this party dissolved and was a noncontender in the 1984 election. Factions of the Conservatives (Partido Conservador Demócrata de Nicaragua [PCDN]) and of the Liberals (Partido Liberal Independiente [PLI]), however, became what might be considered quasi-successor parties to the Somocistas.[41] PCDN candidates, in particular, drew on the PLN's ranks and openly expressed sympathy for the National Guard–based counterrevolution.[42] These parties' reincarnations over the 1980s "had the ignominious distinction of being the heirs to Somoza's Liberal Party."[43] "After 1983, exiled Somocistas, who had no party because the Somoza era [PLN] had disintegrated, began to join the PLC, which gradually became the PLI's successor."[44]

In the 1984 elections, these civil war belligerent parties ran against small and largely uncompetitive opposition groupings that had had no armed role in the war and revolution. These nonbelligerent parties included the Partido

Popular Social Cristiano, Movimiento de Acción Popular Marxista Leninista, Partido Comunista de Nicaragua, and Partido Socialista Nicaragüense. At the same time, according to LASA (1984), "the range of options available to the Nicaraguan voter on most issues was broad." In the electoral campaign, "banners, posters, and billboards for the seven contending parties sprang up throughout Nicaragua, in a riot of contrasting colors and clashing ideologies. . . . Voters were offered a range of choices as broad as those available in Western Europe, ranging from the Far Left to the [conservative] PCD[N]."[45] However, the right-wing Coordinadora group boycotted.

This chapter traces how the main contenders—the rebel successor party and quasi-government-successor parties (FSLN and PCDN/PLI)—positioned themselves to activate prospective voting in their favor. Following decisive military victory, the theory predicts that the rebel winner FSLN would adopt a Restrained Leviathan strategy, and the government loser PCDN/PLI a Tactical Immoderate strategy, and that these equilibrium strategies would prove electorally expedient. The evidence generally aligns with these expectations and casts doubt on partisan and (belligerent) incumbency explanations of postwar electoral strategies and outcomes.

Data Sources

To understand political life in the lead-up to the 1984 elections in Nicaragua, I collected the daily coverage of these congressional and presidential campaigns in *El Nuevo Diario* and *La Prensa*. I gathered the parties' platforms and campaign propaganda from the archives of the Instituto de Historia de Nicaragua y Centroamérica in Managua. I scoured the declassified U.S. cables to and from the embassy, National Security Council committee meetings, situation reports, U.S. pro-Contra propaganda, and Contra organization journals, handbooks, and negotiating position papers available in the U.S. Digital National Security Archives, "Nicaragua: The Making of U.S. Policy, 1978–1990." Given the current security conditions in Nicaragua, I was limited in my ability to conduct personal interviews for this case. However, I was able to interview several important Sandinista activists, family members of Violeta Chamorro, a Contra leader, and member of the Junta of National Reconstruction formed after the FSLN's victory. Survey data collected contemporaneously to the 1984 elections are not available. For dynamics over time, I analyze survey data collected by CID/Gallup, by the Venezuelan polling firm Instituto Doxa,[46] and by Belden and Russonello Research for ABC News and the *Washington Post*.

Campaigning to Secure the Future

If partisanship or incumbency at the start of the Sandinista-Somoza war were determining electoral strategies and performance in 1984, we would anticipate that the right-wing government belligerent's successors would have sought to own the hardline security valence issue and would have run strongmen as their candidates. We may further expect these parties to have converged position-ally on the ideological middle in order to emphasize valence over position, and to electorally target swing voters for whom that valence issue was important. In contrast, we would anticipate the left-wing rebel FSLN to have aimed to own nonsecurity valence issues, to diverge positionally by advancing its revo-lutionary agenda, to electorally prioritize progressive voters, and to run civil-ians as the face of its party. Comparing right- and left-wing parties, we might anticipate the right to have been best able to own the security issue. Compar-ing rebel and incumbent belligerent parties, we might expect the incumbent to have outperformed the rebel party electorally.

If, instead, this book's theory is correct and war outcomes guide strategies irrespective of whether the militarily advantaged party is rebel or government, right-wing or left-wing, then we should observe that the right-wing government successors—who were vanquished in this case—would seek to own nonsecu-rity valence issues, advance a nonmainstream agenda, prioritize ideologically aligned voters, and field civilians. We should observe that the left-wing, rebel successor—victorious in this case—would aim to own the hardline security valence issue, moderate itself positionally, emphasize unaligned voters, and run wartime military figures paired with fresh candidates. The evidence is largely compatible with this second set of observable implications.

Platform: Valence Strategies

Although left-wing and derived from a rebel organization, the Sandinista party nonetheless explicitly made its military victory and the security issue the center-piece of its 1984 electoral campaign.[47] Declassified U.S. cables reveal that FSLN stressed its military "triumph."[48] Sandinista commander Daniel Ortega repeatedly insisted that "the Sandinista National Liberation Front was at the forefront of the struggle against the Somocista dictatorship. It lived through the most bitter mo-ments of the defeat of the Somoza dictatorship; it lived through moments of pain when we lost a brother in combat. . . . With the people of Nicaragua, we conquered the right to freedom, independence and peace on July 19, 1979."[49]

FSLN based its competence on issues of "national defense and public security" primarily on its military record.[50] "The Sandinistas enjoyed a number of political assets. . . . Their greatest asset was the fact that their victory had been unconditional. The old National Guard had been defeated and disbanded."[51] Indeed, the Sandinistas' "mandate to rule was partly moral, deriving from the FSLN's eighteen years of anti-Somoza struggle and military victory over the dynasty's National Guard."[52] Writing at the time of the elections, David Close explained how the Sandinistas' "role in leading the revolt against Somoza gives it a legitimacy no other group can claim. . . . The constant identification of the revolution with the Sandinistas gives the FSLN an unfair political advantage."[53] Against the odds, the Sandinistas had won the war, besting the U.S.-backed National Guard, and thereby demonstrating that it was a power "able to overawe" all other forces. FSLN's reputation for credibility on security issues also lay with the fact that it had the strongest linkages to the "new [post-1979] National Army"—Ejército Popular Sandinista—which was to be "commanded by the military chiefs and leaders of the armed movement that put an end to the dictatorship": the Dirección Nacional of the FSLN.[54] The FSLN party had the ability to control, deploy, and restrain this new coercive institution.[55] FSLN embraced its own wartime use of aggression, arguing that it was justified by the success of its insurrection;[56] however, with atrocities asymmetric in the armed conflict, it did not need to work hard to shift citizens' frames of reference of the violent past.

Despite their right-wing posture and connections to the incumbent government belligerent, PCDN and PLI did not prioritize the security valence issue. Whereas the Sandinistas devoted 16 percent of their party manifesto to security issues, PCDN devoted only 6 percent.[57] PLI had no security section nor even any mention of security or defense in its party program.[58] Contrary to a partisan explanation, neither of these right-wing parties emphasized hard-on-security positions. If anything, PCDN's security policies were soft on security, promising reform and demilitarization. These right-wing (quasi) government successors instead emphasized other valence issues and sought to redirect the discussion away from security, on which the incumbent's military record rendered them weak.[59] The flavor of their preferred topics may be gleaned from PLI slogans painted on walls in the town of San Carlos: "No more rice and beans!"—attacking food shortages and poverty—and "Democracy, yes! Communism, no!"[60] That it was the right-wing parties running on economic and social issues instead of security issues in this election offers support for the book's claims that military outcome, rather than partisanship, influences attempts to own the security issue.

Platform: Positional Strategies

FSLN had fought and come to power to enact a revolutionary agenda of land reform, education, and social welfare. If ideology determined positional placement, we would anticipate the Sandinistas' program to be far left-wing in character. If instead war outcomes incentivized this war-winner party to highlight the security valence issue and downplay position, we would expect FSLN, despite possessing a Marxist identity and policies,[61] to have campaigned on a moderate platform.

After training the ri-le classifier on the Party Manifesto Project text data (as described in the introduction to the case study chapters), I used it to classify the FSLN program into right or left texts.[62] After text cleaning, the classifier found 24.1 percent of the sentences in the manifesto likely to be ideologically "left" and 38.3 percent of them likely to be ideologically "right" in nature. On the −100 to 100 left-right spectrum, this yielded for the FSLN a ri-le score of 14.18, indicating a moderate program leaning slightly to the political right. Given the improbability of a Marxist revolutionary movement converging in such a way, this finding, even if highly noisy, appears consistent with the model's argument that war outcomes drive positional placement. I compare this moderation by victor FSLN with the programmatic positioning of the militarily vanquished (quasi) successor parties. Much of the PLI's program text was, unfortunately, somewhat illegible to machine reading, rendering automated text analysis challenging. However, natural language processing of PCDN's platform[63] proved feasible; it determined 20 percent of PCDN's program likely to be "left" and 46 percent of its platform likely to be "right," yielding a ri-le score of 26, a far more immoderate score than that of the FSLN.

Electoral Targeting

A broad-based coalition achieved the overthrow of Somoza. It included the FSLN's hard-core supporters, and also those who occupied the center and even right flanks of the political spectrum. In the revolution, the FSLN had both "non-Marxists and anti-Marxist allies."[64] The insurgent alliance brought together not only the urban proletariat but also capitalists, the bourgeoisie, the radical Christian ecclesiastical base communities, the middle class, and conservative rural peasantry. In other words, what united the "popular support" of the revolution was anti-Somocismo, not pro-Sandinismo. Thus core Sandinista voters constituted only a smaller proportion of the population. In

1984, the FSLN seems to have recognized that to perform well electorally, it had to win not only its core voters, but also those not aligned ideologically or politically with the Sandinistas.[65] It therefore electorally targeted not its loyal members, but swing and opposition constituencies. It maintained its base through the mobilization capacity it had built during war, that is, its neighborhood-level grassroots organizations, known as Sandinista Defense Committees.[66] In 1984, fifteen thousand block-level committees with a total membership of more than a half million, about one-third of Nicaragua's estimated adult population, provided FSLN a robust capacity to turn out voters.[67] It therefore did not fear dampened turnout if it sought to attract "broad sectors of the society."[68] While radical parties did pop up on its left-wing flank, "charg[ing] the FSLN with allowing the revolution to swing to the right,"[69] these were tiny; having coalesced its three "tendencies" or factions into a unified front, FSLN entered the campaign perceiving itself cohesive and largely invulnerable to coordination problems.

There is, unfortunately, only thinner evidence on the nature of the PLI and PCDN's electoral targeting. Contemporary observers note just that they seemingly sought to strike a chord with "Conservative and Liberal traditions" (their core voters).[70]

Candidates

With respect to party elite in Nicaragua, the evidence runs contrary to that expected by partisanship or incumbency logics. Whereas right-wing, government successors PCDN and PLI fielded only civilians[71]—medical doctor Clemente Guido and lawyer Virgilio Godoy, respectively[72]—left-wing, rebel FSLN put forth its top military "*Comandante* of the Revolution,"[73] the "patriotic and brave"[74] Daniel Ortega, as its presidential candidate.[75] It "stressed . . . [Ortega's] involvement in the insurrection, his revolutionary credentials."[76] Ortega ran in his "traditional comandante's clothing"[77] and campaigned as one intimately linked to the FSLN armed forces.[78] The Sandinista slate was dominated by guerrilla military leaders, members, and activists. Assailants who, in objective terms, had carried out atrocities—kidnapping of unarmed civilians for ransom—were revered for their violent, "revolutionary" actions and appointed to important government posts. For example, Leticia Herrera and Joaquín Cuadra, responsible for the Casa de Castillo hostages, became head of the national network of Sandinista Defense Committees and Chief of Staff of the Sandinista army, respectively.[79] However, as Ortega's running mate,

FSLN chose a civilian, Sergio Ramírez Mercado, a prominent intellectual who was part of the Grupo de los Doce before 1979 and served on the provisional junta. While a FSLN partisan who remained in the party as it became less pluralistic in the early 1980s, Ramírez Mercado's appointment may have provided some indication of prospective restraint.

Persuasion

If state belligerent ties and right-wing partisanship determined media control and capacity for persuasion, we would anticipate PCDN and PLI enjoying such control over the "marketplace of ideas."[80] Instead, war outcomes and de facto incumbency had greater effects: PCDN and PLI had access to the oldest media outlet, right-wing *La Prensa*, which had been anti-Somoza but became anti-Sandinista after the revolution. However, ending the armed conflict victorious, the left-wing rebel FSLN, which had built up its own propaganda apparatus, became the de facto government of Nicaragua and took control of significant state media resources. It therefore gained an equal capacity or even the upper hand in spreading its political messages. The Sandinista Defense Committees also helped distribute FSLN campaign materials and persuade voters.[81]

In sum, the variable of war outcome—military victory—resulted in valence, positional, targeting, candidate, and persuasion electoral strategies for a revolutionary Marxist rebel party that were similar to those of right-wing government belligerent successors in neighboring countries. This is not to suggest that their policies once in office were the same, but rather that their strategies to become elected by conflict-affected populations mirrored each other in ways that defy the logic of arguments centered on right-wing ownership of security and defense or on an incumbency (government belligerent) advantage.

Voters

Polling data are not available for 1984, severely limiting the ability to draw inferences about political behavior. We can, however, glean some insights from later surveys. Despite deteriorating support over time, the left-wing FSLN continued to own the security valence issue.[82] The 1980s Contra War was hugely unpopular: for example, although 85 percent of the population despised Somoza in surveys conducted in 1990, 61 percent felt that life had been better before the 1979 revolution, even under the repressive dictatorship, than during the civil war.[83] Sandinista support dropped over the 1980s as the war took its toll, the economy further stagnated, and the FSLN proved unable to defeat the Contras outright (the latter repeatedly resuscitated by U.S. military aid).[84] Despite this dampened backing, security voters—those who believed that ending the war was the most important issue—strongly favored the Sandinistas to the opposition in 1989 polling (42.5 percent to 18.6 percent), and viewed them as most competent on ending the war and on building peace (41 percent to 26 percent).[85] This preference held not only for FSLN's core— public sector employees and the military—but also for swing voters[86] and for private-sector employees, housewives, and unemployed who said they were voting on security lines. FSLN's perceived advantage on security issues—its ability to keep the country stable, prevent a return of Somocismo, stand up to U.S. imperialism, and avert a U.S. invasion—may well have been even more pronounced in 1984, when it had recently emerged a rebel victor over the Somoza government and the Contras were only just erupting in rebellion, than in 1990 when the Sandinistas had less of a military advantage.[87] Indeed, their margin of electoral victory in 1984 would suggest this.

The final election tallies in 1984 showed the rebel left-wing Sandinistas with 67 percent of the valid vote. Of the vote, 29 percent went to parties ideologically and programmatically to the right of the FSLN, including the government quasi-successor parties, which won one-third of the seats in the National Constituent Assembly.[88] These parties won only their core voters: urban middle- and upper-class constituencies.[89] Without reliable polls, we cannot know the number of core versus swing voters that elected the Sandinistas in 1984. That in 1990 swing voters constituted as much as 50 percent of the electorate and swung away from FSLN suggests that underlying or deep-rooted partisan preferences cannot account for all of FSLN's 1984 vote share.[90] The secondary literature suggests that an important segment of the electorate did not agree ideologically with the Sandinista Marxist platform in 1984, but nonetheless voted for the Sandinistas, rewarding the FSLN for winning the revolution and overthrowing the dictatorship, and prospectively perceiving the FSLN to be most likely to keep order, provide stability, and protect Nicaraguan sovereignty.[91]

Conclusion

This chapter traced political life after the Nicaraguan revolution, where the belligerent that emerged victorious from the prior war was not an ideologically right-wing or a government belligerent but instead a left-wing and a rebel one.

The goals of this chapter were limited: to test the theory's proposition that the dynamics of rebel victory largely mirror those of government victory, and to test whether issue ownership is tied more to partisanship—in particular, the political right—or instead, as the book argues, to war outcomes.

In essence, it sought support for the book's decision to strip the belligerents of their ideological and incumbency status. While parsimony makes this appealing, we may ask whether it is giving too little weight to these factors. The book does not deny the importance of incumbency for affording an advantage, particularly in political communication and thus persuasion. The Nicaraguan case, in fact, suggests no different; it merely confirms that the definition of incumbency merits nuance in war and postwar environments when it is, by definition, under attack. Nicaragua makes this abundantly clear: the rebels in the 1961–1979 war became the incumbent thereafter and the previous incumbent, in turn, became the rebels (Contras). What is more, after the successful revolution in 1979, the Sandinista rebels had become the de facto government even before the founding elections, thereby benefiting, as rebels, from the assets of "incumbency." The model also does not deny the role of ideology or partisanship, but argues that certain empirical patterns can be explained only by considering how the war ended, militarily. The case of Nicaragua clearly demonstrates that the right had no monopoly on the security valence issue, even in its hard-line manifestations. In 1984, the left decisively owned issues of national defense, law and order, and citizen protection. It is true, however, that in a country in which a majority was poor, the Sandinistas did not face the same trade-off as Latin America's political right would face between its stances on redistribution and the interests of the broader electorate. Despite this, the Sandinistas nonetheless emphasized security issues and moderated programmatically in the campaign, suggesting the importance of war outcomes. This book argues that these outcomes are more influential than belligerent identity in guiding optimal political strategies for campaigning to secure the future. This does not mean that rebel victors mirror government ones in all ways, however, and recent research has revealed important differences in how rebel victors, in particular, rule once in office.[92]

In Nicaragua, rebel victory in 1979 did not lead to lasting peace because external intervention incentivized the vanquished incumbent to become a counterrevolutionary rebel force, and began a proxy war "between Nicaraguan nationalism and U.S. hegemony."[93] This Contra War claimed the lives of more than one of every sixty inhabitants of Nicaragua. The FSLN largely succeeded in preventing the rebel forces, other than Indigenous groups, from gaining a territorial foothold; eventually, it won the "military and political collapse of the counterrevolution."[94] This second war terminated with the Esquipulas Peace Process and the Tela Accords.[95]

However, after the Contra War's termination, but before the founding postwar democratic elections of 1990, external U.S. intervention again altered the balance of power. Usually, when such a military balance inverts outside of the context of war, it becomes difficult for citizens to update their understandings of who is the most powerful and best able to secure the future. But, in the Nicaraguan case, the power shift was (unusually) legible to lay, undecided voters, and thus these voters updated their perceptions of the power balance accurately and voted accordingly. This prevented a return to war.

During the electoral campaign for the 1990 Nicaragua elections, the United States decided to change course and double down on its support for the Contras.[96] It did so in a very public fashion; it engaged in aggressive, broadcast rhetoric and bellicose behavior. President Bush issued clear statements that the war and embargo would end only if the U.S.-backed opposition party, UNO,[97] won the election.[98] The United States further reduced its support for Contra disarmament, and threatened to engage in direct war against Nicaragua (following its invasion of nearby Panama, a highly legible event for the citizenry). This generated the sense that "Washington could extend the conflict at will"[99] and thus that the balance of power was actually a "frustrated peace and stagnated war" between the United States and Sandinistas, rather than a Sandinista victory over the defeated, and thus disarming, Contras.[100] The Sandinistas were able to best the Contras militarily,[101] but the FSLN could not beat the United States.[102]

This meant that, whereas security voters who decided their vote before the start of the campaign used the heuristic of "who won the war" and thus strongly favored the Sandinistas over UNO (43 percent to 19 percent), security swing voters—those who made their electoral selection over the course of the campaign[103]—updated their assessments of security competence as the balance of power shifted, and elected the newly empowered party, UNO.

Of those who made up their minds during the campaign, 71.6 percent voted for UNO and 12.4 percent voted for FSLN; approximately 36 percent of the Nicaraguan electorate decided to vote for UNO over the course of the campaign.[104] This electoral "middle" gave up on the (Sandinista) Frente being able to solve the "U.S. problem," deciding that only voting for the U.S.-allied party would lead to a sustainable end to war.[105] Indeed, a large majority of all voters (76 percent) agreed in postelection polls that "if the Sandinistas had won [the election], the war would never have ended."[106] In all, 90 percent believed that the "principal accomplishment" of UNO was terminating the conflict and securing peace. Winning the accurately updated security swing vote enabled UNO, unpopular ideologically relative to the FSLN, to amass 54 percent of the vote when the Nicaraguan electorate went to cast their ballots on February 25, 1990. The incumbent Sandinistas' loss—41 percent of the vote[107]—which reflected not the war outcome but an altered postwar power balance—was variously described as a "stunning electoral defeat," a "stunning upset," which "stunned many political analysts," and produced "stunned Sandinistas."[108] In the aftermath of this electoral loss, the Sandinistas did not, however, engage in revisionist remilitarization. Instead, they updated on the U.S.-upset power distribution, calculating that a return to war would yield neither a superior subsequent war outcome given the American preponderance of force nor a boosted future electoral result. A recalibrated peace thus emerged.[109]

Other dynamics in Nicaragua accord with the book's propositions. After winning the 1984 elections, the belligerent Sandinistas did little to illuminate the truths of the violence, despite their own relatively restrained human rights record; indeed, dossiers were burned and amnesties were widespread.[110] At the same time, rebel victory and the constitution of new armed forces did mean that effective security-sector reform took place. Scholars have attributed to this factor Nicaragua's ability to remain an oasis of nonviolence amid skyrocketing crime and homicide in countries all around it.[111] Born of war, the FSLN transformed into a durable party, institutionalizing a party system around it.[112] While the opposition did not experience the same party strength, the legacy of Somoza in party politics endured, manifest in different reincarnations over time.

The book now departs Nicaragua and zooms out from the Central American nations to all cases of postwar politics 1970–2015 globally. It evaluates the book's observable implications across countries of the world, and relaxes the book's assumptions and scope conditions to test the limitations of the theory's explanatory power.

8

Political Life After War
Globally, 1970–2015

THIS CHAPTER EXTENDS beyond the civil wars of Latin America to assess whether the book's framework can be generalized to all belligerents that transitioned from civil war between 1970 and 2015 around the world. It introduces an original cross-national dataset that traces the postwar political trajectories of all civil war belligerents, identifies their successor parties, charts their electoral performance, and identifies their nonbelligerent opponents. It uses this dataset to establish the universe of cases and to test the framework's cross-national hypothesis: that war outcomes are powerful predictors of belligerent party performance, irrespective of the belligerents' use of mass atrocities, and that, if war winning, abusive belligerent parties perform well, even where elections are clean, free, and fair.

The results offer support for the proposed relationship between war outcomes and founding electoral success. They reveal a general pattern of populations electing their tormenters to govern their countries, if the latter have been militarily successful, even those guilty of heinous crimes against humanity, and even absent electoral coercion. At the same time, the analyses reveal variation in election outcomes even among cases with similar war outcomes. While there are many other determinants of electoral results, a share of such variation may be accounted for by choices of party strategy.

I use these cross-national data to explore selection bias and confounding variables that may pose threats to inference, and to test the cross-national implications of alternative explanations, explored in earlier chapters in depth. I consider factors that might affect selection into the universe of cases including conflict duration, the nature of the warring parties' incompatibility, and internal and external security guarantees provided by power sharing or UN intervention. I examine variables that might influence both war outcomes and electoral performance in the founding elections, particularly incumbency status, popular support, organizational cohesion, and financing. The models illustrate the added value of the book's war outcome variable even when controlling for these alternative frameworks.

Victimization, war termination, and voting patterns are not evenly distributed across regions of countries, rendering the cross-national analyses potentially affected by ecological inference problems. Therefore, I present data on atrocities, war outcomes, and postwar elections, disaggregated by belligerent, at the provincial or municipal level, to evaluate whether the null effects of atrocities and significant effects of war outcomes hold in a cross-national, subnational analysis. The data suggest that militarily successful bloodstained parties perform well even in the localities in which they carried out brutalities, and that winning the war at the local level correlates with greater vote share at this disaggregated level.

The book's model rests on the premise that, as a country emerges from civil war, security is salient to political life; it posits that security voters deem winning belligerents, even if highly abusive, best positioned to keep societal peace. I use data from the World Values Survey[1] to probe the salience of security in countries facing founding postwar elections, and ask of these data whether security voters across countries prove more likely to choose the militarily advantaged party. For the nineteen countries for which such data are available, I find that, on average, 54 percent of the population deem maintaining order to be the most important issue facing their nation, and that these security voters are, on average, significantly more likely to vote for the war-winner party over either war-loser or nonbelligerent parties.

My argument performs best where the model's assumptions hold: that is, where the population was affected by the conflict, security is salient, contested and swing voters exist, the electorate is singular (not bifurcated, as after successful secession), and politics are, at least partially, programmatic. Relaxing each of these assumptions in turn, the chapter discusses whether the logic also has explanatory power in contexts more challenging for the theory: contexts in which victimization was bounded geographically or demographically; those emerging from ethnic wars in which allegiances may prove less fluid; those in which secession succeeded, dividing the electorate, and those in which politics is centered on clientelism. Across regions of the world, following ethnic and nonethnic wars, and in systems of programmatic politics and those of patronage, the data reveal a strong relationship between war outcomes and performance in the founding postwar elections. I skim shadow cases to suggest how war outcomes guide optimal electoral strategies and vote choice in these contexts, and to identify the limits of the theory's applications.

Tracing Political Life after War Globally

To study the broad contours of postwar election outcomes and the generalizability of the patterns revealed in the book thus far requires data on political life after war: the war outcomes, parties, voters, and election results globally. No off-the-shelf data existed to study post-civil-war elections. Data had been collected on postwar democratization,[2] the timing of postwar elections,[3] and the institutions governing the elections.[4] However, the political parties that ran in these elections and the outcomes of the elections remained underexplored.[5] Critical recent data advances facilitated our knowledge of whether rebels participated in elections[6] and how they performed from 1990 to 2016,[7] but the other key belligerent—the government[8]—and nonbelligerent parties were missing from these quantitative studies of postwar politics. Additionally, these new datasets covered only the post–Cold War period, leaving decades of postconflict politics unstudied.

I therefore constructed the Civil War Successor Party (CWSP) dataset, which tracks electoral politics after mass violence in war from 1970 to 2015.[9] The dataset traces the political postwar trajectories of 205 civil war belligerents in fifty-seven different states across all regions of the world. It follows both the parties derived from the rebel side and those born from the government side, and places both civil war successor parties in their natural habitat of political contestation with parties that do not have violent pasts. In this way, it provides a comprehensive picture of political life after civil wars.

The dataset follows the book's definitions of civil war and of war termination detailed in Chapter 2. To determine whether the conflict terminated, I consulted the UCDP Conflict Termination Dataset v.2–2015.[10] Of these terminated conflicts, 56 percent "ended" neither in victory nor with a peace agreement. Of these, 43 percent are coded as ending in "low activity." To assess which of the former should be characterized as termination and which as mere lulls in active fighting, I relied on the UCDP Conflict Encyclopedia and extensive qualitative sources to verify whether each belligerent had transitioned from violence and to record the date of conflict termination (peace accord, ceasefire, victory, or other meaningful end of hostilities).

Identifying the Belligerent Successors and Nonbelligerent Parties

Determining the postwar trajectories of civil war belligerents and nonbelligerents requires coding decisions that are open to dispute. The CWSP data offer
transparency about the decisions for each case in the detailed online appendix
materials, to enable replication and reassessment of the coding process. Several specific coding challenges merit discussion here.

The dataset adopts the definitions of belligerent and nonbelligerent parties
laid out in Chapter 2. In cases where the state ceased to function meaningfully
during hostilities, the government belligerent party refers to the party, group,
or organization that controlled the forces most closely associated with the
previously constituted state's coercive apparatus. Different groups may hold
influence or authority over different coercive ministries, or one group may
control provincial capitals while another controls the national capital. In
such cases, multiple government belligerent actors are reflected in the dataset. Especially in long-lasting conflicts, different parties may control the coercive apparatus at different periods of the war. Where the government
changed hands over the conflict, but only one ruled during the conflict's high-
intensity periods, I treat only this party as the government belligerent, and as
responsible for its violence (e.g., Bangladesh). If multiple parties represented
the government belligerent during the conflict's violence, I combine their
vote shares (e.g., Tajikistan). Rebel groups are similarly subject to splits and
splinters. If multiple rebel groups formed a confederation and ran as a coalition, I treat their vote share as joint (e.g., FMLN in El Salvador). If one
splinter rebel group remilitarized while the others demilitarized and entered
legal politics, I treat the former as party to an ongoing war and exclude it
(e.g., FRUD-AD in Djibouti), while the latter enters the universe of postwar
cases (e.g., FRUD).[11] At times, as illustrated in the case study chapters, belligerent parties adopt nonbelligerent party strategies. Additionally, nonbelligerent parties may share the cause (e.g., autonomy), but not the (violent)
means of the belligerents (e.g., Tamil National Alliance [TNA] advances
Tamil self-determination in Sri Lanka, but not through terror as did the Liberation Tigers of Tamil Eelam [LTTE] insurgents).[12] It is the party's history
during the armed conflict, not its electoral strategies postwar, that defines a
party as belligerent or nonbelligerent for the purposes of this study. Many
cases, inevitably, are gray. As a robustness check, I exclude gray cases from
the analyses.

Postwar Election Results

The dataset traces the successor parties' electoral fates in the founding postwar elections. It also summarizes the electoral outcomes for parties without a violent past. This chapter focuses on the founding postwar legislative elections.[13] It collects the total valid votes and seats for each party based on information collected from various print and electronic sources.[14] The electoral results on all sides ranged dramatically: some belligerent successor parties swept the elections and others performed dismally; some nonbelligerents won landslides, while others secured only a small political foothold.

Selection and Bias

In addition to definitional selection issues, stemming from the book's focus on founding postwar elections after episodes of high-intensity civil war (which I laid out in Chapter 2), other sources of selection bias may affect the analyses. I examine the full universe of conflicts that ended and that were followed by democratic elections. However, war termination and democratic elections are nonrandomly assigned. While several factors discussed in Chapter 2 moderate these selection concerns—even unpopular groups tried their hands at the polls, few boycotted,[15] and elections took place in nearly all postconflict countries—the concerns remain.

To address these sources of potential selection bias, I specify control variables appropriately in the statistical analyses. The literature on conflict and peace suggests five variables that might influence the likelihood of conflict termination, specific terms of termination, and the holding of elections: external guarantees, power sharing, number of veto players, conflict type, and war duration.

International interventions are predicted to provide external guarantees to ease the commitment problem, enabling the actors to end their armed struggles,[16] and are also posited to render elections and successor parties more likely, because belligerents' participation in politics has become part of the UN's peace-building recipe.[17] In the analyses, I include a UN intervention variable, derived from Brancati and Snyder (2012), which captures whether and how the UN intervened, through mediation, observation, peacekeeping, or enforcement. Existing scholarship identifies power sharing as, similarly, facilitating conflict termination by enabling internal guarantees of the peace terms.[18] I use the Peace Agreement Dataset's *shagov* variable,[19] indicating the presence of such power-sharing provisions. For missing cases, I use data on political power sharing from Hartzell and Hoddie (2015) and the Power-Sharing Event Dataset.[20] This variable also helps control for the nature of the electoral system. As an alternative measure of this system, I use the Varieties of Democracy indicator *v2elparlel*, which captures whether the system was majoritarian or proportional.[21] Cunningham (2006) convincingly demonstrates that a greater number of veto players (belligerents who were clearly autonomous, cohesive, and viable) renders bargaining more challenging and war longer. The number of civil war players may also affect war outcomes and the number of political parties in the system, and thus influence the civil war successors' decisions whether to run in the elections. It may also influence the challenge of attributing blame for atrocities. I include the number of such veto players from Cunningham's dataset.[22] Finally, longer-lasting conflicts and those fought over territory tend to be harder to resolve.[23] From the UCDP dataset, therefore, I include a variable capturing war duration and another indicating the nature of the incompatibility.

Measuring War Outcomes, Wartime Violence, and Electoral Coercion

This book argues that war outcomes guide whether citizens vote for rebel and government actors who behaved toward the population in a violent and even brutal manner, or instead say "good riddance" to them, and that this relationship can be seen even in democratic elections. Testing this key claim requires that I characterize war outcomes, wartime violence, and postwar electoral coercion. Measuring concepts is an imperfect procedure; some of the indicators provide a reasonable approximation of the underlying ideas, whereas others are only rough proxies. Here I outline potential issues with each of the explanatory measures, the solutions I employ, and the remaining shortcomings.

WAR OUTCOMES

The book conceives of war outcomes on a spectrum ranging from outright government victory to outright rebel victory, with relative government victory and military draw in between. To operationalize these war outcomes, I employed data from the UCDP dataset on conflict termination. I verified that all cases experienced meaningful ends to fighting, and excluded any that did not. I then created an ordinal variable with the UCDP outcome variable that ranges from 0 (government victory) to 3 (rebel victory). "No activity" (a rebellion that petered out) assumes a value of 1, and conflicts that ended in "peace agreements/ceasefire" I coded as 2. However, some cases in the UCDP "no activity" category involved significant concessions in frozen conflicts, and some cases in the "peace agreements and ceasefires" category involved negotiated surrenders. I therefore created an alternative operationalization of the book's indecisive war outcomes, those involving relative government victory or military draw. To do so, I relied on the indicator *rebstrength* from the Non-State Actor (NSA) dataset, on the strength of the rebels relative to the government at war's end.[24] This is a five-point indicator, which ranges from much weaker to much stronger, based on information on the rebel group's ability to target government forces, or its "offensive strength." I collapsed the "weaker" and "much weaker" categories into relative government victory (1) and used the "equally strong" or parity category to proxy for a draw (2). On the one hand, this alternative scale has the benefit of capturing whether the indecisive outcomes were asymmetric or symmetric. On the other hand, strength is an imperfect proxy for war outcomes, as illustrated by cases in which relatively weaker rebels nonetheless won the wars (e.g., in East Timor). The correlation between the two war outcome proxies is .7. Figure 8.1 shows the distribution of the first war outcome scale. The scale is increasing in outcomes favorable to the rebels; therefore in the analyses of the determinants of electoral performance, the theory anticipates a positive coefficient on *war outcome* for rebel successor parties and a negative coefficient on *war outcome* for government belligerent parties. To explore heterogenous effects, for sample size considerations, I reverse the *war outcome* measure for the government belligerent, such that it runs from outright defeat to outright victory for all observations.

WARTIME VIOLENCE

To operationalize atrocities, I constructed a dummy variable—*belligerent's atrocities*—which captures whether the belligerent used the most severe forms of civilian abuse, or instead refrained from this behavior by engaging in "deliberate efforts to avoid attacking civilian targets." To construct these variables, I relied on the coding criteria and data of Stanton (2016), which define indiscriminate violence against civilians as "massacres; scorched earth campaigns; cleansing of a particular ethnic or religious group; or deliberate bombing and shelling of civilian targets."[25] If a belligerent—rebel or government—did not engage in any of these four forms of violence, it is coded as restrained.[26]

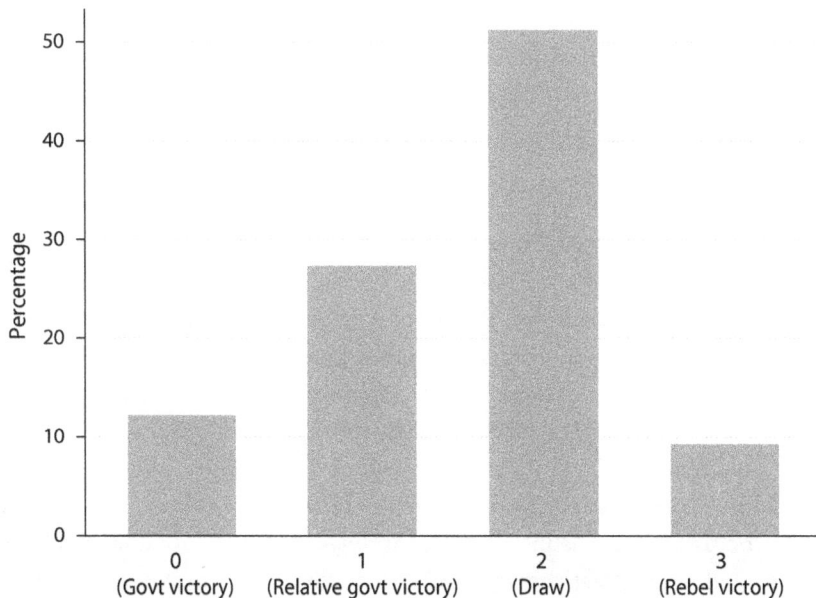

FIGURE 8.1. Frequency of War Outcomes in the CWSP Dataset.

In all, 41 percent of rebels and 37 percent of government actors exhibited such "restraint" in their use of atrocities (in 78 percent of conflicts one or both actors carried out indiscriminate violence).

This is a blunt measure and does not capture the demographic and geographic spread of the violence nor its levels.[27] However, alternative measures, such as UCDP's one-sided Violence Dataset, exhibit a great deal of missingness and, based on widely uneven media reporting, have large levels of variance.[28] I nonetheless use these data as a robustness check and turn to more fine-grained, subnational data on violence below.

ELECTORAL COERCION

To assess whether the puzzling frequency of votes for actors with violent pasts can be explained by coercion in the postwar democratic elections, I evaluate several indicators. I use the Varieties of Democracy indicator *v2xel_ frefair*, which is a clean election index ranging from 0 to 1, capturing the extent to which there was an absence of registration fraud, systematic irregularities, government intimidation of the opposition, vote buying, and election violence.[29] I look separately at whether government electoral coercion can account for government successor party performance, and whether rebel electoral coercion can explain rebel party vote share, based on NELDA data indicators.[30]

Endogeneity and Spuriousness

Threats to inference stem from endogeneity and spuriousness, because war outcomes are not random. To assess the explanatory weight of war outcomes on election results accurately, therefore, I pay close attention to factors that might affect both war outcomes and performance in the founding elections. Earlier chapters have reviewed scholarship on several factors that might confound this relationship or independently drive electoral results. First, (relatively) victorious belligerents might be better positioned to engage in electoral coercion, or better able to restrain their use of atrocities. In this sense, coercion and atrocities operate as intervening variables, and war outcomes might be capturing these alternative variables, a possibility I analyze statistically. Two, war outcomes may be capturing the role of incumbency. Government belligerents enjoy institutionalized advantages through their control of the state apparatus, and this might drive both war outcomes and electoral performance. There are two ways to think about incumbency: (1) as the government belligerent (i.e., the forces of the incumbent government at the start of the conflict) and (2) as the electoral incumbent (i.e., the party in office at the time of the elections). As the case studies clearly demonstrated, these are often not the same party, which mitigates the potential effect of this confounder. Even so, I analyze the determinants of rebel successor party electoral performance and that of government successor electoral performance separately. Three, as discussed in the theoretical and empirical chapters, it might be that wartime popular support or rebel governance can account for both military war results and electoral success in the founding elections.[31] To explore this possibility cross-nationally, I use a pretreatment measure: *mobcap*, the NSA dataset indicator for wartime rebel mobilization capacity, rated relative to the government.[32] According to Reed Wood, "This variable represents a crude accounting of the popularity of the organization among the population of the conflict state and reflects the size of the constituency from which the organization can potentially draw support and resources."[33] For ease of interpretation, I reverse the indicator for the government belligerent observations. I also use Reyko Huang's dummy variable for wartime rebel public goods provision, which assumes a value of 1 if the rebels provided education or created their own schools, if they offered health care, built hospitals, or founded clinics, or if they engaged in relief operations to address war-related humanitarian issues; and o otherwise. This could also capture successor party competence on nonsecurity issues. Four, another alternative mechanism explored qualitatively in the case study chapters centers on wartime organizational weapons. Military organizations that win wars may just be better at organizing, which is why they win elections. Victorious belligerents, for example, might exhibit higher levels of unity, which serve their successor parties well in postwar elections, and likely enjoy more robust funding, which can later be used to bankroll postwar clientelism and campaigns, boosting electoral performance.[34] For cohesion, I employ a pretreatment indicator from the NSA dataset, *strengthcent*, measuring the extent to which a central command exercised control over the constituent groups of an insurgent movement. For rebels' access to resources, I use Huang's pretreatment variable, which assumes a value of 1 if, during war, the rebel group systematically depended on profits from the extraction, sale, or trade of natural resources, such as diamonds, minerals, timber, and metals; or from illicit activities, such as narcotics trading and other contraband.[35] These variables constitute only rough proxies of the concepts, but together with the qualitative evidence explored in the case study chapters, they enable an evaluation of these important explanations.[36]

Analysis

As the dependent variable, this research uses the valid vote share of a successor party. To test the cross-national hypotheses, I consider a series of regression models.[37] My main specifications use ordinary least squares. A number of countries in the dataset have experienced multiple civil wars. I account for the nonindependence of these observations within countries by presenting robust standard errors clustered on the country unit.[38]

Table 8.1, models 1 and 2 test the influence of war outcomes, atrocities, and electoral coercion on rebel and government successor-party success respectively; models 3 and 4 include an interaction term for rebel and government belligerents' atrocities and war outcomes. Models 5 and 6 control for confounding variables. In the appendix, Table A8.2 provides specifications with alternative operationalizations of war outcomes and controls for voter turnout, the electoral system, and per capita income.[39] After presenting the cross-national results in Table 8.1, I examine more fine-grained, subnational data on wartime violence, war outcomes, and voting.

TABLE 8.1. Correlates of Civil War Successor Party Success Around the World

	(1)	(2)	(3)	(4)	(5)	(6)
	Rebel Vote Share	Govt Belligerent Vote Share	Rebel Vote Share	Govt Belligerent Vote Share	Rebel Vote Share	Govt Belligerent Vote Share
War outcomes	15.44***	−18.07***	14.31**	−15.27**	16.33***	−15.57**
	(3.56)	(3.39)	(5.52)	(7.13)	(5.98)	(7.29)
Belligerent's atrocities	−3.12	1.61	−5.68	8.51	−5.37	8.42
	(5.48)	(6.28)	(10.21)	(13.88)	(10.64)	(14.94)
War outcomes × atrocities			1.70	−4.38	−1.62	−4.03
			(7.01)	(8.33)	(7.72)	(8.74)
Free and fair elections	−3.98	−18.94	−3.04	−17.41	−9.38	−15.62
	(12.07)	(12.06)	(12.62)	(12.09)	(13.98)	(12.36)
UN intervention	1.55	−8.85	1.81	−8.49	−3.81	−7.70
	(5.47)	(6.58)	(5.67)	(6.59)	(7.10)	(6.60)
Power sharing	−0.97	4.86	−0.98	5.35	−0.35	4.86
	(6.92)	(9.74)	(7.12)	(9.95)	(8.56)	(10.32)
Number of vetoes	−4.56*	−4.49	−4.54*	−4.56	−3.48	−4.47
	(2.61)	(6.09)	(2.65)	(6.11)	(4.76)	(5.94)

	(1)	(2)	(3)	(4)	(5)	(6)
Incompatibility	12.81***	10.57	13.07**	10.62	18.80***	9.50
	(4.76)	(6.51)	(5.38)	(6.35)	(5.97)	(6.42)
War duration	−0.11	−0.54*	−0.10	−0.57*	−0.10	−0.57*
	(0.18)	(0.27)	(0.19)	(0.28)	(0.23)	(0.29)
Rebel governance					1.31	
					(5.49)	
Rebel cohesion					3.99	
					(4.65)	
Rebel finances					−3.57	
					(7.22)	
Popular support					10.81*	3.94
					(5.90)	(4.05)
Constant	−14.21	75.74***	−13.56	70.70***	−29.90*	66.21***
	(10.47)	(17.13)	(9.74)	(20.26)	(15.53)	(20.51)
Observations	82	62	82	62	74	61
R^2	.36	.41	.36	.41	.45	.42

Note: Robust standard errors in parentheses.

*$p < .1$. **$p < .05$. ***$p < .01$.

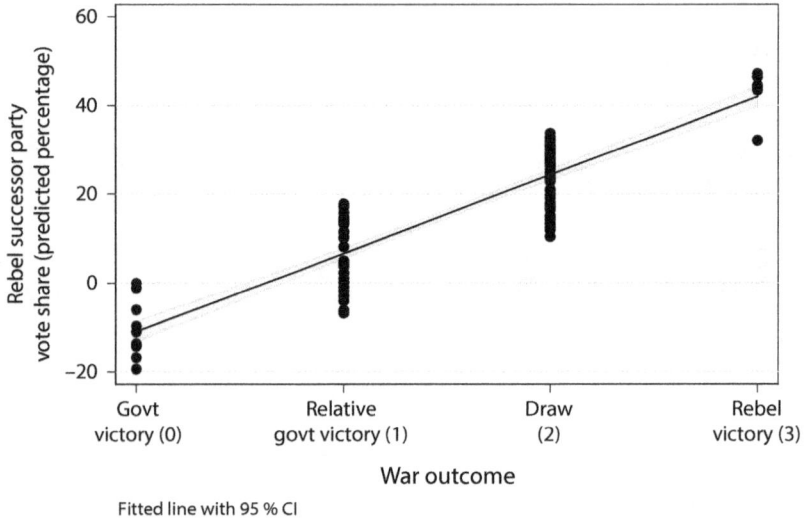

Fitted line with 95 % CI

FIGURE 8.2. War Outcomes and Rebel Vote Shares in Founding Elections.

Results: Cross-National Data

The central finding of the cross-national analysis is that war outcomes prove a powerful predictor of the performance in founding postwar elections of successor parties to belligerents that committed atrocities—both rebel and government. The measure of war outcomes is highly correlated with these belligerent parties' electoral results across all specifications of the model. Cross-nationally, if militarily advantaged at war's end, bloodstained belligerents perform significantly better in postwar voting than do militarily disadvantaged ones. Figures 8.2 (rebels) and 8.3 (government) illustrate this result.

Table A8.3 and Table 8.1, models 5 and 6 explore omitted variables and endogeneity, and evaluate the cross-national implications of alternative explanations. The results in Table A8.3, models 1 and 2 suggest that actors who are indiscriminately violent are just as likely to be successful in war as those that are restrained, and that winning the war is not associated with belligerents being more likely to rig or coerce the elections.[40] This means that those who won the wars were not necessarily the nicest; that the nicest did not become militarily victorious because of their restraint in the use of violence.[41] More "popular," legitimate, and organizationally equipped belligerents should perform better, both in war and in elections, than less popular, illegitimate, and organizationally depraved belligerents. Model 3 regresses war outcomes on popular wartime support, and model 4 analyzes the relationship between war

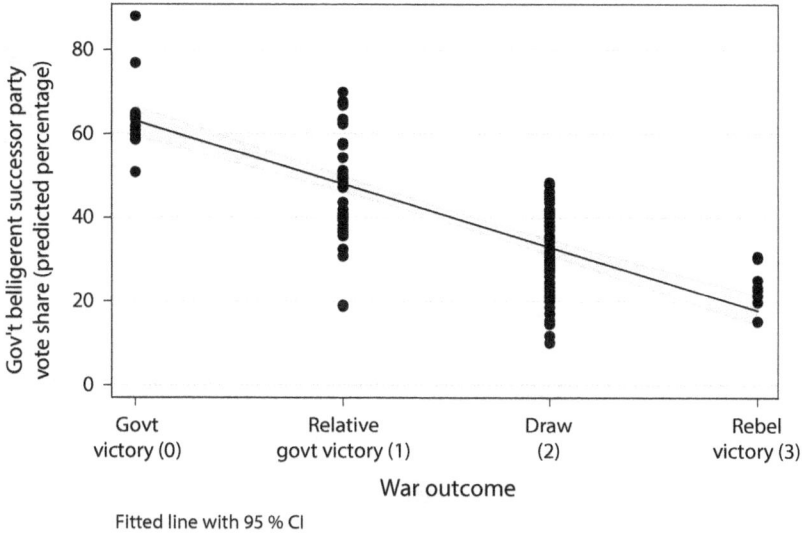

FIGURE 8.3. War Outcomes and Government Belligerent Vote Shares in Founding Elections.

outcomes and wartime rebel governance. In Table A8.3, models 5 and 6, I find that pretreatment rebel cohesion and finances are unrelated to war outcomes using conventional levels of significance, also raising doubts as to whether a better organizational toolkit can account for both war outcomes and electoral performance. Table 8.1, models 5 and 6 then use as the outcome the vote share for rebel and government successor parties. Their results reinforce the null findings for organizational assets, and show a positive correlation between popular support and war outcomes for rebel belligerents, but not for government belligerents, a relationship that the book argues may be, at least partially, interpreted as a finding that it is victory in the war, not underlying political allegiances, that drives popularity and postwar voting.[42] These models demonstrate that the relationship between war outcomes and performance in the founding postwar election is robust to controlling for these potentially confounding variables. The analysis raises questions about the ability of these alternative mechanisms to account for significant variation in postwar electoral success. Aside from that on popular support in the rebel vote share model, each of the coefficients' 95 percent confidence intervals include the possibility of no effect. These cross-national analyses have potential limitations: they may present ecological inference issues, the null effects could be explained by classical measurement error, or the correlational analyses might not lend

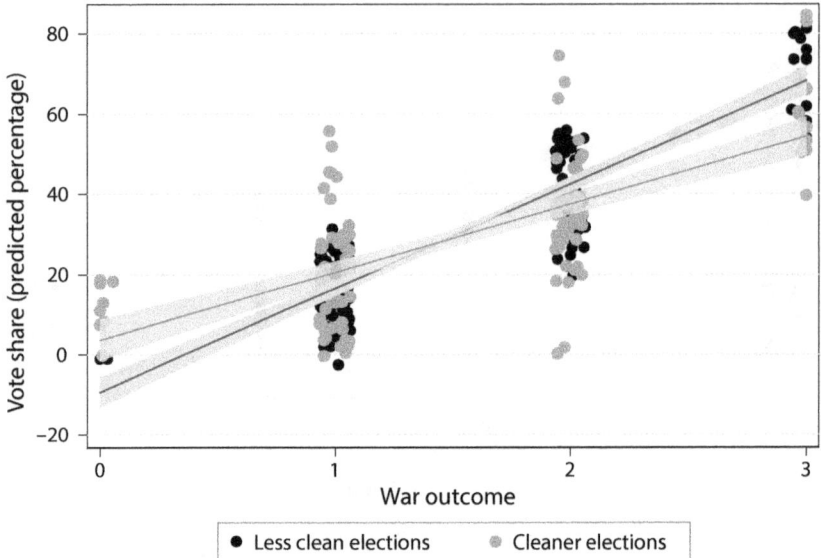

FIGURE 8.4. War Outcomes and Electoral Performance in Cleaner and Less Clean Elections. *Note*: For sample size reasons, for these subanalyses, I consider the full universe of rebel and government observations together and reverse the military outcome scale for government belligerents such that it ranges from defeat (o) to victory (3) for all cases. Elections are coded as cleaner if they fall above 0.5 on the Varieties of Democracy clean elections index. Less clean elections are those below 0.5 on the index.

themselves to mechanism testing. However, the qualitative and subnational evidence from the case study chapters, together with these cross-national analyses, casts doubt on arguments that victimization, coercion, incumbency, popular support, wartime governance, resources, or unity are driving postwar electoral performance or driving the robust relationship between war outcomes and this performance. While they may account for the success of specific cases and a share of the postwar vote, they leave significant variation unexplained, for which my theory may help account.

ELECTORAL COERCION

Militarily successful violent belligerents performed well in elections against militarily unsuccessful violent belligerents and nonbelligerents, not only in less clean elections, but also in cleaner ones (see Figure 8.4). The average vote share for successor parties competing in more free and fair elections and those competing in less free and fair elections did not differ to a statistically significant degree.[43] I look separately at whether government electoral coercion can account for government successor party performance, and whether rebel electoral coercion can explain rebel party vote share, based on NELDA data.[44] I find null results in both analyses.[45]

WARTIME VIOLENCE

The cross-national analysis further reveals that rebel and government wartime use of atrocities cannot account for citizens' decisions whether to vote for or against these belligerents' successor parties. Figure A8.1 shows that parties derived from belligerents that executed high levels of wartime brutality win elections when they won the war; in fact they do so as well as war victors who exercised restraint in their use of violence. In the book's framework, war outcomes offset the belligerents' use of atrocities, irrespective of the extent of those atrocities. Consistent with this claim, Table 8.1, models 3 and 4, shows an insignificant interaction term between the use of atrocities and war outcome.

Subnational Data from Around the World

I next consider whether the cross-national results are mirrored at the subnational level; that is, whether tormentors were performing electorally as well in the specific *regions* where they carried out carnage as in those where they exercised relative restraint, and whether winning the war at the local level bolstered the belligerent party's vote share at that level as well. Significant issues of endogeneity remain. Additionally, such fine-grained data on local violence exist for only certain conflicts. For these conflicts, I collected data on wartime violence, voting, and war outcomes, disaggregated by belligerent, at the most micro administrative unit possible. I derived electoral outcome data by scraping National Election Registrars and using the Constituency-Level Elections Archive. In certain cases, these were available only for the rebel or only the government belligerent successor party. I used georeferenced maps of the electoral districts to merge the subnational election data with information on wartime violence from truth commissions and violent-event databases for each individual country. For countries for which such micro violence data were not available, I used the UCDP Georeferenced Event Database Global version 18.1 (2017).[46] For subnational war outcomes, I gathered existing data scraped from military and UN disarmament maps. Table A8.3 documents the sources of data

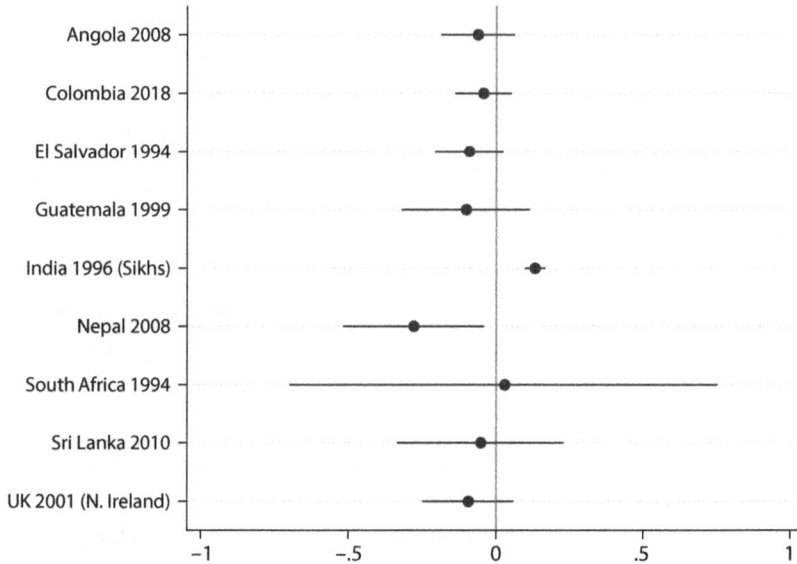

FIGURE 8.5. Subnational Wartime Victimization by Rebels and Postwar Rebel Successor Party Vote Share.
Note: This plot shows the coefficient estimates of ordinary least squares models where the dependent variable is the valid vote share for the rebel belligerent successor party and the independent variable is relative atrocities, which captures the proportion of the total violent events against civilians attributed to the rebel belligerent. Both variables are measured at the most disaggregated administrative unit available. The bars indicate a 95 percent confidence interval.

on violence, war outcomes, and elections and the administrative level used for each analysis.

Figure 8.5 provides the graphical representation of the effect of greater rebel violence at the subnational level on rebel party vote share at that level. Figure 8.6 demonstrates the impact of greater government violence at the municipal or provincial level on government party vote share at that level.[47] Figure 8.7 then displays the coefficient plots for the effect of war outcomes in the local (subnational) area on the local valid vote share of the belligerent successor parties. Coefficient estimates for each country and belligerent are displayed separately. For comparison, I also include the subnational analyses presented in the case study chapters.

Across the elections for which subnational data are available, as predicted by the book's theory and echoing the findings at the cross-national level, there is no consistent relationship between belligerents' relative civil war violence

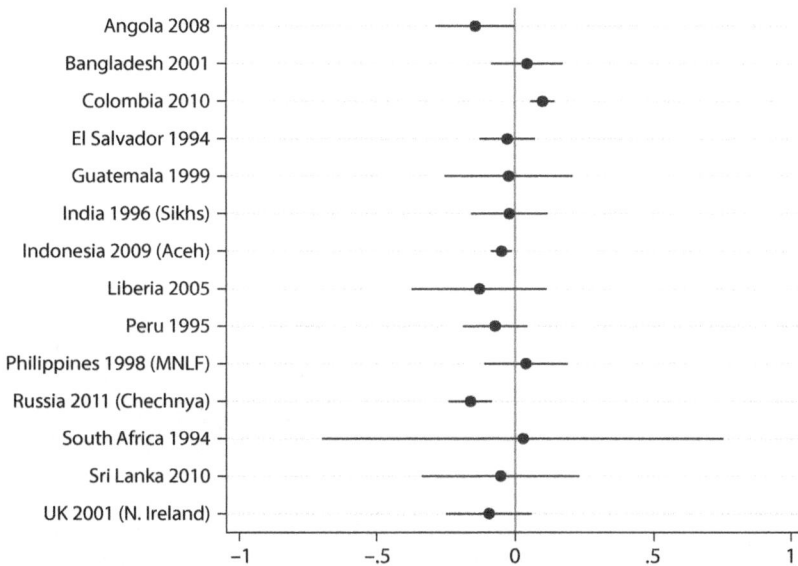

FIGURE 8.6. Subnational Wartime Victimization by Government and Postwar Government Successor Party Vote Share.
Note: This plot shows the coefficient estimates of ordinary least squares models where the dependent variable is the valid vote share for the government belligerent successor party and the independent variable is relative atrocities, which captures the proportion of the total violent events against civilians attributed to the government belligerent. Both variables are measured at the most disaggregated administrative unit available. The bars indicate a 95 percent confidence interval.

against civilians and their successor parties' later electoral success at the municipal or provincial levels.[48] Victimized regions did not vote against the perpetrators whereas nonvictimized ones could account for the vote share for victimizers. Instead, terrorized regions of countries voted for the successor parties in proportions similar to regions unscathed by the belligerents' wartime campaigns.

In the four cases for which subnational war outcome data were available and variation existed—that is, outcomes were not decisive—the data suggest that winning the war locally translated into positive electoral performance in the founding postwar elections, raising the belligerent successor's local vote share by, on average, 25 percent (see Figure 8.7). Violence and war outcomes are not (and cannot be) randomized, posing a threat to inference. However, overall, these results track with those anticipated by the theory.

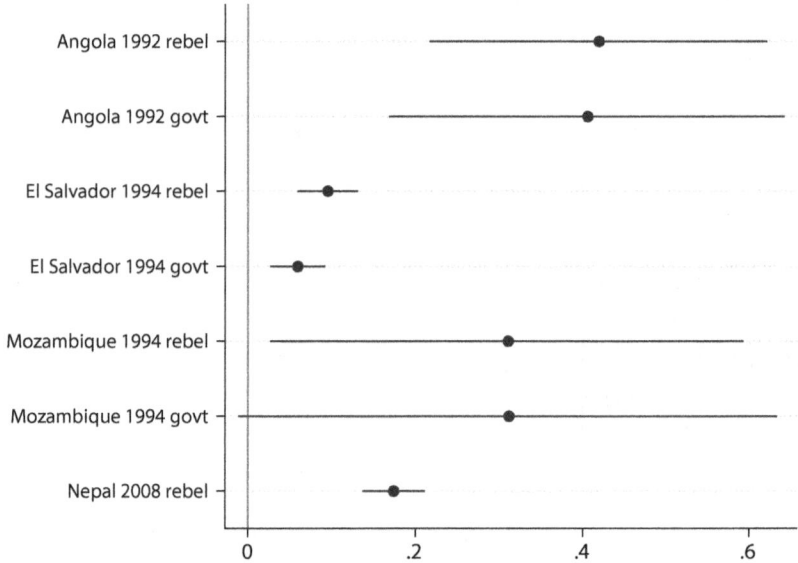

FIGURE 8.7. Subnational War Outcomes and Belligerent Successor Party Vote Share. *Note*: This plot shows the coefficient estimates of ordinary least squares models where the dependent variable is the valid vote share for the rebel or government belligerent successor party and the independent variable is a binary indicator, local war outcome, which captures whether the belligerent won the war locally. These subnational war outcome data are available only for these four conflicts and, in Nepal, only for the rebel belligerent. The bars indicate a 95 percent confidence interval. The analysis suggests that winning the war locally translated into between a 6 percent and a 42 percent increase in the local vote share of the rebel and government belligerent parties.

In sum, new data provide support for the book's cross-national and subnational observable implications that war outcomes guide party fates in the first postwar elections. Whereas the relationship holds both for the more intuitive cases of outright victory and defeat, and also for the indecisive, war outcomes, some combatant parties fall squarely on the regression line whereas others do not. The choice among strategies by the belligerent and nonbelligerent parties may be able to account for some of this convergence or divergence from the equilibrium path. Future inquiry should study these party strategies and their electoral implications for a broad set of cases.

Generalizability and Relaxing the Book's Assumptions

The book makes several assumptions. I explore the generalizability of these assumptions and implications of relaxing them.

Security Voting

The framework's central assumption is that security is salient for an important segment of the population and becomes the basis for this segment's vote choice. These "security voters," the theory predicts, are more likely to cast votes for the militarily winning belligerent successor party, perceiving it to be best able to secure the country going forward. To evaluate the generalizability of these propositions, I analyze data from the World Values Survey (WVS).[49] The WVS project realized surveys at approximately the same times as sixteen of the cross-national CWSP cases of founding elections and, across time and space, asked comparable questions of issue salience for political life.[50]

Figure 8.8 displays the proportion of respondents who viewed "maintaining order in the nation" to be the most important issue facing the country. Across the cases for which WVS data exist, an average of 54 percent of respondents were most concerned with securing the future. While elections were multivalent and voters cast ballots along diverse dimensions, security proved important to a majority of voters emerging from civil war. I consider these individuals to be security voters.

To probe whether security voters do in fact use war outcomes as an informational cue to judge security competence, I examine whether these voters were more likely to vote for the winning belligerent. For nine of the WVS cases, the surveys also included questions about vote choice. For each of these cases of recorded vote choice, I run a simple bivariate analysis to determine the effect of being a security voter on the likelihood of voting for the militarily advantaged belligerent party in that election (as coded by the CWSP dataset's *war outcome* variable). Figure 8.9 displays the regression coefficients from each of these election-level analyses. The data suggest that, in most cases, security voters, who are a sizeable share of the electorate, were between 6 and 16 percent more likely to cast their ballots for the winning combatant party over either militarily losing or nonbelligerent parties.

Security, however, is not equally salient across contexts, because of the nature of the war, or the nature of the recovery.[51] In certain cases, conflict affected only certain regions and only minority populations. In these cases, only specific demarcated parts of the countries or demographics might fall within the theory's scope condition of experiencing and then emerging from mass violence. The book's theory might still shed light on the subnational electoral performance of belligerent successors and nonbelligerent parties in those regions considered "postconflict,"[52] even if this would not describe the whole country, but it has less explanatory power in explaining national-level elections

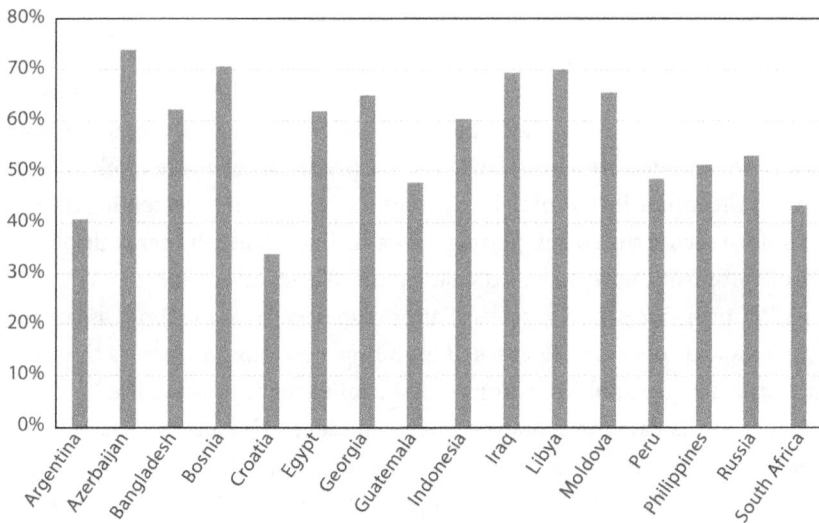

FIGURE 8.8. Proportion of Security Voters around the World.

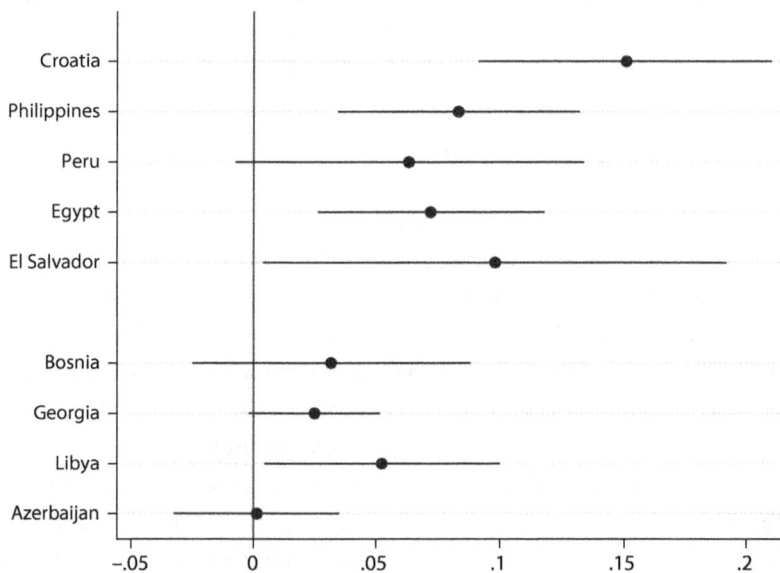

FIGURE 8.9. Marginal Effect of Being a Security Voter on Voting for the Militarily Winning Belligerent Party.

in these cases, and particularly in accounting for the vote choice of the majority, which may have remained nonvictimized and unaffected by large-scale violence. Normal politics centered on economic voting, clientelism, and partisanship will be more likely to dictate vote choices in these elections. We lack surveys to confirm public opinion in most such cases, but it seems plausible, for example, that wars in noncontiguous or satellite territories would exhibit such a dynamic. For example, the majority of the national populations of the Philippines, the United Kingdom, and Indonesia—those living in Luzon, England, or Java—likely did not acutely feel the civil war violence taking place in the separate island territories of Mindanao, Northern Ireland, and East Timor, or the relief of the peace that followed the violence in those territories. Accordingly, it is less likely that security voting was a powerful force in the national elections in these three countries; rather other dimensions of voting likely dominated.[53] This demonstrates the limits to the theory when the assumption of widespread conflict impact and resulting security salience is relaxed.

Next, I consider whether the book's logic holds if the framework's other core assumptions are relaxed.[54] These include ethnic wars where swing voters may have been erased, successful secessionist wars in which the electorate may become bifurcated, and clientelistic systems in which programmatic politics may play a minor role. These exploratory analyses should be viewed as suggestive of the theory's generalizability and its limits, rather than proof of it. Future in-depth research is merited to determine precisely whether and how the theory works in environments in which the framework's assumptions apply more loosely or not at all.

Ethnic Wars

The book assumes that war leaves an "uncommitted middle":[55] populations that are undecided in their electoral allegiance and preferences. It is on this uncommitted middle's attitudes and behavior that the argument has the greatest explanatory power. What happens if party affiliation is not fluid and malleable, but instead ethnicized, racialized, and frozen, and there are no unaligned voters? In such cases, there may exist only core voters, whose vote choice may be determined more by underlying political preferences or identities than by war outcomes. Specifically, for instance, they might vote for coethnic belligerent successor parties whether those parties' predecessors won or lost the war. Examples in which a cursory look suggests that identities exhibited little fluidity include the separate Black and white elections held after the violent death of

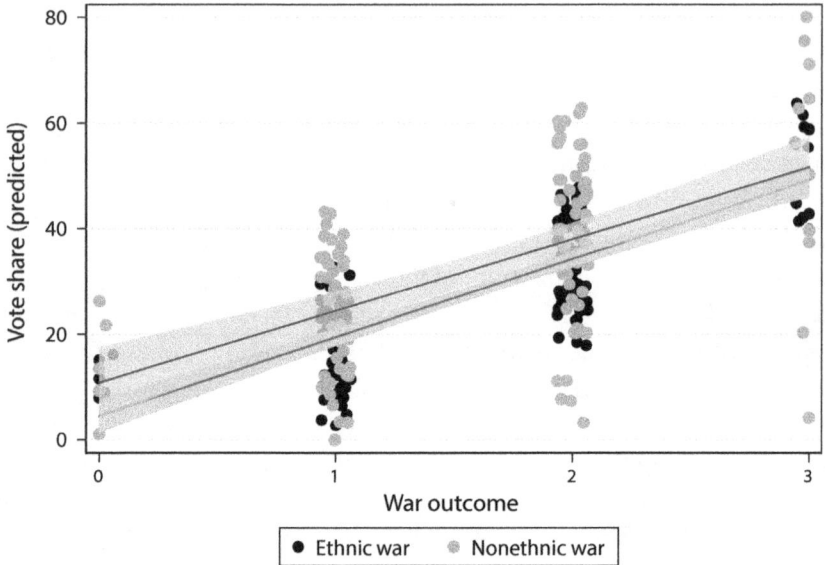

FIGURE 8.10. War Outcomes and Vote Shares in Founding Elections following Ethnic versus Nonethnic Conflicts.

Rhodesia, birth of Zimbabwe, and establishment of majority rule in 1980,[56] and South Africa's 1994 "ethnic elections"[57] following the conflict to end apartheid. Here the theory seems to reach its limits.

However, that such cases fall outside of the theory's scope does not necessarily mean that the framework lacks explanatory power in all cases of ethnic wars. I pause to analyze whether war outcomes guide postwar electoral performance following conflicts that are defined by ethnic cleavages. To do so, I adopt Cederman, Wimmer, and Min's (2010) classification: wars are categorized as ethnic if they seek ethnic aims, predominantly recruit fighters among their leaders' own ethnic group, and forge alliances on the basis of ethnic affiliation. I examine the subsamples of ethnic and nonethnic wars separately. For sample size considerations, I reverse the war outcome scale for government belligerents, rendering it comparable to the scale for rebels—that is, from defeat to victory—and analyze the rebel and government belligerent observations together. As displayed in Figure 8.10, the cross-national data reveal a link between war outcomes and electoral performance following ethnic conflicts as well, a correlation that is nearly indistinguishable from that following nonethnic ones.

This may reflect the fact that mass violence also hardens nonascriptive cleavages in some nonethnic wars. For example, seven civil conflicts in

Colombia between Independence and 1958 rendered the two belligerents—Liberals and Conservatives—like "two races" that, according to historian Robert Dix, "live side by side and hate each other eternally."[58] Party allegiance was inherited and party carnets resembled ethnic passports.[59] (At the same time, even such a tradition of "hereditary hatreds," was "deactivated" by the National Front peace accord; a new overarching class cleavage subsumed the partisan one.)[60]

The finding that, on average, war outcomes also guide electoral results in ethnic contexts makes more sense if we assume a constructivist rather than primordial approach to identity, taking not the pundits' "ancient hatreds" view[61] but instead one consistent with recent scholarship on the multiplicity and fluidity of identities, which may be more appropriate to some, but not all ethnic conflicts.[62] Such a shift in paradigm reveals that, in certain ethnic wars, not all violence occurs along ethnic lines; rather belligerents oftentimes commit violence against coethnics.[63] As a result, in the aftermath of such violence, the belligerents, even if constituted as ethnic parties, may need to seek the votes of populations they victimized. A constructivist view further shows that not all ethnic kin necessarily support their coethnic belligerent. Many prefer nonviolence; many object to the violence committed; many support noncombatant parties. These noncombatant parties constitute viable alternatives. And, despite being coethnic, they push the belligerent successors to reckon with their violent past and to make plausible promises that they will not revictimize in the future. Even if swing voters do not cross ethnic belligerent lines with their ballots, how the war ends may influence whether they choose a belligerent or instead a nonbelligerent party with these voters likely to flock to a war winner (if coethnic), but to a nonbelligerent if their ethnic belligerent loses the war. Finally, a constructivist rendering suggests that people hold multiple identities and thus, in peacetime following some ethnic wars, cleavages deactivated during the wars may resurface, or new overarching identities may make their way to the fore. Several illustrative examples of ethnic wars support these conjectures; however, an in-depth analysis of war outcomes and party strategy in ethnic contexts remains beyond the scope of this book. It would be a fertile subject for future inquiry.

In Rwanda, the internecine brutality included rebel Tutsi violence against Hutus and extremist Hutu genocide against Tutsis, but also an extremist Hutu genocide against moderate coethnic Hutus who did not side with the radical Hutu belligerent. The rebel Tutsi-RPF (Rwandan Patriotic Front) won the war. Victorious, hegemonic, and with an incontestable hold on political power, it could have embraced its violent past, offered security only to coethnics, and sought the votes only of coethnics, even though the Tutsis were a minority in Rwanda. Instead, in the campaign for the 2003 elections, RPF sought to win the support of security, moderate, and victimized Hutu voters. It strategized to spin the wartime atrocities as one-sided, committed *only* by the extremist Hutu genocidaires.[64] At the same time, it opted to mitigate its own violence as justified by its provision of security and peace. This worked; RPF became "credited by many Rwandans—Hutu and Tutsi alike—with having ended the 1994 genocide."[65] RPF sought to translate its military success into a reputation for competence on future protection not only for Tutsis, but also for Hutus. Terrence Lyons writes of how, on the one hand, "the defeat of genocidal forces by the Rwandan Patriotic Front provided RPF substantial initial endowments of legitimacy," while, on the other hand, its own past record of victimization against Hutus meant that "the perceived ethnic character of the RPF raised doubts among some [swing Hutus] about the nature of their new protectors."[66] To sell itself as a prospective restrained sovereign for the whole Rwandan population, including its former adversary ethnic group and victims,[67] the RPF decided to play the constructivist card and stretch its constituency from just Tutsis to an overarching Rwandan identity. To do so, it promoted a "powerful" brand of Rwandan "civic nationalism," constructing and elevating a new identity of "national unity" based on territory to supplant the wartime cleavage of ethnicity,[68] a process rendered easier by the ruling party's ability to ban discussions of ethnicity.[69] The RPF also allowed a moderate Hutu to assume the post of interim president. Meanwhile, the RPF undermined perceptions of its opponents' competence on security by claiming that they were prospective revictimizers, likely to incite ethnic tensions and violence again. RPF commander and later president Paul Kagame explained that the people "wanted security first of all. Even people who didn't know the RPF program in detail saw us as the party that would guarantee that [security]."[70] As a result, albeit in only minimally democratic, postwar elections, Tutsi-RPF gained the vast majority of its large number of votes from swing Hutus, who fueled its electoral landslide.[71]

In other post–ethnic war contexts, it appears that security and swing voters also existed and that belligerent parties sought to capture these votes across ethnic lines, at times, with the strategies the book posits as equilibria to persuade voters of their ability to consolidate peace. In Burundi, for instance, Hutu-dominated CNDD-FDD[72] "presented the party as the guardian against any possible threat to the [population's] security." It sought to "guarantee the security of the country's institutions in service to the *whole* Burundian nation," not just that of the majority Hutus,[73] by establishing a "truly national army" with equal participation by Tutsis and Hutus.[74] For a sustainable end to the war, Burundi's Hutus therefore voted nearly unanimously against their ethnic interests for quotas that would grant Tutsis—constituting only 15 percent of the population—half of the upper house of Congress and 40 percent of the lower house. In the 2005 elections, despite its past use of violence, Hutu belligerent successor party CNDD-FDD drew Hutu voters away from the nonbelligerent FRODEBU party, and it also seems to have drawn some Tutsi voters—victims of that violence—to its side.[75] According to a voter in Bujumbura, "For me this election means voting peace in the country."[76]

In Iraq's 2018 elections, despite fomenting a decade of sectarian conflict against Sunnis, Shiite cleric Muqtada al-Sadr's political list Sa'iroun (Moving Forward) and the Da'wa Shia sectarian party appealed across ethnic belligerent lines to Sunni voters. To do so, it ran on its effective fight against and victory over ISIS and on rebuilding war-torn social services.[77] To render credible the party's political transformation from a protector of only Shias to a leader of all Iraqis, including Sunnis, Sadr established an unlikely alliance with communists and secular Iraqis, a costly move, to demonstrate to the public his formal renunciation of sectarian politics and his adoption instead of an overarching Iraqi civic nationalism.[78] Large numbers of Sunnis crossed ethnic lines and voted for this party. It received almost 30 percent of its votes from Sunnis and won the 2018 elections.[79]

It appears likely that war outcomes and party strategies helped guide postwar election results even in these ethnic contexts seemingly inhospitable for the book's theory because these contexts exhibited features consistent with a more constructivist reading of identity and, as such, better approximated the scope conditions of the book. In other cases of ethnic war (potentially more common following wars in which the casus belli concerned "the status of a specified territory . . . e.g., secession or autonomy") undecided voters seemingly rarely crossed ethnic lines in the founding elections, but they still swung between belligerent and nonbelligerent (coethnic) parties; war outcomes may have mattered to this decision. I touch on several cases that illustrate how the theory might be adapted to shed some light on these contexts.

Following the military defeat of Serb separatism in Croatia, many Serbs did not cross over belligerent (ethnic) lines to vote for the Croat government belligerent successor party, HDZ[80] (i.e., they did not augment the victor's vote share), yet they still voted *against* the vanquished Serb belligerent successor, reducing its share of the vote. These Serb voters instead "supported nonethnic parties, especially the SDP and the HSLS," deeming these nonbelligerent parties better able to secure the future. "It would be wrong to assume that members of the Serb . . . communities uniformly support[ed] the political parties that claim[ed] to speak in their name";[81] instead, war outcomes guided whether they voted *against* their coethnic combatant parties and instead *for* noncombatant ones.

At the same time, the war-winner Croat-HDZ sought to appeal beyond its radical core supporters to undecided and opposition Croat voters who were more closely aligned politically with moderate, nonbelligerent parties. Because these nonbelligerent parties could raise "human rights concerns related to [HDZ's] Operation Storm"—the ethnic cleansing that resulted in the death of 200,000 Serbs—HDZ opted to spin its violent past and brandish its Leviathan credentials to appeal to these voters.[82] Its propaganda asserted, "We are forced to listen to the 'theory' of common guilt, of two 'sides in war,'" and claimed that it was actually a "Homeland War" of "heroic defense" against one-sided terrorism. HDZ scapegoated all the "murderous and destructive components" of the war on the Serbs. Its own violence, which, although targeted disproportionately against non-coethnics, assumed atrocious forms, it mitigated with the boast that it had achieved war termination, the "final defeat of the enemy." HDZ campaign posters showed "a newborn baby in the muscular arms of a Croatian bodybuilding champion" labeled, "in the arms of a safe future."[83] Its war win and electoral strategy earned it the support of Croat swing and security voters.

In Sri Lanka, after the LTTE's military defeat, Tamils did not cross ethnic lines and choose to vote for the war-winning Sinhalese belligerent successor party. Instead they cast their votes for nonbelligerent TNA (albeit no successor party to the belligerent Tamil emerged to contest the elections). Sinhalese swing and security voters, meanwhile, did shift disproportionately to the Sinhalese government combatant party, United People's Freedom Alliance, which had been indiscriminately violent (mostly against Tamils), rewarding its military victory and security provision.

A final (and rarer) set of cases—where rebels win their wars of secession—defies another of the theory's assumptions: that the electorate is singular, not bifurcated. In such cases, the rebels' coethnics significantly bolstered the rebel victors' electoral fates (for example, Fretilin in East Timor and SWAPO in Namibia),[84] while coethnics of the government belligerent appeared, on average, less likely to cast their ballots for successors to that belligerent, and voted instead for nonbelligerent parties (such as Namibia's Democratic Turnhalle Alliance).

These anecdotal examples suggest that the theory—if revised—may be able to apply to ethnic conflicts in which the voters only swing so far (and not across ethnic lines) and where the assumption of a unitary and shared electorate after mass violence is violated.

Patronage Politics

I conclude this chapter by asking whether the theory can usefully be applied to postwar contexts in which programmatic politics is overtaken by other forms of linkages. If voters cast their ballots based on entrenched clientelistic networks,[85] rather than based on the performance of politicians in delivering collective or public goods, then "swing voting—that a voter's ballot is up for grabs by any number of political parties—should become an empirical anomaly, especially along nonclientelistic lines."[86] As a crude attempt to evaluate the applicability of the theory to contexts of nonprogrammatic politics, I rely on the Varieties of Democracy indicator of party-constituent linkages, which "refers to the sort of 'good' that the party offers in exchange for political support and participation in party activities." Linkages are considered clientelistic if constituents are rewarded in a targeted, contingent fashion with goods, services, cash, or jobs in exchange for political support. Linkages are coded as programmatic if "constituents respond to a party's positions on national policies, general party programs, and visions for society."[87] I analyze whether the relationship between war outcomes and electoral performance holds not only in political systems deemed more programmatic (above the mean of this index), but also in those deemed more clientelistic (below the mean). The analysis displayed in Figure 8.11 suggests that although, as anticipated, it is more muted, the relationship does indeed hold in clientelistic contexts. Whether, following a given war outcome, electoral strategies that would be optimal in programmatic contexts also prove so in nonprogrammatic ones is a topic worthy of additional research.

Conclusion

This chapter introduced an original cross-national Civil War Successor Party (CWSP) dataset that traces the postwar political trajectories of all belligerents that transitioned from civil war over forty-five years. It used this dataset to

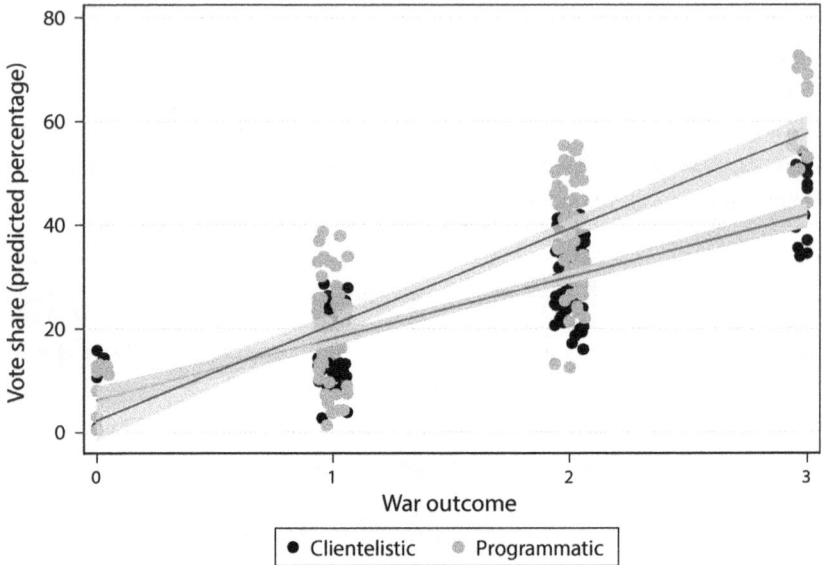

FIGURE 8.11. War Outcomes and Vote Shares in Founding Elections with Clientelistic and Programmatic Linkages.

establish the contours of the universe of cases and to provide evidence for the cross-national applicability of the book's framework. The dataset also enabled an assessment of selection issues and confounding variables that pose threats to inference. After accounting for endogeneity and controlling for alternative hypotheses centered on incumbency, popular support, and organizational weapons, the data showed that there exists a strong relationship between war outcomes and bloodstained successor party performance, irrespective of the belligerent's use of mass wartime atrocities, and even where elections were clean.

Moving to the subnational level, the chapter analyzed data and provided evidence that responsibility for local atrocities did not seem to alter the belligerents' vote share—belligerents won the regions they most brutalized—but local war outcomes did.

Disaggregating further, to the individual level of analysis, the chapter showed the prevalence of security voters and the general pattern in which they elect the successor party to the belligerent that won the war. The chapter reaffirmed that the theory works best in postwar contexts in which security remained salient and politics programmatic, but that it may extend even where political linkages center on clientelism. At the same time, the chapter

discussed the nuances and opportunities of future research rigorously apply-
ing the theory broadly to cases of ethnic wars. In so doing, scholars may wish
to identify the precise limits of the theory's generalizability and adapt its inner
workings to these diverse settings, which are critical to a more comprehensive
understanding of political life after large-scale violence. In particular, tracing
the role of war outcomes and parties' political strategies for campaigning to
secure their countries' future in these settings would be a fruitful avenue for
additional scholarship.

Before I turn to a more extended discussion of areas ripe for inquiry, I use
the CWSP cross-national dataset and a rich subnational dataset for an additional purpose: to illuminate the important *implications* of the founding elections for patterns of peace, justice, democracy, and governance. It is to this task
that I go next, in the book's penultimate chapter.

9

Implications for Postwar Peace, Justice, Democracy, and Governance

THIS BOOK DRAWS on the experiences and outcomes of war to explain the *results* of the first postwar elections: who wins, who loses, how, and why. This chapter takes these results as given, and examines their critical implications for fundamental questions of successful peace building, democratization, justice, rule of law, and social welfare. To do so, it uses the book's global record of founding election outcomes, cross-national data on remilitarization, transitional justice, and liberal democracy, and local-level data from Colombia on public goods provision. Given the scale of this undertaking, the discussion and analyses are more abbreviated and circumscribed than those of earlier chapters (I undertake more comprehensive analyses in related work).[1]

Aligned with the implications of the book's framework, the chapter finds that, absent military power upsets, belligerents do not return to war if they lose the elections; rather, peace consolidates. In voting for stability, however, the evidence indicates that the citizenry may elect to delay or forgo near-term justice and a liberal variant of democracy. Finally, the data suggest that the election of belligerent politicians may generate a reduction in public insecurity, but with likely pernicious effects on the provision of other public goods, especially education.

Do Postwar Elections of Belligerents Bring a More Lasting Peace?

Many associate the process of consolidating war termination with the ballot box, but express well-merited concern that the advent of elections in postwar societies also brings risk.[2] A journalist in Angola in 1994 aptly summarized the concern: "Who cares who wins? . . . The losers won't accept it."[3] Some dramatic exemplars include NPFL warlord Charles Taylor in Liberia and UNITA rebel Jonas Savimbi in Angola. In the words of Terrence Lyons, "A great many Liberians believed that Taylor would return to war if he lost the election."[4] Because he won, the country progressed toward peace (albeit one that was short-lived). In contrast, following the Bicesse Accords in Angola in 1991, Savimbi allegedly told a British television crew, "If I lose . . . I will send my men back to the bush to fight again. We will not accept [electoral] defeat."[5] This did come about: when Savimbi lost the UN-monitored election, he refused to accept the result and Angola plunged back into civil war.[6]

Despite the conventional wisdom that electoral "losers will refuse to accept the results peacefully" and remilitarize,[7] it remains unexplored whether election *results* really affect the durability of a country's transition from conflict to peace, and whether combatant parties that lose these postwar electoral contests prove more prone to return to war. By measuring belligerents' performance at the polls and their subsequent decision whether to resume hostilities, the book sheds light on an important posited link between elections and war.

The book's theory implies that postwar elections increase the chance of renewed conflict if there is an inversion in the military balance of power after war, and the war loser performs poorly in the elections. If instead relative military power remains stable (or citizens accurately update on changes to it), civil war actors prove unlikely to remilitarize if they lose the elections.

Qualitative evidence in Chapters 5 to 7 substantiated this proposed logic. The Salvadoran and Guatemalan cases illustrated how a sustained postwar power balance and electoral results aligned with military power led to "Leviathan Peace." In the Nicaraguan case, the United States' highly public military shoring up of the Contras after the 1989 peace accord resulted in (empirically rare) "Recalibrated Peace"; the citizens accurately updated on the change in power, as did the Sandinistas. Security voters therefore issued the war-winner Sandinista party a stunning electoral defeat, which it conceded nonviolently. Chapter 8's brief mentions of places in which security was not highly salient (e.g., UK 2001), war winners adopted nonequilibrium strategies (e.g., Kosovo 2001), or voters preferred rule of law (e.g., Liberia 2005) suggested a scenario in which the military power balance held, the war winner lost the election, but the belligerents nonetheless allowed "Residual Peace" to consolidate.[8]

The emblematic case of revisionist war—Angola—further corroborates the argument: the demobilization process "upset the balance of power between the two militaries ... [and] worked decisively in UNITA's favor." Accordingly, "Savimbi was confident that UNITA could win the [next] war."[9] Voters did not engage in this type of updating; instead they used the war outcome as their heuristic. As a result, they split their vote and the newly militarily empowered UNITA rebels narrowly lost the founding postwar elections. "Fearing [the] consequences of this *discrepancy* between military power and electoral support, [U.S. Assistant Secretary of State Herman] Cohen admitted that it was not hard to wish for a UNITA [electoral] victory."[10] UNITA perceived that it could return to the next postwar ballot box the military victor, a title that, through security voting, would significantly raise its prospects of an electoral landslide in future elections.[11] Accordingly, it resumed its military offensives.[12]

Evaluating the Relationship between Power Upsets, Election Outcomes, and Remilitarization Globally

To probe the generalizability of the postulated relationship between power upsets, electoral results, and the decision to reinitiate fighting beyond these illustrative cases, I rely on the book's CWSP dataset on postwar election results, and new data on whether the belligerents returned to war and, if they did, *who* initiated the new fighting. This belligerent-level coding of remilitarization enables analysis of whether electoral winners or losers are more likely to restart war. To distinguish remilitarization from violence caused by new belligerents and wars, I carefully trace the actors after conflict termination. Of the belligerents that transitioned from violence from 1970 to 2015, 30 percent experienced a return to war with the same combatants.

An ideal operationalization of a power upset would code whether there was a shift, changing which military organization was dominant (and thus the anticipated war outcome from a subsequent bout of fighting, and prospective results from future elections). Such data are not available, however, and I therefore analyze a variable, *power shift*, that measures changes in the postwar balance of military power and indicates which side it favored.[13] Unfortunately, these data exist for only those conflicts that ended between 1990 and 2009 ($n = 88$). But within this subset, the data are available for all cases, suggesting little selection bias. In this subsample, I find that 14 percent of war losers gained power during the postwar period, destabilizing the power balance of 28 percent of the belligerent cases. In the remaining cases, the power balance was maintained or reinforced (i.e., the war winner became stronger).

Assessing the Risk of War Recurrence

This section shows the risk of war recurrence associated with each of the scenarios that intersect the stability of the distribution of power with the postconflict election outcomes (Table 9.1). Given that the scenarios are experienced at the country level, this analysis employs conflict-level data.

Of the thirty-one conflicts for which data on power shifts are available, five fell back into war within five years, two did so thereafter, and twenty-four consolidated peace. The theory accurately predicts the outcomes in twenty-eight of the thirty-one cases. Confirming my book's hypothesis, it is more likely for belligerents to demilitarize and for a Leviathan peace to emerge if the power balance stabilized and the war winner won the election. Where the power balance inverted and the war winner nonetheless won the election, the belligerents tended to plunge their states back into revisionist war. Scenarios in which the war winner lost the election—with either a stable or upset power balance—were rarer, but faced a negligible risk of remilitarization, substantiating the logic of what I call "residual" and "recalibrated" peace. In only three cases does the framework inaccurately predict the outcome.

These findings are largely consistent with the predictions. However, selection bias may have affected this analysis, and omitted determinants of power shifts, election outcomes, and remilitarization could be confounding the results. I therefore employ multivariate models to test the effects of power shifts and election results on a binary variable, *reinitiated war*, controlling for possible selection, endogeneity, and spuriousness.[14] Table A9.1 shows the results of this series of logistic regression models.

The basic pattern revealed in Table 9.1 generally holds in the multivariate analyses. The remilitarization risk rises dramatically when the balance of power inverts, but the war winner nonetheless wins the election. Holding the other variables at their means, the predicted probability of remilitarization in this scenario is 56 percent, compared to 0.4 percent if the power balance sustains or shifts and the newly empowered war loser wins the election. The data

TABLE 9.1. Empirical Cases of Postconflict War and Peace

		Postwar Balance of Power			
		Stable Power Balance		*Upset Power Balance*	
Election Outcome	*War Winner Wins Election / Stalemated Belligerents Split Vote*	Leviathan Peace		Revisionist War	
		Peace	*War*	*Peace*	*War*
		19	1	2	4
	War Winner Loses Election / Stalemated Belligerents Do Not Split Vote	Residual Peace		Recalibrated Peace	
		Peace	*War*	*Peace*	*War*
		4	0	1	0

suggest that, against oft-cited fears, electoral losers, even those contesting quick elections under plurality rules, without guarantees of shared power and absent UN oversight, do not necessarily return to war.

How Do Founding Election Results Influence Postwar Justice and Democracy?

In electing peace, the book's framework implies that citizens tend to forgo justice and liberal democracy. Selecting belligerent successors to take political office in the founding elections may help transform them into democratic actors, as they preserve a political system that serves them. At the same time, these parties born of war are unlikely to consolidate a type of democracy imbued with liberalism, as the work of Caroline Hartzell and Matthew Hoddie convincingly demonstrates,[15] and they are likely to solidify perpetrators' impunity to legal accountability. This book's case study chapters hinted at these potential perversities of belligerents' electoral victories. Here, I explore in suggestive terms whether, in a broader set of cases, the election of belligerent successor parties does, in fact, tend to stall prosecution and democratic deepening.

I operationalize transitional justice with a binary indicator—*amnesty*—that I take from the Post-Conflict Justice dataset.[16] This measure captures whether or not amnesty processes were put into place that promised not to prosecute or punish past violators. It includes amnesty processes in the postwar period up to five years after the termination of the internal armed conflict. The dataset verifies whether the amnesty began during the conflict termination process or rather in the postconflict stage, and it records the date of the process; I use these variables to verify that the amnesties were measured posttreatment.

To capture the extent to which the ideal of liberal democracy was achieved, I use the Varieties of Democracy liberal democracy index *vdem_libdem*, averaged over the five years following the founding postwar election. The index defines the liberal principle as "the importance of protecting individual and minority rights against the tyranny of the state and the tyranny of the majority. . . . This is achieved by constitutionally protected civil liberties, strong rule of law, an independent judiciary, and effective checks and balances that, together, limit the exercise of executive power."[17]

Table 9.2 presents the results. Model 1 engages in logistic regression with *amnesty* as the dependent variable. Model 2 uses ordinary least squares regression with *liberal democracy* as the outcome. For these analyses, the unit of analysis is the country-election year. As the explanatory variable, I use the belligerent successor parties' vote share. The analyses control for factors that might influence the electoral performance of belligerent parties in the founding election, and also independently influence the likelihood of advancing justice and liberal democracy thereafter. They include war outcomes, wartime incompatibility, war duration, UN intervention, veto players, and per capita GDP (proxying for state capacity).

Aligned with the implications of the book's framework, the results of the founding postwar elections, and in particular the success of bloodstained parties, appear to matter not only for the durability of peace but also for justice and democracy. A 1 percent increase in the belligerent parties' margin of victory corresponds with a 2 percent increase in the likelihood of an amnesty process. Among cases that implemented amnesties, the average combined vote share of the belligerent parties was 66 percent, compared to 46 percent in places that opted not to protect human rights abusers from future prosecution and punishment. This provides preliminary evidence that bloodstained parties may shield themselves from retribution, wrap themselves in blanket immunity, and block transitional justice, at least in the short to medium term. The theory suggests, and the case study evidence supports, that after the consolidation of security, possibilities for justice may increase over the longer term. Future research should establish the generalizability of these longer term patterns.

As displayed in Table 9.2, model 2, the coefficient on belligerent party success, while of small magnitude, is negative and significant, providing suggestive evidence that postwar election results may dampen liberal democracy in the five years following these founding contests. This analysis, cursory in nature, underscores the utility in seeking rigorous, more causally identified research designs to investigate further the effects of these critical elections on legal accountability and regime type.

TABLE 9.2. Effects of Founding Election Results on Postwar Justice and Democracy

	(1) Amnesty	(2) Liberal Democracy
Margin of victory of belligerent successor parties	0.02* (0.01)	−0.001* (0.00)
Constant	1.19 (4.81)	−0.23 (0.31)
Observations	56	66
R^2/Pseudo R^2	0.20	0.34

Note: Standard errors in parentheses. Robust standard errors account for country clustering. Analyses control for war outcomes, wartime incompatibility, war duration, UN intervention, per capita GDP (proxying for state capacity), and veto players.

*$p < .05$.

How Do Elections of Belligerent-Tied Politicians Influence Public Safety and Other Social Services?

In electing belligerent successor parties, the framework predicts that the citizenry is likely to gain in the short term in the domain in which the successful belligerent has a comparative advantage, competence, and expertise—security—but is likely to sacrifice social welfare.

Studying the implications of belligerents' electoral selection on public goods provision is challenging because insecurity and lack of development might have facilitated the electoral success of politicians with violent ties rather than these politicians, once elected to office, causing changes in insecurity and development. Moreover, there could be a variety of unobserved factors influencing both the likelihood of belligerents winning the elections and of belligerents governing in a specific fashion.

I seek to overcome this challenge by analyzing Colombian mayoral elections to compare the administrations of coercive politicians with those of politicians without coercive ties. An original database of 784 paramilitary-allied mayors, based on over 42,000 pages of Colombian Supreme Court sentencing documents,[18] enables a comparison of the administrations of paramilitary-tied candidates who barely won with those who barely lost the elections, using a regression discontinuity (RD) design. On either side of the electoral victory threshold, the outcomes of winners can be viewed as valid counterfactuals for the outcomes of losers. In the analysis, the unit of analysis is the municipality. I restrict the sample to the races in which a paramilitary politician and a non-paramilitary politician were the top two finishers (515 observations). I look at the paramilitary politician's vote share minus that of its strongest contender.[19] After verifying the validity of the design,[20] I examine the local average effects on provision of public security and of other public services at the cutoff of a locality being "treated" with a paramilitary-tied mayor against the "control" case in which it received a non-paramilitary mayor.

To measure levels of insecurity and crime, I employ three Policía Nacional indicators: (1) the total number of thefts (of cars, motorcycles, stores, people, banks, and residences); (2) the number of robberies against people; and (3) the number of incidents of bodily harm (interpersonal violence), averaged over the mayors' tenures in office.

For municipal performance in nonsecurity public goods provision, I examine levels of development as captured by infant mortality rates from the Departamento Administrativo Nacional de Estadísticas Vitales. I also derive the rate of educational coverage calculated as the total number of enrolled students divided by the total number of school-age individuals, provided by the Colombian Ministerio de Educación. Given the slow-moving nature of development indicators, I further examine expenditures as a proxy for nonsecurity public goods provision. These data derive from the Panel de Buen Gobierno data of the Universidad de los Andes. For these measures, I compute the means during the mayors' administrations.

To analyze the effect of a paramilitary politician barely winning or barely losing a mayoral election on governance outcomes, I estimate the following RD model: $y_{it} = f(margin)_{it} + \beta_1 (parapol)_{it} + \varepsilon$, where y_{it} is the outcome of interest in time t for municipality i, $f(margin)_{it}$ is a function of the paramilitary politician margin of victory (the forcing variable) in the municipal election, and $(parapol)_{it}$ is an indicator variable equal to 1 if the paramilitary politician candidate won and 0 otherwise. The coefficient β_1 represents the local average treatment effect (LATE) at the threshold of the margin of victory forcing variable, which is the difference between the local regressions' two estimated intercepts.

The Governance Records of Paramilitary Mayors

Table 9.3 shows the difference in means across the governance outcomes. In general, paramilitary mayors' municipalities exhibited lower crime rates: lower total thefts, robberies, and interpersonal violence per 1,000 inhabitants. At the same time, relative to their non-paramilitary counterparts, these mayors tended to perform poorly in terms of social welfare with,

TABLE 9.3. Difference in Means: Security and Public Goods Outcomes

Variable	(1) Non-paramilitary Politician	(2) Paramilitary Politician	(3) Difference
Thefts	−0.2	−0.6	−0.8***
	(2.1)	(1.7)	(0.3)
Robberies (of people)	−0.3	−1.3	−1.0***
	(2.1)	(1.7)	(0.3)
Bodily harm	0.1	−0.8	−0.9***
	(1.9)	(1.7)	(0.2)
Education coverage	70.9	70.9	−0.0
	(22.9)	(23.0)	(2.5)
Education spending	4.3	3.7	−0.6***
	(1.6)	(1.4)	(0.2)
Infant mortality rates	21.9	25.4	3.6***
	(7.9)	(9.4)	(1.3)
Observations	157	358	515

Note: Standard errors in parentheses. Thefts, robberies, and bodily harm are measured in logs per person.

***$p < .01$.

on average, higher infant mortality rates and lower educational coverage and expenditures.

Table 9.4 shows the RD coefficients for the security outcomes. For all three outcomes—thefts, robberies, and personal injuries—and for every bandwidth choice, there is a negative effect of a narrow paramilitary-tied politician win, suggesting that having this type of mayor in office caused a reduction in crime and an improvement in security. As the dependent variable is logged, for substantive interpretation, I exponentiate the coefficients. The analysis presented in the first column reveals that, when a paramilitary-linked politician barely won an election, the municipality experienced, on average, a $(\exp(-1.90) - 1) \times 100 = 85$ percent reduction in thefts, compared to when this type of politician barely lost the election. This effect is statistically significant at the .05 level for the three models. Moreover, the effects are also pronounced and significant for rates of victimization and bodily harm. Figure 9.1 illustrates the jump at the discontinuity with a RD plot of thefts where the dots are optimally chosen binned means and the line is a linear fit that includes the 95 percent confidence interval.

At the same time, the analyses presented in Table 9.5 show that a paramilitary politician barely winning a closely fought election tended to harm the

TABLE 9.4. RD Estimates: Security Outcomes

	Thefts			Robberies of People			Bodily Harm		
Outcomes	(1)	(2)	(3)	(4)	(5)	(6)	(7)	(8)	(9)
Paramilitary mayors	-1.90*	-1.45**	-1.68*	-2.62***	-1.86***	-2.25**	-1.82**	-1.19**	-1.60*
	(1.10)	(0.66)	(0.98)	(0.99)	(0.62)	(0.91)	(0.86)	(0.57)	(0.85)
Bandwidth	Opt (0.081)	0.1	0.05	Opt (0.074)	0.1	0.05	Opt (0.085)	0.1	0.05
Observations	100	115	66	79	101	59	107	120	70

Note: Standard errors in parentheses. Columns 1, 4, and 7 use the package "rdrobust" developed by Calonico et al. (2017), the computed optimal bandwidth, and a triangular kernel; these columns report robust point estimates and standard errors. The other models use a local linear regression with robust standard errors.

*p < .1. **p < .05. ***p < .01.

TABLE 9.5. RD Estimates: Public Goods Outcomes and Spending

	Education Coverage			Infant Mortality			Education Spending		
Outcomes	(1)	(2)	(3)	(4)	(5)	(6)	(7)	(8)	(9)
Paramilitary mayors	-17.36**	-7.07	-16.66**	4.50	4.27	5.36	-1.05**	-0.96**	-1.05*
	(7.38)	(5.65)	(6.94)	(4.48)	(3.47)	(4.81)	(0.48)	(0.38)	(0.55)
Bandwidth	Opt (0.087)	0.1	0.05	Opt (0.11)	0.1	0.05	.078 (Opt.)	0.1	0.05
Observations	179	198	113	142	121	70	135	164	98

Note: Standard errors in parentheses. Columns 1, 4, and 7 use the package "rdrobust" developed by Calonico et al. (2017), the computed optimal bandwidth, and a triangular kernel; these columns report robust point estimates and standard errors. The other models use a local linear regression with robust standard errors.

*p < .1. **p < .05.

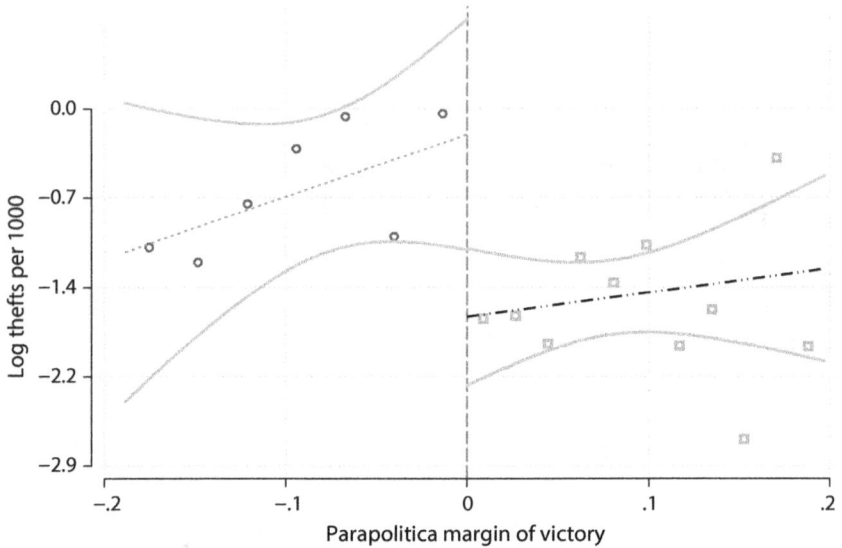

FIGURE 9.1. Effect of Paramilitary Politician Win on Thefts.
Note: The horizontal axis displays the winning margin of the paramilitary mayors (winners and runners-up). The dashed lines are the linear fit. The solid lines are the 95 percent confidence intervals, at both sides of the threshold.

municipality on dimensions of public goods, such as education coverage, though the results are weaker. All the point estimates are consistently negative. Models 1 and 3, in particular, show that, among municipalities that elected paramilitary mayors, educational coverage was 17 percentage points lower compared to municipalities in which such mayors narrowly lost. The coefficients on education in these specifications are significant at conventional levels. For infant mortality rates, we see that the effect points in the same direction: paramilitary mayors tended to increase these rates, but the results are not statistically significant. The education coverage results are illustrated in Figure 9.2. These effects, on variables that tend to be slow to change, manifested during these mayors' short administrations. I analyze the effect of a narrow paramilitary mayor win on expenditures on public goods, a variable more mutable over a four-year term. Models 7 to 9 reveal a strong negative effect; paramilitary mayors spent approximately $\exp(-0.94) - 1) \times 100 = 60.9$ percent less on education. The coefficients and differences in the means on public services and spending on these services may indicate, but

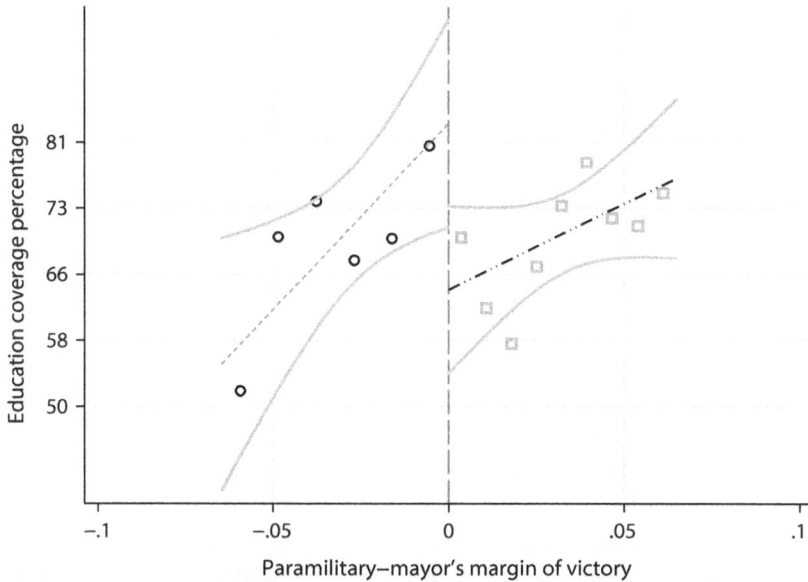

FIGURE 9.2. Effect of Paramilitary Politician Win on Education Coverage.
Note: The horizontal axis displays the winning margin of the paramilitary mayors (winners and runners-up). The dashed lines are the linear fit. The solid lines are the 95 percent confidence intervals, at both sides of the threshold.

by no means prove, that paramilitary politicians' rule may produce longer-term adverse effects on development outcomes. Elsewhere, I show with data on politicians' density of ties to the paramilitaries, police reinforcements, municipal expenditures, and public discourse that these narrow wins by paramilitary-tied mayors influenced crime rates and the provision of nonsecurity public goods through mechanisms of security capacity—a wider repertoire of security enforcers to keep sources of disorder under an iron fist and security prioritization—diversion of social spending from other public services. Given the limited sample size, these are strong results on security and education.

While the local-level design enables causal inference on a generally intractable question of belligerent party governance, it also reduces the generalizability of the findings. The Colombian paramilitary politics phenomenon exhibited many particularities; investigating how elected politicians with violent linkages govern in other contexts is a topic that merits further scholarly attention.

Conclusion

This chapter underscored the scope and significance of the political processes sparked by pivotal founding postwar elections in which bloodstained parties, if war winners, perform well. The cross-national and subnational evidence suggests that these elections tend to dissuade war recurrence and, under certain conditions, encourage ironfisted public safety. However, in so doing, the elections may legitimize coercive actors, undermine the Justice Cascade,[21] arrest burgeoning rule of law, and limit public goods provision.

If the elections are free and fair, their outcomes represent the preferences of war-ravaged voters. They suggest that, with their ballots, these voters prioritize stability and "negative peace";[22] they opt to "prevent victims of tomorrow rather than [addressing] victims of yesterday."[23] The question becomes how to enhance "positive peace" over time: how to generate conditions for transitional legal accountability, to protect and deepen democracy, to establish rule of law, and to enhance social development. The book's concluding chapter attempts a preliminary answer, delineating avenues for research and policy that may improve the chances that postwar elections yield not only peace, but also justice, liberalism, and welfare.

10

Conclusion

THIS BOOK'S analytic framework of violent-victors can potentially be applied widely around the globe, and several building blocks of the theory may suggest actionable interventions. The elections studied in this book shape postwar political order: citizens tend to elect peace, but at a sacrifice of justice, liberalism, and social welfare. Specifying the project's implications for future scholarly inquiry and policy is the task of these concluding pages.

This book is about a real puzzle: how parties with blood on their hands seek votes from populations they victimized, and why people so often vote for the very political actors guilty of violence against civilians. This has happened in every corner of the world, in every period of history, after every type of armed conflict, and in every form of regime including electoral democracy. The research presented in this book shows that it does not matter how much violence the perpetrators committed, nor whether they were associated with the government or with the rebels, incumbent or opposition, political right or political left. A pattern emerges: in founding postwar elections, belligerent successor parties win votes from abused populations and even from their own victims over nonbelligerent parties that present a viable alternative.

The answer to this puzzle centers on war outcomes. Militarily winning belligerents, and even those that have reached a stalemate at best, earn a most potent electoral weapon: credit for ceasing the wartime violence. They may wield this weapon to shift voters' views of even heinous past violence, and even in the face of nonbelligerent parties' campaigns for legal accountability. As a result, voters may reward the belligerent parties for the stability of peace rather than blame them for the carnage of war.

This credit for war termination makes the bloodstained parties' effective record of forcible coercion an electoral advantage rather than a liability. It is transmuted into a reputation for competence on security. With careful programmatic scripting, electoral targeting, and candidate selection, the militarily victorious parties can brandish this advantage to persuade voters that they can provide societal peace even better than could the less violent belligerents who lost the war, and better even than nonbelligerents, untainted by war, who credibly promise to follow the rules meant to protect the population from abuse.

Why does this work? Citizens emerging from war desire security and must decide which party they trust to handle securing their future. Persuaded that the winning belligerent can do better than the nonbelligerents, they elect these violent victors running as Restrained Leviathans: sovereigns promising sufficient strength to "overawe" threats to order and "to control the governed," and with restraint enough "to control [themselves]" and not revictimize in the future. (If the war ended in a draw, the successors of the stalemated belligerents would instead share these security votes unless, even if equal in war, they are unequal in their persuasive abilities.) The electoral performance of the successor to the war loser, meanwhile, is limited by its weak military showing. If, however, it advances a nonviolent, nonmainstream platform, it might earn a small place in the postwar political landscape, and foster a reputation that could bolster its prospects in future elections.

By opening the black box of postwar elections, this book offers a first attempt to understand how noncombatant and war-successor parties campaign and victimized voters cast their ballots in the postwar political arena, and to predict who is likely to dominate this arena. It examines not only the postwar parties that represent the ideological and organizational characteristics of the rebel side, as much of the literature does, but also nonbelligerent parties and those parties arising from the government side of the conflict. Thus, it indicates a bridge between scholarship on successor parties emerging from transitions from war to peace and scholarship on those born of transitions from authoritarianism to democracy.[1] In underscoring the impact of war outcomes, it contributes to a body of scholarship on conflict termination that points to the importance of *how* wars end for a variety of key political and economic outcomes.[2]

Implications for Scholarship

The book's framework suggest areas that remain rich for research; these center on advancing the international relations literature that uses the tools of political behavior, and pushing beyond the scope of the book both chronologically and geographically.

Security and Political Behavior

This book's examination of the electoral consequences of violence and military success in civil wars speaks to scholarship on the domestic politics of belligerence in the international domain. It suggests a research agenda that might integrate the two.

The book's results align with prominent findings in the study of public opinion about the use of force in foreign policy. They bolster the view that a "logic of consequences" (rather than a "logic of appropriateness") guides public attitudes toward belligerence, proportionality, and noncombatant immunity.[3] In the international arena, it has been shown that battlefield successes, winning wars, and military utility affect public opinion toward the use of force.[4] Analogously, the book suggests, war outcomes and military performance also shift public reactions to the use of force in civil war.[5] Parties play an important role in framing this public reaction and, through their programs, elite selection, and messaging, influence how battlefield effectiveness translates into electoral consequences, an argument echoing the foreign policy scholarship.[6]

Finding some commonality among patterns of support for use of force in intrastate wars and that in foreign relations suggests a potential avenue for future inquiry. To what extent does the reputation for competence on security that belligerent successor parties derive from winning a positive military outcome translate into domestic credibility on foreign policy and national defense? Such a line of inquiry suggests further research directions: (1) What affects public perceptions of the credibility of parties and candidates on countering different types of security threats (e.g., interstate, rebel, criminal, terrorist)? And (2) how does the election of belligerent parties and leaders affect security outcomes abroad?[7] While most countries covered by this book are not great powers, many are regional powers that engage in international relations. Understanding how the elections at the core of the book influence not only their domestic law and order but also their foreign policy and hence international stability merits investigation.[8]

This book focuses on the successor parties born of domestic rebel and government belligerents in intrastate war. However, many current wars are neither intrastate nor interstate, but rather internationalized civil conflicts in which foreign governments are active or proxy combatants.[9] Even though these foreign interveners commonly withdraw their troops at war's end, there are likely to be strong local, political and electoral legacies of the interveners' use of force. When countries pick sides and dedicate blood or treasure to other states' internal conflicts, they retain a continuing interest in preserving political influence on the ground through empowered local party allies. Their ability to do so depends, in part, on how such foreign belligerence in civil wars affects public opinion in the war-torn societies, the electoral fortunes of local political actors, and the conflict-state's cooperation with international powers after the international troops' withdrawal. This line of investigation could illuminate the foreign "audience costs" and benefits to intervenors of projecting hard power abroad, a fundamental instrument of world politics.

The sizeable toolbox of political behavior theory exhibits great promise in unlocking key questions of international security, not just economic voting. Deepening our understanding of security voting could further enhance the usefulness of canonical voting models in settings in which stability is the paramount issue.

Research Beyond the Scope of the Book, in Space and Time

Chapter 2 delineated the scope of the theory conceptually, and Chapter 8 did so empirically, skimming contexts at the boundaries: ethnic wars, cases of successful secession, environments defined by patronage politics, and places in which violence was more limited geographically. A deeper dive into these contexts would further enrich our understanding of political life after war.

The research reported in this book suggests some tentative predictions about how long belligerent successor parties may last. Data on the results of second postwar legislative election results reveal a significant correlation (0.8) between the vote share in the founding election and that in the second election. This underscores the impact of the first elections on the short- and medium-term political trajectories of battle-scarred countries.

However, longer-term dynamics merit future investigation. Additional research could seek to reveal the conditions under which belligerent successor parties retain their political foothold over multiple electoral cycles. As seen in the Latin American case studies, the effectiveness of the security brand tends to erode over time, compelling parties born of war to start campaigning on other issues. Why and how certain parties are better able to build effective political machines and to continue to compete successfully after politics normalize is a question ripe for research. Associated prospects for judicial progress or regression, and the deepening or debasement of democracy over time should also be examined.

Another direction for future inquiry is the question of what precisely happens to the security brand over the longer term. My research suggests that the brand's power diminishes, but it does not seem to collapse completely. Rather, as seen in the country studies, it may often lie dormant, where it can be resuscitated during future spells of insecurity. Understanding when, why, and how such a brand may be reactivated, and how and when it succeeds politically—that is, when voters opt with their ballots for "law and order" over the rule of law—are worthwhile inquiries.[10] This line of questioning suggests that insights from this book may apply beyond postwar environments to other elections in which security is highly salient.

Attempts and some successes at reviving a latent security brand that brought "order," even when that brand was built on the commission of atrocities, can be seen in campaigns around the world. Ironfisted candidates use propaganda to spin a narrative in which the strong break the law so as to provide stability. For example, in Peru, Keiko Fujimori ran in 2016 on her father Alberto Fujimori's "double-edged" legacy, decades old, of having defeated the Sendero Luminoso insurgency, which he had done with human rights abuses.[11] In the Dominican Republic in 2020, the grandson of brutal dictator Rafael Trujillo, Ramfis Domínguez-Trujillo, evoked "memories of a bygone era" with a promise of rule by a similar firm hand.[12] In the Philippines, the "Punisher," President Rodrigo Duterte, a merciless firebrand, built a reputation of being able to clean up a crime-riddled nation based on his record of extrajudicial killings.[13] His dynasty more recently joined with that of prior dictator Ferdinand Marcos to win the 2022 election by "airbrushing . . . the sins of [Marcos'] 20-year rule," arguing that it brought "order . . . [and] peace."[14] In Brazil, "dictatorship-praising, pro-torture" army captain Jair Bolsonaro argued in 2018 that what his violence-plagued nation needed was "a government with authority . . . similar to the one we had 40, 50 years ago,"[15] a government that "saved the country," but at the cost of thousands of victims.[16] In Nigeria in 2015, Muhammadu Buhari activated a security brand built upon his credentials as a former military dictator who had waged a vicious "war against indiscipline" from 1983 to 1985. Thirty years later, he sought "to convince voters that he wield[ed a] sufficient iron fist to beat the [more recent] insurgency by the Islamist militants."[17] In Sri Lanka in the aftermath of the 2019 Easter Sunday terror attacks, Gotabaya Rajapaksa projected himself as the only leader able to secure the country based on his credentials of "bringing peace to Sri Lanka in 2009 by defeating the Tamil Tigers" despite allegations of war crimes. His party's founder asserted that "the people have requested a leader who can ensure their security."[18] In India, as of May 2011, approximately one-third of the 545 elected lawmakers in the lower house had a track record of violent crime,[19] which signaled to voters that they would be hard on threats to security.[20]

In many postwar and postauthoritarian environments, and even beyond, parties often play the law-and-order card, seeking to heighten the salience or urgency of "anarchy" to justify adherence to a savior-strongman.[21] They argue they should not be blamed for the suffering but instead should be rewarded with votes for preventing greater turmoil; they canvass surrounded by military uniforms; and they act as if they were above the law.[22] Core voters, and sometimes even swing voters, may respond to these appeals with their security-motivated votes. Insights into such voter behavior may therefore shed light more generally on why, when feeling threatened, people prove willing to forgo rights, and favor hardline approaches to security and defense, and why, at times, people vote seemingly against their self-interests.

Policy Implications

The theory presented in this book reveals forces that influence postwar electoral outcomes, and suggests instruments that could help amplify the stabilizing power of these political contests while mitigating their potential for harm.

The theory may seem to imply perverse incentives for belligerents to engage in ruthless violence in war to obtain the upper hand militarily and then electorally. The theory does suggest dangerous incentives to start wars if victory seems assured. It indicates that, if winning in war, belligerents can escape electoral retribution for their transgressions in the short run. However, such transgressions are unlikely to increase prospects for wartime military success (indeed countless studies have demonstrated the counterproductive nature of indiscriminate violence in war), and in the long run ghosts from the past tend to catch up with their victimizers.[23] It is not their atrocities that bolster belligerent parties in postwar elections; it is winning the war that does so.

The theory may revise, but does not completely undercut, the conventional wisdom that actors guilty of egregious acts of violence will try not to end their wars, because they fear what will happen to them in the wars' aftermath.[24] The book's logic does imply that weaker belligerents—who will face most of the blame for the war—have a greater incentive to hold out than do war winners, who are better positioned to shield themselves from prosecution. At the same time, notable research implies that internationally imposed justice and the

International Criminal Court could penetrate these war winners' shield of impunity, the prospect of which could alter their decision to cease fire.[25]

The book's discussion of the effects of elections on peace, justice, democracy, and governance reinforces our knowledge of the trade-offs inherent in transitions that have been noted by numerous scholars: that what is necessary to avert instability and recurrent war in the aftermath of mass violence may, perversely, protect human rights abusers from justice, prevent the country from effectively resolving its "torturer problem,"[26] and hinder the deepening of democracy.[27] Uncovering the tensions and dilemmas inherent in the inclusion of violent perpetrators in democratic politics is an important policy contribution of this book. It is voters themselves who ultimately must weigh these trade-offs and choose between peace or justice and democratization in the short term. The good news of the book suggests that, even if voters prioritize peace, justice and democratization may also eventually become possible.

While respecting the agency of the electorates living through the turbulent war-to-peace transitions, outsiders' actions may be able to speed up the normalization of politics after violence. Interventions aimed at securing the peace, buttressing the balance of power, preventing waves of criminality, reducing the urgency of security issues, and countering strategic efforts to spin the violent past may be able to dampen the perverse electoral potency of war outcomes and amplify opportunities for justice and liberalism. I discuss such potential actionable conclusions and instruments for policy makers suggested by the theory advanced in this book.

Helping Elections Keep the Peace

The book's analyses suggest that citizens tend to elect peace, but that preventing perilous shifts in the power balance in the lead-up and aftermath of the elections is critical to consolidating this peace. The international community could do so, for example, by averting asymmetric demobilization processes that strengthen certain belligerents while weakening others.[28] It could further deter foreign interveners from using elections as their exit, a strategy that destabilizes because, when power shifts as a result of their withdrawal, belligerents gain incentives to remilitarize in order to establish the new power balance prior to future elections. Delaying the postwar polls to allow time to bolster democratic institutions may prove beneficial, although such a delay risks increasing the possibility of dangerous power shifts. Finally, while it may confer other benefits, power sharing appears unable to prevent electoral losers from returning to war if they face a power shock. If power sharing were rendered endogenous to changing power dynamics after war, it could be more effective at averting the resumption of hostilities.

Stabilizing the power balance after war is critical, and where instability is unavoidable, detecting and communicating the new military distribution of power to the decisive audience of voters could make it more likely that they will elect the stabilizing power. Overall, understanding the electoral incentives and disincentives for remilitarization could reveal ways to ballast a country weathering the stormy seas of the transition.

Bolstering Nonbelligerent Parties and the Rule of Law

A second set of actionable conclusions for policy makers concerns nonbelligerent parties. Security voting gives war winners, even if blood soaked, the upper hand in the elections. To render the electoral playing field more competitive, enhance the prospects of nonbelligerent parties, and strengthen the appeal of rule-abider platforms, several potential interventions could be entertained. First, since belligerent parties' electoral success requires that security remain salient, consolidating the transition, preventing spikes in crime, and otherwise reducing the urgency of security issues could take away the electoral power of winning the war. Citizens who perceive themselves safe are more likely to prioritize civil liberties and the rule of law. Second, belligerent successor parties have incentives to run on security and thus also to sustain the salience of security in voters' minds through scary rhetoric and, potentially, a persisting threat of low-level violence; therefore, steps to counter fear-mongering politics and belligerents' protection rackets may be valuable.[29] Third, electoral performance tracks with party strategies, so parties that adopt off-equilibrium paths tend to disappoint and disappear. Accordingly, interventions should seek to help nonbelligerents adopt an optimal Rule Abider strategy: promising security within the confines of the law, running candidates with clean human rights records, advancing moderate policies, and targeting the median voter. Outsiders also could help to strengthen these parties' advantages on nonsecurity valence issues, particularly economic recovery, to further boost their electoral successes.

Advancing Justice

The election of violent victors can forestall legal accountability for the perpetrators of crimes against humanity, particularly of those shielded by acquiring elected political power. However, the mitigating role of security on desires for retribution against war winners for their carnage may wane over time, and demands for prosecution may expand. Unfortunately, the international justice community has tended to disengage just at the moment when it might have the most impact: in the medium term, when changes in citizens' preferences render an expansion of accountability more feasible. Over the longer term, supporting civil society and victims' mobilization in pursuit of punishment, truth, and reparations may prove advantageous.

The research in this book reflects and supports Margaret Somers's observation: "which kinds of narratives will socially predominate . . . will depend in large part on the distribution of power."[30] Propaganda and persuasion can produce a fissure between "forensic truth" and "narrative truth."[31] Interventions aimed at ensuring balanced media access, increasing the pluralism of voices, countering misinformation, and enhancing competition in the "marketplace of ideas" may facilitate justice. As such, they merit greater international investment.

Conclusion

This book lays bare the electoral rewards of raw abuses of coercive power. It reveals the underlying logic, that the winner of a war also wins a powerful electoral weapon: credit for war termination. The party with this weapon, acting as a Restrained Leviathan, can shift voters' frames of reference, even for the most brutal atrocities, and even when confronted with nonbelligerents' demands for retribution. As a result, voters reward the combatant party for peace rather than blame it for violence. The militarily successful party's blood-stained war record, laundered by this credit for conflict termination, may become not an electoral disadvantage, but instead a reputation for competence on future security. The war-winner party, with programmatic convergence, electoral prioritization of unaligned voters, and a choice of candidates who will act as controlled sovereigns, can brandish this reputation to convince voters that it will do better at securing societal peace than could parties untainted by war, who credibly guarantee to obey the laws written to safeguard the citizenry from harm.

Populations battered by war elect such Restrained Leviathans. In so doing, they gain an end to anarchy, but lose justice and liberalism. Absent intervention, only time can heal this tension, but action by outsiders may accelerate the clock.

Chapter 4

Table A4.1 displays the final survey sample. In addition to the sampling procedures outlined in the main text, in the case of refusals or failure to contact the selected adult after two attempts, the household was replaced with the adjacent household and the interval sampling recommenced from that household. It merits mention that the survey sought to capture attitudes in *post*war contexts. This meant that, for both theoretical and safety considerations, municipalities in which violence was present were to be excluded and replaced within the homogeneity strata. Our random draw did not include zones of active violence at the time of sampling. However, violence morphs constantly, and thus an uptick in violence did prevent our survey from being conducted in three municipalities prior to enumeration, which we replaced within the homogeneity strata. Throughout the research, the safety of our enumerators and respondents was the guiding principle.

TABLE A4.1. Descriptive Statistics of Survey Sample

Variable	(1) Nonvictim	(2) Victim	(3) Difference
Age 18–25	0.207	0.210	0.003
	(0.405)	(0.408)	(0.021)
Age 26–35	0.216	0.244	0.028
	(0.412)	(0.430)	(0.022)
Age 36–45	0.179	0.184	0.005
	(0.384)	(0.388)	(0.020)
Age 46–55	0.156	0.154	−0.002
	(0.363)	(0.361)	(0.019)
55+	0.242	0.208	−0.034
	(0.429)	(0.406)	(0.022)
SES 1 (low)	0.208	0.307	0.099***
	(0.406)	(0.461)	(0.023)

Continued on next page

Variable	(1) Nonvictim	(2) Victim	(3) Difference
SES 2	0.268	0.190	−0.078***
	(0.443)	(0.393)	(0.022)
SES 3	0.126	0.077	−0.049***
	(0.332)	(0.267)	(0.015)
SES 4	0.037	0.022	−0.015*
	(0.188)	(0.147)	(0.009)
SES 5	0.020	0.002	−0.018***
	(0.140)	(0.048)	(0.005)
SES 6 (high)	0.014	0.004	−0.010**
	(0.117)	(0.059)	(0.005)
Female	0.528	0.501	−0.028
	(0.500)	(0.500)	(0.026)
Urban	0.671	0.602	−0.069***
	(0.470)	(0.490)	(0.025)
Elementary school	0.204	0.239	0.036
	(0.403)	(0.427)	(0.022)
Middle school	0.193	0.229	0.036*
	(0.395)	(0.420)	(0.021)
High school	0.446	0.418	−0.028
	(0.497)	(0.493)	(0.026)
College	0.106	0.063	−0.043***
	(0.308)	(0.243)	(0.014)
Observations	657	857	1,514

*$p < .1$. **$p < .05$. ***$p < .01$.

TABLE A4.2. Offsetting Experiment: All Outcomes

	(1) Violence Justified	(2) Anger	(3) Jail	(4) Jail (Years)
Army–security	0.603***	−0.255***	−0.123***	−7.484***
	(0.148)	(0.080)	(0.025)	(2.044)
Army	0.299**	−0.149*	−0.075***	−4.099**
	(0.150)	(0.081)	(0.026)	(2.035)
FARC–security	0.374**	−0.154*	−0.028	−4.541**
	(0.148)	(0.080)	(0.026)	(2.040)
Constant	1.042***	2.709***	0.922***	38.209***
	(0.107)	(0.058)	(0.018)	(1.431)
Observations	1,510	1,510	1,436	1,082
R^2	.011	.007	.018	.013

Note: All models use OLS regression with robust standard errors and include age, education, socioeconomic level, and gender covariates. All models calculate the ATE of each condition relative to the baseline condition of *FARC–no security*.

*$p < .1$. **$p < .05$. ***$p < .01$.

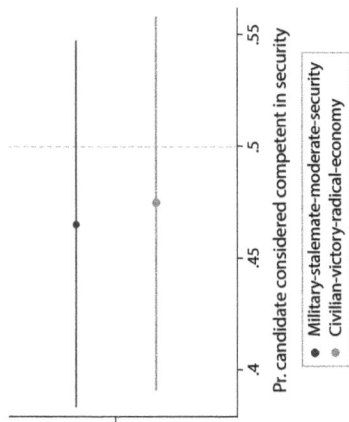

Panel A. Switch military/civilian

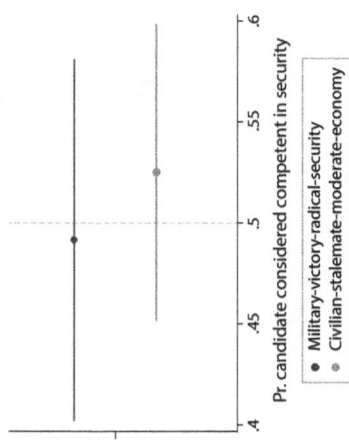

Panel D. Switch security/economy

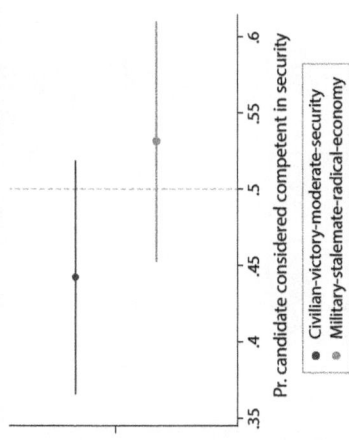

Panel B. Switch moderate/radical

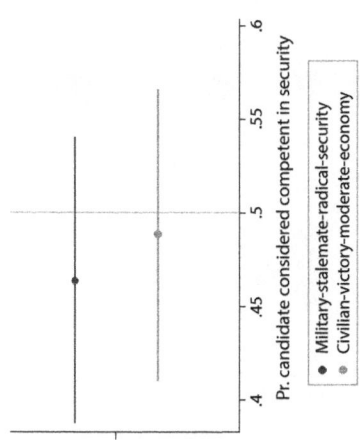

Panel E. Switch war outcome and position

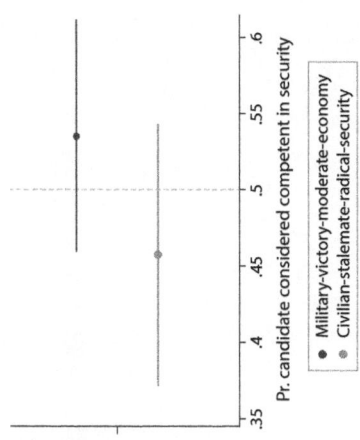

Panel C. Switch victory/stalemate

FIGURE A4.1. Alternative Combinations of Party Strategy on Perceived Competence on Security.
Note: The panels present probability estimates for alternative combinations of attributes to indicate the extent to which the specific interaction drives the results versus individual aspects of the profile. Consistent with the theory, only the Restrained Leviathan profile produces the boost in perceptions of security competence (Figure 4.5). Bars represent 95 percent confidence intervals.

	% of Words	
Topic	Uribismo (Duque)	Santismo (De La Calle)
Disarmament / decreasing military expenditures	0 (0)	2.8 (0.9)
Rearmament / strengthening military / increasing military expenditures	12.1 (3.9)	0 (4.7)
Emphasis on human and civil rights / freedom from coercion	23.0 (15.6)	17.0 (2.2)
Soft on crime (prevention, rehabilitation, reducing penalties)	12.4 (6.2)	38.0 (17.5)
Hard on crime (strong government, strict law enforcement, tough actions against domestic crime, increasing support and resources for the police, importance of internal security)	24.3 (0.7)	13.0 (4.4)

Note: To contrast the security agendas of Santismo and Uribismo, research assistants, blind to the book's expectations, hand coded the sections of their respective candidates' party manifestos devoted to security topics. They classified each word and estimated the proportion that fit the prespecified categories. The analysis, displayed, illustrates that Santismo was much more likely to emphasize rule of law, Uribismo law and order.

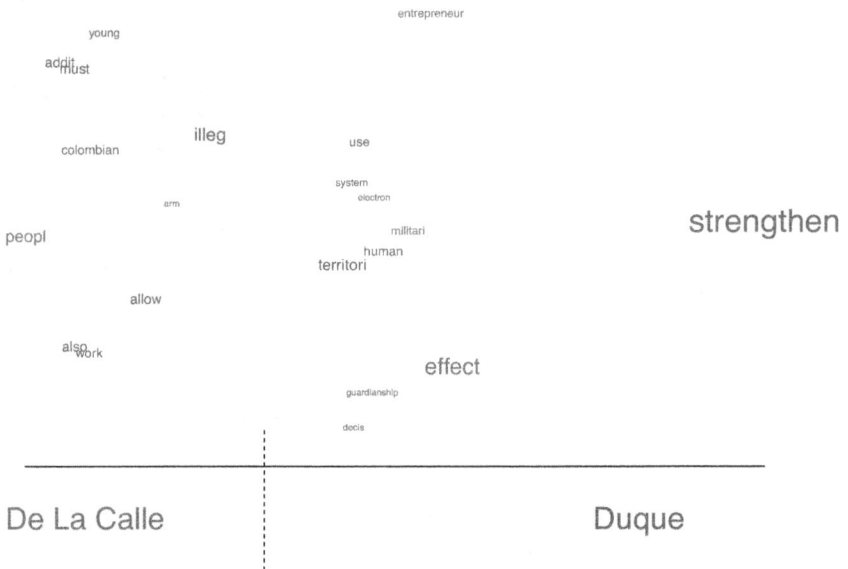

FIGURE A4.2. Santismo's Rule of Law versus Uribismo's Law and Order.

Note: This figure illustrates the results of natural language processing (described in the introduction to Chapter 5) of the 2018 candidates' security platforms. (See the online appendix for similar analyses of nearly half a million Twitter posts of the 2018 candidates.) It shows the stemmed words associated with a topic, grouped by whether the topic was discussed by Santista de la Calle (left quadrant) or Uribista Duque (right quadrant). The larger the words, the more frequently they appeared. The larger, further from the center, to the left or right, and darker in tone the words appear, the more strongly associated those words are with one party or the other. They show that, in 2018, Santistas were more likely to emphasize rule-based security; Uribistas strongarm security.

TABLE A5.1. Party Manifesto Project Variables: Right-Left Party Positions

rile	Right-left position of party as given in Laver and Budge (1992).
	The procedure adapts version 5 of the coding instructions: $(per104 + per201\_1 + per201\_2 + per305\_1 + per305\_2 + per305\_3 + per305\_4 + per305\_5 + per305\_6 + per401 + per505 + per601\_1 + per605\_1 + per605\_2) - (per103\_1 + per103\_2 + per105 + per106 + per202\_1 + per412 + per413 + per504)$

per104	Military: positive
per105	Military: negative
per106	Peace
per103_1	Anti-imperialism: state-centered anti-imperialism
per103_2	Anti-imperialism: foreign financial influence
Per201_1	Freedom
per201_2	Human rights
per202_1	Democracy general: positive
per305_1	Political authority: party competence
per305_2	Political authority: personal competence
per305_3	Political authority: strong government
per305_4	Transition: predemocratic elites: positive
per305_5	Transition: predemocratic elites: negative
per305_6	Transition: rehabilitation and compensation
per401	Free market economy
per412	Controlled economy
per413	Nationalization
per504	Welfare state expansion
per505	Welfare state limitation
per601_1	National way of life general: positive
per605_1	Law and order: positive
per605_2	Law and order: negative

Note: This table lists the Party Manifesto Project variables used to build the right-left party position classifier.

Chapter 8

TABLE A8.1. Summary Statistics, Civil War Successor Party Dataset

Variable	Mean	Std. Dev.	Min.	Max.	N
Vote share	25.80	28.72	0	75.33	180
War outcome	1.58	0.82	0	3	205
War outcome (alternative)	1.26	0.79	0	3	189
Belligerent's atrocities	0.61	0.49	0	1	161
Free and fair elections	0.51	0.18	0.22	0.93	194
UN intervention	0.43	0.50	0	1	200
Power sharing	0.14	0.35	0	1	196
Number of vetoes	2.24	0.60	2	5	192
Incompatibility	1.59	0.49	1	2	202
War duration	10.21	12.84	0	65	203
Incumbent electoral coercion (NELDA)	0.22	0.42	0	1	156
Opposition electoral coercion (NELDA)	0.48	0.50	0	1	162
Rebel governance	0.45	0.50	0	1	101
Rebel cohesion	1.22	0.62	0	2	97
Rebel finances	0.52	0.50	0	1	101
Popular support	0.95	0.70	0	2	188
Election timing	4.36	3.77	0	18	185
Voter turnout	66.92	16.84	30.35	96.48	150
Per capita GDP	8.00	1.07	5.59	10.47	178
PR system	0.38	0.49	0	1	182

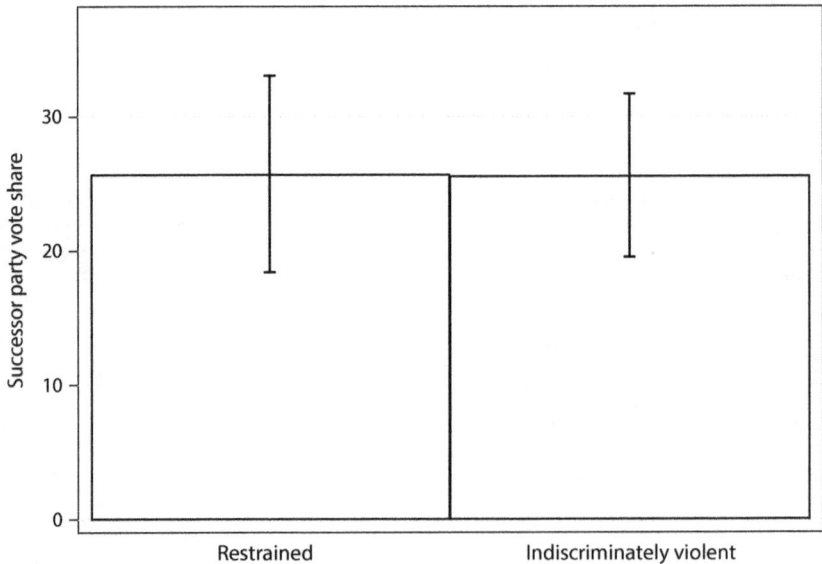

FIGURE A8.1. Wartime Victimization and Successor Party Vote Share.
Note: This figure illustrates the overall null result of wartime victimization on post-civil-war party success.

TABLE A8.2. Correlates of Civil War Successor Party Success, Robustness Checks

	(1)	(2)	(3)	(4)
	Rebel Vote Share	Govt Belligerent Vote Share	Rebel Vote Share	Govt Belligerent Vote Share
War outcomes			10.26*** (3.73)	−11.56** (5.52)
War outcomes (alternative measure)	25.31*** (3.35)	−21.52*** (3.59)		
Belligerent's atrocities	−1.91 (3.58)	2.82 (5.70)	−4.53 (5.08)	1.19 (6.78)
Free and fair elections	5.99 (8.70)	−24.26* (12.13)	−8.04 (16.60)	−36.12 (22.18)
UN	1.74 (4.55)	−8.24 (6.19)	0.29 (6.29)	−11.20 (7.56)
Power sharing	−9.07 (5.46)	12.40 (9.73)		
Number of vetoes	−1.99 (2.33)	−6.82 (6.43)	−7.10** (2.92)	−5.00 (5.82)
Incompatibility	17.26*** (3.87)	7.33 (6.33)	9.49 (5.88)	2.56 (10.38)
War duration	−0.13 (0.17)	−0.46 (0.28)	−0.19 (0.15)	−0.62* (0.34)
Voter turnout			9.95* (5.10)	10.69 (7.82)
Per capita GDP			0.24 (0.20)	0.08 (0.28)
PR system			−0.37 (3.60)	−0.37 (4.36)
Constant	−36.96*** (9.71)	84.73*** (15.24)	−11.33 (41.50)	85.75 (57.79)
Observations	82	62	64	48
R^2	.58	.41	.37	.33

Note: Standard errors in parentheses. Robust standard errors account for country clustering. Models 1–2 provide specifications with alternative operationalizations of war outcomes. Models 3 and 4 control for voter turnout, proportional representation arrangements, and per capita GDP.

*$p < .1.$ **$p < .05.$ ***$p < .01.$

TABLE A8.3. Alternative Explanations and Endogeneity

	(1)	(2)	(3)	(4)	(5)	(6)
	War Outcomes	Postwar Free and Fair Elections	War Outcomes	War Outcomes	War Outcomes	War Outcomes
War outcomes (defeat to victory)		−0.00 (0.01)				
Belligerent's wartime atrocities	−0.01 (0.28)					
Wartime popular support			0.82*** (0.28)			
Wartime rebel governance				0.16 (0.42)		
Wartime rebel cohesion					−0.17 (0.31)	
Wartime rebel finances						0.36 (0.33)
cut1	−2.35*** (0.31)		−1.54*** (0.30)	−1.84*** (0.36)	−2.07***	−1.73***
cut2	0.18 (0.17)		0.96*** (0.28)	−0.31 (0.31)	−0.64 (0.39)	−0.18 (0.32)
cut3	2.33*** (0.34)		2.99*** (0.46)	2.40*** (0.37)	2.22*** (0.47)	2.53*** (0.43)
Constant		0.39*** (0.04)				
Observations	159	180	187	101	97	101

Note: Robust standard errors in parentheses. All models use ordinal logit regression except Model 2, which uses ordinary least squares.

***p < .01.

TABLE A8.4. Sources of Data on Subnational Violence, War Outcomes, and Postwar Elections

Country-Election	Source of Subnational Violence Data	Source of Subnational Voting Data	Data on Rebel, Govt, or Both Parties	Source of Subnational War Outcome Data	Administrative Level of Subnational Analysis: First Level (Department) or Second Level (Municipality)
Angola 1992		CLEA	Both	Gromes and Ranft 2016	First level
Angola 2008	UCDP	CLEA	Both		First level
Bangladesh 2001	UCDP	CLEA	Govt		Second level
Colombia 2010	Daly 2012; El Centro de Estudios sobre Desarrollo Económico (CEDE)	Registraduría Nacional del Estado Civil / CEDE Base de Datos Electorales	Militias		Second level
Colombia 2018	Daly 2012; El Centro de Estudios sobre Desarrollo Económico	Registraduría Nacional del Estado Civil	Rebel		Second level
El Salvador 1994	Informe de la Comisión de la Verdad para El Salvador	Tribunal Supremo Electoral	Both	Cienfuegos 1982; McElhinny 2006	Second level
Guatemala 1999	Centro Internacional para Investigaciones en Derechos Humanos	Tribunal Supremo Electoral[a]	Both		Second level
India 1996 (Sikhs)	UCDP	CLEA	Both		Second level
Indonesia 2009 (Aceh)	UCDP	CLEA	Govt		Second level

Continued on next page

TABLE A8.4. (*continued*)

Country-Election	Source of Subnational Violence Data	Source of Subnational Voting Data	Data on Rebel, Govt, or Both Parties	Source of Subnational War Outcome Data	Administrative Level of Subnational Analysis: First Level (Department) or Second Level (Municipality)
Liberia 2005	Liberian Truth and Reconciliation Commission[b]	CLEA	Govt		First level
Mozambique 1994		Comissão Nacional de Eleições		Ishiyama[c]	First level
Nepal 2008	Informal Sector Service Centre (INSEC)[d]	Electoral Commission of Nepal[e]	Rebel	Ishiyama and Widmeier 2013	Second level
Peru 1995	Truth and Reconciliation Commission (CVR)[f]	Registro Nacional de Identificación y Estado Civil[g]	Govt		First level
Philippines 1998 (MNLF)	UCDP	CLEA	Govt		First level
Russia 2011	UCDP	CLEA	Govt		Second level
South Africa 1994	UCDP	CLEA	Both		First level
Sri Lanka 2010	UCDP	CLEA	Both		Second level
UK 2001 (N. Ireland)	Northern Ireland Research Initiative[h]	CLEA	Both		Second level

a. I am grateful to Regina Bateson for these data.
b. See Cibelli, Hoover, and Krüger 2009.
c. I am grateful to John Ishiyama for these data.
d. Data are available from INSEC 2006. See Ishiyama and Widmeier 2013.
e. I am grateful to Binod Paudel for these data.
f. I am grateful to Hillel Soifer for these data.
g. I am grateful to José Incio for these data.
h. See Loyle, Sullivan, and Davenport 2014.

TABLE A8.5. World Values Survey and Founding Election Dates

	Year of Founding Election	Year of World Values Survey
Argentina	1983	1984
Azerbaijan	1996	1997
Bangladesh	2001	2002
Bosnia	1996	2001
Croatia	1995	1996
Egypt	2000	2001
Georgia	1995	1996
Guatemala	1999	2004
Indonesia	2009	2006
Iraq	2010	2012
Libya	2012	2014
Moldova	1994	1996
Peru	1995	1996
Philippines	1998	1996
Russia	2011	2011
S. Africa	1994	1996

Note: This table lists the date of the World Values Surveys and of the elections to show how accurately the polls took the pulse of public opinion.

Chapter 9

TABLE A9.1. Correlates of Remilitarization after Postwar Elections

	(1)	(2)[a]	(3)	(4)	(5)	(6)	(7)
				Reinitiate War			
Power upset and war winner wins election	5.87*** (1.61)	7.00*** (1.64)					
Belligerent party vote share			0.00 (0.02)	−0.03 (0.02)	0.01 (0.01)	−0.11*** (0.03)	−0.01 (0.02)
Power sharing		−0.67 (2.20)	0.40 (1.14)				
Vote share × Power sharing			0.00 (0.02)				
PR system				1.73 (0.98)			
Vote share × PR system				−0.00 (0.03)			
Election timing		−0.14 (0.14)			0.11 (0.07)		
Vote share × Election timing					−0.01** (0.00)		
UN intervention		3.72* (1.54)				−1.12 (0.71)	

Vote share × UN intervention						0.12*** (0.03)	
Organizational capacity							0.21 (0.72)
War duration	0.03 (0.04)	0.10 (0.11)	0.01 (0.04)	-0.00 (0.02)	-0.02 (0.03)	0.00 (0.02)	-0.00 (0.05)
Incompatibility	-2.79 (1.66)		-1.26 (0.90)	-0.85 (0.82)	-0.33 (0.59)	-0.38 (0.60)	0.48 (0.88)
War violence	-0.38 (0.57)	-0.33 (0.57)		0.57* (0.29)	0.22 (0.30)	0.28 (0.29)	0.40 (0.27)
Number of vetoes	0.80 (0.71)	0.41 (0.63)	0.54 (0.46)	-0.54 (0.57)	-0.25 (0.61)	-0.19 (0.53)	-0.72 (0.73)
Per capita GDP (logged)	-1.58** (0.60)	-0.89 (1.64)		0.02 (0.44)	0.09 (0.46)	0.07 (0.41)	0.38 (0.53)
Free and fair elections	-11.99 (7.74)	-14.98** (5.79)	-5.08** (1.78)	-2.88 (1.68)	-0.76 (1.68)	-1.14 (1.63)	-0.47 (2.04)
Constant	14.79** (5.39)	4.19 (12.05)	-0.17 (1.28)	-0.43 (4.85)	-2.14 (4.68)	-1.08 (4.26)	-5.32 (5.74)
Observations	67	55	103	126	133	133	71

Note: Standard errors in parentheses. Robust standard errors account for country clustering.

a. Due to multicollinearity, incompatibility must be dropped from this analysis. The result for *power upset* and *war winner wins election* holds irrespective of which variables are included/excluded from the analysis.

*p < .05. **p < .01. ***p < .001.

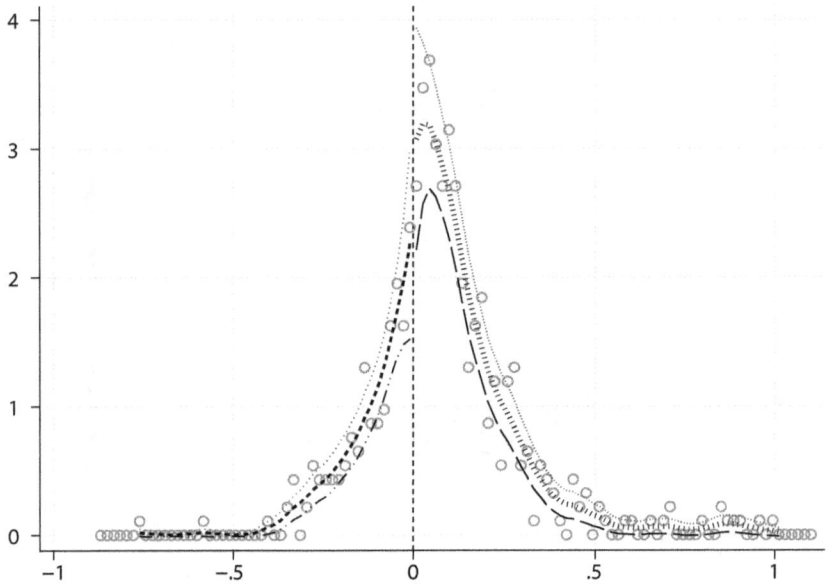

FIGURE A9.1. Validating the Regression Discontinuity Design: McCrary Test.
Note: This figure shows the graphical results of the McCrary test, which analyzes possible anomalous jumps in the distribution of the running variable: paramilitary politician's margin of victory (bandwidth 0.1). The jump at the threshold is not statistically significant (the p value of the log difference in heights is higher than 0.1), suggesting that it is a normal jump that also exists at different values of the distribution. This indicates that candidates could not precisely influence close elections and that mayors' administrations on either side of the cutoff may be comparable (McCrary 2008). I also use Cattaneo, Frandsen, and Titiunik's (2015) local polynomial density estimator to estimate whether the density of the margin-of-victory variable is continuous in the neighborhood of the threshold. The p value of .34 confirms that the test fails to reject the null hypothesis that the density of the running variable is continuous at the cutoff.

TABLE A9.2. Validating the RD Design: Continuity Tests, Lagged Outcomes

	(1)	(2)	(3)	(4)	(5)	(6)
Outcomes	Education	Infant Mortality	Education Spending	Thefts	Robberies	Bodily Harm
Paramilitary mayor	6.48 (9.75)	−0.81 (8.34)	−0.65 (0.65)	−0.85 (1.42)	−1.19 (1.27)	−1.25 (1.23)
Obs.	199	62	100	48	49	48

Note: Standard errors in parentheses. The models use a triangular kernel and the optimal bandwidth calculated with the package "rdrobust," which uses the algorithm developed by Calonico et al. (2017). Robust point estimates and robust standard errors are estimated with a local polynomial regression-discontinuity. The RD model uses one-period lagged outcomes as the dependent variable to check whether there is a significant effect of having a paramilitary mayor on pre-treatment outcomes. None of the RD estimates are significant, suggesting that there is not a pretrend on the outcomes that may explain the treatment effects. In the placebo tests, there exist no discontinuities, further validating the RD design and suggesting, in particular, that places with paramilitary and non-paramilitary mayors did not differ in their pretreatment levels of insecurity and public goods provision.

NOTES

Chapter 1

1. Stoll 1990.
2. Garrard-Burnett 2010.
3. U.S. Department of State 1999.
4. Organization of American States 2000.
5. Garrard-Burnett 2010, 10.
6. LAPOP 1999.
7. Kobrak 2013.
8. ARENA is the Nationalist Republican Alliance.
9. Pyes 1983.
10. International Foundation for Electoral Systems 1994.
11. FMLN stands for the Farabundo Martí National Liberation Front.
12. Daly 2019.
13. LAPOP 1995.
14. International Foundation for Electoral Systems 1994.
15. Human Rights Watch 2015 describes this systematic practice: "Army brigades across Colombia routinely executed civilians. . . . Soldiers and officers abducted victims or lured them to remote locations under false pretenses—such as with promises of work—killed them, placed weapons on their lifeless bodies, and then reported them as enemy combatants killed in action."
16. The transitional justice regime found the paramilitaries responsible for over 60 percent of the disappearances, massacres, and assassinations in a conflict that left over nine million victims. Centro Nacional de Memoria Histórica 2020.
17. Between 2005 and 2007, the International Organization for Migration (IOM) administered a survey to nearly 3,000 civilians living in 450 Colombian communities with a significant ex-paramilitary presence. For details, see Daly 2016.
18. Author interview, Bogotá, March 2017. According to LAPOP 2009, paramilitary victims and nonvictims in equal proportions expressed support for the ex-paramilitaries.
19. Camilo Echandía, author interview, Bogotá, November 2015. International observers confirmed this knowledge (author interviews, Aguachica, June 2008; Valledupar, March 2017). The vote share of paramilitary-politicians in places with high risk of electoral manipulation and displacement was equal to that in places with low displacement and zero risk of manipulation,

according to data from the Misión Observatorio Electoral (MOE) and Centro de Estudios sobre Desarrollo Económico (CEDE).

20. This is consistent with Barry Weingast's model: "When the sovereign [or rebel] transgresses against one group, he shares some of the benefits with the other group in exchange for their support" (1997, 248).

21. On coercion in elections, see Hafner-Burton, Hyde, and Jablonski 2014; Mares and Young 2016; Wilkinson 2004.

22. Voting patterns in such elections have been meticulously studied by Magaloni 2006.

23. As tackled in Chapter 2 and documented in Chapter 8, elections took place in the vast majority of postconflict countries, and nearly every case of civil war that ended in the period 1970 to 2015 witnessed participation by belligerent successors in these postwar elections.

24. See, for example, Calvo and Murillo 2019; Lewis-Beck and Paldam 2000; Lupu 2016; Stokes et al. 2013.

25. Berinsky 2007; Gartner 2008; Gelpi, Feaver, and Reifler 2009; Getmansky and Zeitzoff 2014; Howell and Pevehouse 2007; Kertzer and Zeitzoff 2017; Mueller 1973; Press, Sagan, and Valentino 2013; Tomz, Weeks, and Yarhi-Milo 2020.

26. This is consistent with Madison's argument that the ability to control the government, or oblige it to control itself, is essential. *Federalist No. 51*. See Madison 1788 (Madison 2008, 257). This focus on restraint echoes John Locke, who argued, "No one ought to harm another in his life, health, liberty or possessions" (Locke 1824).

27. Kahneman and Tversky 1979. If it fumbles at this game, it finds itself on the ash heap of history, as off-equilibrium case studies in the book show.

28. Hobbes 1996.

29. Madison 2008, 257.

30. Weber 1946. This is not to suggest that voters necessarily deem the Weberian ideal feasible in practice, but rather seek its pursuit. Institutional capacity and political will limit statebuilding theories' applicability to the Global South, as Herbst 2000 points out.

31. If, instead, the war ended in stalemate, both or all of the belligerent successors will share these prospective security votes unless, even if equal in war outcome, they are unequal in their persuasive abilities.

32. Hobbes 1996. This is a Madisonian variant of Hobbes, in that the sovereign must exhibit both strength and restraint. Chapter 3 develops this concept in depth.

33. Davenport 2007; Diamond and Plattner 2006.

34. Walter 2004.

35. Goodwin 2001; Hegre et al. 2001; Przeworski 1991; Wood 2003.

36. Mansfield and Snyder 2007; Paris 2004, Flores and Nooruddin 2012.

37. Brancati and Snyder 2012.

38. UNITA leader Jonas Savimbi in Angola constitutes a dramatic example of a loser who returned to war.

39. Manning and Smith 2016; Marshall and Ishiyama 2016; Söderberg Kovacs 2007.

40. Brancati and Snyder 2012.

41. Bush and Prather 2017; Hyde 2011; Matanock 2017.

42. Cammett and Malesky 2012; Hartzell and Hoddie 2007; Toft 2010; Walter 2002 build on Lijphart's 1977 writings on democracy in divided societies. They argue that there are benefits to

peace of institutions that guarantee electoral losers some degree of political power, for example, through proportional representation, vetoes, autonomy, or seat/cabinet quotas.

43. See Daly 2022.

44. Werner 1999.

45. Galtung 1969 differentiated "negative peace"—an absence of war and manifest violence—from "positive peace"—the absence of structural violence. I argue not that these societies become immediately "peaceful" but that large-scale war does not recur.

46. Flores and Nooruddin 2012.

47. Fearon 1995 argues that war is costly and therefore both sides should be able to negotiate an agreement that will leave each side better off than the inefficiency of fighting.

48. Fortna and Huang 2012; Huang 2016; Wood 2000b. See also Gurses and Mason 2008; Wantchekon 2004.

49. Flores and Nooruddin 2016; Hartzell and Hoddie 2015; Wantchekon 2004. Matanock 2017 offers insights into the impact on democratization of provisions for rebel participation in postwar elections. Roeder and Rothchild 2005 weigh the potentially pernicious effects of power-sharing institutions on democratic quality. Berman 2007 documents the origins of many democracies in violent conflict.

50. Rueschemeyer, Stephens, and Stephens 1992, 57 were speaking of the relationship between class cleavages and support for democracy, but this statement also appears plausible in the context of postwar elections. In Chapter 8, I evaluate selection issues empirically: whether belligerents allow competitive elections only if they believe they will win. I show empirically that war winners do not control whether there are competitive elections, how competitive the elections are, or when the elections take place. I also show that the relationship between war outcomes and election results holds irrespective of the extent to which the elections are competitive.

51. Huntington 1993; Levitsky and Way 2012; Lopez-Alves 2000; Slater and Smith 2016. For example, strong parties consolidated from revolutionary and counterrevolutionary struggles in Latin America (Uruguay, Colombia, El Salvador, Honduras, Costa Rica, Mexico, Nicaragua, and Bolivia), in Africa (Angola, Ethiopia, Cape Verde, Mozambique, and Zimbabwe), and in Asia (Taiwan, India, and China).

52. A party system is defined as "a set of patterned interactions in the competition among parties" having varying levels of institutionalization (Mainwaring and Scully 1995). See Roberts and Wibbels 1999.

53. Democratic transitions under a pact or agreement, in which authoritarian and military rulers gain space in the new democratic system, have been found to prevent these rulers from "spoiling" the path to peaceful democracy but have negative ramifications for the quality of democracy (Hagopian 1990; Karl 1986; O'Donnell and Schmitter 1986; Stepan 1988).

54. Hartzell and Hoddie 2015.

55. For example, see Arriola and Lyons 2016; Levitsky and Way 2012; Thaler 2017; Lyons 2016.

56. Elster 2004.

57. Vinjamuri and Snyder 2015.

58. Finnemore and Sikkink 1998; Sikkink 2011.

59. Akhavan 2009.

60. Huntington 1993.

61. Balcells 2012; Lupu and Peisakhin 2017; Rozenas, Schutte, and Zhukov 2017 demonstrate that descendants of victims form hostile attitudes and electorally punish the perpetrators. These studies look intergenerationally at victims' preferences, rather than in the aftermath of war. Related scholarship looks at how citizens form judgments of violence during (not after) civil war (Condra and Shapiro 2012; Kupatadze and Zeitzoff 2021; Levy 2022; Lyall, Blair, and Imai 2013) and at whether wartime victimization results in an increase in political participation, but does not study who gets the votes of these victimized populations (Bateson 2012; Bellows and Miguel 2009; Blattman 2009; Dorff 2017).

62. Nalepa 2010; Snyder and Vinjamuri 2003; Vinjamuri and Snyder 2015. Simmons 2009 assumes that both logics are at play.

63. Snyder and Vinjamuri 2003. In this sense, the book agrees more with Thomas Hobbes than with David Hume.

64. Nalepa 2010; Peskin 2008.

65. International Center for Transitional Justice (ICTJ) 2004, 2006; Samii 2013b; Stover and Weinstein 2004.

66. The mitigating effect of the provision of security on the attribution of blame likely erodes. With time, the citizenry begins to compare the belligerents' wartime atrocities to a world in which no atrocities ever occurred, and its desire for justice may increase.

67. Mintz 1993; Powell 1993; Sexton, Wellhausen, and Findley 2019.

68. Ahnen 2007; Arias and Ungar 2009; Holland 2013; Lessing 2017; Moncada 2013; Rivera and Zarate-Tenorio 2016.

69. Howell and Pevehouse 2007; Tomz, Weeks, and Yarhi-Milo 2020. On public opinion and foreign policy, see also Milner and Tingley 2013.

70. See, for example, Gartner 2008; Kertzer and Zeitzoff 2017; Mueller 1973.

71. Wantchekon 1999a, 1999b; Wood 2000b.

72. Brancati and Snyder 2012; Flores and Nooruddin 2012; Hartzell and Hoddie 2007; Toft 2010; Walter 2002.

73. Cunningham, Gleditsch, and Salehyan 2009; DeRouen and Sobek 2004; Fortna 2015; Lyall and Wilson 2009.

74. Eichenberg 2005.

75. Gelpi, Feaver, and Reifler 2009.

76. Press, Sagan, and Valentino 2013 and Sagan and Valentino 2017. Other studies establish that democratic leaders suffer public backlash if they lose wars (Chiozza and Goemans 2004; Croco 2015; Snyder and Borghard 2011). In selectorate theory, meanwhile, expectations about public opinion make democratic leaders avoid military operations that might fail (Bueno de Mesquita et al. 2003). An alternative approach holds that norms of noncombatant immunity and just war doctrine guide public attitudes toward the use of force (Crawford 2013).

77. Baum and Groeling 2009.

78. Gadarian 2010; Getmansky and Zeitzoff 2014.

79. Berinsky 2007; Saunders 2015; Zaller 1992.

80. Key 1966.

81. Innumerable analyses have demonstrated a robust relationship between voters' assessments of the economy and how they vote for all levels of government (Berry and Howell 2007; Healy and Malhotra 2013; Kinder and Kiewiet 1979; Kramer 1983; Lewis-Beck and Paldam 2000;

Markus 1988). They show that sociotropic (national) economic voting is generally stronger than egotropic (personal) economic voting (Kinder and Kiewiet 1979), that voter assessments of recent events are more influential than those of more distant ones (Ferejohn 1986), and that voters tend to react to past events (Fiorina 1981) more than to expected conditions (MacKuen, Erikson, and Stimson 1996; Miller and Wattenberg 1985).

82. Such nonmaterial factors include crime, corruption, foreign policy, and social issues (Aldrich et al. 2006).

83. See Lewis-Beck and Ratto 2013 on Latin America.

84. Pettersson, Högbladh, and Öberg 2019. The number of people wounded, maimed, and disabled is many multiples greater (Fazal 2014).

85. See, for example, Arce 2003; Carlin, Love, and Martínez-Gallardo 2015; Holmes and Gutiérrez de Piñeres 2002; Kibris 2011; Weyland 2000.

86. Berrebi and Klor 2008; Carlin, Love, and Martínez-Gallardo 2015; Gassebner, Jong-A-Pin, and Mierau 2008; Getmansky and Zeitzoff 2014; Hetherington and Nelson 2003; Ladd 2007; Merolla and Zechmeister 2009; Williams, Koch, and Smith 2013.

87. Berinsky 2007; Karol and Miguel 2007; Koch 2011; Mueller 1973; Nickelsburg and Norpoth 2000.

88. Drago, Galbiati, and Sobbrio 2020; Ley 2017; Marshall 2018.

89. McDermott and Panagopoulos 2015.

90. Rozenas, Schutte, and Zhukov 2017.

91. Abadeer et al. 2022; Bateson 2012; Carreras 2013; Ceobanu, Wood, and Ribeiro 2010; Davis and Silver 2003; Hou and Quek 2019; Pepinsky 2017; Pérez 2003; Visconti 2020.

92. Vaishnav 2017.

93. Acemoglu, Robinson, and Santos 2013; Fergusson, Vargas, and Vela 2013; Kaltenthaler 2018.

94. Marten 2007; Reno 1998.

95. Arias et al. 2022; de Figueiredo, Hidalgo, and Kasahara 2013.

Chapter 2

1. UCDP definitions are available at https://www.pcr.uu.se/research/ucdp/definitions/.

2. The universe of conflicts that did not cumulatively reach this threshold over their course may exhibit divergent postwar trajectories. For example, they may involve lower-capacity rebel groups that chose to participate in politics informally or non-electorally through sociopolitical associations (Daly 2016). To determine this threshold, the dataset, like the UCDP project, relies on battle-related-death reporting, which may be uneven.

3. Christia 2012; Daly 2016.

4. Kreutz 2010.

5. This temporal bound covers periods both during and after the Cold War, but excludes early Cold War cases and those preceding 1945, which may be systematically different. I find that rebel and government successor party electoral competition was common both during and after the Cold War. A central role for war outcomes, and political strategies for reckoning with the past and securing the future, can be seen even in the campaigns of much earlier postwar elections, including those in the United States and Mexico (see Buchenau 2011; Hesseltine 1957).

6. See Daly 2021b.

7. Petersen 2002, 19, 25.

8. Author interview, Tolima, Colombia, May 2008.

9. This is different than one-sided state repression because no "side" can feel safe, unaffected, or only benefit from the violence. For example, non-indigenous people in Guatemala City were largely spared the ruthlessness the military unleashed against the Mayan population of the Western Highlands, but they lived in fear of guerrilla terrorism. Some Colombian large landowners stood to gain from paramilitary atrocities, but suffered rebel kidnapping, extortion, and killings.

10. Following successful secessionist conflicts, electorates may become bifurcated into two separate states.

11. Hobbes 1996, 111.

12. Former Burundian president Domitien Ndayizeye, quoted in Watt 2008.

13. Crime often follows armed political conflict (Blattman and Annan 2016; Call 2007).

14. I am not assuming that these are "single-issue" voters, such as those who "allow one issue [such as abortion, gun control, or climate change] to guide his or her participation in politics" (Conover, Gray, and Coombs 1982). Here, security is a highly salient issue, as is recovery, in the same way that the economy is important in mainstream elections.

15. Birch 2020; Calvo and Murillo 2019; Stokes et al. 2013.

16. Sartori 2005, 56.

17. Jhee 2008.

18. Examples include Ellen Johnson Sirleaf's Unity Party in Liberia and Aung San Suu Kyi's National League for Democracy Party in Myanmar.

19. Kydd and Walter 2002. Rebel movements tend to be the radical arms of social movements that believed that violent means were necessary to achieve the desired ends; war tends to elevate extremist hawks over moderate doves within government belligerent forces. Nonbelligerent parties may span the political spectrum, but the main contenders following war tend to represent more moderate voices.

20. Schumpeter 1976, 260. In this, I follow the thoughtful approach of Caroline Hartzell and Matthew Hoddie in "The Art of the Possible" (Hartzell and Hoddie 2015).

21. Schumpeter 1976, 271. This definition is compatible with other work on postwar democratization, which looks at competition based solely on the procedure by which a government is chosen (e.g., Wantchekon 2004).

22. In the book's time period, Eritrea never held elections. In Congo, war resumed before elections could be held.

23. These cases include Iran, Iraq, Laos, Russia, Sudan, and Yemen.

24. Langer 1982.

25. Magaloni 2006.

26. Fergusson, Vargas, and Vela 2013.

27. Inflated armies, irregular forces, distorted civil-military relations, states of siege, exceptional law, and the fog of war often further undermine the freedom and fairness of wartime elections.

28. This proves important especially in contexts in which the wars fizzled out long before their official ends through negotiated settlement.

29. Fortna and Huang 2012; Huang 2016; Weinstein 2007.

30. The founding of postwar political order often takes place under the auspices of international interventions that push for elections (Brancati and Snyder 2011; Krasner 2005; Paris 2004). Election monitors are also now an international norm (Hyde 2011).

31. Lipset and Rokkan 1967. See also Boix 1997.

32. According to Lupu 2016, "When these countries returned to democracy, political parties that had contested prior elections also returned. These parties were already well established, with long, albeit interrupted, histories of mobilizing voters and building party attachments." See also Dix 1992.

33. Mainwaring and Shugart 1997.

34. Duverger 1954.

35. Cox 1997; Riker 1982. Strategic voting captures the fact that voters vote for parties only in ways where their votes are not wasted. Strategic entry represents the fact that, if candidates and parties decide whether or not to enter a race partly on the basis of their chance of winning a seat (or seats), expectations about who will win under various entry scenarios are crucial influences on who will actually enter, and whether parties will join forces if they can coordinate their respective positions.

36. At the same time, Riker 1982 posits that voting is not necessarily always strategic. Sometimes voters vote for parties that support their preferred ideological programs, and if these ideological parties can win locally, they can exist for a while. Strategic voting assumes that there are many parties that voters could find to fully or partially represent those voters' interests, but if a certain interest becomes very salient to a group of voters, there may be only one party that could represent them, for example, their ethnic party. The militarily disadvantaged belligerent parties may be in this category, even under first-past-the-post (FPP) rules, and especially because they often compete in what Sartori 2005 would classify as weak party systems.

37. Hyde 2011; Paris 2004.

38. Álvaro de Soto, author interview, New York, September 2018.

39. Lupu 2016; Mainwaring and Shugart 1997; Samuels 2003.

40. This definition tracks closely with Fortna 2015, but omits the ongoing war category and posits that rebellions that fizzle out may have peace agreements and those that conclude in a draw may end without peace agreements.

41. Betts 1994; Daly 2012; DeRouen and Sobek 2004; Fearon and Laitin 2003; Fortna 2015.

42. Christia 2012; Kalyvas 2006; Staniland 2012.

43. Many electorally successful belligerent parties represented relatively small elites rather than the masses; the repressive origins of many rendered them objectively "unpopular," and especially so prewar. Others represented ethnic minorities (e.g., in Rwanda). Even where public support is fixed and overwhelming (e.g., Blacks in South Africa), it is not determinative of war outcomes.

Chapter 3

1. This chapter employs the American politics literature because it underlies dominant concepts and theories in political behavior (given biases toward the study of voting in the Global North). However, I adapt this scholarship to my context of transitional elections in postconflict

and developing countries, in which the rules of the game are far less stable than in the U.S. context.

2. Aldrich 1995; Stokes et al. 2013; Kitschelt and Wilkinson 2007.

3. Hobbes 1996, 111.

4. These do not fit the spatial model because all parties take the same position for or against the issues. On issue positions and ideology, see Enelow and Hinich 1982.

5. Most define valence as expertise, skill, competence. The term "valence" has been used as a proxy for economic performance ratings, leadership ratings (Groseclose 2001), and for candidate trustworthiness and honesty (Enelow and Hinich 1982).

6. Petrocik 1996. See also Egan 2008.

7. William Riker (1986) defined heresthetic as parties structuring the political process so they may win through (1) agenda control, (2) strategic voting, and (3) manipulations of salient dimensions.

8. Sides 2006, 411.

9. Calvo and Murillo 2019.

10. Huntington 1993.

11. Huntington 1993. See also Moravcsik 2000.

12. Hume 2007.

13. Mockus 2010, emphasis added.

14. Sergio Fajardo (Antanas Mockus's vice presidential candidate), author interview, September 2016.

15. Mockus 2010, emphasis added.

16. Madison 2008.

17. Baum and Groeling 2009; Berinsky 2007.

18. This model follows the work of Köszegi and Rabin 2009 and the experimental evidence of Abeler et al. 2011 and assumes that the reference point is endogenously determined in equilibrium, given the behavior and related expectations of players.

19. The model assumes that voters know the nature of the violence conducted in the first stage. Accordingly, I am not arguing that voters are ignorant or hoodwinked, nor that they fail to attribute blame objectively because the violent facts are unknown. While there invariably exists variation in the extent to which voters are informed, and the extent to which the facts are discoverable, I argue that, after war, the fog of war begins to lift, and the population usually knows and may even broadly agree on the facts of the violence. If voter ignorance were driving the results, revelations about the atrocities would shift voters' attribution of blame. However, my prediction (validated in Chapter 4) is that they would not.

20. This follows the payoff function of Acharya and Grillo 2019.

21. $u_1 = E\{u(1,d)|h=1\}$ is a linear combination of $u(1,1)$ and $u(1,0)$. Both are deemed possible, so the expected payoff is in between the two, with $u(1,0) > u_1 > u(1,1)$. Therefore, when the belligerent doubles down on violence, the material payoff is below the reference point, sparking a negative psychological payoff: *disappointment*.

22. Alternatively, these parties could deny outright that they spilled blood. While deniers abound in these contexts (Fisher and Taub 2019), thousands or hundreds of thousands of people witnessed the violence. Outright denial therefore often lacks credibility and is thus ineffective. They could deflect references to the violence and change the subject, emphasizing

other issues such as the economy, or they could engage in truth telling, formal apology, symbolic reparations, and acceptance of responsibility (Vollhardt, Mazur, and Lemahieu 2014). However (as I substantiate below), the belligerents may want to burnish their wartime credentials. Doing so, they might embrace and boast of their violence. Or they might distance themselves from the stain of the atrocities and scapegoat the weaker adversary (Carlin, Love, and Martínez-Gallardo 2015). Below, I discuss what happens when the actors adopt off-equilibrium strategies rather than the strategies that are most electorally expedient.

23. Author interview, Medellín, March 5, 2008.

24. See Defensoría del Pueblo, ACNUR, and EUROPEAID 2004.

25. Yarce 2002; author interviews, Antioquia, January–June 2008.

26. Yarce 2003.

27. For example, the number of reported killings in Antioquia fell by 47 percent in 2003.

28. Yarce 2003.

29. Ex-combatants, author interviews, Caurallo, July 3, 2008.

30. Author interview, Comuna 3, Medellín, March 2008.

31. Author interview, Comuna 3, Medellín, March 2008.

32. Author interview, Comuna 1, Medellin, March 2008.

33. Quoted in Castrillón 2005.

34. Programa Paz y Reconciliación 2006.

35. *Revista Semana* 2005.

36. Author interview, Montería, April 2017.

37. Paramilitary commander Manuel de Jesús Pirabán, author interview, La Picota prison, Bogotá, September 2008.

38. Paramilitary commander Jorge Pirata, author interview, La Picota Prison, Bogotá, September 2008.

39. Coordinator of the ex-combatants, author interview, Medellín, 2008.

40. Conflict analyst, author interview, Medellín, 2008.

41. I measure subnational paramilitary war outcomes with an original indicator: the proportion of the local paramilitary brigade's combatants who defected to the state in the year prior to the peace accords based on an IOM survey of all 35,310 ex-paramilitaries and classified mappings of each paramilitary group's zone of operation. See Daly 2016 for details. Municipal-level vote shares are constructed based on the original paramilitary-politics dataset described in Chapter 9.

42. Petersen and Daly 2010a.

43. Steimer 2002.

44. Aranguren Molina 2001.

45. It should be noted that, at times, the belligerents' rhetoric involves intentional manipulation, lies, and fake news; this is done for electoral purposes, but often the belligerents themselves believe their own propaganda, as a way of justifying themselves and their actions. In such cases, the rewriting of history is experienced by the protagonists—parties (and even voters alike)—as fact. On lying and spin, see, for example, Mearsheimer 2013.

46. Belligerent parties equate civil war with anarchy to invoke a Hobbesian defense. However, rich scholarship on rebel governance and wartime orders during civil war reveals a complex and varied picture of order during civil conflict (Carnegie et al. 2022; Huang 2016; Mampilly 2011; Staniland 2012).

47. Hobbes 1996.

48. TVM Television Maputo 1994.

49. Gadarian 2010; Getmansky and Zeitzoff 2014.

50. Chiozza and Goemans 2004. See also Debs and Goemans 2010.

51. Research on the Democratic Republic of Congo (DRC) reveals that, as their security providers, people prefer to have perpetrators of domestic violence because they are seen as more credible at protection (Lindsey 2019). Similarly, in the Indian context, Vaishnav 2017 shows that a criminal past signals candidates' willingness to get their hands dirty to provide security.

52. For example, consistent with this, all six presidents eventually elected after conflict in Central Africa had previously led battalions of the army or rebels. See Frére 2007.

53. McDermott and Panagopoulos 2015.

54. Teigen 2013 found little evidence that voters perceived these military candidates as more capable leaders in general, nor that they expressed greater ideological attachment toward military-veteran candidates. See also Flores-Macías and Zarkin 2021.

55. Hobbes 1996. For an application of Max Weber's related concept of charismatic authority, see Gerdes 2013.

56. Teten 2004, emphasis added.

57. *Harper's Weekly* 1868. Another cartoon by Thomas Nast encapsulated the prospective vote: it showed Ulysses Grant receiving official thanks from Congress for his military service, emphasizing "the continuity between Grant's military leadership for the Union cause and the nominee's anticipated political leadership in working for the nation's best interests as president" (Nast 1886).

58. Madison 2008, 257. Ikenberry 2019 examines strategic restraint and institutions after victory in interstate wars.

59. Hobbes 1996, 118, emphasis added.

60. In Ethiopia, for example, the EPRDF had to find ways to build support among the electorate in the south, with which it had had few linkages or appeal during the war (Lyons 2016).

61. Its mitigation rhetoric, which whitewashes its murderous record, may help, but actions speak louder than words, and costly words speak louder than cheap words. It should be noted that this concept differs from Acemoglu and Robinson's 2020 Shackled Leviathan one, which explores the conflict between state and society, and its implications for liberal democracy.

62. Shafik Handál, author interview, San Salvador, July 2018.

63. Powell 1993; Sexton, Wellhausen, and Findley 2019.

64. Grzymala-Busse 2002, 169. On managerial competence, see also Calvo and Murillo 2019.

65. Hobbes 1996, 84.

66. Madison 2008.

67. "Moderation" and "extremism" are always relative to the context, as Walter 2017 renders clear.

68. The pioneering spatial voting models of Black 1958; Downs 1957; Hotelling 1929 show that parties' platforms will tend to converge on some centrally located point, such as the preferences of the median voter. Cox 1990 extends the classical "median voter theorem" to different electoral systems and shows that, in noncumulative systems, increases in the number of votes per voter, outlawry of partial abstention, and decreases in the district magnitude create centripetal (convergent) incentives leading political parties to advocate centrist policies as opposed to more extreme positions.

69. Groseclose 2001, 863. See also Soubeyran 2006. Some ironfisted politicians diverge from this equilibrium playbook and advocate extremist positions, as I discuss below.

70. Ansolabehere and Snyder 2000; Groseclose 2001.

71. Grzymala-Busse 2002.

72. This is not to say that the belligerent successors will become centrist parties, which would undermine their credibility, but that they will move toward greater moderation and, for the founding elections, seek to deemphasize position.

73. Ansolabehere and Snyder 2000; Aragones and Palfrey 2002; Groseclose 2001.

74. Cox 2009. Scholars define swing/core voters in different ways. Dixit and Londregan 1996, for example, instead define core voters as "those [a party] knows well and to whom it can more effectively and credibly target benefits."

75. See Dunning and Harrison 2010; Posner 2004.

76. Cruz 2000, 275.

77. Lyons 2016.

78. Christia 2012; Corstange 2020; Posner 2004. Mozambique presents an example: despite wartime antagonisms, after the war Frelimo downplayed this antagonism and played up over-arching values and identities (Bertelesen 2003).

79. Not everyone votes (Smithies 1941). Accordingly, as Cox 2009, 353, shows, when parties "contemplate a move toward the center, they anticipate more vote losses due to abstention on their extreme wing than vote gains from centrists." Diluting their brand through moderation undermines claims to their base that they stand for something distinctive and superior (Lupu 2016). As a result, their core will not turn out.

80. Parties can splinter (Palfrey 1984), and therefore "if the number of parties is not fixed, [parties] worry that they might be outflanked by a splinter or new party if they move toward the center" (Cox 2009, 353). Accordingly, Cox 2009 expects parties to invest little (if anything) in opposition groups (including, in my case, direct victims), somewhat more in swing groups, and more still in their core support groups (see also Cox 1999).

81. Cox and McCubbins's 1986 "core voter model" pitted against Lindbeck and Weibull's 1987 "swing voter model" highlights these tensions. Dixit and Londregan 1996 present an alternative distributive theory of electoral targeting in which parties favor their core constituencies to whom they can more effectively deliver patronage benefits in exchange for votes.

82. Hale 2006, 12. See Lupu 2016.

83. Panebianco 1988.

84. Belligerents' territorial organizations also help get out the vote: boots on the ground to disseminate the narrative, mobilize their followers, canvass before the election, transport voters, and generate personal reminders on election day. See Cox 1999 and Samuels and Zucco 2014.

85. LeBas 2011, 46.

86. Levitsky and Way 2012. Brand-new parties can emerge but do not have the organizational and reputational assets to succeed in the founding election. Studies of party building suggest that new parties are more likely to succeed when they build upon an infrastructure inherited from preexisting movements or organizations (Ziblatt 1998).

87. The nature of belligerent party leaders may also help prevent splinters because their word is treated as law internally, and externally their appeal presents high barriers to competition (Van Dyck 2014).

88. Kayser and Wlezien 2011.

89. On candidate selection, see Krasa and Polborn 2010.

90. Ansolabehere and Snyder 2000; Aragones and Palfrey 2002.

91. Stone 2017, 18 defines leadership valence as the "attributes, skills, and qualities that voters intrinsically value in candidates other than the policy positions they take."

92. In closed party-list proportional representation, voters effectively vote only for political parties as a whole and thus have no influence on the party-supplied order in which party candidates are elected.

93. Ishiyama 2019. This strategy proves effective because presidential elections usually have higher voter turnout and more undecided voters, and because presidential candidates are highly vetted, whereas legislative elections exhibit greater partisan and clientelistic voting.

94. This candidate selection model follows the work of Galasso and Nannicini 2011 and conforms with the findings of Ishiyama and Marshall 2015.

95. Werner 1999.

96. Wantchekon 2004.

97. Jaime Bustamante (ex-M19), author interview, Bogotá, July 2006; Álvaro Villarraga Sarmiento (ex-EPL), author interviews, Santa Marta, May 2009 and Bogotá, May 2009.

98. Alape Pastor (ex-FARC), author interview, Bogotá, February 2019; FMLN commander, author interview, San Salvador, July 2019.

99. Walter 2002.

100. In attribution error theory (Pettigrew 1979), group members make situational versus dispositional attributions for negative acts (e.g., Rosenberg and Wolfsfeld 1977). If my argument is wrong, we would observe voters finding the more violent side most culpable (irrespective of war outcomes); or deciding that war is messy, victims are inevitable, and thus no one is to blame; or blaming all sides equally.

101. Groseclose 2001; Soubeyran 2006.

102. Ansolabehere and Snyder 2000.

103. One of the best explanations for immoderation is that the candidates themselves hold ideological preferences. Calvert 1985 and Wittman 1977 show that when candidates have such preferences, under uncertainty, their programs do not converge, although they may move from their ideal points. Aldrich 1983 maps the role of party activists; Cox 1984 the role of candidates' personal policy beliefs; and Roemer 2009 the role of partisan purists in generating such non-convergent equilibria.

104. One may argue that strategic positioning is limited by parties' deep commitments to wartime ideologies and organizations. However, that the winning side moderates programmatically, despite similar wartime allegiance to a raison d'être, suggests the ability of belligerent successors to position for tactical electoral gain.

105. Eguia and Giovannoni 2019.

106. See Hirsch and Shotts 2015.

107. Below, I discuss nonequilibrium cases, party splits, and multiple parties in each category, which complicate the model, and I show when and how losing belligerents may pursue alternative strategies, including moderation.

108. Eguia and Giovannoni 2019.

109. Transitional justice (truth, reparations, and accountability) seeks to provide an antidote to anger by reconciling the balance between the victim and perpetrator, restoring victims' self-esteem, and closing the books on a traumatic period. See Bass 2002; Daly 2018; Elster 2004; Sikkink 2011, Petersen and Daly 2010a, 2010b.

110. Grzymala-Busse 2002.

111. On conflict frames, see Canetti et al. 2019.

112. This view of the war loser's optimal strategy is consistent with the literature on postcommunism and on party reform outside of civil war contexts (Grzymala-Busse 2002). In general, parties remain conservative and reform their party image only in response to "calamitous" or "disappointing" electoral performance (Janda et al. 1995).

113. Riker 1986.

114. The narratives are manifested in, for example, memorials, monuments, and museums (Hagopian 2009; Novick 1999); textbooks; official apologies (Schuman, Vinitzky-Seroussi, and Vinokur 2003); and truth commission reports (Gibson 2006).

115. Chong and Druckman 2007. Extensive research has demonstrated that political communication and campaign advertising have a substantial potential to shape voters' preferences and behavior (Alt, Lassen, and Marshall 2016; Greene 2011; Lawson and McCann 2005). They reduce voter uncertainty about the policy positions and characteristics of different candidates (Lenz 2009) and are useful for influencing swing voters (Ackerberg 2001). Mass media proves especially effective at shaping public attitudes toward war as well as retrospective assessments of security successes and failures (Carlin, Love, and Martínez-Gallardo 2015; Entman 2004; Gadarian 2010).

116. Snyder and Ballentine 1996.

117. Lasswell 1938. Propaganda to spin the past usually builds on a wartime legacy of manipulating public opinion.

118. Downs 1957.

119. Durante and Knight 2012; Lawson and McCann 2005.

120. Carlin, Love, and Martínez-Gallardo 2015; Chong and Druckman 2007. It is worth noting that changes in information and communications technology (ICT), social media, and more widespread availability of cell phones, SMS messaging, and the internet may level the persuasion playing field or render it subject to divergent inequalities than those present with older technologies. These revolutions in ICT may increase polarization in political consumption, render spin and fake news easier to propagate, or multiply voices and amplify those formerly silenced. The effect of these media changes on postwar electoral campaigns is a topic fertile for future research.

121. Djankov et al. 2003; Hughes and Lawson 2005; Magaloni 2006.

122. There are exceptions in which the media remain in private hands.

123. The belligerent party derived from the coercive apparatus of the government side of the conflict does not necessarily control the executive or legislature at the end of the conflict; these may be held by a nonbelligerent party.

124. In places in which rebels control territory (and win the war locally), they may be the de facto incumbents and hence enjoy some of the advantages of incumbency.

125. Garrard-Burnett 2010, 4.

126. Elster 2004.

127. Catatumbo 2018.

128. It may be that citizens perceive a stalemated rebel party as more competent than a stalemated government party given the notion that, for rebels to be perceived as effective, they have to only avoid defeat, but governments lose unless they win. While there may be imbalances, in general belligerents at a draw are anticipated to share the security vote.

129. Ansolabehere and Iyengar 1994.

130. Grzymala-Busse 2002.

131. For example, if the nonbelligerent chooses a suboptimal strategy—"forgive and forget"—"embracing the past" becomes a preferable (because it is less costly) strategy for the militarily advantaged belligerent. If the advantaged belligerent party opts for contrition (a suboptimal strategy), the disadvantaged belligerent can embrace its violent past. Similarly, if the nonbelligerent opts for a noncentrist position, the advantaged belligerent may converge toward the noncentrist position.

132. Niche parties arise as electoral vehicles for severely disadvantaged political outsiders in systems that bias elections in favor of the incumbent party. Their ideological extremism serves them well during their struggles to survive but is detrimental to their electoral prospects after the transition, when moderating to appeal to a broader electorate proves necessary (Greene 2016).

133. In founding elections, "electoral parties" tend to outperform mass and catchall parties (Manning 2008).

134. Greene 2016.

135. On centralization, see Grzymala-Busse 2002 and Ishiyama 2019. On elite-based parties, see Gunther and Diamond 2003. On personalistic candidacies and resultingly shallow investments in organization building, see Hale 2006; Kalyvas 1996.

136. Balcells 2012; Lupu and Peisakhin 2017; Petersen and Daly 2010b; Rozenas, Schutte, and Zhukov 2017.

137. Chaturvedi 2005; Collier and Vicente 2014; Hafner-Burton, Hyde, and Jablonski 2014; Mares and Young 2016; Robinson and Torvik 2009; Wilkinson 2004. Wantchekon 1999a and Lyons 2005 argue that voters fear that, were they not to vote for the former belligerents, the belligerents would carry out retribution or return to war.

138. These parties might harbor their own sins such as corruption but are not guilty of crimes against humanity.

139. Huang 2016; Mampilly 2011; Stewart 2018; Weinstein 2007.

140. Christia 2012; Kalyvas 2006; Staniland 2012.

141. A variant on this would be that success in war itself breeds popularity not because it signals competence on security, but because success begets success and citizens join the winning side.

142. Studies of former autocrats, such as "post-communist parties," "ex-authoritarian parties," "recycled dictators," and "authoritarian successor parties," emphasize cohesion and managerial competence as the core of these parties' positive "inheritance" that bolsters their electoral performance after the transitions (Grzymala-Busse 2002; Jhee 2008; Kyle 2016; Ziblatt 1998). Many communists, however, suffered initial electoral defeats (Grzymala-Busse 2002).

143. Berry and Howell 2007; Healy and Malhotra 2013; Kinder and Kiewiet 1979; Kramer 1983; Lewis-Beck and Paldam 2000; Markus 1988.

144. Gadarian 2010; Getmansky and Zeitzoff 2014.

145. Lee 2008.

146. According to Collier 1999, 175, "A 15-year civil war . . . reduce[s] per capita GDP by around 30%."

147. Petrocik 1996.

148. For parsimony, I conceive of the balance of power between the belligerents as either stable/reinforced or instead inverted. In the former case, the war winner remains militarily superior or becomes more so (in the case of a draw, the military symmetry sustains). In the latter case, the wartime loser becomes more militarily powerful than the wartime winner (in the case of a draw, the military symmetry becomes military asymmetry). I focus on a shock to the distribution of military power *after* the civil war ends but *before* the first election.

149. Werner 1999.

150. Fearon 1995; Powell 2006.

151. Sources of shocks to the power balance include changes in external military sponsorship including intervener entry or exit (Sawyer, Cunningham, and Reed 2017), shifting domestic alliances involving third-party violent actors, and differential processes of DDR and security sector reform (Christia 2012; Toft 2010; White 2020).

152. During the war-to-peace transition, high levels of uncertainty exist. This means that if the military balance changes outside of the context of war, it becomes difficult for citizens to update their understandings of who is the most militarily powerful. Many power shifts are also illegible to the population. The lay voters therefore still tend to rely on "who won the war" as their heuristic for which party can sustain future stability. If the power shift is legible and voters instead update their estimates of postwar power accurately and vote for the newly empowered war-loser party, I predict that the war winner (which is now weaker militarily) will concede the electoral loss and a recalibrated peace will emerge.

153. See Daly 2022.

154. Huntington 2006, 417.

155. Lopez-Alves 2000, 69.

156. On the logic of parties for mobilization and coordination of votes, see Aldrich 1995. Over time, young populations, in particular, who did not experience war as deeply, may put civil liberties and pocketbook concerns ahead of prospects for physical security or underestimate the risks of a new conflict.

157. Mainwaring and Scully 1995; Weyland 1999.

158. Samuels and Shugart 2010.

159. Potentially, if the electoral tides turn against the belligerent successors, they may foster a backsliding from democracy to preserve their political standing. This suggests the potential value of international democracy promotion and election monitors not just in the immediate aftermath of conflict, but also over longer periods of time.

160. Chowanietz 2011.

161. Weyland 2000.

162. Consistent with behavioral voting theory, evidence suggests that retrospective voters have short memories, use cognitive shortcuts (Healy and Malhotra 2013), and rely on judgments about recent events (Huber, Hill, and Lenz 2012).

163. Call 2007.

164. Ahnen 2007; Lessing 2017.

165. Mintz 1993; Sexton, Wellhausen, and Findley 2019.

166. Rivera and Zarate-Tenorio 2016. Investment in human capital, among other welfare policies, addresses the social roots of criminal offending and thereby enhances public safety.

167. Drago, Galbiati, and Sobbrio 2020; Ley 2017.

168. Through media framing and priming, parties can alter the political salience of different issues (Krosnick and Kinder 1990).

169. Sides 2006. See also Glazer and Lohmann 1999.

170. Petrocik 1996. See also Egan 2008.

171. Riker 1996.

172. Hammond and Humes 1993.

173. Fortna 2019.

174. Cases such as those of Peru's Alberto Fujimori—a violent past, a landslide in his favor in the founding elections, but ultimate rejection and imprisonment—show that the possibilities of transitional justice increase over time, after transitions are consolidated.

175. Seawright 2016, 9.

176. Yashar 2018. These cases and the outcomes in them were not fully independent of one another; rather they were intertwined with spillover effects. See, for instance, Gleditsch and Beardsley 2004; LeoGrande 1998; Pastor 2018.

177. While irregularities existed and turnout was, in certain cases, low, these were real political contests, extensively monitored, and deemed to be free and fair. They were multiparty elections and presented alternatives to voters: rebel and incumbent successor parties, and also options without roots in the violent organizations of the war.

178. Kitschelt and Wilkinson 2007.

179. These include ethnic wars, successful secessionist wars, contexts in which politics centered on patronage, and places in which security was not highly salient after the war.

180. FARC stands for the Revolutionary Armed Forces of Colombia.

181. Conjoint analysis is an experimental design that estimates the causal effects of multiple treatment components and assesses several causal hypotheses simultaneously (Hainmueller, Hopkins, and Yamamoto 2014).

Chapter 4

1. Sandra Ramírez (ex-FARC commander), author interview, Bogotá, January 2019.

2. Author interview, Bogotá, February 2019.

3. Centro Nacional de Memoria Histórica 2016.

4. Human Rights Watch 2015. Human Rights Watch interviews with military officers confirm the established nature of this practice: the government had "systems in place for committing false positives" and officers would "meet with their battalion commander on a weekly basis to plan false positives." The victims "included farmers, children, unemployed people, homeless people, people . . . dependent on drugs, people with mental disabilities, community leaders, people with criminal records, petty criminals." See also Acemoglu et al. 2020.

5. Tellez 2019. Between 2012 and 2016, FARC and the government held negotiations, reaching accords in August 2016. Two months later, in October, the peace deal was put to a plebiscite,

in which the "no" campaign won; voters deemed the concessions to FARC too great. Nonetheless, despite losing this referendum, in November 2016 President Santos pushed the deal through Congress.

6. FARC was guaranteed five seats in the Senate and five seats in Congress for two election cycles, and its members were granted amnesty or reduced prison sentences in exchange for truth telling.

7. In practice, it is challenging to classify individuals as "unaffected by conflict." One might argue, for example, that Bogotá was relatively untouched by the armed conflict; an individual living there had a lower probability of being a victim of the conflict than those in other parts of the country. While Bogotá never fell under guerrilla or paramilitary control, it did experience high-profile bombings, kidnappings, and sieges that kept its population living in fright. The false positive scandal terrorized Bogotá's poorer quarters. The arbitrary and indiscriminate nature of this violence instilled chilling fear. Therefore, to claim that only certain places or individuals "felt" a conflict may be to deny the psychological experience of populations faced with objectively lower levels of conflict and violence. Thus "unaffected by violence" is only a relative term.

8. This step helped ensure that the sample was representative of many factors that covary with region, including political affiliation and whom the perpetrators of violence were.

9. Alternative indices, used in the application of the Territorially Focused Development Plans, include poverty, weak institutions, and illicit economies, which, while correlated with violence, are inferior to direct measures of atrocity.

10. An alternative would have been to stratify based on the percentage of the population who were victims. However, this could have yielded only receptor municipalities of displaced victims, instead of conflict zones that may have had net out-migration. Victims who have been displaced from the places in which the violent acts transpired and have relocated may differ from those who stayed (Steele 2017).

11. Extensive piloting and enumerator feedback guided the final version of the survey. Enumerator training took place with the researchers and also with the survey firm's statistical and operations teams.

12. The survey was enumerated using tablets that we programmed to randomize the survey versions, in order to minimize enumerator error in administering the survey experiments.

13. Members of FARC and government delegations to Havana, author interviews, Bogotá, January–March 2019.

14. President Andrés Pastrana, author interview, Washington, DC, June 2006. From 2000 to 2012, Colombia received nearly $8 billion in U.S. aid. See Shifter 2012.

15. Long 2015.

16. During his time in office, Uribe reduced FARC from nearly 21,000 to roughly 9,000 fighters.

17. In interviews, the FARC leadership conceded that, by 2016, they were at a relative military loss (author interviews, January–March 2019).

18. This proved unnecessary; our random draw did not include zones of active ELN operations (see the appendix for more details).

19. Right-wing militias, self-defense groups, and paramilitaries proliferated in the 1980s and 1990s to counter the rebel threats, protect the status quo, and offer security that the state was unwilling and unable to provide. These illegal nonstate armies achieved significant military

successes against the rebels. Between 2003 and 2006, each of the thirty-seven paramilitary brigades signed separate peace accords with the government and disarmed their troops (Daly 2016).

20. This generated widespread national protests centered not on security issues but on social and economic grievances such as pensions.

21. Potegal, Stemmler, and Spielberger 2010.

22. Anger is an approach emotion, and therefore dampened anger would correspond with less support for standing up to a belligerent victor. See Kupatadze and Zeitzoff 2021.

23. To ensure that the results are not driven by the inclusion of these covariates, I also include the less-efficient covariate-free models; the results do not change.

24. As a manipulation check, I evaluate whether the security information was internalized by respondents. Posttreatment, respondents were asked how much they believed each of the belligerents—FARC and the army—had contributed to improving security in Colombia. Unfortunately, nonresponse was very high ($n = 1,065$), potentially because the question appeared at the end of the survey and therefore suffered survey fatigue. A high share of respondents in the control group answered that the army had greatly improved security, and this share was roughly equal to that in the "army-security" treatment group. By comparison, a low share of respondents believed that the FARC had improved security, but the difference across the "security" and "no-security" conditions was greater, albeit not to a statistically significant degree. This suggests that priors—already knowing that the army was winning and credited with security—may have influenced the extent to which respondents internalized the offsetting information and could have attenuated the results of army offsetting on judgments of the violent past.

25. The observational survey data suggest that few credited FARC with such security improvements.

26. In a parallel experiment, I evaluated whether belligerent provision of welfare had a similar offsetting effect as that of security, as predicted by the rebel governance and electoral violence literature (Huang 2016; Gutiérrez-Romero and LeBas 2020). I found no effect.

27. Humberto de la Calle, author interview, Bogotá, February 2019.

28. Victims are not necessarily punitive as is often assumed. The observational data indicate that, on average, half of victims and half of nonvictims expressed support for punishing perpetrators of violence; half did not support retribution. Victims, moreover, were 10 percentage points more likely to favor forgetting as opposed to learning the truth of the violent past.

29. Following best practices laid out by Hainmueller, Hopkins, and Yamamoto 2014, as a robustness check, respondents answered a pair of questions that asked them to rate each candidate on a seven-point scale.

30. Hainmueller, Hopkins, and Yamamoto 2014.

31. Hainmueller, Hangartner, and Yamamoto 2015.

32. On this methodology, see Cooperman, Richey, and Seim 2018.

33. I opted not to compare the candidates associated with the government belligerent directly with those associated with the FARC belligerent, for two reasons. One, the founding election results—FARC's dismal performance—were known at the time of the survey's enumeration. Two, if I had opted for a single experiment and included belligerent identity—government or rebel—as an additional attribute treatment, this would have demanded that

belligerent identity be interacted with each of the other strategy attributes. Such a design would have proven very draining on statistical power given the sample size of 1,500, likely rendering null results due to underpowering. Accordingly, conducting the paired experiments was preferable.

34. EJE21 2021; Gaviria 2017.

35. Observationally, the survey found that 44 percent of respondents believed the conflict might have ended through outright government victory, whereas 56 percent believed that it could be resolved only through negotiation, even if the government was militarily stronger.

36. I realize a randomization balance check by regressing important respondent demographic variables (gender, household income, education level, age, and victim status) on indicator variables for the candidate profile attributes. Overall, the test shows good balance.

37. Appropriate operationalization of the concept of "swing voter" is a subject of scholarly debate. Here, I code respondents as swing voters simply if they answered that they were unaffiliated with a political party.

38. I code respondents as "security voters" if they listed as the most salient issue facing the country one of the following: armed conflict, crime, human rights violations, forced displacement, war against terrorism, guerrillas, paramilitaries, emerging criminal gangs, peace, peace accord, gangs, narcotrafficking, kidnapping, (lack of) security, terrorism, or violence; if they listed security—violence, crime, conflict, and narcotrafficking—as the most important issue facing their community; or if they named maintaining order in the country as the most important goal for the country in the next ten years.

39. Here, a voter is coded as "victimized" if they or their community were affected by any of the forms of violence listed above (e.g., assassination, forced disappearance, etc.). Being conflict-affected increases the odds of being a security voter in the founding elections by 47 percent.

40. Groseclose 2001, 863.

41. The survey finds that 53 percent of respondents saw security as a precondition for growth.

42. Green, Ha, and Bullock 2010.

43. The predicted probability of being attributed with credit for peace increased from 49 percent for a Tactical Immoderate to 63 percent for a Restrained Leviathan.

44. In contrast, only 18 percent responded that they had very little confidence in the armed forces or army; 9 percent answered 2 on this 1–10 confidence scale.

45. Acemoglu et al. 2020.

46. Uribistas, including the son of General Jaime Uscátegui, convicted of the massacre of forty-nine people in Mapiripán, began a Twitter campaign claiming that "there were no false positives, only false victims."

47. Sebastián Velásquez Vélez, Director Ejecutivo Fevcol, author interview, emphasis added.

48. Sofia Gaviria, author interview, March 2019.

49. There likely exists heterogeneity in the information treatments that my different experiments were providing (Alt, Lassen, and Marshall 2016). Albeit a potentially information-saturated environment, parts of the sample were likely more marinated in prior information than others. Unfortunately it was impossible to exploit either natural spatial variation using exogenous discontinuities in TV coverage related to the reach of TV antennas or temporal variation generated by new campaign information disseminated in the midst of polling.

I leverage variation in media consumption provided within my survey itself. Likely correlated with other covariates and, as such, not well identified, it suggests that individuals with weaker prior beliefs updated their assessments more than those with strong preconceptions, though the effect is not significant by conventional standards (Arias et al. 2022).

50. Administration insiders claim that Santos wished to be more important than Uribe, sparking a rift reminiscent of Colombia's political feuds of centuries past between the elite of Bogotá (Santismo) and that of the "regions" (Uribismo) (author interview, Bogotá, January 2019). Additionally, Santos "wanted to be the president to sign the peace accords" (author interview, New York, January 2020). Even after losing the referendum, Santos reaffirmed, "I'll continue [to] search for peace until the last moment of my mandate" (Domonoske 2016).

51. Cabinet members in both Uribe and Santos administrations, author interviews, Bogotá, February 2019.

52. Indeed, in his 2010 successful election campaign, Santos had run on these security improvements. Santos's party manifesto began by claiming "a reduction in the number of kidnappings by 90%, terrorist acts by more than 90%, subversive acts by 64%" (Santos Calderón 2010). According to my interviewees, in this year he ran "not on a right-wing or left-wing platform" but as "the security candidate" (author interview, New York, February 2020).

53. Author interview, Bogotá, February 2020.

54. Compromiso Cuidadano is part of the Green Alliance.

55. Santos's family owned one of the largest media companies in Colombia (Alsema 2017).

56. Elements of the Fajardo coalition strategies included "anti-polarization," rule-based security, anticorruption and education valence issues, and running clean civilians (Fajardo's campaign strategists Johanna Peters and Alejandro Fajardo, author interviews, January–March 2019). See Garbiras-Días 2018.

57. Juan Manuel Santos, "From Hawk to Dove" (George W. Ball Lecture, Columbia University, April 13, 2022).

58. Luis Echeverri, Uribista campaign strategist, author interview, Bogotá, February 2019.

59. Author interview, January 2020. According to a Santos administration member, Santos's popularity had fallen to 11 percent; he was even consider resigning. Then, Santos received the Nobel Peace Prize and "became fixated on his legacy. . . . FARC exploited this and got more concessions. . . . FARC played their hand right" (author interview, New York, January 2020).

60. Alfonso Prada, Santos's chief of staff, author interview, Bogotá, February 2019.

61. Santos 2022.

62. Gamboa 2018. See *Verdad Abierta* 2019.

63. Reconciliation with the armed left, a movement supported by Venezuela and Cuba (Colombians' international enemies), yielded campaign smears of Santistas as "unpatriotic" (*El Espectador* 2018). Santos claims that he understood that his political strategy would lead him to being called a traitor (Santos 2022).

64. Robayo 2016; Cosoy 2016.

65. *Revista Semana* 2016.

66. Marcos 2015.

67. Juanita Goebertus, Congresswoman, author interview, March 2019. De la Calle's Liberal party distanced itself from Santos, and Vargas Lleras's Cambio Radical defected from the National Unity coalition. Vargas Lleras ran on the ticket of the Mejor Vargas Lleras movement.

But, as Santos's peace negotiator and vice president, respectively, de la Calle and Vargas Lleras were widely seen as Santos's successors. See *France 24* 2018.

68. Party strategist, author interview, January 2019.

69. De la Calle 2018.

70. Hobbes 1996.

71. Luis Echeverri, author interview, Bogotá, February 2019. Echeverri told of how they improvised the party from scratch.

72. International Crisis Group 2018.

73. Johanna Peters described how, whereas nonbelligerent Fajardo canvassed as "a civilian" in jeans and a white shirt with no bodyguards, Uribista Duque was accompanied at all campaign encounters, even in very safe locations, by an entourage of military officers in fatigues with assault weapons; this generated the image that "he represented the military" and that the other candidates were "up against something militarized." A member of Duque's campaign team confirmed Duque's tactical decision to bring armed escorts along with him on the campaign trail (author interview, Bogotá, February 2019).

74. See Bhatia 2005.

75. CD Senator María Fernanda Cabal, author interview, Bogotá, February 2019.

76. CD Senator Paloma Valencia, author interview, Bogotá, February 2019.

77. President Iván Duque appointed, as the new director of the CNMH, Darío Acevedo, who "has indicated that the armed conflict did not exist, that the false positives were not a State policy" (Quintero 2019).

78. Youkee 2018.

79. María Fernanda Cabal, author interview, Bogotá, February 2019.

80. Villamizar 2019.

81. @IvanDuque. CD's government plan, displayed as a tree, consisted of 203 proposals that it claimed would grow a blossoming Colombia. The proposals began with the seed of the tree—"Liberty and Order"—and its roots: "Security and Justice." These order and security issues occupied the first fifty-seven proposals; only after that did other programmatic issues appear (Centro Democrático 2018).

82. María Fernanda Cabal, author interview, Bogotá, February 2019.

83. María Fernanda Cabal, author interview, Bogotá, February 2019.

84. Paloma Valencia, author interview, Bogotá, February 2019.

85. María Fernanda Cabal, author interview, Bogotá, February 2019.

86. Clara López, 2014 presidential candidate for the Alternative Democratic Pole Party, author interview, Bogotá, February 2019.

87. Luis Echeverri, author interview, Bogotá, February 2019.

88. Interview with Andrés Pastrana, CNN *Conclusiones*. An estimated two million refugees poured over the border from Venezuela between 2015 and 2018. According to the opposition, when CD could find no other insecurity to report on, it would tweet about rampant cattle thefts to keep the salience of security heightened (Santos minister, author interview, New York, January 2019).

89. Paloma Valencia, author interview, Bogotá, February 2019.

90. Author interview, Bogotá, February 2019.

91. Centro Democrático 2018.

92. Johanna Peters, author interview, March 2019. The scandal of paramilitary politics took down many of Uribe's closest allies and family members (*BBC News* 2016; Isacson 2010). Uribe's political enemies called him a "paramilitary," and his allies did not deny that the accusations had some merit: one of his campaign strategists acknowledged that "Uribe is called a paramilitary internationally and in Colombia" (CD party strategy, author interview, Bogotá, February 2019). In my survey, 53 percent of respondents saw Uribista parties as those closest to the false positive scandal, and 62 percent saw Uribista parties as closest to the paramilitaries. There were other elements to the dark side of Uribe's administrations: for example, he was accused of using the secret police to spy on and target judges, opposition politicians, and journalists. Uribe would face 28 charges in Colombia's Supreme Court based on his alleged responsibility in the false-positive scandal and 276 additional investigations for ties to the paramilitary groups. In 2020, he was placed under house arrest.

93. Johanna Peters, author interview, March 2019.

94. Luis Echeverri, author interview, Bogotá, February 2019.

95. Johanna Peters, author interview, March 2019.

96. Luis Echeverri, author interview, Bogotá, February 2019. See Sánchez 2018; Lewin 2017. As its congressional candidates, CD ran Uribe at the top of its ticket and hid, on its closed list, several caudillos; in more competitive districts, it ran unblemished faces.

97. Luis Echeverri, author interview, Bogotá, February 5, 2019.

98. Greene 2016.

99. Alape Pastor, FARC commander, author interview, Bogotá, February 2019.

100. Juanita Goebertus, author interview, March 2019: "In general . . . throughout the negotiation, the [FARC] sounded very confident that it had the support of the population."

101. Ishiyama 2019.

102. Marco Calarcá, FARC commander, author interview, Bogotá, February 2019.

103. Londoño 2018.

104. Sandra Ramírez, FARC commander, author interview, Bogotá, February 2019.

105. Juanita Goebertus, author interview, March 2019. See Casey 2018.

106. Only after its campaign was met with "rejection, repudiation . . . insults . . . aggressions . . . hatred"—a wakeup call—did FARC begin to adopt more contrite language, too little and too late (Londoño 2018).

107. Pastor Alape, author interview, Bogotá, February 2019.

108. *InSight Crime* 2017.

109. *CNN Español* 2017. FARC's closed legislative list comprised almost exclusively FARC commanders, many accused of crimes against humanity (U.S. Department of State, Bureau of International Narcotics and Law Enforcement Affairs Narcotics Reward Program 2001–2009). Its mayoral candidates were mostly FARC combatants, selected for their "long trajectory in the ranks [and] fidelity." Sandra Ramírez, author interview, Bogotá, February 2019.

110. Paloma Valencia, author interview, Bogotá, February 2019.

111. Names proposed by these reformists included "Recall New Colombia" and "Hope" (Marco Calarcá, FARC commander, author interview, Bogotá, February 2019).

112. Pastor Alape, author interview, Bogotá, February 2019.

113. Pastor Alape, author interview, Bogotá, February 2019. As its new symbol, FARC selected the rose, which was said to represent "the flower of [socialist] struggle." A red rose, it also symbolized the color of blood (unacknowledged by FARC).

114. Pastor Alape, author interview, Bogotá, February 2019.

115. Marco Calarcá, author interview, Bogotá, February 2019.

116. Polimétrica 2018c.

117. Invamer 2018.

118. Alberto Cienfuegos, Petro's campaign strategist, author interview, Bogotá, February 2019.

119. Johanna Peters, author interview, Bogotá, March 2019.

120. To the extent that the population heard FARC's mitigation narrative first, moreover, the narrative survey experiment above suggests that an order effect might have played an electoral role, increasing retributive voting against FARC.

121. Rodrigo Londoño Echeverri (Timochenko) dropped out of the race, ostensibly due to health complications, but mass rejection surely had something to do with it. FARC commander, author interview, Bogotá, February 2019.

122. *BBC News* 2018.

123. *Revista Semana* 2015.

124. Alfonso Prada, author interview, Bogotá, February 2019.

125. As successors to the incumbent Santos, both benefited from access to the state and from the Santos family's media advantage. They possessed broad patronage networks and endorsement from traditional politicians. These assets did serve their parties well in the congressional elections in which political machinery and clientelism, not the "thermometer of public opinion," drove votes. Paloma Valencia, author interview, Bogotá, February 2019. On the other end of the ideological spectrum, Clara López confirmed this (author interview, Bogotá, February 2019).

126. In May 2017, 21.5 percent said they would vote for Vargas Lleras (Datexco-Opinómetro 2018). By May 2018, only 6.6 percent said they would vote for him (Invamer 2018). De la Calle polled at 10 percent in November 2017, sinking to 1 percent by May 2018 (Polimétrica 2017, 2018d). Polls show that if the run-off had been between Duque and either Vargas Lleras or de la Calle, Duque would have had twice as many votes as either of the Santistas (Guaruma–Ecoanalíticas 2018).

127. Alfonso Prada, author interview, Bogotá, February 2019.

128. Yanhaas 2018b.

129. Yanhaas 2018a. This poll found that 73 percent said that insecurity, the peace process, and the armed conflict were the most important issues.

130. Alfonso Prada, author interview, Bogotá, February 2019.

131. Johanna Peters, author interview, March 2019. Only 48 percent of the population voted for the same party for the Senate and for Congress (Polimétrica 2018a). A mere 6 percent said partisan affiliation determined their vote (Polimétrica 2018b).

132. Author interview, January 2018. Duque performed equally well across social sectors (Polimétrica 2018b) and across rural and urban areas (Invamer 2018).

133. Humberto de la Calle, author interview, February 2018.

134. For each party, respondents were asked, on a scale of 1–4, how competent they believed the party was at providing security.

135. On economic and managerial competence, see Calvo and Murillo 2019. For each party, respondents were asked, on a scale of 1–4, how competent they believed the party was at

administering the economy. Other work has shown that voters support corrupt or even violent candidates if they are seen as effective (see, e.g., De Vries and Solaz 2017; Grzymala-Busse 2002; Vaishnav 2017).

136. Respondents were asked to place themselves on an ideological spectrum ranging from 1 to 10, where 1 was extreme left and 10 was extreme right. They were asked to do the same for each party.

137. Respondents were asked, for each party, how likely, on a scale of 1 to 10, a candidate from that party would be to provide them food, clothes, or public-sector jobs. I also measured partisan networks, but these questions exhibited very high nonresponse rates.

138. Given the sampling design and particularly the oversample of victims and conflict-affected nonvictims in my sample, I also run the analysis by reweighting the sample.

139. E.g., Steele 2011, 2017.

140. Matanock and García-Sánchez 2018.

141. Carreri and Dube 2017.

142. Quoted in Greenwald 2019, emphasis added.

143. Macías 2018. See also MOE 2018. The MOE index takes into consideration "active" risk factors—electoral violence such as attacks and threats against or homicides and kidnappings of candidates or current politicians; forced displacement of voters; and presence of illegal armed group(s)—and also "passive" ones less perceptible to electoral observers, including atypical electoral participation, anomalies in null votes, limitations on electoral competition, and voter intimidation.

144. Party logos were included next to the party names, as piloting revealed that voters often recognized the logos more quickly than the names, and this also helped respondents with limited literacy.

145. Matanock and García-Sánchez 2018.

146. This methodology was developed and implemented by Daniel Corstange to gauge support for the brutal Syrian regime and for jihadi groups during active warfare in Syria (Corstange 2022).

147. Piloting confirmed that there was little design effect: the "nonsensitive" items did not produce ceiling effects (where respondents said "yes" to all nonsensitive items) or floor effects (where respondents said "no" to all nonsensitive items). Ceiling and floor effects would reduce the privacy of the list experiment by increasing the possibility that the respondent would not answer the sensitive item truthfully. Piloting also ensured that the sensitive item did not stand out too much; it was placed in the third position to decrease its conspicuousness. I followed recommendations by Glynn 2013 and Blair and Imai 2012 to use nonsensitive items that were negatively correlated (to improve efficiency) and that were clear and unambiguous, to minimize design effects.

148. See Lyons 2005.

149. Invamer 2018.

150. Berinsky 2007.

151. This experiment presented ethical challenges. Given the importance of establishing an accurate national historiography, all facts of the violence revealed in the survey were truthful. Interviews suggested knowledge of the facts of the violence. For example, international observers described that the population "knew about the alliances with paramilitarism" (author

interview, Aguachica, June 2008). One shared that the atrocity "was known but many people [still] preferred the [paramilitary politicians]" (Alejandrina Ayastuy, author interview, Valledu-par, March 2017).

152. Centro Nacional de Memoria Histórica 2020.

153. Piloting suggested respondent discomfort with conflating paramilitary and army violence, despite the collaboration between the belligerents being well established.

Chapter 5

1. Additional justification for the case selection may be found in Chapter 3.

2. To prepare the text corpus, I converted the manifestos using AWS's textract API; removed numbers, special characters, and punctuation, and standard Spanish stop words (e.g., "the," "a," "an," "in"); and stemmed words, omitting inflectional affixes (e.g., "victor" instead of "victory," "victories," "victorious").

3. Grimmer and Stewart 2013. I used the R-program Structured Topic Models (STM) (Roberts, Stewart, and Tingley, 2019). This is an unsupervised machine learning method; that is, the algorithm identifies the underlying prevalence of topics in the text without human intervention. A key advantage of this method is that it allows the incorporation of metadata (which can be understood as arbitrary covariates about each document) into the topic models. This enables discovery of latent relationships between the document's metadata and topic clusters.

4. As the input data themselves came from a relatively clean source (party manifesto security sections where I knew specifically that they were talking about security), initializing with a large number of topics did not prove necessary. I ran a selection model with different numbers of topics requested (from 2 to 10) and then chose the model producing topics that scored highest on both semantic coherence and exclusivity. The overall prevalence of each topic in the corpus ranged from 10 to 20 percent.

5. Gabel and Huber 2000.

6. I divided the text into the PMP categories and subcategories, following the codes assigned by the Manifesto Project (see Table A5.1). A data imbalance issue arose: most categories had many Spanish-language texts, whereas several (in particular, 202_2 and 305_4) had only a few texts. To address this issue, I down-sampled all categories with more than 500 texts to 500 texts. I then added texts translated from other languages to categories that had fewer than 100 texts. I translated them into Spanish using Google's Cloud Translation API. Category 202_2 thereby increased from 7 to 145 texts and category 305_4 increased from 23 to 45 texts.

7. The specific pipeline of the model consisted of three steps: (1) vectorize, which converted the texts to a matrix of token counts; (2) transform, which normalized the count matrix; and (3) model, which classified the normalized count matrix using the Multinomial Naive Bayes algorithm. I used a tenfold cross-validated grid search to optimize the hyperparameters. Hyperparameters decide the detailed structure of a model; the goal was to establish which set had the best performance. Therefore, I divided the training set into ten folds. For each possible set of hyperparameters, nine folds were used for training and one fold was used for testing. The set of hyperparameters with the highest average was used in my model. The best set of hyperparameters for the model were obtained using unigram, bigram, and trigram; using raw counts instead of tf-idf; and using a smoothing coefficient of 0.1.

8. I randomly split the texts into a training set (80 percent of the data) and a testing set (20 percent of the data). The model learned from the training text how to predict whether a right or left label should be assigned to a text. The test set was then used to examine how well the classifier learned and to compare the classifier's prediction with the true answers. Given that accuracy can be misleading in cases with class imbalance, I also look at performance metrics. The precision of the weighted average was 0.7993; the recall was 0.7958; the F1 was 0.7863.

9. I used the classifier on the extracted and cleaned text to predict the right-left label (ri or le) of each sentence. For each party, I then calculated the percentages of ri and le sentences, respectively. Replication code and classifications of all text are available in the online appendix.

10. These include surveys conducted by LatinoBarometer, Latin American Public Opinion Project (LAPOP), Instituto Universitario de Opinión Pública (IUDOP), and Consultoría Interdisciplinaria en Desarrollo S.A. / Gallup conducted for the United States Information Agency.

11. Anderson 1971.

12. Montgomery 1983a

13. Brockett 1988; Muller and Seligson 1987.

14. Coatsworth 1994.

15. Barry and Preusch 1990.

16. Daly 2011.

17. Geovani Galeas, author interview, San Salvador, July 2018.

18. Webre 1979.

19. Paolo Luers, author interview, San Salvador, July 2018. See Americas Watch Committee and American Civil Liberties Union 1982.

20. These death squads answered directly to the civilian elite. They included the White Warriors' Union, Anti-Communist Armed Forces of Liberation by Wars of Elimination, and Secret Anticommunist Army, to name a few. See Arnson 2000.

21. Loxton 2014. See also Pyes 1983.

22. See Daly 2011; Armstrong and Shenk 1982; McClintock 1998; Pearce 1986; Villalobos 1984.

23. Goodwin 2001; Mason and Krane 1989; Wood 2003.

24. The militias were called the Nationalist Democratic Organization, ORDEN.

25. Jung 1980; McClintock 1985.

26. Stanley 1996; Williams and Walter 1997.

27. Author interview, San Salvador, August 2018.

28. Stanley 1996.

29. LeoGrande 1998.

30. Karl 1988.

31. Herman and Brodhead 1984.

32. Wood 2000b, 82.

33. Diskin and Sharpe 1986, 54.

34. Americas Watch 1991; Stanley 1996.

35. Allison 2010.

36. United Nations Commission on the Truth for El Salvador 1993.

37. Stanley 1996.

38. Binford 1996; Danner 1994.

39. Loxton 2014.

40. See, for example, *La Prensa Gráfica* 1982.

41. Daly 2011; U.S. Congress, Subcommittees on International Organizations of the Committee on International Relations 1977.

42. Rubén Zamora (FMLN presidential candidate in 1994), author interview, San Salvador, July 2018. See Commission for the Defense of Human Rights in Central America 1990.

43. Author interview with David Escobar Galindo, San Salvador, July 2018. IUDOP found that, in 1993, 86 percent of the population knew of the Truth Commission (IUDOP 1993b).

44. Williams and Seri 2003.

45. Wood 2003.

46. Montgomery 1983b.

47. Manning 2008.

48. Ameringer 1992, 290.

49. In this book, I consider El Salvador's war to have ended at a military draw. This differs slightly from my 2019 *World Politics* article, in which I categorized the belligerents as stalemated, but the government stronger relative to the FMLN. The difference stems from a shift in the coding of the explanatory variable: from relative military strength to war outcomes (Daly 2019).

50. Álvaro de Soto, author interview, New York, September 2018. See also Harding 1993. Discovery of arms caches in Nicaragua in May 1993 threatened this, but the overall balance was preserved (Spear 1999).

51. Spear 1999.

52. These were the first democratic elections. Many scholars considered the 1980s elections to have been less than free and fair because, in the context of the ongoing civil war, ideological pluralism was limited, the military retained power over the elected civilian authorities, and fear and intimidation were widespread (Barnes 1998; Herman and Brodhead 1984; Karl 1995; Seligson and Booth 1995).

53. Wade 2008.

54. International Foundation for Electoral Systems 1994.

55. Author interview with Rubén Zamora, San Salvador, July 2018.

56. Wolf 2009.

57. Deputies were elected in the fourteen constituencies of the country and in a single national district.

58. Cruz and González 1997. In 1993, 88.6 percent of the population perceived crime to be increasing (IUDOP 1993a).

59. IUDOP 1994; LAPOP 1995. See also Azpuru 2010.

60. IUDOP 1994.

61. LAPOP 1991.

62. Webre 1979.

63. Dunkerley 1988.

64. Duarte 1986.

65. Williams and Walter 1997.

66. Partido Demócrata Cristiano n.d.

67. *La Prensa Gráfica* 1982.

68. Partido Demócrata Cristiano, "Plataforma Electoral," emphasis added.

69. The fight between Fidel Chávez Mena and Julio Adolfo Rey Prendes split the party. Rey Prendes left and formed the Authentic Christian Movement (MAC) (Ameringer 1992).

70. Williams and Seri 2003.

71. Bird and Williams 2000, 37.

72. Nonbelligerent PDC won only 16.4 percent in the first round presidential vote and 17.9 percent of the legislative vote.

73. CD constituted a more minor player. Whereas the FMLN secured 21 percent of the vote in the legislative elections, CD gained only 4 percent.

74. Salvador Samayoa, author interview and subsequent email exchange, San Salvador, July 2018.

75. The PCN was originally called the Revolutionary Party of Democratic Unification.

76. Pyes 1983.

77. Loxton 2014.

78. Ameringer 1992, 293.

79. Mauricio Sandoval, ARENA party strategist, author interview, San Salvador, July 2018.

80. Galeas 2004.

81. Quoted in Loxton 2014.

82. Quoted in Loxton 2014.

83. Loxton 2014. See also Blachman and Sharpe 1988/1989.

84. Stanley 1996.

85. Mauricio Sandoval, author interview, San Salvador, July 2018. In its first presidential contest, in 1984, ARENA had won 46.4 percent of the vote, an outcome made possible by building on the organizational capacity of the PCN.

86. I am extremely grateful to Ricardo Simán for making these archives available to me.

87. While some ARENA hardliners favored outright denial and a "war" on the truth commission, the legitimacy of this commission sidelined such a strategy (Ching 2016).

88. David Escobar Gaviria, author interview, San Salvador, July 2018.

89. Quoted in Dickey 1982.

90. Facundo Guardado, author interview, San Salvador, July 2018.

91. General Mauricio Vargas, author interview, San Salvador, July 2018.

92. Interview with Calderón Sol, November 8, 1993.

93. ARENA described itself as comprising not "death squad" members but "warriors of liberty," to quote the title of a book by one ARENA founder (Panamá 2005).

94. *Diario de Hoy*, March 9, 1994, ad by ARENA.

95. Author interview, San Salvador, July 2018.

96. Mauricio Sandoval, author interview, San Salvador, July 2018.

97. ARENA 1994.

98. Quoted in Loxton 2014, 394.

99. Sprenkels 2011.

100. Robert White, quoted in Paige 1997, 34.

101. LAPOP 1995.

102. Anderson 1988; Artiga González 2001; Loxton 2014; Wood 2000a.

103. Wood 2000a.

104. Dunkerley 1988, 351. See also Stanley 1996; Wolf 2009.

105. For example, the themes it planned for campaign ads presenting its economic plan were "to protect consumers; modernize the state institutions; guarantee the availability of basic nourishment."

106. ARENA, "Más Empleos con Calderón Sol," January 23, 1994.

107. ARENA, "Estrategia de Comunicaciones, Campaña '94."

108. In October 1992, 62 percent of the Salvadoran electorate was unaligned. In October 1993, 51 percent remained undecided and neither party commanded a partisan majority (IUDOP 1994).

109. IUDOP 1994.

110. Alfredo Cristiani, author interview, San Salvador, July 2018.

111. Loxton 2014.

112. Wood 2000a, 248.

113. Mauricio Sandoval, author interview, San Salvador, July 2018.

114. ARENA, "Puntos de Copy Para Posicionar al Dr. Calderón Sol Como El Presidente En Quien Todos Confiamos," June 1993.

115. ARENA 1994.

116. Mauricio Sandoval, author interview, July 17, 2018, San Salvador.

117. ARENA established internal groupings for each sector of society: professional, agricultural, entrepreneurial, female, youth, campesino, labor. "It was easier for somebody to be recruited. Everyone felt they had an entry. For example, if I'm a campesino, [ARENA could] say 'Why don't you join the party, there is a campesino sector, and through that sector, the party listens to your needs.'" President Alfredo Cristiani, author interview, San Salvador, July 2018.

118. *El Diario de Hoy* 1994a.

119. *El Diario de Hoy* 1994c.

120. ARENA internal document, "Puntos de Copy Para Posicionar al Dr. Calderón Sol Como El Presidente En Quien Todos Confiamos," June 1993.

121. Without primaries in the party, the nominations depended only on D'Aubuisson's choices.

122. Alfredo Cristiani was the first untainted civilian presidential candidate chosen by ARENA; with a clean record, he was ostensibly selected to appease the United States, but faced opposition from hardliners. Calderón Sol appeared as a consensus candidate for the founding postwar elections.

123. Manuel Meléndez, author interview, San Salvador, July 2018.

124. Alfredo Cristiani, author interview, San Salvador, July 2018.

125. Salvador Samayoa, author interview, San Salvador, July 2018.

126. Alfredo Cristiani, author interview, San Salvador, July 2018.

127. Salvador Samayoa, author interview, San Salvador, July 2018.

128. General Mauricio Vargas (ARENA senator), author interview. Candidate lists, albeit incomplete, confirm this.

129. Alfredo Cristiani, author interview, San Salvador, July 2018.

130. Manuel Meléndez, author interview, San Salvador, July 2018.

131. Vickers, Spence, and Huff 1994. Referenced in author interview with Manuel Meléndez, San Salvador, July 2018.

132. Acosta Oertel 1994.

133. *El Diario de Hoy* 1994d.

134. *El Diario de Hoy* 1994c.

135. Girón S. 1994, 84, emphasis added.

136. See, for example, Girón S. 1994.

137. Albertson and Gadarian 2015. According to President Cristiani, ARENA sought to pursue "a very emotional campaign in the media, aimed at elevating people's emotions." It played the anticommunist anthem first, to generate anger and fear toward the FMLN, and then "happy, enthusiastic music" associating sentiments of hope with ARENA (President Alfredo Cristiani, author interview, San Salvador, July 2018).

138. CIDAI 2004.

139. *Prensa Gráfica*, archives, January 1994. Archived interview with ARENA presidential candidate Armando Calderón Sol, November 8, 1993.

140. ARENA internal document, "Puntos de Copy Para Posicionar al Dr. Calderón Sol Como El Presidente En Quien Todos Confiamos," June 1993.

141. Acosta Oertel 1994.

142. Bruch 1994.

143. "Subversión y derechos humanos," *El Diario de Hoy*, March 1, 1994, 15.

144. *El Diario de Hoy*, March 1, 1994.

145. Secretaria de Relaciones y Plan Electoral, "FMLN 92 memo on party image communication strategy," September 28, 1992.

146. Frente Farabundo Martí para la Liberación Nacional FMLN, "Estatutos del Partido Político."

147. Shafik Handál, author interview, San Salvador, July 2018.

148. Sebastián Alejos, author interview, San Salvador, July 2018.

149. Secretaria de Relaciones y Plan Electoral, "FMLN 92 memo on party image communication strategy," September 28, 1992.

150. McClintock 1985, 173. See also Villalobos 1984.

151. Having fought against the state's armed forces and having been these forces' primary victims, FMLN did not, in its security platform, advance using these same forces and mano dura to provide security, but instead pushed for public safety accompanied by security sector reform.

152. Sebastián Alejos, author interview, San Salvador, July 2018.

153. Shafik Handál, author interview, San Salvador, July 2018.

154. Facundo Guardado, author interview, San Salvador, July 2018.

155. Sebastián Alejos, author interview, San Salvador, July 2018.

156. Sebastián Alejos, author interview, San Salvador, August 2018.

157. Secretaria de Relaciones y Plan Electoral, "FMLN 92 memo on party image communication strategy," September 28, 1992, emphasis added.

158. Zamora 1998, 227.

159. FMLN, "Propuesta de Plataforma."

160. Dada 1994.

161. FLACSO 1995. FMLN's overall authority was a consensus-based mechanism involving the leaders of the five groups that made up the FMLN: Fuerzas Populares de Liberación

Farabundo Martí (FPL), Ejército Revolucionario del Pueblo (ERP), Fuerzas Armadas de Resistencia National (RN), Partido Comunista Salvadoreño (PCS), and Partido Revolucionario de los Trabajadores Centroamericanos (PRTC).

162. Grenier 1999.

163. Galeas, author interview, San Salvador, July 2018. One organization of the FMLN was the moderate-leaning ERP, comparable to social democrats (Villalobos 1999).

164. FMLN also included the PCS and FPL, which divided further into orthodox revolutionaries and renovators (Sprenkels 2019). See also McClintock 1985; White 1973.

165. According to Sprenkels 2019, "The leadership settled on postponing the ideological debates until after the founding elections."

166. Secretaria de Relaciones y Plan Electoral, "FMLN 92 memo on party image communication strategy," September 28, 1992, emphasis added.

167. Azpuru 2010.

168. Shafik Handál, author interview, San Salvador, July 2019, emphasis added.

169. FMLN Secretaria de Relaciones y Plan Electoral, "FMLN 92 memo on party image communication strategy," September 28, 1992.

170. FMLN, "Propuesta de los comunicadores sociales para la asamblea nacional del PRS," emphasis added.

171. ARENA sought to turn even this benign slogan on its head. Its propaganda countered that FMLN put the "people first," as targets of its violence. One ad blasted the population: "First it was the people, then it was the electric towers . . . then it was the bridges . . . and last the cows." *El Diario de Hoy*, March 9, 1994. See also Girón S. 1994.

172. Wade 2008.

173. FMLN Secretaria de Relaciones y Plan Electoral, "FMLN 92 memo on party image communication strategy," September 28, 1992.

174. FMLN, "Propuesta de los comunicadores sociales para la asamblea nacional del PRS."

175. The two most powerful factions—the ERP and the FPL—were strongly discordant (Giovanni Galeas, author interview, San Salvador, August 2018). "FMLN's Achilles' heel . . . [was its] lack of unity" (Vickers, Spence, and Huff 1994). The FMLN splintered in the aftermath of the founding elections, and shed its more moderate elements (Shafik Handál, author interview, San Salvador, July 2018). See Allison and Martín Alvarez 2012.

176. FMLN, "Propuesta de los comunicadores sociales para la asamblea nacional del PRS." See also FMLN Secretaria de Relaciones y Plan Electoral, "FMLN 92 memo on party image communication strategy," September 28, 1992.

177. The choice of Zamora may also have resulted from an inability to reach consensus among the FMLN constituent organizations as to which faction would field the presidential candidate.

178. Manuel Meléndez, author interview, San Salvador, July 2018.

179. Sebastián Alejos, author interview, San Salvador, July 2018. Putting forth a civilian candidate also made the FMLN less vulnerable to rhetorical attack by ARENA (Manuel Meléndez, author interview, San Salvador, July 2018).

180. The candidates were taken evenly from the five insurgent organizations that composed the FMLN (Facundo Guardado, author interview, San Salvador, July 2018). Its national party slate, for example, included the leader of the PRTC, the second in command of the ERP, the

sister of one of the founders of the FPL, one of the most prominent members of the RN, and a member of the PCS leadership. I am grateful to Salvador Samayoa, FMLN commander and peace negotiator, for sharing with me the FMLN list of candidates for 1994.

181. This played well to the base, but in some places backfired with undecided voters (Facundo Guardado, author interview, San Salvador, July 2018).

182. Sebastián Alejos, author interview, San Salvador, August 2018.

183. Rubén Zamora, author interview, San Salvador, July 2018.

184. Manuel Meléndez, author interview, San Salvador, July 2018. FMLN did try to play one radio piece "with Monseñor Romero sermon clips, and the slogan: 'Do not vote for those that assassinated Monseñor Romero,' but it was very naïve. It had no impact." Sebastián Alejos, author interview, San Salvador, August 2018.

185. A study by Hemisphere Initiatives conducted midway through the founding postwar campaign found that ARENA's advertising time on television and radio averaged five to fourteen times that of the FMLN.

186. It was estimated that ARENA spent approximately US$12 million on the founding postwar campaign; the FMLN spent only $270,000. Quoted in Stahler-Sholk 1994, 24.

187. Vickers, Spence, and Huff 1994. This broadcasting advantage proved especially helpful to ARENA's strategy to target swing voters. By contrast, the FMLN proved unable to "adequately target specific campaign messages to key sectors of the electorate, in particular women, youth, and rural voters, in which it knew its support was weak."

188. Loxton 2014; Wood 2000a.

189. FMLN Secretaria de Relaciones y Plan Electoral, "FMLN 92 memo on party image communication strategy," September 28, 1992.

190. Wasow's 2020 work on civil rights protests shows how the media plays a huge role in determining how the population at large thinks about contentious events and how they vote.

191. ARENA internal document, "ARENA Estrategia de Comunicaciones Campaña '94."

192. FMLN Secretaria de Relaciones y Plan Electoral, "FMLN 92 memo on party image communication strategy," September 28, 1992.

193. FMLN, "Propuesta de Plataforma"; FMLN, "Propuesta de los comunicadores sociales para la asamblea nacional del PRS."

194. Rubén Zamora, author interview, San Salvador, July 2018.

195. Snyder and Ballentine 1996. FMLN's rigorous attempts to break through inequalities in media access has interesting parallels to Chile, where a failure to democratize or pluralize control of mass media outlets since the 1990 transition from military rule has led to persistent problems of accountability for state violence. See Bonner 2014.

196. Shafik Handál, author interview, San Salvador, July 2018.

197. Vickers, Spence, and Huff 1994.

198. IUDOP 1991.

199. IUDOP 1994.

200. Alfredo Cristiani, author interview, San Salvador, July 2018, emphasis added.

201. Facundo Guardado, author interview, San Salvador, July 2018.

202. LAPOP 1991.

203. Giovanni Galeas, author interview, San Salvador, July 2018.

204. Alfredo Cristiani, author interview, San Salvador, July 2018.

205. This survey, conducted before the war ended in 1992, likely exhibits bias. Indeed, non-response and "do not know" answers were high. Unfortunately, no similar data exist for the post-1992 period. My in-depth interviews were consistent with this poll, expressing a divergence between perceptions of objective and subjective violence. Given that conditions when the survey was taken in 1991 were insufficient for an unbiased statement of political opinions, I draw on later data wherever possible.

206. IUDOP 1994; LAPOP 1995. See also Azpuru 2010.

207. ARENA's candidate choice seems to have paid off. Only 12 percent of the population had a negative image of Calderón Sol (IUDOP 1994).

208. IUDOP 1994.

209. Alfredo Cristiani, author interview, San Salvador, July 2018.

210. IUDOP 1993b.

211. Ameringer 1992, 293.

212. IUDOP 1994.

213. IUDOP 1994; LAPOP 1995.

214. Security issues concerned various socioeconomic groups in roughly equal proportions in surveys by IUDOP 1994 and LAPOP 1995. See Yashar 2018.

215. President Alfredo Cristiani, author interview, San Salvador, July 2018.

216. LAPOP 1991.

217. Cienfuegos 1982; McElhinny 2006.

218. Azpuru 2010.

219. Loxton 2014.

220. Wood 2000a.

221. Azpuru 2010.

222. Shafik Handál, author interview, San Salvador, July 2018.

223. FMLN won 25.6 percent of the electorate's votes in the first round, 31.7 percent in the second round; it won 15 of 262 municipalities.

224. ARENA won 200 of 262 municipalities.

225. I am extremely grateful to Michael Allison for sharing these election data and to the University of North Texas for digitizing the Commission on the Truth for El Salvador data. It merits mention that the commission's documentation of wartime violence suffered from bias: participation by rural victims varied, depending on whether the locally dominant insurgent faction urged residents to come forward. As a result, testimonies of wartime abuse were quite uneven across El Salvador. I seek to follow the approach of Allison and use data on whether any family member died during the war, taken from a survey reported in Seligson and McElhinny 1996, but these data are available only at the department level and cannot be disaggregated by perpetrator. See Allison 2010.

226. David Escobar Galindo, author interview, San Salvador, July 2018. (IUDOP 1993b).

227. For illustrations of these results, see Daly 2019.

228. Andrés Suster, author interview, New York City, June 2018.

229. The war prompted significant transformations in demographic patterns. At least 750,000 citizens were displaced during the war, many from rural to urban areas, and more than one million Salvadorans migrated abroad (Zamora 1998). On displacement and elections, see Kasara 2016.

230. Author interviews, San Salvador, July 2018.

231. For example, ARENA Alfredo Cristiani and FMLN presidential candidate Facundo Guardado, author interviews, San Salvador, July 2018. See IUDOP 1994.

232. Petrocik 1996. See Tavits and Potter 2015.

233. LAPOP 1995.

234. See Daly 2019.

235. Álvaro de Soto, author interview, New York, September 2018. To the extent that there was asymmetry in the demobilization process, rebalancing of power was achieved. For example, according to President Alfredo Cristiani, during delays in the purging of the officer corps, the government allowed the FMLN to retain its air-to-surface missiles (author interview, San Salvador, July 2018). On the sustained balance of power, see Harding 1993; Karl 1992; Wood 2003.

236. FMLN Secretaria de Relaciones y Plan Electoral, "FMLN 92 memo on party image communication strategy," September 28, 1992.

237. French 1994.

238. Cagan 1994.

239. Author interviews with FMLN leaders Shafik Handál and Facundo Guardado, and FMLN presidential candidate Rubén Zamora, San Salvador, July 2018.

240. Author interviews with President Alfredo Cristiani and with government peace negotiator David Escobar Galindo, San Salvador, July 2018.

241. Trejo, Albarracín, and Tiscornia 2015.

242. Ching 2016.

243. Yashar 2018.

244. LAPOP 2010.

245. Mauricio Sandoval, author interview, San Salvador, July 2018.

246. @ARENAOFICIAL, September 29, 2019.

247. Pocasangre 2022.

248. For example, in 2006, ARENA built a plaza in San Salvador in D'Aubuisson's honor. It was inaugurated by President Antonio Saca, who praised D'Aubuisson for having saved El Salvador from "the tragedy of Marxist totalitarianism" (Loxton 2014).

249. Collier and Collier 1991. On the institutionalization of parties in new democracies, see Hicken 2009. Since 2018, this party system stabilization has been blown up by Nayib Bukele and the party, Nuevas Ideas.

250. Wood 2000a.

251. Author interview, San Salvador, July 2018.

252. McClintock 1985, 38; see also Loxton 2014.

253. Mauricio Sandoval, author interview, San Salvador, July 2018.

254. Party leader, author interview, San Salvador, July 2018.

255. Manning 2008.

256. Sprenkels 2019, 550. See Almeida 2010.

257. Manning 2008. The rate of partisan identification with the FMLN grew after the war (LAPOP 2006–2010): over time, this enabled the FMLN to win over the swing voters (Azpuru 2010). See Colburn 2009.

258. ARENA secured 52 percent in the 1999 presidential election, 58 percent in the 2004 election, and 48.7 percent in the 2009 election. While its legislative presence declined from its

1994 high of 39 seats, it consistently hovered at around 30 out of 84 seats. FMLN, meanwhile, increased its political foothold over time, gaining 29.4 percent of the vote in 1999 and 35.6 percent in 2004 and winning the presidency in 2009 with 51.3 percent of the vote. Its seats in the legislature increased from 21 in 1994 to consistently matching ARENA with around 30 seats in each subsequent election. *Keesing's Record of World Events* 1987.

259. Stanley 2006.

260. The presence of the PCN may have made it easier for ARENA to distance itself from the bloody past (relative to cases in which no split occurred).

261. Alfredo Cristiani, author interview, San Salvador, July 2018.

262. *NotiSur,* July 30, 1993.

263. Manuel Meléndez, author interview, San Salvador, July 2018.

264. "*Crónica del mes*" 1993.

265. "Central America Report" 1993.

266. In the hypothetical election, PCN received the lowest vote of the major parties on the dimension of honoring human rights. Only 1.3 percent claimed they would vote for it on this competency (IUDOP 1993b).

267. According to Loxton 2014, "inside-out" denotes the unusual status of these parties' founders: they formerly held positions of power in the military regimes but had been displaced. Finding themselves on the outside and sidelined from power, they turned to party building in an attempt to regain influence.

268. Manuel Meléndez, author interview, San Salvador, July 2018.

269. Wood 2000b. See Johnson 1993; Paige 1997.

270. Francisco de Sola, author interview, San Salvador, July 2018.

271. Alfredo Cristiani, author interview, San Salvador, July 2018.

272. General Mauricio Vargas, author interview, San Salvador, July 2018, and Giovanni Galeas, author interview, San Salvador, July 2018.

273. Ameringer 1992, 295.

274. Mauricio Sandoval, author interview, San Salvador, July 17, 2018.

Chapter 6

1. Yashar 1997.

2. Cullather 1999; REMHI 1999.

3. Wilkinson 2002.

4. Anderson 1988, 26–27.

5. The four armies were the Ejército Guerrillero de los Pobres, Fuerzas Armadas Rebeldes, Organización del Pueblo en Armas, and Partido Guatemalteco de Trabajo.

6. Garrard-Burnett 2010, 38.

7. Schirmer 1998, 44.

8. U.S. Department of State 1983.

9. Schirmer 1998, 45.

10. For a quantitative analysis of the state terror, see Ball, Kobrak, and Spirer 1999.

11. La Comisión para el Escalarecimiento Histórico CEH 1999.

12. REMHI: Recovery of Historical Memory Project 1999.

13. These projects gathered and built on more than 37,000 testimonies.

14. Garrard-Burnett 2010, 6.

15. Garrard-Burnett 2010, 3, 7.

16. In May 2013, a Guatemalan court found Ríos Montt guilty of genocide, based on evidence that the military under his direction had intentionally sought to exterminate the Ixil ethnic group. There is disagreement among scholars about whether the actions of the military during this period meet the legal definition of genocide. Sanford 2003, 155, for example, argues in the affirmative. Schwartz and Straus 2018 weigh in, claiming that the strategic logic of the violence was not genocidal in nature.

17. Garrard-Burnett 2010, 16. Stoll 1993 has advanced the case that while the rebels were not directly responsible for the violence, they provoked the genocidal state violence against the highlands by planting themselves there and then failing to protect the population from the violence. Nonetheless, the TRCs found them responsible for only a small share of the violence.

18. La Comisión para el Escalarecimiento Histórico CEH 1999. See also Jonas 2000.

19. U.S. Department of Defense 1991.

20. Hectór Rosada Granados, author interview, Guatemala City, August 2018.

21. The cable acknowledged "it was difficult to determine the exact number of combatants . . . due to the fact that the guerrillas here are farmers by day and guerrillas by night" (U.S. Department of Defense 1994).

22. Garrard-Burnett 2010, 89.

23. Figueroa Ibarra and Martí i Puig 2007, 46.

24. Allison 2016; Jonas 2000. In May 1999, a referendum ("Consulta Popular") was held on the reforms related to the Peace Accords. The packages of policy changes voted upon included recognizing indigenous languages and customary law, demilitarizing the state, and improving democratic accountability. With a very low turnout (18.5 percent), the "no vote" prevailed by a margin of 55 percent (Carey 2004). Right-wing propaganda, racism, and the extent to which people had "felt the devastating effects of the war" have been used to explain the rejection of the referendum (Pico 1999b).

25. Luciak 2001. The United Nations Verification Mission in Guatemala was established in November 1994.

26. Organization of American States 2000.

27. Quoted in *New York Times* 1999.

28. The 113 deputies were elected in a two-tiered voting system. Voters cast separate ballots for members of congress from multimember constituencies corresponding to the country's departments, and through proportional representation in a single national list.

29. Gálvez Borrell 1996.

30. Steinberg et al. 2006 show the distribution of massacres in Guatemala 1978–1995; these were clearly distributed across the country.

31. Gunson 1996; Rohter 1996b. See Jonas 2000.

32. Daly, Paler, and Samii 2020.

33. Borge and Associates poll, cited in Pico 1999a. An alternative survey, conducted by ASIES, found 56 percent of respondents cited economic well-being and 28 percent cited crime as the most important issues facing Guatemala ahead of the 1999 elections (Lehoucq 2002).

34. Loeb 1999.

35. Lehoucq 2002.

36. In a 1999 poll, on a left-right ideological scale, nearly one-fourth set themselves cleanly in the center (24.4 percent). Only 9.3 percent located themselves solidly on the left, and only 8.2 percent on the right. Another 16.6 percent of those polled defined themselves as center-left and 17.4 percent as center-right. One-fourth did not respond (Pico 1999a).

37. LAPOP 1999.

38. Trudeau 1993, 147.

39. Loxton 2014.

40. Sanchez 2008.

41. These included the parties (PID, PR, CAN, CAO) that had supported the various military dictatorships; the Movimiento Emergente de Concordia party of retired officers Benedicto Lucas García and Ríos Montt military junta member Colonel Luís Gordillo Martínez; the "party of organized violence," Movimiento de Liberación Nacional; and the party of Ríos Montt's private secretary Francisco Bianchi, Acción Reconciliadora Democrática. Bianchi notoriously had told the *New York Times* that if the indigenous people sympathized with the guerrillas, they must be killed, even if they were civilians (Pico 1999a). See also Garrard-Burnett 2010, 36. These parties largely mirrored PCN in El Salvador; they exhibited terminal birth defects, unfavorable strategies, and poor electoral outcomes.

42. ANN comprised URNG and two minor progressive parties: Desarrollo Integral Auténtico (DIA) and Unidad de Izquierda Democrática (UNID). Frente Democrático Nueva Guatemala had exited the coalition before the 1999 election. See Alianza Nueva Nación 1999; Holiday 2000.

43. Madison 2008. See CIDOB 2018.

44. CIDOB 2018. See Loxton 2014.

45. Partido de Avanzada Nacional 1999.

46. Loxton 2014.

47. See *New York Times* 1996.

48. See Ajenjo Fresno and García Díez 2001; Loxton 2014; Trudeau 1993.

49. They did not seek prosecution; there was a 1996 amnesty law for most politically motivated crimes committed during Guatemala's thirty-six-year civil war (Ruhl 2004).

50. Guatemala News and Information Bureau Archive (1963–2000) 1999.

51. Quoted in Rohter 1996a; Guatemala News and Information Bureau Archive (1963–2000) 1999.

52. Williams and Seri 2003.

53. Pico 1999a.

54. Guatemala News and Information Bureau Archive (1963–2000) 1999.

55. Partido de Avanzada Nacional 1999.

56. CIDOB 2018.

57. McCleary 1997, 132.

58. "Who's Who in the 1995 Elections" 1995.

59. Trudeau 1992, 343. See Loxton 2014.

60. Among other goals, PAN advanced integration into the global economy, infrastructure projects, and support for the peace deal ("Who's Who in the 1995 Elections" 1995), and promised to "attack poverty and unemployment" (*Infopress* 1999).

61. ASIES 2004; McCleary 1997.

62. Partido de Avanzada Nacional 1999.

63. CIDOB 2004.

64. Frente Republicano Guatemalteco 1999. This symbol implied an iron fist, or law and order (Loxton 2014).

65. Loeb 1999.

66. Stoll 1990.

67. Jonas 1995.

68. Garrard-Burnett 2010, 81.

69. American Embassy 1983.

70. Weld 2014, 5.

71. Given the extent of the harm, accepting responsibility for the violence risked this asset and provoking significant retribution.

72. Weld 2014, 5.

73. Garrard-Burnett 2010, 39. See also Schirmer 1998, 61.

74. Schirmer 1998, 62.

75. Garrard-Burnett 2010, 49–50.

76. Stoll 1990.

77. Schirmer 1998, 21.

78. Ríos Montt, quoted in Kuchuj Voz Ciudadana 1999.

79. Jonas 1995.

80. Ríos Montt's FRG had initially been an outsider to the military inner circle and was an outsider again after the coup that ousted him, but among the parties that were competitive in 1999, the FRG had the closest ties to the armed forces.

81. Stoll 1990. Ríos Montt therefore decided to campaign in uniform, accompanied by a strong police and military presence (U.S. Department of State, Guatemala Embassy 1997).

82. Malone 2010. See also Trudeau 1993.

83. Madison 2008.

84. These text analyses follow the approach of McClendon and Riedl 2019 in their meticulous study of Pentecostal and Catholic sermons in Africa.

85. Roberts, Steward, and Tingley 2019.

86. Riker 1996. The dominance principle anticipates that candidates will run on issues over which they can claim ownership and will ignore those issues on which other parties have a competency advantage.

87. Ansolabehere and Iyengar 1994. The "riding the wave" logic predicts that candidates from all parties will tend to run on the same issues, namely those salient in the public's mind.

88. Hobbes 1996.

89. *Infopress* 1999, emphasis added.

90. Frente Republicano Guatemalteco 1999.

91. See Jonas 1995.

92. Carey 2004. The right's slogan on the referendum was "If you want peace, vote no."

93. Carey 2004. In a survey, 31 percent believed that ethnic war in the future was very probable; 32 percent believed it was somewhat probable (LAPOP 1999).

94. Bateson 2022.

95. Kuchuj Voz Ciudadana 1999.

96. Loeb 1999.

97. Molina Mejía 2000. See *Guatemala Hoy* 1999; *Infopress* 1999.

98. Ríos Montt, June 27, 1999, quoted in Kuchuj Voz Ciudadana 1999.

99. American Embassy 1983.

100. Gruson 1989.

101. Ríos Montt, June 27, 1999, quoted in Kuchuj Voz Ciudadana 1999.

102. U.S. Department of State, Guatemala Embassy 1997.

103. www.frg.org.gt, accessed through the Wayback Machine internet archive.

104. See Rohter 1996a.

105. ASIES 2004.

106. PAN, quoted in Guatemala News and Information Bureau Archive (1963–2000) 1999.

107. ANN, quoted in Guatemala News and Information Bureau Archive (1963–2000) 1999, emphasis added.

108. Garrard-Burnett 2010, 9.

109. Guatemala News and Information Bureau Archive (1963–2000) 1999.

110. Internal documents are not available to shed light on whether FRG would have selected Alfonso Portillo as its candidate anyway, had Montt been eligible to run.

111. Carter Center 2003, 11.

112. Rohter 1996a.

113. Portillo also had "security" credentials. Midway through the campaign, it was revealed that during a street fight in Mexico in the early 1980s, he had killed two men (allegedly in self-defense). He had fled to avoid prosecution (La Comisión para el Escalarecimiento Histórico CEH 1999). FRG used this to showcase "his willingness to stand up to any threat," that since he was above the law he was therefore able to impose the law and that he would use any means necessary to provide security (Carey 2004, 76). An FRG slogan declared, "If Portillo can defend himself, he can defend you and your family" (Holiday 2000, 82).

114. "Who's Who in the 1995 Elections" 1995.

115. Barrera Ortiz 2014.

116. Molina Mejía 2000.

117. Loeb 1999.

118. Lehoucq 2002.

119. *Guatemala Hoy* 1999.

120. Palma Lau 2010.

121. Guatemala News and Information Bureau Archive (1963–2000) 1999.

122. Pico 1999a.

123. Unfortunately, there was missingness in the data. Kuchuj Voz Ciudadana gave information on civilian/military backgrounds for 39 percent of the FRG candidates, 74 percent of the PAN candidates, and 69 percent of the ANN candidates (Kuchuj Voz Ciudadana 1999).

124. Author interview, Guatemala City, August 2018.

125. FRG conceded that there was war, but claimed there was "no genocide" (Weld 2014). It called the violence "the situation" (Garrard-Burnett 2010). Even when, in 2013, Ríos Montt faced threats of conviction for directing the military to intentionally exterminate the Ixil ethnic group, the rallying call of his supporters became "no hubo genocidio!"—there was no genocide (Fisher and Taub 2019).

126. Jonas 2000.

127. Guatemala News and Information Bureau Archive (1963–2000) 1999.

128. See Alianza Nueva Nación 1999.

129. Kuchuj Voz Ciudadana 1999.

130. Quoted in Guatemala News and Information Bureau Archive (1963–2000) 1999.

131. Figueroa Ibarra and Martí i Puig 2008.

132. URNG 1995, 14.

133. Guatemala News and Information Bureau Archive (1963–2000) 1999.

134. Loeb 1999. The ANN candidate had a 36 percent favorable rating and a 15 percent unfavorable rating, and 32 percent did not know him, indicating that URNG had succeeded in selecting a fresh, untainted public face (LAPOP 1999).

135. Álvaro Colom's brother had been a former URNG leader, but the candidate himself had been a Social Democrat. See Pico 1999a.

136. Carey 2004.

137. LAPOP 1999.

138. Guatemala News and Information Bureau Archive (1963–2000) 1999.

139. Loxton 2014.

140. Figueroa Ibarra and Martí i Puig 2008.

141. Guatemala News and Information Bureau Archive (1963–2000) 1999.

142. Loeb 1999.

143. Garrard-Burnett 2010, 12–13.

144. *Guatemala Hoy* 1999.

145. Author interview, Guatemala City, August 2018.

146. Pico 1999b. Rosada Granados confirmed, "The peace *accords* were not an important electoral issue" (author interview, Guatemala City, August 2018).

147. Ricardo Sáenz de Tejada, author interview, Guatemala City, August 2018, emphasis added.

148. See Schirmer 1998, 45. Polling is not available to explicitly test whether frames of reference shifted from no terror to ongoing terror.

149. Ricardo Sáenz de Tejada, author interview, Guatemala City, August 2018.

150. Trudeau 1992, 343.

151. LAPOP 1999.

152. United States Information Agency (USIA) 2000.

153. LAPOP 1999.

154. Garrard-Burnett 2010, 11.

155. Gruson 1989.

156. USIA 1991.

157. LAPOP 1999.

158. LAPOP 1999.

159. Stoll 1990.

160. LAPOP 1999.

161. Stoll 1990. The Guatemalan constitution gives the military the responsibility to maintain internal as well as external security (Ruhl 2004).

162. LAPOP 1999.

163. The efficacy of the war-winner's Restrained Leviathan message lies with its credibility against all threats. The theory suggests how the security brand may evolve as the country moves away from war and other forms of insecurity may rival and trump that stemming from political violence.

164. Lehoucq 2002, emphasis added.

165. Rosada Granados, author interview, Guatemala City, August 2018.

166. Stoll 1990, emphasis added.

167. Azpuru 2016.

168. LAPOP 1999. Of those who believed there was a need for strong-arm government, 66 percent intended to vote for FRG, compared to 31 percent of those who did not perceive this need. The 39 percent of the population that expressed indifference between a civilian and military regime or who favored an authoritarian government were twice as likely to vote FRG.

169. LAPOP 1999.

170. Molina Mejía 2000; Stoll 1990.

171. Copeland 2011.

172. Lehoucq 2002, citing polling data from Borge y Asociados's 1999 Encuesta Nacional de Opinión Pública.

173. LAPOP 1999.

174. U.S. Department of State 1990. See Weyland 1999.

175. U.S. Department of State 1990.

176. Molina Mejía 2000.

177. LAPOP 1999.

178. Lehoucq 2002; Loeb 1999.

179. According to a December 1999 survey, 66 percent of respondents believed that a PAN administration would "defend the interests of the rich."

180. Loeb 1999.

181. Lehoucq 2002.

182. Ball 1999.

183. I am grateful to Regina Bateson for sharing the digitalized municipal-level election results. Given the skew in the distribution of violence, I take the log of the violent events.

184. In one of these places, Guatemala City, it was not the FRG that won in 1999, but instead the nonbelligerent PAN.

185. Schirmer 1998, 61.

186. Molina Mejía 2000. See also Loeb 1999.

187. See LAPOP 1999.

188. Loxton and Mainwaring 2018; Lupu 2016.

189. Loeb 1999.

190. *Guatemala Hoy* 1999.

191. Guatemala News and Information Bureau Archive (1963–2000) 1999.

192. Sáenz de Tejada 2004.

193. Organization of American States 2000.

194. Ideology as a vote determinant is negatively correlated with voting for PAN, a party with a better-defined ideological position to the right of the spectrum's center. This could reflect the success of FRG's strategy of positional convergence.

195. See ASIES 2012.

196. Ríos Montt's sentence was overturned on procedural grounds; he died in 2018 during the retrial.

197. Yashar 2018.

198. UN Office on Drugs and Crime's International Homicide Statistics database.

199. Bateson 2022.

200. Ríos Montt's own daughter Zury also sought to resurrect the brand, running on her father's law-and-order laurels.

201. Sáenz de Tejada, author interview, Guatemala City, August 2018.

202. Sáenz de Tejada, author interview, Guatemala City, August 2018.

203. Over time, the security brand might prove less expedient against candidates promising redistribution and social services, as suggested by the 2009 Salvadoran election in which ARENA's mano dura candidate, the former director of the police, lost to the FMLN candidate, who emphasized *mano amiga* (friendly hand).

204. Loxton and Mainwaring 2018; Lupu 2016.

205. See Allison 2010; Bateson 2022.

206. Garrard-Burnett 2010, 101.

207. Sáenz de Tejada 2004.

208. Spence et al. 1998.

209. Allison 2010.

210. In 2003, FRG won 19.7 percent of the legislative vote. Ríos Montt, its presidential candidate, failed to advance beyond the first round. In 2007, Ríos Montt was elected again to Congress and FRG won 9.8 percent of the vote, but by 2011, FRG won only 2.7 percent of the vote and only a single seat in Congress. In 2013, the party dissolved and renamed itself Partido Republicano Institucional (PRI) (ASIES 2012). In 2015, receiving few votes, this party too disappeared (Sáenz de Tejada, author interview, Guatemala City, August 2018). URNG's trajectory was similarly in decline: in 2003, it did not compete with ANN; it won 4.2 percent of the vote. In 2007, it earned 3.56 percent of the vote, after which it became noncompetitive in national elections. See also Nohlen 2005a.

211. Sanchez 2008.

Chapter 7

1. Kuant and O'Kane 1990.

2. Following the 1972 earthquake, for example, as reconstruction funds and international assistance flooded the country, Anastasio Somoza embezzled these resources, alienating not only the masses but also the business elite.

3. Margarita Vaninni, historian, author interview, Managua, April 22, 2019. On December 27, 1974, Sandinista commandos stormed a Somoza Christmas party and seized many of the country's most prominent figures as hostages. In exchange for the release of these hostages, the Sandinistas extracted from Somoza funds for the armed struggle, including $1 million in ransom; restoration of their leaders, to be freed from prison; and a propaganda triumph—the ability to disseminate the Sandinista raison d'être across Nicaragua on the official state radio network and in the opposition newspaper.

4. Kuant and O'Kane 1990. See Close and Martí i Puig 2012.

5. *New York Times* 1979.

6. Paul, Clarke, and Grill 2010.

7. Margarita Vannini, author interview, Managua, April 22, 2019.

8. Nuñez de Escorcia 2014.

9. Margarita Vannini, author interview, Managua, April 22, 2019.

10. Nicaragua never had a truth commission, neither for the Somoza regime and revolutionary uprising, nor for the civil war in the 1980s. See Nuñez de Escorcia 2014.

11. Walker 1991.

12. Booth 1985; Walker 1982.

13. Everingham 1996.

14. Margarita Vannini, author interview, Managua, April 22, 2019.

15. These forces organized as the 15th of September Legion, Nicaraguan Democratic Union and eventually the combined Nicaraguan Democratic Force (FDN).

16. Margarita Vannini, author interview, Managua, April 22, 2019.

17. Barbosa-Miranda 2010; Millett 1977.

18. Booth 1985.

19. Latin American Studies Association 1984.

20. Anderson and Dodd 2005, 115.

21. Latin American Studies Association 1984.

22. Booth 1985, 219.

23. Margarita Vannini, author interview, Managua, April 22, 2019. See also *Revista Envío* 1984a.

24. Latin American Studies Association 1984.

25. Shugart 1987.

26. I use the years after the elections for Nicaragua, Guatemala, and El Salvador because of how V-Dem registers the full impact of elections in the year subsequent to the elections.

27. The Social Christian Party united with the business organization COSEP and tiny groups of dissident liberals and conservatives to form the CDN.

28. *New York Times* 1984. Declassified U.S. cables from the Digital National Security Archive confirm that CDN decided to boycott because of U.S. pressure.

29. Latin American Studies Association 1984.

30. U.S. Department of State, Nicaragua Embassy 1984.

31. Even declassified U.S. cables, while condemning the elections on all fronts, do not make this claim. Some have argued that, had the CDN remained in the race, it could have undercut the FSLN's majority. However, Latin American Studies Association 1984 concluded otherwise: "There is no evidence that the Coordinadora [CDN] parties possessed a mass base comparable to that of such parties as the [liberal] PLI and the [conservative] PCD, which were tested in the November 4 election. Even if the Coordinadora alliance had participated and received 15 percent of the votes—more than any of the opposition parties that actually competed in the election—the FSLN would still have won a majority." It also remains unclear whether CDN voters abstained or whether they instead voted for other parties. On the one hand, abstention was on average 24.6 percent and higher in the interior of the country, where the opposition was stronger. On the other hand, this abstention level mirrors that in 1990 when all flavors of the opposition ran, and some won.

32. Former Barricada journalist Guillermo Cortés claimed in 1984 that "power was not in play"; rather, elections were adopted only as a means to undercut U.S. political pressure and criticisms (Cruz 2021).

33. Even some former FSLN leaders admitted that the elections were not free and fair and never intended to bring actual electoral democracy. For perspectives from former commanders including Luis Carrion, Jaime Wheelock, and Victor Hugo Tinoco, see https://watson.brown.edu/events/2019/conference-nicaragua-1979-2019-sandinista-revolution-after-40-years.

34. Booth 1985.

35. Reding 1991, 25.

36. Close 1995, 53.

37. U.S. Embassy Managua 1984. See Booth 1985.

38. Author interview, April 2020.

39. Castro and Prevost 1992.

40. See Anderson and Dodd 2005, 145. Other studies found that 35 percent of the electorate were undecided voters (Castro and Prevost 1992).

41. Hoyt 2004. On October 21, just two weeks before the election, Virgilio Godoy ultimately announced that his party PLI was withdrawing from the elections (seemingly under intense U.S. pressure). It nonetheless remained on the ballot with its votes counted (*Revista Envío* 1984b).

42. Instituto Histórico Centroamericano 1985.

43. Latin American Studies Association 1990.

44. Hoyt 2004, 19.

45. Reding 1991, 27–28.

46. The DOXA polling organization, located in Caracas, Venezuela, conducted a series of public opinion surveys in the three months prior to the 1990 election. These were the only ones to forecast correctly a victory for the opposition and, as such, are deemed the most reliable (Anderson 1995).

47. Weaver and Barnes 1991.

48. U.S. Department of State, Nicaragua Embassy 1984.

49. U.S. Department of State, Nicaragua Embassy 1990.

50. Walker 1985.

51. Walker 1991, 9.

52. Booth 1985, 198.

53. Close 1985.

54. Booth 1985, 198.

55. "Estatuto Fundamental de la República," Articulo 24 and 26.

56. Frente Sandinista de Liberación Nacional (FSLN) 1984. The party manifesto, for example, stated, "The Sandinista Front will educate future generations in respect for all the men and women of our country who have shed their blood throughout all our struggles for the conquest of a future of justice and peace. They are the ones who died fighting tirelessly against foreign domination and its instrument, the genocidal dictatorship. They are the ones who, after a revolutionary triumph, have fallen in defense of our sacred rights of freedom and independence"; peace through rebel victory offset the use of violence.

57. FSLN 1984; Partido Conservador Demócrata de Nicaragua 1984.

58. Partido Liberal Independiente 1984. PLI did ostensibly promise that it would "bring peace to the country if elected, although it [did] not specif[y] how it [would] go about this"; it lacked security credentials (*Revista Envío* 1984c).

59. FSLN further undermined the legacy of Somoza credibility on security issues by emphasizing, in its party manifesto for example, that these forces "signified terror, threats. . . . They murdered and tortured. Police chiefs and commanders were also leaders of gangs and implicated in drug trafficking, the prostitution business, and gambling." It thus implied that these forces, if elected, would bring only further brutality and criminality (FSLN 1984).

60. Close 1991, 155.

61. Three "tendencies" emerged within the FSLN in 1975: the orthodox Proletarian (Jaime Wheelock) and Prolonged Popular War (Tomas Borge) factions, and the moderate Terceristas (Daniel and Humberto Ortega) (Kuant and O'Kane 1990). The Terceristas won out during the split between the tendencies, successfully pushing the organization to soften its radical stances in 1978–1979. This helped contribute to the broader popular uprising and multiclass coalition behind the revolutionary victory. In the revolution's aftermath and lead-up to the founding elections, the tendencies reunited and FSLN moderated further, leading to discontent among many on the left in Nicaragua who thought the revolution was not going far enough. See La Botz 2016.

62. FSLN 1984.

63. Partido Conservador Demócrata de Nicaragua 1984.

64. Close and Martí i Puig 2012, 4.

65. Author interview, Costa Rica, December 2019.

66. Serra 1991.

67. These included 70,000 activists for door-to-door campaigning (*Revista Envío* 1984c).

68. *Revista Envío* 1984c.

69. *Revista Envío* 1984a. Movimiento de Acción Popular Marxista Leninista accused the FSLN of "socialism with the bourgeoisie, socialism in negotiations with the imperialists, and socialism behind the workers' backs." In contrast, it offered "proletarian socialism and communism." The far-left PCdeN party also promised, if elected, to realize "the dictatorship of the proletariat, as well as the development of socialism and a communist society in Nicaragua" (*Revista Envío* 1984c). See also Comité Central del MAP-ML 1984; PCdeN 1984.

70. *Revista Envío* 1984a.

71. Booth 1985.

72. Even the Coordinadora opposition group—more closely tied to the Contras—which was not participating in the elections, had put forth a civilian rather than military presidential candidate: Arturo Cruz J.

73. *Revista Envío* 1984c.

74. Anderson and Dodd 2005, 182.

75. Payne 1985.

76. Anderson and Dodd 2005, 65.

77. This stands in contrast to 1990, when, following a different war outcome, the Sandinistas depicted Ortega "as a man of peace" rather than a military general; his military uniform "was shunned in favor of livelier, more youthful-looking civilian dress" (Latin American Studies Association 1990). In this latter election, the FSLN "tried to have a 'new' Daniel: to distance Ortega from the military" (Barnes 1992).

78. Barnes 1992.

79. Martí i Puig 2010.

80. Snyder and Ballentine 1996.

81. Serra 1991.

82. Oquist 1992, Weaver and Barnes 1991.

83. Instituto DOXA Venezuela 1990.

84. The Contra war left 61,884 victims, amounting to 1.72 percent of the Nicaraguan population of 3.6 million inhabitants. Material damage was estimated at $12.2 billion (Close 1991).

85. Instituto DOXA Venezuela 1989.

86. Of swing voters, 55 percent were undecided about who was more credible on security issues and implementation of peace (Instituto DOXA Venezuela 1989).

87. Anderson 1995.

88. Latin American Studies Association 1984. Of the government successor parties, PCD won 14 percent of the vote and PLI 10 percent of the vote in the presidential election. In the election for the National Constituent Assembly, PCD won 14 and PLI 9 of the 96 total seats (Booth 1985).

89. Booth 1985.

90. See Oquist 1992 for evidence of the extent of swing constituencies in Nicaragua.

91. Anderson 1995; Close 1991; Oquist 1992.

92. Lyons 2016; Thaler 2017.

93. Oquist 1992.

94. Serra 1991. See also Robinson and Norsworthy 1987, 253.

95. Close 1991.

96. At the same time, Soviet patronage for the Sandinistas was drying up as the Cold War wound down.

97. UNO constituted an unwieldy, fractious conglomerate of opposition parties spanning the entire political spectrum from the extreme left to the extreme right (Dye et al. 1995), but tilted to the right and pro-Contras (Weaver and Barnes 1991). It assumed the rebels' acronym, United Nicaraguan Opposition (UNO) (Trainor 1987), but changed the name to National Opposition Union (see Kondracke 1987). UNO had key Contras on its slate and won its largest victories in Contra areas (Oquist 1992; Coordinadora Regional de Investigaciones Económicas y Sociales 1990). Margarita Vannini described, "UNO was the political arm of the Contras," but others saw a greater break with, if not full separation from, the rebels (author interview, Managua, April 22, 2019).

98. Martí i Puig 2010.

99. Close 1991, 71–72.

100. Anderson and Dodd 2005, 82–83.

101. U.S. Department of State, Nicaragua Embassy 1990. See also Robinson and Norsworthy 1987, 253, Serra 1991, Close 1991.

102. See Oquist 1992, Paul, Clarke, and Grill 2010; Vickers 1990.

103. At the start of the campaign, approximately 30–50 percent of the electorate remained undecided, most concerned with the issue of "political stability," and unsure who was more credible on security issues (Anderson and Dodd 2005; Castro and Prevost 1992).

104. Oquist 1992.

105. Castro and Prevost 1992.

106. Oquist 1992.

107. Latin American Studies Association 1990, 34–35; CSE Managua 1990.

108. Quoted in Huntington 1993, 151.

109. Daly 2022. This peace in Nicaragua, too, was short-lived because the United States again shocked the balance of power. It used the 1990 elections as its exit strategy, withdrawing its support from the Contras in the elections' aftermath. As a result, the Sandinistas launched an offensive against the Contras. In response, the Contras began to organize in military formation as the "Re-Contras." See Brown 2001.

110. Nuñez de Escorcia 2014.

111. Cruz 2009; Yashar 2018.

112. Martí i Puig 2010.

Chapter 8

1. Inglehart et al. 2014.

2. Bermeo 2003; Fortna and Huang 2012; Hartzell and Hoddie 2015; Huang 2016; Wantchekon 2004.

3. Brancati and Snyder 2012; Flores and Nooruddin 2012.

4. Hartzell and Hoddie 2007; Manning and Smith 2016; Marshall and Ishiyama 2016; Walter 1999.

5. Country case studies of postwar parties and outcomes include Allison 2010; Curtis and Sindre 2019; De Zeeuw 2008; Dresden 2017; Holland 2015; Ishiyama and Widmeier 2013; Manning 2008; Neumann 2005; Shugart 1992; Söderberg Kovacs 2007.

6. Manning and Smith 2016; Söderberg Kovacs and Hatz 2016.

7. Manning and Smith 2019.

8. Themner 2017 provides insightful cases of ex-military leaders' political participation in Africa.

9. Daly 2021b.

10. Kreutz 2010.

11. FRUD stands for Front for the Restoration of Unity and Democracy, FRUD-AD for Front for the Restoration of Unity and Democracy–Ahmed Dini.

12. In this case, there was not a clear rebel belligerent successor party, as discussed below.

13. Where there is a bicameral system, the dataset examines the lower house. Where there is a two-round electoral system, it studies the first round. This enables comparable data across the greatest possible number of cases, as first-round legislative elections took place regardless of the political system, and had lower barriers to participation. For conflicts fought over territory, as explored in more depth below, the dataset examines the national elections in the original state if secession failed (e.g., Sri Lanka) or in the new state in which the war took place if it succeeded (e.g., Namibia). I also code, but analyze separately, regional elections where these determined governance in autonomous zones (e.g., Palestine).

14. These include Banks et al. 1999; Birch 2003; Grotz, Hartmann, and Nohlen 2001; Nohlen 2005a, 2005b; Nohlen, Krennerich, and Thibaut 1999; Nohlen and Stöver 2010; African Elections Database; Political Database of the Americas; and Parties and Elections in Europe. I also

consulted *Keesing's Record of World Events*; Lexis-Nexis Academic; Pro-Quest Historical Newspapers; CIA *World Factbook*; U.S. State Department Reports; Library of Congress Country Reports; BBC Country Profiles; Latin American Election Statistics; and Economist Intelligence Unit Country Profiles. In several elections, such as those in Pakistan (1985) and Yemen (1971), all candidates ran as independents, although they were publicly associated with specific parties. Where party affiliations of the candidates are unavailable, election results are omitted.

15. In the analyses, I code these results as 0 and, as a robustness check, drop them from the sample.

16. Fortna 2008; Gilligan and Sergenti 2008; Howard 2008; Walter 2002.

17. United Nations Peacebuilding Commission 2009.

18. Walter 2002.

19. Högbladh 2011.

20. Ottmann and Vüllers 2015.

21. Lindberg et al. 2014.

22. At times, for practical reasons, groups are lumped together as one because they are too numerous to count (e.g., Kashmir insurgents; Sikh insurgents). I recode these.

23. Fearon 2004.

24. Cunningham, Gleditsch, and Salehyan 2012.

25. To supply data where missing, I consulted the UCDP One-Sided Violence Dataset (Pettersson, Högbladh, and Öberg 2019) and qualitative sources.

26. It should be noted that restraint does not mean that the group did not employ violence against civilians; all did.

27. Humphreys and Weinstein 2006.

28. I verify that, for the cases for which OSV data are nonmissing, there is a correlation between these data and the atrocity measure based on the Stanton 2016 data.

29. Lindberg et al. 2014.

30. Hyde and Marinov 2012.

31. Huang 2016; Mampilly 2011; Stewart 2018.

32. Cunningham, Gleditsch, and Salehyan 2012.

33. Wood 2014.

34. Levitsky and Way 2012.

35. For missing values, I use data from Rustad and Binningsbø 2012 and Fearon 2004.

36. Unfortunately, comparable indicators for wartime public goods provision, financing, and cohesion do not exist for government belligerents.

37. Table A8.1 presents summary statistics.

38. There are more than fifty clusters in the data. Nonetheless, as a robustness check, I follow Cameron, Gelbach, and Miller's 2008 recommendations and use a wild bootstrap to estimate clustered standard errors. The results do not change.

39. For voter turnout, I use the variable *ideavt_legvt* from the Voter Turnout Database (International Institute for Democracy and Electoral Assistance 2019). I extract data on electoral systems and the logged GDP per capita (*e_migdppcln*) from the V-Dem Project (Lindberg et al. 2014).

40. Daly 2019 tests whether electoral coercion does not correlate with war outcomes because the relationship is nonlinear: whether government victory and rebel victory—but not indecisive war outcomes—predict coercion.

41. Given that indiscriminate violence is well established to be counterproductive, there may be a selection effect whereby if belligerents that committed atrocities are militarily successful, it is because they were stronger in other ways, and won the war despite their atrocities. Thus, winners with blood-soaked pasts would be stronger militarily than war victors that were restrained in their use of violence. I divide the sample into restrained and indiscriminately violent belligerents, and use the NSA data to evaluate whether, within the war-winning category, the latter surpass the former in terms of military strength. I find that they do not.

42. Where the other inputs—arms, resources, sanctuary, training, etc.—are equally distributed among the belligerents, but the number of unwavering activists is highly skewed, public support likely tilts the scales and explains both a share of war outcomes and electoral performance. However, even in these cases, few may support the armed option until it is proven to be viable. For example, as seen in Chapter 7, in Nicaragua, few backed the Sandinistas until they proved they could beat Somoza. Defining "underlying support," even in this emblematic case of a highly popular movement, proves challenging. Further complicating this definitional process are Timur Kuran's ideas of preference falsification and opinion/participation cascades (Kuran 1991). In a negative coalition aimed at toppling a dictator such as Somoza, citizens tend to support the most powerful challenger to the status quo and may be unwilling to express their support publicly while the dictator is still in power.

43. There is no significant correlation between war outcomes and free and fair elections (even if captured posttreatment).

44. I use two indicators from Hyde and Marinov 2012: (1) *nelda_15*, which indicates the level of harassment of the opposition, including detaining opposition leaders, disrupting opposition political rallies with state forces, and shutting down opposition newspapers and offices; and (2) *nelda_33*, which indicates whether there was violence during elections. If there was any significant violence relating to the elections that resulted in civilian deaths, a "yes" is coded.

45. See Daly 2019.

46. I relied on the UCDP "best estimates" of violence; as robustness checks, I ran the analyses using the low and high estimates, but the results did not change. While the UCDP data allow uniformity across cases, they were not available for all cases for which I had subnational election data. Moreover, in some cases they existed only for a more aggregated level than that for which I had election data; covered only the post-1989 period, truncating the data on wartime violence for certain wars; or, reliant on media reporting, tended to underestimate the violence. Accordingly, wherever possible, I used the country-specific violence data from truth commissions or event databases.

47. I also examine absolute atrocities, which reveal similar results. I restrict the sample to administrative units in which violence occurred. This differentiates the zeros that signal that a belligerent carried out none of the violence from the zeros that indicate that no violence occurred in the locality altogether. As an alternative model, I ran the analyses with the full sample of electoral units in all countries, including those unscathed by wartime atrocities, and the results did not change.

48. Violence was often systematically targeted, usually in reaction to a population's political allegiances. This may bias the results. Most often, combatants targeted their adversaries' civilian base, and they abstained from inflicting violence on their own sympathizers (Kalyvas 2006). This suggests that any bias should go against my hypothesis and amplify any negative correlation

between victimization and voting. Thus, observing a null or weakly positive relationship between victimization and voting would suggest support for my hypothesis that the tormentors, if militarily victorious, also won votes in places their forces brutalized.

49. Inglehart et al. 2014.

50. For nine of the cases, the surveys asked about vote choice; Table A8.5 lists the survey and election dates to show how accurately the polls reflect public opinion.

51. War outcomes do not predict the length of time between the end of conflict and holding of elections.

52. An analysis of electoral performance in regions seeking autonomy or secession, for example, reveals a strong relationship between war outcomes and this performance.

53. For example, in Indonesia, the Golkar ruling party had a relatively strong showing against the PDI-P in 2004, despite losing to the rebels in East Timor (McDowell 2009). Pakistan shows a similar result: after "losing" Bangladesh, the Pakistan People's Party experienced relatively little backlash and emerged victorious in the 1977 Pakistani election (although the extent to which the latter election was democratic is also subject to doubt).

54. This exercise is particularly important because the in-depth analyses of Latin America hold constant a critical dimension: the goals of the violence. All belligerent protagonists in Latin America fought over control of the central government either to impose a communist revolutionary regime or to retain a capitalist order. While Guatemala and Nicaragua presented an ethnic dimension (El Salvador and Colombia were nonethnic), the violence was motivated by ideology rather than ethnicity. In Latin America, ethnic polarization is low, ethnic parties have succeeded by generating broad and inclusive constituencies, and class remains the dominant cleavage (Madrid 2012). See Huber 2017. Additionally, wartime violence was widespread, security a critical dimension of postwar vote choice, and politics at least partially programmatic in the region.

55. Tilly 2003, 22.

56. Associated Press 1980. In "separate white elections," the government belligerent Rhodesian Front Party secured all twenty seats in the legislature, which were reserved for the 4 percent white population (Edlin 1980).

57. These elections followed the 1992 "white referendum" (Pilyatskin 1994).

58. Dix 1987.

59. Fernán González, author interview, August 2006.

60. Pizarro Leongómez 2004.

61. See, for example, Burleigh 2014; Kaplan 1994.

62. Abdelal et al. 2009; Chandra 2012; Posner 2004.

63. See Bakke, Cunningham, and Seymour 2012; Christia 2012; Kalyvas 2008; Rudloff and Findley 2016.

64. Brehm and Fox 2017.

65. Meierhenrich 2006.

66. Lyons 2016.

67. IHS Global Insight 2003.

68. Kalinaki 2003.

69. Nation may, in public expression, have supplanted ethnicity, but, given incentives to falsify public beliefs, this may not have trickled down into people's lives and personal preferences (Kuran 1991).

70. Kinzer 2008.

71. Hutus constituted approximately 83 percent of Rwanda's population (*Economist* 2003).

72. CNDD-FDD is the National Council for the Defence of Democracy–Forces for the Defence of Democracy.

73. Canadian Press 2003.

74. Nindorera 2012; Samii 2013a.

75. CNDD-FDD won approximately 60 percent of the vote, FRODEBU 22 percent, and the Tutsi-dominated UPRONA 7.21 percent (ElectionGuide 2005).

76. Niyoyita 2005.

77. Jalabi and Georgy 2018.

78. Al-Marashi 2018.

79. Coker 2018; Kaltenthaler 2018.

80. HDZ is the Croatian Democratic Union party.

81. Commission on Security and Cooperation in Europe 1996.

82. These observations are based on fieldwork conducted in Croatia and Bosnia, June–July 2019. Most quotations in this paragraph, unless otherwise noted, come from the museum exhibition "Dubrovnik during the Homeland War, 1991–1995," Empire's Fort, Dubrovnik. The exhibit includes over five hundred original photographs, documents, and objects from the war.

83. Swain 1995. Adoption of nonequilibrium strategies seems to have engendered election results off the regression line in wars over autonomy as well. In Kosovo, for example, the KLA carried the prestige "of having led [and won] the war of liberation against Serbia," but nonetheless lost to the nonbelligerent LDK in the founding elections because KLA's successor (PDK) failed to moderate, stretch its constituency, or signal restraint (International Crisis Group 2001).

84. FRELETIN is the Revolutionary Front for an Independent East Timor; SWAPO is the South West Africa People's Organisation.

85. Stokes et al. 2013; Vicente 2014.

86. Weghorst and Lindberg 2013.

87. Coppedge et al. 2018, 91.

Chapter 9

1. Daly 2021a, 2022.

2. Brancati and Snyder 2012; Lyons 2005; Mansfield and Snyder 2007; Paris 2004.

3. McCullum 1992.

4. Lyons 1998.

5. Spears 2010, 201.

6. Stedman 1997, 5.

7. Brancati and Snyder 2012.

8. Remilitarizing would not change the three primary reasons that war winners lose elections in this scenario; it would be unlikely to render security salient for the national population (if the first war failed to do so). It would not amend a war winner's electoral missteps; instead, running an alternative campaign with an equilibrium strategy in future elections would more likely do so. And remilitarizing would not make rule-of-law over law-and-order voters reverse their preferences.

9. Stedman 1997, 37, 40.

10. Spears 2010, 201, emphasis added

11. UNITA's plan ultimately proved ill-fated, as it "underestimated the resolve and capability of the MPLA to fight" (Stedman 1997).

12. Human Rights Watch Arms Project and Human Rights Watch/Africa 1994.

13. I constructed this variable from the Gromes and Ranft (2016) Post–Civil War Power and Compromise dataset, which provides information on changes in power due to demobilization/recruitment of troops, (de)acquisition of arms/equipment, and shifts in patterns of territorial control.

14. I again consider factors that might affect selection into the universe of cases—war duration, incompatibility, extent of wartime violence, veto players, development levels, and democracy scores—and factors that might confound the relationship or independently drive the resumption of hostilities—the absence of power sharing, of UN intervention, and of delayed elections. Additionally, groups with strong organizational capacity may resume war irrespective of the election results, a possibility I analyze statistically. For additional discussion of the variables, data sources, and models, see Daly 2022.

15. Hartzell and Hoddie 2015.

16. Binningsbø et al. 2012.

17. Coppedge et al. 2018.

18. To identify the paramilitary-politicians, I reviewed official data I received from the Colombian Supreme Court on politicians who were being investigated or were convicted for relationships with illegal armed groups. I then verified information for each paramilitary-politician case with the public datasets of *Verdad Abierta*'s Parapolíticos project (2013), Misión de Observación Electoral (2013), Congreso Visible reports; Fundación Paz y Reconciliación publications; national and regional newspapers; and 60 sentences issued by the Supreme Court, totaling nearly 6,000 pages, provided to me by the Colombian attorney general. Electoral data were obtained from the CEDE. For more details on the dataset, see Daly 2021a.

19. The margin of victory therefore ranged from −1 to 1; the paramilitary-politician won when its vote margin was positive and lost when it was negative.

20. For validity of the design and robustness checks, see Figure A9.1, Table A9.2, and Daly 2021a.

21. Sikkink 2011.

22. Galtung 1969.

23. Eduardo Pizarro Leongómez (head of the Colombian National Commission for Reparations), author interview, Santa Marta, May 2008.

Chapter 10

1. On authoritarian successor parties, see, for example, Grzymala-Busse 2002, Levitsky and Way 2012; Loxton and Mainwaring 2018.

2. Doyle and Sambanis 2000; Reiter 2009; Toft 2010.

3. March and Olsen 1989. This accords with Press, Sagan, and Valentino's 2013 model of nuclear aversion and Snyder and Vinjamuri's 2003 argument about international justice. Advancing a logic of appropriateness, Pinker 2011 and Thomas 2001 contend that the public's internalization of the Just War Doctrine principle of noncombatant immunity has shaped public aversion to targeting or killing civilians.

4. Eichenberg 2005; Gelpi, Feaver, and Reifler 2009; Sagan and Valentino 2017, Downes 2008.

5. Where foreign policy issues may be relatively removed from the domestic audience's lives (Rosenau 1965), by contrast, internal defense issues are far more immediate, and so their electoral consequences may be greater. Moreover, unlike in foreign policy, in civil war, casualties disproportionately involve national civilians, and these noncombatant victims may be part of the debating and voting public.

6. Baum and Groeling 2009; Berinsky 2007.

7. The work of Horowitz, Stam, and Ellis 2015; Saunders 2015; Colgan 2013 shows how leaders' characteristics shape decisions about international war.

8. Gleditsch, Salehyan, and Schultz 2008.

9. Approximately 42 percent of current wars in 2019 were internationalized, and such foreign interference is becoming more prevalent: 2019 witnessed the largest number of internationalized civil wars since World War II. These conflicts were internationalized in that troops from external states supported one or both sides in the conflict, as secondary warring parties (Pettersson, Högbladh, and Öberg 2019).

10. Smith 2018.

11. Zarate and Casey 2016.

12. Roddy 2019.

13. Jenkins 2016.

14. McCarthy 2021.

15. Elliott and Phillips 2018.

16. Phillips 2019. See also Londoño and Andreoni 2018.

17. Smith 2015.

18. Shah and Aneez 2019.

19. Chemin 2012.

20. Vaishnav 2017.

21. Daly 2020. In 2020, Trump bet on this playbook. As his former counselor Kellyanne Conway said explicitly, "The more chaos and anarchy and vandalism and violence reigns, the better it is for the very clear choice on who's best on public safety" (Vigdor 2020).

22. An example was President Donald Trump's appearance in Lafayette Square during Black Lives Matter protests, accompanied by the chairman of the Joint Chiefs of Staff dressed in military fatigues, a decision that the chairman later publicly regretted (Kagan 2020).

23. Condra and Shapiro 2012; Daly 2011; Fortna 2015; Kalyvas 2006; Kocher, Pepinsky, and Kalyvas 2011; Kupatadze and Zeitzoff 2021; Lyall, Blair, and Imai 2013 show that indiscriminate violence causes mass attitudes to turn against the perpetrator. Lupu and Wallace 2019; Rozenas, Schutte, and Zhukov 2017 show that the past tends to catch up with victimizers.

24. Snyder and Vinjamuri 2003.

25. Simmons 2009.

26. Huntington 1993.

27. Hagopian 1990; Loxton and Mainwaring 2018; O'Donnell and Schmitter 1986; Stepan 1988.

28. Daly 2016.

29. Lake and Rothchild 1996.

30. Somers 1994.

31. Oglesby 2004.

REFERENCES

Abadeer, Caroline, Alexandra Domike Blackman, Lisa Blaydes, and Scott Williamson. 2022. "Did Egypt's Post-Uprising Crime Wave Increase Support for Authoritarian Rule?" *Journal of Peace Research.*

Abdelal, Rawi, Yoshiko M. Herrera, Alastair Iain Johnston, and Rose McDermott, eds. 2009. *Measuring Identity: A Guide for Social Scientists.* New York: Cambridge University Press.

Abeler, Johannes, Armin Falk, Lorenz Goette, and David Huffman. 2011. "Reference Points and Effort Provision." *American Economic Review* 101 (2): 470–492.

Acemoglu, Daron, Leopoldo Fergusson, James A. Robinson, Dario Romero, and Juan F. Vargas. 2020. "The Perils of High-Powered Incentives: Evidence from Colombia's False Positives." *American Economic Journal: Economic Policy* 12 (3): 1–43.

Acemoglu, Daron, and James A. Robinson. 2006. *Economic Origins of Dictatorship and Democracy.* Cambridge: Cambridge University Press.

———. 2020. *The Narrow Corridor: States, Societies, and the Fate of Liberty.* New York: Penguin.

Acemoglu, Daron, James A. Robinson, and Rafael J. Santos. 2013. "The Monopoly of Violence: Evidence from Colombia." *Journal of the European Economic Association* 11 (S1): 5–44.

Acharya, Avidit, and Edoardo Grillo. 2019. "A Behavioral Foundation for Audience Costs." *Quarterly Journal of Political Science* 14 (2): 159–190.

Ackerberg, Daniel A. 2001. "Empirically Distinguishing Informative and Prestige Effects of Advertising." *RAND Journal of Economics* 32 (2): 316–333.

Acosta Oertel, Mario. 1994. "Las posibilidades del Lic. Rubén Zamora." *El Diario de Hoy,* March 12.

Ahnen, Ronald E. 2007. "The Politics of Police Violence in Democratic Brazil." *Latin American Politics and Society* 49 (1): 141–164.

Ajenjo Fresno, Natalia, and Fátima García Díez. 2001. "Guatemala." In *Partidos Políticos de América Latina: Centroamérica, México y República Dominicana,* edited by Manuel Alcántara Sáez and Flavia Freidenberg, 277–376. Salamanca: Ediciones Universidad de Salamanca.

Akhavan, Payam. 2009. "Are International Criminal Tribunals a Disincentive to Peace: Reconciling Judicial Romanticism with Political Realism." *Human Rights Quarterly* 31 (3): 624–654.

Albertson, Bethany, and Shana Kushner Gadarian. 2015. *Anxious Politics: Democratic Citizenship in a Threatening World.* New York: Cambridge University Press.

Aldrich, John H. 1983. "A Downsian Spatial Model with Party Activism." *American Political Science Review* 77 (4): 974–990.

———. 1995. *Why Parties? The Origin and Transformation of Political Parties in America*. Chicago: University of Chicago Press.

Aldrich, John H., Christopher Gelpi, Peter Feaver, Jason Reifler, and Kristin Thompson Sharp. 2006. "Foreign Policy and the Electoral Connection." *Annual Review of Political Science* 9 (1): 477–502.

Alianza Nueva Nación. 1999. *Programa de gobierno 2000–2004*. Guatemala City: INCEP.

Allison, Michael E. 2006. "Leaving the Past Behind? A Study of the FMLN and URNG Transitions to Political Parties." PhD diss., Florida State University.

———. 2010. "The Legacy of Violence on Post–Civil War Elections: The Case of El Salvador." *Studies in Comparative International Development* 45 (1): 104–124.

———. 2016. "The Guatemalan National Revolutionary Unit: The Long Collapse." *Democratization* 23 (6): 1042–1058.

Allison, Michael E., and Alberto Martín Alvarez. 2012. "Unity and Disunity in the FMLN." *Latin American Politics and Society* 54 (4): 89–118.

Al-Marashi, Ibrahim. 2018. "How Iraq's Elections Proved 'Status Quo' Expectations Wrong." *Al Jazeera*, May 14.

Almeida, Paul D. 2010. "El Salvador: Elecciones y movimientos sociales." *Revista de ciencia política* 30 (2): 319–334.

Alsema, Adriaan. 2017. "Power through Manipulation: The Story of the Santos Family." *Colombia Reports*, May 26.

Alt, James E., David D. Lassen, and John Marshall. 2016. "Credible Sources and Sophisticated Voters: When Does New Information Induce Economic Voting?" *Journal of Politics* 78 (2): 327–342.

Americas Watch. 1991. *El Salvador's Decade of Terror: Human Rights since the Assassination of Archbishop Romero*. New Haven, CT: Yale University Press.

Americas Watch Committee and American Civil Liberties Union. 1982. *Report on Human Rights in El Salvador*. New York: Random House.

Ameringer, Charles D., ed. 1992. *Political Parties of the Americas, 1980s to 1990s: Canada, Latin America, and the West Indies*. Westport, CT: Greenwood.

Anderson, Leslie E. 1995. "Elections and Public Opinion in the Development of Nicaraguan Democracy." In *Elections and Democracy in Central America, Revisited*, edited by Mitchell A. Seligson and John A. Booth. Chapel Hill: University of North Carolina Press.

Anderson, Leslie E., and Lawrence C. Dodd. 2005. *Learning Democracy: Citizen Engagement and Electoral Choice in Nicaragua, 1990–2001*. Chicago: University of Chicago Press.

Anderson, Thomas P. 1971. *Matanza: El Salvador's Communist Revolt of 1932*. Lincoln: University of Nebraska Press.

———. 1988. *Politics in Central America: Guatemala, El Salvador, Honduras, and Nicaragua*. New York: Praeger.

Ansolabehere, Stephen, and Shanto Iyengar. 1994. "Riding the Wave and Claiming Ownership over Issues: The Joint Effects of Advertising and News Coverage in Campaigns." *Public Opinion Quarterly* 58 (3): 335–357.

Ansolabehere, Stephen, and James M. Snyder, Jr. 2000. "Valence Politics and Equilibrium in Spatial Election Models." *Public Choice* 103 (3–4): 327–336.

Aragones, Enriqueta, and Thomas R. Palfrey. 2002. "Mixed Equilibrium in a Downsian Model with a Favored Candidate." *Journal of Economic Theory* 103 (1): 131–161.

Aranguren Molina, Mauricio. 2001. *Mi confesión: Carlos Castaño revela sus secretos.* Bogotá: Editorial Oveja Negra.

Arce, Moisés. 2003. "Political Violence and Presidential Approval in Peru." *Journal of Politics* 65 (2): 572–583.

ARENA. 1994. "Seguridad con Calderón Sol." *La Prensa Gráfica*, February 1.

Arias, Enrique Desmond, and Mark Ungar. 2009. "Community Policing and Latin America's Citizen Security Crisis." *Comparative Politics* 41 (4): 409–429.

Arias, Eric, Horacio Larreguy, John Marshall, and Pablo Querubín. 2022. "Priors Rule: When Do Malfeasance Revelations Help and Hurt Incumbent Parties." *Journal of European Economic Association.*

Armstrong, Robert, and Janet Shenk. 1982. *El Salvador: The Face of Revolution.* Boston: South End.

Arnson, Cynthia J. 2000. "Window on the Past: A Declassified History of Death Squads in El Salvador." In *Death Squads in Global Perspective: Murder with Deniability*, edited by Bruce B. Campbell and Arthur D. Brenner, 85–124. New York: St. Martin's.

Arriola, Leonardo R., and Terrence Lyons. 2016. "Ethiopia: The 100% Election." *Journal of Democracy* 27 (1): 76–88.

Artiga González, Álvaro. 2001. "El Salvador." In *Partidos políticos de América Latina: Centroamérica, México y República Dominicana*, edited by Manuel Alcántara Sáez and Flavia Freidenberg, 137–178. Salamanca: Ediciones Universidad de Salamanca.

ASIES. 2004. *Guatemala: Monografía de partidos políticos, 2000–2004.* Guatemala: Asociación de Investigación y Estudios Sociales.

———. 2012. *Monografía de partidos políticos de Guatemala, 2012.* Guatemala: Asociación de Investigación y Estudios Sociales.

Associated Press. 1980. "Blacks Vote in Second Day of Rhodesian Election." February 28.

Azpuru, Dinorah. 2010. "The Salience of Ideology: Fifteen Years of Presidential Elections in El Salvador." *Latin American Politics and Society* 52 (2): 103–138.

———. 2016. "To Understand Donald Trump's Law-and-Order Appeal, Look South of the Border." *Washington Post*, August 17.

Bakke, Kristin M., Kathleen Gallagher Cunningham, and Lee J. M. Seymour. 2012. "A Plague of Initials: Fragmentation, Cohesion, and Infighting in Civil Wars." *Perspectives on Politics* 10 (2): 265–283.

Balcells, Laia. 2012. "The Consequences of Victimization on Political Identities. Evidence from Spain." *Politics & Society* 40 (3): 311–347.

Ball, Patrick. 1999. "AAAS/CIIDH Database of Human Rights Violations in Guatemala" (ATV20.1).

Ball, Patrick, Paul Kobrak, and Herbert F. Spirer. 1999. *State Violence in Guatemala, 1960–1996: A Quantitative Reflection.* Washington, DC: American Association for the Advancement of Science.

Banks, Arthur S., Hal Smith, Thomas C. Muller, William Overstreet, and Sean M. Phelan, eds. 1999. *Political Handbook of the World.* Washington, DC: CQ Press.

Barbosa-Miranda, Francisco José. 2010. *Historia militar de Nicaragua antes del siglo XV al XXI*. Managua: Hispamer.

Barnes, William A. 1992. "Rereading the Nicaraguan Pre-election Polls in Light of the Election Results." In *The 1990 Elections in Nicaragua and Their Aftermath*, edited by Vanessa Castro and Gary Prevost. Lanham, MD: Rowman & Littlefield.

———. 1998. "Incomplete Democracy in Central America: Polarization and Voter Turnout in Nicaragua and El Salvador." *Journal of Interamerican Studies and World Affairs* 40 (3): 63–101.

Barrera Ortiz, Byron. 2014. *Portillo: La democracia en el espejo*. Guatemala: F&G Editores.

Barry, Tom, and Deb Preusch. 1990. *AIFLD in Central America: Agents as Organizers*. Albuquerque, NM: Resource Center.

Bass, Gary Jonathan. 2002. *Stay the Hand of Vengeance: The Politics of War Crimes Tribunals*. Princeton, NJ: Princeton University Press.

Bateson, Regina. 2012. "Crime Victimization and Political Participation." *American Political Science Review* 106 (3): 570–587.

———. 2022. "Voting for a Killer: Efraín Ríos Montt's Return to Politics in Democratic Guatemala." *Comparative Politics* 54 (2): 203–228.

Baum, Matthew A., and Tim Groeling. 2009. "Shot by the Messenger: Partisan Cues and Public Opinion Regarding National Security and War." *Political Behavior* 31 (2): 157–186.

"BBC Country Profiles." http://news.bbc.co.uk/2/hi/country_profiles/default.stm.

BBC News. 2016. "Colombia Ex-President Alvaro Uribe's Brother Arrested." March 1. https://www.bbc.com/news/world-latin-america-35693440.

———. 2018. "Colombia Election: Farc Fails to Win Support in First National Vote." March 12. https://www.bbc.com/news/world-latin-america-43367222.

Bellows, John, and Edward Miguel. 2009. "War and Local Collective Action in Sierra Leone." *Journal of Public Economics* 93 (11–12): 1144–1157.

Berinsky, Adam J. 2007. "Assuming the Costs of War: Events, Elites, and American Public Support for Military Conflict." *Journal of Politics* 69 (4): 975–997.

Berman, Sheri. 2007. "How Democracies Emerge: Lessons from Europe." *Journal of Democracy* 18 (1): 28–41.

Bermeo, Nancy. 2003. "What the Democratization Literature Says—or Doesn't Say—About Postwar Democratization." *Global Governance* 9 (2): 159–177.

Berrebi, Claude, and Esteban F. Klor. 2008. "Are Voters Sensitive to Terrorism? Direct Evidence from the Israeli Electorate." *American Political Science Review* 102 (3): 279–301.

Berry, Christopher R., and William G. Howell. 2007. "Accountability and Local Elections: Rethinking Retrospective Voting." *Journal of Politics* 69 (3): 844–858.

Bertelsen, Bjørn Enge. 2003. "'The Traditional Lion Is Dead': The Ambivalent Presence of Tradition and the Relation between Politics and Violence in Mozambique." *Lusotopie* 10 (1): 263–281.

Betts, Richard K. 1994. "The Delusion of Impartial Intervention." *Foreign Affairs* 73 (6): 20–33.

Bhatia, Michael V. 2005. "Fighting Words: Naming Terrorists, Bandits, Rebels and Other Violent Actors." *Third World Quarterly* 26 (1): 5–22.

Binford, Leigh. 1996. *The El Mozote Massacre: Anthropology and Human Rights*. Tucson: University of Arizona Press.

Binningsbø, Helga Malmin, Cyanne E. Loyle, Scott Gates, and Jon Elster. 2012. "Post-Conflict Justice Dataset Codebook."

Birch, Sarah. 2003. *Electoral Systems and Political Transformation in Post-Communist Europe.* New York: Palgrave Macmillan.

———. 2020. *Electoral Violence, Corruption, and Political Order.* Princeton, NJ: Princeton University Press.

Bird, Shawn L., and Philip J. Williams. 2000. "El Salvador: Revolt and Negotiated Transition." In *Repression, Resistance, and Democratic Transition in Central America*, edited by Thomas W. Walker and Ariel C. Armony, 25–46. Rowman & Littlefield.

Blachman, Morris J., and Kenneth E. Sharpe. 1988/1989. "Things Fall Apart: Trouble Ahead in El Salvador." *World Policy Journal* 6 (1): 107–139.

Black, Duncan. 1958. *The Theory of Committees and Elections.* Cambridge: Cambridge University Press.

Blair, Graeme, and Kosuke Imai. 2012. "Statistical Analysis of List Experiments." *Political Analysis* 20 (1): 47–77.

Blattman, Christopher. 2009. "From Violence to Voting: War and Political Participation in Uganda." *American Political Science Review* 103 (2): 231–247.

Blattman, Christopher, and Jeannie Annan. 2016. "Can Employment Reduce Lawlessness and Rebellion? A Field Experiment with High-Risk Men in a Fragile State." *American Political Science Review* 110 (1): 1–17.

Boix, Carles. 1997. "Political Parties and the Supply Side of the Economy: The Provision of Physical and Human Capital in Advanced Economies, 1960–90." *American Journal of Political Science* 41 (3): 814–845.

Bonner, Michelle D. 2014. *Policing Protest in Argentina and Chile.* Boulder, CO: Lynne Rienner.

Booth, John A. 1985. *The End and Beginning: The Nicaraguan Revolution.* 2nd ed. Boulder, CO: Westview.

Brancati, Dawn, and Jack L. Snyder. 2011. "Rushing to the Polls: The Causes of Premature Post-conflict Elections." *Journal of Conflict Resolution* 55 (3): 469–492.

———. 2013. "Time to Kill: The Impact of Election Timing on Postconflict Stability." *Journal of Conflict Resolution* 57 (5): 822–853.

Brehm, Hollie Nyseth, and Nicole Fox. 2017. "Narrating Genocide: Time, Memory, and Blame." *Sociological Forum* 32 (1): 116–137.

Brockett, Charles D. 1988. *Land, Power, and Poverty: Agrarian Transformation and Political Conflict in Central America.* Boston: Allen & Unwin.

Brown, Timothy C. 2001. *The Real Contra War: Highlander Peasant Resistance in Nicaragua.* Norman: University of Oklahoma Press.

Bruch, Hermann W. 1994. "Primero la gente? Una campaña engañosa y demagógica." *El Diario de Hoy.*

Buchenau, Jürgen. 2011. *The Last Caudillo: Alvaro Obregón and the Mexican Revolution.* Malden, MA: Wiley-Blackwell.

Bueno de Mesquita, Bruce, Alastair Smith, Randolph M. Siverson, and James D. Morrow. 2003. *The Logic of Political Survival.* Cambridge, MA: MIT Press.

Burleigh, Michael. 2014. "The Ancient Muslim Hatreds Tearing Apart the Middle East." *Daily Mail*, June 12.

Bush, Sarah Sunn, and Lauren Prather. 2017. "The Promise and Limits of Election Observers in Building Election Credibility." *Journal of Politics* 79 (3): 921–935.

Cagan, Steve. 1994. "Election Diary: El Salvador Tries to Vote." *Nation* 258 (15): 526.

Call, Charles T. 2007. *Constructing Justice and Security After War.* Washington, DC: United States Institute of Peace Press.

Calonico, Sebastian, Matias D. Cattaneo, Max H. Farrell, and Rocío Titiunik. 2017. "rdrobust: Software for Regression-Discontinuity Designs." *Stata Journal* 17 (2): 374–404.

Calvert, Randall L. 1985. "Robustness of the Multidimensional Voting Model: Candidate Motivations, Uncertainty, and Convergence." *American Journal of Political Science* 29 (1): 69–95.

Calvo, Ernesto, and Maria Victoria Murillo. 2019. *Non-Policy Politics: Richer Voters, Poorer Voters, and the Diversification of Electoral Strategies.* New York: Cambridge University Press.

Cameron, Adrian Colin, Jonah B. Gelbach, and Douglas L. Miller. 2008. "Bootstrap-Based Improvements for Inference with Clustered Errors." *Review of Economics and Statistics* 90 (3): 414–427.

Cammett, Melani, and Edmund Malesky. 2012. "Power Sharing in Postconflict Societies: Implications for Peace and Governance." *Journal of Conflict Resolution* 56 (6): 982–1016.

Canadian Press. 2003. "Commission Declares Former Rebels Winners of Burundi Parliamentary Elections." July 5.

Canetti, Daphna, Ibrahim Khatib, Aviad Rubin, and Carly Wayne. 2019. "Framing and Fighting: The Impact of Conflict Frames on Political Attitudes." *Journal of Peace Research* 56 (6): 737–752.

Carey, David, Jr. 2004. "Maya Perspectives on the 1999 Referendum in Guatemala: Ethnic Equality Rejected?" *Latin American Perspectives* 31 (6): 69–95.

Carlin, Ryan E., Gregory J. Love, and Cecilia Martínez-Gallardo. 2015. "Security, Clarity of Responsibility, and Presidential Approval." *Comparative Political Studies* 48 (4): 438–463.

Carnegie, Allison, Kimberly Howe, Adam Lichtenheld, and Dipali Mukhopadhyay. 2022. "The Effects of Foreign Aid on Rebel Governance: Evidence from a Large-Scale US Aid Program in Syria." *Economics & Politics* 34 (1): 41–66.

Carreras, Miguel. 2013. "The Impact of Criminal Violence on Regime Legitimacy in Latin America." *Latin American Research Review* 48 (3): 85–107.

Carreri, Maria, and Oeindrila Dube. 2017. "Do Natural Resources Influence Who Comes to Power, and How?" *Journal of Politics* 79 (2): 502–518.

Carter Center. 2003. "Guatemala Election Observation 2003: Final Report."

Casey, Nicholas. 2018. "Colombia Rebels Suspend Election, Putting Peace into Limbo." *New York Times*, February 9.

Castrillón, Gloria. 2005. "La Mano Invisible de 'Don Berna.'" *Cromos*, June 5.

Castro, Vanessa, and Gary Prevost, eds. 1992. *The 1990 Elections in Nicaragua and Their Aftermath.* Lanham, MD: Rowman & Littlefield.

Catatumbo, Pablo. 2018. "Definitivamente son quienes padecieron en carne propia la guerra." @PCatatumbo_FARC. Twitter, February 26.

Cattaneo, Matias D., Brigham R. Frandsen, and Rocío Titiunik. 2015. "Randomization Inference in the Regression Discontinuity Design: An Application to Party Advantages in the U.S. Senate." *Journal of Causal Inference* 3 (1): 1–24.

Cederman, Lars-Erik, Andreas Wimmer, and Brian Min. 2010. "Why Do Ethnic Groups Rebel? New Data and Analysis." *World Politics* 62 (1): 87–119.

"Central America Report." 1993. Guatemala: Inforpress Centroamericana, October 29.

Centro Democrático. 2018. "203 Propuestas: Iván Duque y Marta Lucía Ramírez." Bogotá.

Ceobanu, Alin M., Charles M. Wood, and Ludmila Ribeiro. 2011. "Crime Victimization and Public Support for Democracy: Evidence from Latin America." *International Journal of Public Opinion Research* 23 (1): 56–78.

Chandra, Kanchan, ed. 2012. *Constructivist Theories of Ethnic Politics*. New York: Oxford University Press.

Chaturvedi, Ashish. 2005. "Rigging Elections with Violence." *Public Choice* 125 (1–2): 189–202.

Chemin, Matthieu. 2012. "Welfare Effects of Criminal Politicians: A Discontinuity-Based Approach." *Journal of Law & Economics* 55 (3): 667–690.

Ching, Erik. 2016. *Stories of Civil War in El Salvador: A Battle over Memory*. Chapel Hill: University of North Carolina Press.

Chiozza, Giacomo, and Hein E. Goemans. 2004. "International Conflict and the Tenure of Leaders: Is War Still 'Ex Post' Inefficient?" *American Journal of Political Science* 48 (3): 604–619.

Chong, Dennis, and James N. Druckman. 2007. "Framing Theory." *Annual Review of Political Science* 10 (1): 103–126.

Chowanietz, Christophe. 2011. "Rallying Around the Flag or Railing Against the Government? Political Parties' Reactions to Terrorist Acts." *Party Politics* 17 (5): 673–698.

Christia, Fotini. 2012. *Alliance Formation in Civil Wars*. New York: Cambridge University Press.

"CIA World Factbook." https://www.cia.gov/library/publications/the-world-factbook/.

Cibelli, Kristen, Amelia Hoover, and Jule Krüger. 2009. "Benetech / Human Rights Data Analysis Group Database of Victim and Witness Statements Collected by the Liberian Truth and Reconciliation Commission."

CIDAI. 2004. "La campaña subterránea de ARENA." *Proceso* 1085.

CIDOB. 2004. "Óscar Berger Perdomo." http://www.cidob.org/en/documentacio/biografias_lideres_politicos/america_central_y_caribe/guatemala/oscar_berger_perdomo.

———. 2018. "Álvaro Arzú Yrigoyen." https://www.cidob.org/biografias_lideres_politicos/america_central_y_caribe/guatemala/alvaro_arzu_yrigoyen/(language)/esl-ES.

Cienfuegos, Fermán. 1982. *Commander Ferman Cienfuegos Speaks*. Los Angeles: Solidarity Committee.

Close, David. 1985. "The Nicaraguan Elections of 1984." *Electoral Studies* 4 (2): 152–158.

———. 1991. "Central American Elections 1989–90: Costa Rica, El Salvador, Honduras, Nicaragua, Panama." *Electoral Studies* 10 (1): 60–76.

———. 1995. "Nicaragua: The Legislature as Seedbed of Conflict." In *Legislatures and the New Democracies in Latin America*, edited by David Close, 49–69. Boulder, CO: Lynne Rienner.

Close, David, and Salvador Martí i Puig. 2012. "The Sandinistas and Nicaragua since 1979." In *The Sandinistas and Nicaragua since 1979*, edited by David Close, Salvador Martí i Puig and Shelley A. McConnell. Boulder, CO: Lynne Rienner.

CNN Español. 2017. "¿Quién es 'Timochenko', el líder de las FARC?" July 3.

Coatsworth, John H. 1994. *The United States and Central America: The Clients and the Colossus*. New York: Twayne.

Coker, Margaret. 2018. "U.S. Takes a Risk: Old Iraqi Enemies Are Now Allies." *New York Times*, May 11.

Colburn, Forrest D. 2009. "The Turnover in El Salvador." *Journal of Democracy* 20 (3): 143–152.

Colgan, Jeff D. 2013. "Domestic Revolutionary Leaders and International Conflict." *World Politics* 65 (4): 656–690.

Collier, Paul. 1999. "On the Economic Consequences of Civil War." *Oxford Economic Papers* 51 (1): 168–183.

Collier, Paul, and Pedro C. Vicente. 2014. "Votes and Violence: Evidence from a Field Experiment in Nigeria." *Economic Journal* 124 (574): 327–355.

Collier, Ruth Berins, and David Collier. 1991. *Shaping the Political Arena: Critical Junctures, the Labor Movement, and Regime Dynamics in Latin America*. Princeton, NJ: Princeton University Press.

Comité Central del MAP-ML. 1984. *Programa político del MAP-ML*. Managua.

Commission for the Defense of Human Rights in Central America (CODEHUCA). 1990. *Condoning the Killing: Ten Years of Massacres in El Salvador*. Washington, DC: Ecumenical Program on Central America and the Caribbean (EPICA).

Commission on Security and Cooperation in Europe. 1996. *1995 Parliamentary Elections in Croatia*. Washington, DC: CSCE.

Condra, Luke N., and Jacob N. Shapiro. 2012. "Who Takes the Blame? The Strategic Effects of Collateral Damage." *American Journal of Political Science* 56 (1): 167–187.

Conover, Pamela Johnston, Virginia Gray, and Steven Coombs. 1982. "Single-Issue Voting: Elite-Mass Linkages." *Political Behavior* 4 (4): 309–331.

Cooperman, Alicia, Alexandra S. Richey, and Brigitte Seim. 2018. "Drivers of Successful Common Pool Resource Management: A Conjoint Experiment on Groundwater Management in Brazil." AGU Fall Meeting, Washington, DC, December 10–14.

Coordinadora Regional de Investigaciones Económicas y Sociales. 1990. *Nicaragua, Elecciones 1990. Cronologia*. Managua: CRIES.

Copeland, Nick. 2011. "Guatemala Will Never Change': Radical Pessimism and the Politics of Personal Interest in the Western Highlands." *Journal of Latin American Studies* 43 (3): 485–515.

Coppedge, Michael, John Gerring, Carl Henrik Knutsen, Staffan I. Lindberg, Jan Teorell, Kyle L. Marquardt, Juraj Medzihorsky, Daniel Pemstein, Nazifa Alizada, Lisa Gastaldi, Garry Hindle, Johannes von Römer, Eitan Tzelgov, Yi-ting Wang, and Steven Wilson. 2018. "V-Dem Codebook v8, Varieties of Democracy (V-Dem) Project."

Corstange, Daniel. 2020. "National and Subnational Identification in the Syrian Civil War." *Journal of Politics* 82 (3): 1176–1181.

———. 2022. "Mass Dissimulation in the Syrian Civil War." *Journal of Politics*. 84 (3).

Cosoy, Natalio. 2016. "Juan Manuel Santos: 'Personalmente hubiera querido que los responsables de los crímenes de lesa humanidad tuvieran un mayor castigo.'" *BBC News*, September 26.

Cox, Gary W. 1984. "An Expected-Utility Model of Electoral Competition." *Quality and Quantity* 18 (4): 337–349.

———. 1990. "Centripetal and Centrifugal Incentives in Electoral Systems." *American Journal of Political Science* 34 (4): 903–935.

———. 1997. *Making Votes Count: Strategic Coordination in the World's Electoral System.* New York: Cambridge University Press.

———. 1999. "Electoral Rules and the Calculus of Mobilization." *Legislative Studies Quarterly* 24 (3): 387–419.

———. 2009. "Swing Voters, Core Voters, and Distributive Politics." In *Political Representation,* edited by Ian Shapiro, Susan C. Stokes, Elisabeth Jean Wood, and Alexander S. Kirshner, 342–357. Cambridge: Cambridge University Press.

Cox, Gary W., and Matthew D. McCubbins. 1986. "Electoral Politics as a Redistributive Game." *Journal of Politics* 48 (2): 370–389.

Crawford, Neta. 2013. *Accountability for Killing: Moral Responsibility for Collateral Damage in America's Post-9/11 Wars.* Oxford: Oxford University Press.

Croco, Sarah, E. 2015. *Peace at What Price? Leader Culpability and the Domestic Politics of War Termination.* New York: Cambridge University Press.

"Crónica del mes Julio–agosto." 1993. Estudios centroamericanos, July–August 1993.

Cruz, Consuelo. 2000. "Identity and Persuasion: How Nations Remember Their Pasts and Make Their Futures." *World Politics* 52 (3): 275–312.

Cruz, Eduardo. 2021. "Daniel Ortega, el candidato que no hace campaña electoral." *La Prensa,* March 7.

Cruz, José Miguel. 2009. "Democratization under Assault: Criminal Violence in Post-Transition Central America." APSA Annual Meeting, Toronto.

Cruz, José Miguel, and Luis Armando González. 1997. "Magnitud de la violencia en El Salvador." *Estudios Centroamericanos* 52 (588): 953–966.

Cullather, Nick. 1999. *Secret History: The CIA's Classified Account of Its Operations in Guatemala, 1952–1954.* Stanford, CA: Stanford University Press.

Cunningham, David E. 2006. "Veto Players and Civil War Duration." *American Journal of Political Science* 50 (4): 875–892.

Cunningham, David E., Kristian Skrede Gleditsch, and Idean Salehyan. 2009. "It Takes Two: A Dyadic Analysis of Civil War Duration and Outcome." *Journal of Conflict Resolution* 53 (4): 570–597.

———. 2012. "Non-State Actor Data." http://privatewww.essex.ac.uk/~ksg/eacd.html.

Curtis, Devon E. A., and Gyda M. Sindre. 2019. "Transforming State Visions: Ideology and Ideas in Armed Groups Turned Political Parties—Introduction to Special Issue." *Government and Opposition* 54 (3): 387–414.

Dada, Héctor. 1994. "El Salvador: Elecciones y democracia." *Revista Nueva Sociedad* 132 (July–August): 22–28.

Daly, Sarah Zukerman. 2011. "The Roots of Coercion and Insurgency: Exploiting the Counterfactual Case of Honduras." *Conflict, Security & Development* 11 (2): 145–174.

———. 2012. "Organizational Legacies of Violence: Conditions Favoring Insurgency Onset in Colombia, 1964–1984." *Journal of Peace Research* 49 (3): 473–491.

———. 2016. *Organized Violence after Civil War: The Geography of Recruitment in Latin America.* New York: Cambridge University Press.

———. 2018. "Determinants of Ex-Combatants' Attitudes toward Transitional Justice in Colombia." *Conflict Management and Peace Science* 35 (6): 656–673.

———. 2019. "Voting for Victors: Why Violent Actors Win Post-War Elections." *World Politics* 71 (4): 747–805.

———. 2020. "Trump Is Running for Reelection as a 'Strongman,' Promising Protection from Anarchy. That Might Not Work." *Washington Post*, September 23.

———. 2021a. "How Do Violent Politicians Govern? The Case of Paramilitary-Tied Mayors in Colombia." *British Journal of Political Science.*

———. 2021b. "Political Life after Civil Wars: Introducing the Civil War Successor Party Dataset." *Journal of Peace Research* 58 (4): 839–848.

———. 2022. "A Farewell to Arms? Election Results and Lasting Peace after Civil War." *International Security* 46 (3): 163–204.

Daly, Sarah Zukerman, Laura Paler, and Cyrus Samii. 2020. "Wartime Ties and the Social Logic of Crime." *Journal of Peace Research* 57 (4): 536–550.

Danner, Mark. 1994. *The Massacre at El Mozote: A Parable of the Cold War*. New York: Vintage.

Datexco-Opinómetro. 2018. "Pulso País Colombia April." *Pinómetro* 11413.

Davenport, Christian. 2007. "State Repression and Political Order." *Annual Review of Political Science* 10 (1): 1–23.

Davis, Darren W., and Brian D. Silver. 2004. "Civil Liberties vs. Security: Public Opinion in the Context of the Terrorist Attacks on America." *American Journal of Political Science* 48 (1): 28–46.

Debs, Alexandre, and Hein E. Goemans. 2010. "Regime Type, the Fate of Leaders, and War." *American Political Science Review* 104 (3): 430–445.

Defensoría del Pueblo, ACNUR, and EUROPEAID. 2004. "Desplazamiento intraurbano como consecuencia del conflicto armado en las ciudades." Bogotá.

de Figueiredo, Miguel F. P., Fernando Daniel Hidalgo, and Yuri Kasahara. 2013. "When Do Voters Punish Corrupt Politicians? Experimental Evidence from Brazil." University of Texas at Austin, School of Law.

de la Calle, Humberto. 2018. "Seguridad para una vida tranquila." Bogotá.

DeRouen, Karl R., Jr., and David Sobek. 2004. "The Dynamics of Civil War Duration and Outcome." *Journal of Peace Research* 41 (3): 303–320.

De Vries, Catherine E., and Hector Solaz. 2017. "The Electoral Consequences of Corruption." *Annual Review of Political Science* 20 (1): 391–408.

De Zeeuw, Jeroen. 2008. *From Soldiers to Politicians: Transforming Rebel Movements after Civil War*. Boulder, CO: Lynne Rienner.

Diamond, Larry, and Marc F. Plattner, eds. 2006. *Electoral Systems and Democracy*. Baltimore, MD: Johns Hopkins University Press.

Dickey, Christopher. 1982. "Salvadoran Rightist Mounts Vigorous Election Campaign." *Washington Post*, February 7.

Diskin, Martin, and Kenneth Evan Sharpe. 1986. *The Impact of U.S. Policy in El Salvador, 1979–1985*. Policy Papers in International Affairs 27. Berkeley: Institute of International Studies, University of California.

Dix, Robert H. 1987. *The Politics of Colombia*. New York: Praeger.

———. 1992. "Democratization and the Institutionalization of Latin American Political Parties." *Comparative Political Studies* 24 (4): 488–511.

Dixit, Avinash, and John Londregan. 1996. "The Determinants of Success of Special Interests in Redistributive Politics." *Journal of Politics* 58 (4): 1132–1155.

Djankov, Simeon, Caralee Mcliesh, Tatiana Nenova, and Andrei Shleifer. 2003. "Who Owns the Media?" *Journal of Law and Economics* 46 (2): 341–381.

Domonoske, Camila. 2016. "Colombian President Juan Manuel Santos Awarded Nobel Peace Prize." *NPR*, October 7.

Dorff, Cassy. 2017. "Violence, Kinship Networks, and Political Resilience: Evidence from Mexico." *Journal of Peace Research* 54 (4): 558–573.

Downes, Alexander B. 2008. *Targeting Civilians in War*. Ithaca, NY: Cornell University Press.

Downs, Anthony. 1957. *An Economic Theory of Democracy*. New York: Harper & Row.

Doyle, Michael W., and Nicholas Sambanis. 2000. "International Peacekeeping: A Theoretical and Quantitative Analysis." *American Political Science Review* 94 (4): 779–801.

Drago, Francesco, Roberto Galbiati, and Francesco Sobbrio. 2020. "The Political Cost of Being Soft on Crime: Evidence from a Natural Experiment." *Journal of the European Economic Association* 18 (6): 3305–3336.

Dresden, Jennifer Raymond. 2017. "From Combatants to Candidates: Electoral Competition and the Legacy of Armed Conflict." *Conflict Management and Peace Science* 34 (3): 240–263.

Duarte, José Napoleón. 1986. *Duarte: My Story*. New York: G.P. Putnam's Sons.

Dunkerley, James. 1988. *Power in the Isthmus: A Political History of Modern Central America*. New York: Verso.

Dunning, Thad, and Lauren Harrison. 2010. "Cross-Cutting Cleavages and Ethnic Voting: An Experimental Study of Cousinage in Mali." *American Political Science Review* 104 (1): 21–39.

Durante, Ruben, and Brian Knight. 2012. "Partisan Control, Media Bias, and Viewer Responses: Evidence from Berlusconi's Italy." *Journal of the European Economic Association* 10 (3): 451–481.

Duverger, Maurice. 1954. *Political Parties: Their Organization and Activity in the Modern State*. London: Methuen.

Dye, David R., Judy Butler, Deena Abu-Lughod, Jack Spence, and George Vickers. 1995. *Contesting Everything, Winning Nothing: The Search for Consensus in Nicaragua, 1990–1995*. Cambridge, MA: Hemisphere Initiatives.

Economist. 2003. "Kagame Won, a Little Too Well; Rwanda's Presidential Election." August 28. "Economist Intelligence Unit Country Profiles." https://www.eiu.com/.

Edlin, John. 1980. "Record 93 Percent Voted in Rhodesian Elections." Associated Press, March 1.

Egan, Patrick. 2008. "Issue Ownership and Representation: A Theory of Legislative Responsiveness to Constituency Opinion." Unpublished manuscript. https://ssrn.com/abstract=1239464.

Eguia, Jon X., and Francesco Giovannoni. 2019. "Tactical Extremism." *American Political Science Review* 113 (1): 282–286.

Eichenberg, Richard C. 2005. "Victory Has Many Friends: U.S. Public Opinion and the Use of Military Force, 1981–2005." *International Security* 30 (1): 140–177.

EJE21. 2021. "Choques con el Ejército dejan 3 campesinos heridos en noroeste de Colombia." March 4. https://www.eje21.com.co/2021/03/choques-con-el-ejercito-dejan-3-campesinos-heridos-en-noroeste-de-colombia/.

El Diario de Hoy. 1994a. "Cristiani pide al pueblo vote por un futuro mejor." March 19.

———. 1994b. "Fidel Castro lleva 35 años como dictador de Cuba." March 18.

———. 1994c. "¡No más niños guerrilleros! ¡No más niños mutilados!" Advertisement by Los Amigos de la Libertad. March 14.

———. 1994d. "Terror y muerte: cara real del FMLN." March 18.

ElectionGuide. 2005. "Republic of Burundi, July 4, 2005." http://www.electionguide.org/elections/id/350/.

El Espectador. 2018. "Humberto de la Calle niega apoyo de FARC a su candidatura." March 9.

Elliott, Lucinda, and Tom Phillips. 2018. "Bolsonaro's Pledge to Return Brazil to Past Alarms Survivors of Dictatorship." *Guardian,* October 22.

Elster, Jon. 2004. *Closing the Books: Transitional Justice in Historical Perspective.* New York: Cambridge University Press.

Enelow, James M., and Melvin J. Hinich. 1982. "Ideology, Issues, and the Spatial Theory of Elections." *American Political Science Review* 76 (3): 493–501.

Entman, Robert M. 2004. *Projections of Power: Framing News, Public Opinion, and U.S. Foreign Policy.* Chicago: University of Chicago Press.

Everingham, Mark. 1996. *Revolution and the Multiclass Coalition in Nicaragua.* Pittsburgh, PA: University of Pittsburgh Press.

Fazal, Tanisha M. 2014. "Dead Wrong? Battle Deaths, Military Medicine, and Exaggerated Reports of War's Demise." *International Security* 39 (1): 95–125.

Fearon, James D. 1995. "Rationalist Explanations for War." *International Organization* 49 (3): 379–414.

———. 2004. "Why Do Some Civil Wars Last So Much Longer Than Others?" *Journal of Peace Research* 41 (3): 275–301.

Fearon, James D., and David D. Laitin. 2003. "Ethnicity, Insurgency, and Civil War." *American Political Science Review* 97 (1): 75–90.

Ferejohn, John. 1986. "Incumbent Performance and Electoral Control." *Public Choice* 50 (1–3): 5–25.

Fergusson, Leopoldo, Juan F. Vargas, and Mauricio A. Vela. 2013. "Sunlight Disinfects? Free Media in Weak Democracies." Serie Documentos CEDE.

Figueroa Ibarra, Carlos, and Salvador Martí i Puig. 2007. "Guatemala: From the Guerrilla Struggle to a Divided Left." In *From Revolutionary Movements to Political Parties: Cases from Latin America and Africa,* edited by Kalowatie Deonandan, David Close, and Gary Prevost, 43–65. New York: Palgrave Macmillan.

———. 2008. "De la lucha guerrillera a la marginalidad electoral. Un análisis de las organizaciones revolucionarias guatemaltecas desde su aparición hasta las elecciones de 2003." *Studia Historica. Historia Contemporánea* 26 (1): 99–117.

Finnemore, Martha, and Kathryn Sikkink. 1998. "International Norm Dynamics and Political Change." *International Organization* 52 (4): 887–917.

Fiorina, Morris P. 1981. *Retrospective Voting in American National Elections.* New Haven, CT: Yale University Press.

Fiorina, Morris P., Samuel Abrams, and Jeremy Pope. 2003. "The 2000 US Presidential Election: Can Retrospective Voting Be Saved?" *British Journal of Political Science* 33 (2): 163–187.

Fisher, Max, and Amanda Taub. 2019. "When Is History a Political Act? (Always)." *New York Times,* August 22.

FLACSO. 1995. *El Salvador: El proceso electoral 1994*. San Salvador: FLACSO.

Flores, Thomas Edward, and Irfan Nooruddin. 2012. "The Effect of Elections on Postconflict Peace and Reconstruction." *Journal of Politics* 74 (2): 558–570.

———. 2016. *Elections in Hard Times: Building Stronger Democracies in the 21st Century*. New York: Cambridge University Press.

Flores-Macías, Gustavo, and Jessica Zarkin. 2021. "Militarization and Perceptions of Law Enforcement in the Developing World: Evidence from a Conjoint Experiment in Mexico." *British Journal of Political Science*.

Fortna, Virginia Page. 2008. *Does Peacekeeping Work? Shaping Belligerents' Choices after Civil War*. Princeton, NJ: Princeton University Press.

———. 2015. "Do Terrorists Win? Rebels' Use of Terrorism and Civil War Outcomes." *International Organization* 69 (3): 519–556.

———. 2019. "Strongman Benefits from Terrorism and Security Concerns in Sri Lanka." *Political Violence at a Glance*, November 20.

Fortna, Virginia Page, and Reyko Huang. 2012. "Democratization after Civil War: A Brush-Clearing Exercise." *International Studies Quarterly* 56 (4): 801–808.

France 24. 2018. "Humberto de la Calle: El candidato que busca consolidar la paz en Colombia." May 26.

French, Howard W. 1994. "Salvador's Ex-Rebels Trail in Polls but Look Ahead." *New York Times*, March 6.

Frente Republicano Guatemalteco. 1999. "Plan de gobierno 2000–2004: Linamientos generales." Guatemala City.

Frente Sandinista de Liberación Nacional (FSLN). 1984. "Plataforma electoral del FSLN: Nicaragua 1984." Managua.

Frére, Marie-Soleil. 2007. *The Media and Conflicts in Central Africa*. Boulder, CO: Lynne Rienner.

Gabel, Matthew J., and John D. Huber. 2000. "Putting Parties in Their Place: Inferring Party Left-Right Ideological Positions from Party Manifestos Data." *American Journal of Political Science* 44 (1): 94–103.

Gadarian, Shana Kushner. 2010. "The Politics of Threat: How Terrorism News Shapes Foreign Policy Attitudes." *Journal of Politics* 72 (2): 469–483.

Galasso, Vincenzo, and Tommaso Nannicini. 2011. "Competing on Good Politicians." *American Political Science Review* 105 (1): 79–99.

Galeas, Geovani. 2004. *Mayor Roberto D'Aubuisson: El rostro más allá del mito*. San Salvador: La Prensa Gráfica.

Galtung, Johan. 1969. "Violence, Peace and Peace Research." *Journal of Peace Research* 6 (3): 167–191.

Gálvez Borrell, Victor. 1996. "Guatemala: Nueva derecha y viejos problemas." *Nueva Sociedad* 142 (March–April): 6–11.

Gamboa, Laura. 2018. "Latin America's Shifting Politics: The Peace Process and Colombia's Elections." *Journal of Democracy* 29 (4): 54–64.

Garbiras-Días, Natalia. 2018. "Colombia: Teaching a New Kind of Politics." *Berkeley Review of Latin American Studies*, Fall.

Garrard-Burnett, Virginia. 2010. *Terror in the Land of the Holy Spirit: Guatemala under General Efraín Ríos Montt, 1982–1983*. Oxford: Oxford University Press.

Gartner, Scott Sigmund. 2008. "The Multiple Effects of Casualties on Public Support for War: An Experimental Approach." *American Political Science Review* 102 (1): 95–106.

Gassebner, Martin, Richard Jong-A-Pin, and Jochen O. Mierau. 2008. "Terrorism and Electoral Accountability: One Strike, You're Out!" *Economic Letters* 100 (1): 126–129.

Gaviria, Ricardo Monsalve. 2017. "Disidencias de las Farc ya están en 8 departamentos." *El Colombiano*, September 12. https://www.elcolombiano.com/colombia/paz-y-derechos -humanos/disidencias-de-las-farc-ya-estan-en-8-departamentos-LI7280692.

Gelpi, Christopher, Peter D. Feaver, and Jason Reifler. 2009. *Paying the Human Costs of War: American Public Opinion of Casualties in Military Conflicts.* Princeton, NJ: Princeton University Press.

Gerdes, Felix. 2013. *Civil War and State Formation: The Political Economy of War and Peace in Liberia.* Frankfurt: Campus Verlag.

Getmansky, Anna, and Thomas Zeitzoff. 2014. "Terrorism and Voting: The Effect of Rocket Threat on Voting in Israeli Elections." *American Political Science Review* 108 (3): 588–604.

Gibson, James L. 2006. "The Contributions of Truth to Reconciliation: Lessons from South Africa." *Journal of Conflict Resolution* 50 (3): 409–432.

Gilligan, Michael J., and Ernest J. Sergenti. 2008. "Do UN Interventions Cause Peace? Using Matching to Improve Causal Inference." *Quarterly Journal of Political Science* 3 (2): 89–122.

Girón S., Carlos. 1994. "'Primero la gente.' . . ." *El Diario de Hoy.*

Glazer, Amihai, and Susanne Lohmann. 1999. "Setting the Agenda: Electoral Competition, Commitment of Policy, and Issue Salience." *Public Choice* 99 (3–4): 377–394.

Gleditsch, Kristian Skrede, and Kyle Beardsley. 2004. "Nosy Neighbors: Third-Party Actors in Central American Conflicts." *Journal of Conflict Resolution* 48 (3): 379–402.

Gleditsch, Kristian Skrede, Idean Salehyan, and Kenneth Schultz. 2008. "Fighting at Home, Fighting Abroad: How Civil Wars Lead to International Disputes." *Journal of Conflict Resolution* 52 (4): 479–506.

Glynn, Adam N. 2013. "What Can We Learn with Statistical Truth Serum? Design and Analysis of the List Experiment." *Public Opinion Quarterly* 77 (S1): 159–172.

Goodwin, Jeffrey. 2001. *No Other Way Out: States and Revolutionary Movements, 1945–1991.* New York: Cambridge University Press.

Green, Donald P., Shang E. Ha, and John G. Bullock. 2010. "Enough Already about 'Black Box' Experiments: Studying Mediation Is More Difficult than Most Scholars Suppose." *Annals of the American Academy of Political and Social Science* 628 (1): 200–208.

Greene, Kenneth F. 2011. "Campaign Persuasion and Nascent Partisanship in Mexico's New Democracy." *American Journal of Political Science* 55 (2): 398–416.

———. 2016. "The Niche Party." In *Challenges of Party-Building in Latin America*, edited by Steven Levitsky, James Loxton, Brandon Van Dyck, and Jorge I. Domínguez, 159–186. New York: Cambridge University Press.

Greenwald, Glenn. 2019. "Interview with Brazil's Ex-President Lula From Prison." *Intercept*, May 22.

Grenier, Yvon. 1999. *The Emergence of Insurgency in El Salvador: Ideology and Political Will.* Pittsburgh, PA: University of Pittsburgh Press.

Grillo, Edoardo, and Carlo Prato. 2021. "Reference Points and Democratic Backsliding." *American Journal of Political Science.*

Grimmer, Justin, and Brandon M. Stewart. 2013. "Text as Data: The Promise and Pitfalls of Automatic Content Analysis Methods for Political Texts." *Political Analysis* 21 (3): 267–297.

Gromes, Thorsten, and Florian Ranft. 2016. "The Dataset on Post–Civil War Power and Compromise, 1990–2012." PRIF Working Papers 33.

Groseclose, Tim. 2001. "A Model of Candidate Location When One Candidate Has a Valence Advantage." *American Journal of Political Science* 45 (4): 862–886.

Grotz, Florian, Christof Hartmann, and Dieter Nohlen. 2001. *Elections in Asia and the Pacific: A Data Handbook*. Vol. 1: *Middle East, Central Asia, and South Asia*. Oxford: Oxford University Press.

Gruson, Lindsey. 1989. "Old Dictator Looks Better to Guatemala." *New York Times*, September 3.

Grzymala-Busse, Anna M. 2002. *Redeeming the Communist Past: The Regeneration of Communist Parties in East Central Europe*. New York: Cambridge University Press.

Guaruma–Ecoanalíticas. 2018. "Elecciones Presidenciales 2018: Medición #6 Mayo 2018." Bogotá.

Guatemala Hoy. 1999. "El proceso electoral de 1999 en Guatemala: Una reflexán." December 15.

Guatemala News and Information Bureau Archive (1963–2000), Civil War Society and Political Transition in Guatemala. 1999. "Guatemala's First Post-war Elections: How Representative and Participatory Will They Be?"

Gunson, Phil. 1996. "Peace Treaty Ends Guatemalan War." *Guardian*, December 30.

Gunther, Richard, and Larry Diamond. 2003. "Species of Political Parties: A New Typology." *Party Politics* 9 (2): 167–199.

Gurses, Mehmet, and T. David Mason. 2008. "Democracy Out of Anarchy: The Prospects for Post-Civil-War Democracy." *Social Science Quarterly* 89 (2): 315–336.

Gutiérrez-Romero, Roxana, and Adrienne LeBas. 2020. "Does Electoral Violence Affect Vote Choice and Willingness to Vote? Conjoint Analysis of a Vignette Experiment." *Journal of Peace Research* 57 (1): 77–92.

Hafner-Burton, Emilie M., Susan D. Hyde, and Ryan S. Jablonski. 2014. "When Do Governments Resort to Election Violence?" *British Journal of Political Science* 44 (1): 149–179.

Hagopian, Frances. 1990. "Democracy by Undemocratic Means? Elites, Political Pacts, and Regime Transition in Brazil." *Comparative Political Studies* 23 (2): 147–170.

Hagopian, Patrick. 2009. *The Vietnam War in American Memory: Veterans, Memorials, and the Politics of Healing*. Amherst: University of Massachusetts Press.

Hainmueller, Jens, Dominik Hangartner, and Teppe Yamamoto. 2015. "Validating Vignette and Conjoint Survey Experiments Against Real-World Behavior." *Proceedings of the National Academy of Sciences* 112 (8): 2395–2400.

Hainmueller, Jens, Daniel J. Hopkins, and Teppei Yamamoto. 2014. "Causal Inference in Conjoint Analysis: Understanding Multidimensional Choices via Stated Preference Experiments." *Political Analysis* 22 (1): 1–30.

Hale, Henry E. 2006. *Why Not Parties in Russia? Democracy, Federalism, and the State*. Cambridge: Cambridge University Press.

Hammond, Thomas H., and Brian D. Humes. 1993. "The Spatial Model and Elections." In *Information, Participation, and Choice: An Economic Theory of Democracy in Perspective*, edited by Bernard Grofman. Ann Arbor: University of Michigan.

Harding, Erika. 1993. "El Salvador: U.N. Observer Mission (Onusal) Announces Conclusion of F.m.l.n. Disarmament." *NotiSur*, August 20.

Harper's Weekly. 1868. "The Modern Gulliver Among the Lilliputians." September 12, 592.

Hartzell, Caroline A., and Matthew Hoddie. 2007. *Crafting Peace: Power-Sharing Institutions and the Negotiated Settlement of Civil Wars*. University Park: Pennsylvania State University Press.

———. 2015. "The Art of the Possible: Power Sharing and Post–Civil War Democracy." *World Politics* 67 (1): 37–71.

Healy, Andrew, and Neil Malhotra. 2013. "Retrospective Voting Reconsidered." *Annual Review of Political Science* 16 (1): 285–306.

Hegre, Håvard, Tanja Ellingsen, Scott Gates, and Nils P. Gleditsch. 2001. "Toward a Democratic Civil Peace? Democracy, Political Chance and Civil War, 1816–1992." *American Political Science Review* 95 (1): 33–48.

Herbst, Jeffrey. 2000. *States and Power in Africa: Comparative Lessons in Authority and Control*. Princeton, NJ: Princeton University Press.

Herman, Edward S., and Frank Brodhead. 1984. *Demonstration Elections: U.S.-Staged Elections in the Dominican Republic, Vietnam, and El Salvador*. Boston: South End.

Hesseltine, William Best. 1957. *Ulysses S. Grant, Politician*. New York: F. Ungar.

Hetherington, Marc J., and Michael Nelson. 2003. "Anatomy of a Rally Effect: George W. Bush and the War on Terrorism." *PS: Political Science & Politics* 36 (1): 37–42.

Hicken, Allen. 2009. *Building Party Systems in Developing Democracies*. New York: Cambridge University Press.

Hirsch, Alexander V., and Kenneth W. Shotts. 2015. "Competitive Policy Development." *American Economic Review* 105 (4): 1646–1664.

Hobbes, Thomas. 1996. *Leviathan*. Oxford: Oxford University Press.

Högbladh, Stina. 2011. "Peace Agreements 1975–2011—Updating the UCDP Peace Agreement Dataset." In *States in Armed Conflict*, edited by Thérése Pettersson and Lotta Themnér. Uppsala: Uppsala University, Department of Peace and Conflict Research Report.

Holiday, David. 2000. "Guatemala's Precarious Peace." *Current History*, February, 99 (634): 78–84.

Holland, Alisha C. 2013. "Right on Crime? Conservative Party Politics and 'Mano Dura' Policies in El Salvador." *Latin American Research Review* 48 (1): 44–67.

———. 2015. "Insurgent Successor Parties: Scaling Down to Build a Party After War." In *Challenges of Party-Building in Latin America*, edited by Steven Levitsky, Brandon Van Dyck, James Loxton, and Jorge I. Domínguez, 273–304. New York: Cambridge University Press.

Holmes, Jennifer S., and Shiela Amin Gutiérrez de Piñeres. 2002. "Sources of Fujimori's Popularity: Neo-Liberal Reform or Ending Terrorism." *Terrorism and Political Violence* 14 (4): 93–112.

Horowitz, Michael C., Allan C. Stam, and Cali M. Ellis. 2015. *Why Leaders Fight*. New York: Cambridge University Press.

Hotelling, Harold. 1929. "Stability in Competition." *Economic Journal* 39 (153): 41–57.

Hou, Yue, and Kai Quek. 2019. "Violence Exposure and Support for State Use of Force in a Non-Democracy." *Journal of Experimental Political Science* 6 (2): 120–130.

Howard, Lise Morjé. 2008. *UN Peacekeeping in Civil Wars*. Cambridge: Cambridge University Press.

Howell, William G., and Jon C. Pevehouse. 2007. *While Dangers Gather: Congressional Checks on Presidential War Powers*. Princeton, NJ: Princeton University Press.

Hoyt, Katherine. 2004. "Parties and Pacts in Contemporary Nicaragua." In *Undoing Democracy: The Politics of Electoral Caudillismo*, edited by David Close and Kalowatie Deonandan, 17–42. New York: Lexington Books.

Huang, Reyko. 2016. *The Wartime Origins of Democratization: Civil War, Rebel Governance, and Political Regimes*. New York: Cambridge University Press.

Huber, Gregory A., Seth J. Hill, and Gabriel S. Lenz. 2012. "Sources of Bias in Retrospective Decision Making: Experimental Evidence on Voters' Limitations in Controlling Incumbents." *American Political Science Review* 106 (4): 720–741.

Huber, John D. 2017. *Exclusion by Elections: Inequality, Ethnic Identity, and Democracy*. New York: Cambridge University Press.

Hughes, Sallie, and Chappell Lawson. 2005. "The Barriers to Media Opening in Latin America." *Political Communication* 22 (1): 9–25.

Human Rights Watch. 2015. *On Their Watch: Evidence of Senior Army Officers' Responsibility for False Positive Killings in Colombia*. New York: Human Rights Watch.

Human Rights Watch Arms Project and Human Rights Watch/Africa. 1994. *Angola: Arms Trade and Violations of the Laws of War since the 1992 Elections* (New York: Human Rights Watch, November 1994), https://www.hrw.org/reports/ANGOLA94N.PDF

Hume, David. 2007. *A Treatise of Human Nature: A Critical Edition*. Edited by David Fate Norton and Mary J. Norton. Oxford: Oxford University Press.

Humphreys, Macartan, and Jeremy M. Weinstein. 2006. "Handling and Manhandling Civilians in Civil War." *American Political Science Review* 100 (3): 429–447.

Huntington, Samuel P. 1993. *The Third Wave: Democratization in the Late Twentieth Century*. Tulsa: University of Oklahoma Press.

———. 2006. *Political Order in Changing Societies*. New Haven, CT: Yale University Press.

Hyde, Susan D. 2011. *The Pseudo-Democrat's Dilemma: Why Election Observation Became an International Norm*. Ithaca, NY: Cornell University Press.

Hyde, Susan D., and Nikolay Marinov. 2012. "Which Elections Can Be Lost?" *Political Analysis* 20 (2): 191–210.

IHS Global Insight. 2003. "Election 2003: Rwanda's Historic Presidential Poll Undermined by Allegations of Foul Play."

Ikenberry, Gilford John. 2019. *After Victory: Institutions, Strategic Restraint, and the Rebuilding of Order after Major Wars*. 2nd ed. Princeton, NJ: Princeton University Press.

Infopress. 1999. "Campaña 1999: muchos temas, poco interés." July 9, 1327.

Inglehart, Ronald, Christian Haerpfer, Alejandro Moreno, Christian Welzel, Kseniya Kizilova, Jaime Diez-Medrano, Marta Lagos, Pippa Norris, Eduard Ponarin, and Bi Puranen, eds. 2014. *World Values Survey: All Rounds—Country-Pooled Datafile Version*. Madrid: JD Systems Institute.

INSEC. 2006. "No. of Victims Killed by State and Maoists in Connection with 'People's War' (13 February 1996–8 October 2006)."

InSight Crime. 2017. "Rodrigo Londoño Echeverri, alias 'Timochenko.'" January 28.

Instituto DOXA Venezuela. 1989. "DOXA Survey # 8977."

———. 1990. "DOXA Survey # 9073."

Instituto Histórico Centroamericano. 1985. "Las elecciones que Reagan quiere enterrar: un análisis del voto popular el 4 de Noviembre." *Revista Envío* (5) 46: 1–30.

International Center for Transitional Justice (ICTJ). 2004. *Iraqi Voices: Attitudes toward Transitional Justice and Social Reconstruction.* Berkeley: University of California.

———. 2006. *Percepciones y opiniones de los Colombianos sobre justicia, verdad, reparación y reconciliación.*

International Crisis Group (ICG). 2001. "Kosovo: Landmark Election." *Balkans Report* 120 (November 21).

———. 2018. "Risky Businesses: The Duque Government's Approach to Peace in Colombia." Latin America and Caribbean Report 67.

International Foundation for Electoral Systems. 1994. "Election Observation—El Salvador, March 20, 1994—April 24, 1994." Washington, DC: IFES.

International Institute for Democracy and Electoral Assistance. 2019. "Voter Turnout Database."

Invamer. 2018. "Elecciones 2018: Medición #7 May 2018."

Isacson, Adam. 2010. "Colombia: Don't Call It a Model." Washington Office on Latin America (WOLA), July 13. https://www.wola.org/2010/07/colombia-dont-call-it-a-model/.

Ishiyama, John. 2019. "Identity Change and Rebel Party Political Success." *Government and Opposition* 54 (3): 454–484.

Ishiyama, John, and Michael Marshall. 2015. "Candidate Recruitment and Former Rebel Parties." *Party Politics* 21 (4): 591–602.

Ishiyama, John, and Michael Widmeier. 2013. "Territorial Control, Levels of Violence, and the Electoral Performance of Former Rebel Political Parties after Civil Wars." *Civil Wars* 15 (4): 531–550.

IUDOP. 1991. "Los salvadoreños ante el año 1990: Una encuesta de opinion pública del 12 al 26 de enero de 1991." San Salvador: Instituto Universitario de Opiníon Pública Universidad Centroamericana José Simeón Cañas.

———. 1993a. "Encuesta exploratoria sobre delincuencia urbana: Una encuesta de opinión pública del 13 al 20 de febrero de 1993." San Salvador: Instituto Universitario de Opiníon Pública Universidad Centroamericana José Simeón Cañas.

———. 1993b. "Encuesta sobre coyuntura política en el país: La Comisión de la verdad y el proceso electoral en la opinión pública salvadoreña: Una encuesta de opinión pública del 19 al 27 de junio de 1993." Informe 35. San Salvador: Instituto Universitario de Opiníon Pública Universidad Centroamericana José Simeón Cañas.

———. 1994. "Public Opinion Surveys." http://uca.edu.sv/publica/iudop.

Jalabi, Raya, and Michael Georgy. 2018. "Cleric Moqtada al-Sadr's Bloc Wins Iraq Election." Reuters, May 18.

Janda, Kenneth, Robert Harmel, Christine Edens, and Patricia Goff. 1995. "Changes in Party Identity: Evidence from Party Manifestos." *Party Politics* 1 (2): 171–196.

Jenkins, Nash. 2016. "Why Did the Philippines Just Elect a Guy Who Jokes about Rape as Its President?" *Time*, May 10.

Jhee, Byong-Kuen. 2008. "Economic Origins of Electoral Support for Authoritarian Successors: A Cross-National Analysis of Economic Voting in New Democracies." *Comparative Political Studies* 41 (3): 362–388.

Johnson, Kenneth L. 1993. "Between Revolution and Democracy: Business Elites and the State in El Salvador during the 1980's." Tulane University.

Jonas, Susanne. 1995. "Electoral Problems and the Democratic Project in Guatemala." In *Elections and Democracy in Central America, Revisited*, edited by Mitchell A. Seligson and John A. Booth, 25–44. Chapel Hill: University of North Carolina Press.

———. 2000. *Of Centaurs and Doves: Guatemala's Peace Process*. Boulder, CO: Westview.

Jung, Harald. 1980. "Class Struggle and Civil War in El Salvador." In *El Salvador: Central America in the New Cold War*, edited by Marvin E. Gettleman, Patrick Lacefield, Louis Menashe, and David Mermelstein. New York: Grove Press.

Kagan, Robert. 2020. "The Battle of Lafayette Square and the Undermining of American Democracy." Brookings Institution Order from Chaos Series.

Kahneman, Daniel, and Amos Tversky. 1979. "Prospect Theory: An Analysis of Decision under Risk." *Econometrica* 47 (2): 263–292.

Kalinaki, Daniel K. 2003. "Rwanda : Presidential Elections: The Good, the Bad and the Ugly." *Africa News*, August 25.

Kaltenthaler, Karl. 2018. "Some Sunnis Voted for a Shiite—and 3 More Takeaways from the Iraqi Election." *The Conversation*, May 24. http://theconversation.com/some-sunnis-voted-for-a-shiite-and-3-more-takeaways-from-the-iraqi-election-86904.

Kalyvas, Stathis N. 1996. *The Rise of Christian Democracy in Europe*. Ithaca, NY: Cornell University Press.

———. 2006. *The Logic of Violence in Civil War*. New York: Cambridge University Press.

———. 2008. "Ethnic Defection in Civil War." *Comparative Political Studies* 41 (8): 1043–1068.

Kaplan, Robert D. 1994. *Balkan Ghosts: A Journey through History*. New York: Vintage.

Karl, Terry Lynn. 1986. "Petroleum and Political Pacts: The Transition to Democracy in Venezuela." In *Transitions from Authoritarian Rule: Latin America*, edited by Guillermo O'Donnell, Philippe C. Schmitter, and Laurence Whitehead, 219. Baltimore, MD: Johns Hopkins University Press.

———. 1988. "Exporting Democracy: The Unanticipated Effects of US Electoral Policy in El Salvador." In *Crisis in Central America: Regional Dynamics and U.S. Policy in the 1980s*, edited by Nora Hamilton, Linda Fuller, Jeffry A. Frieden, and Manuel Pastor, Jr., 173–192. Boulder, CO: Westview.

———. 1992. "El Salvador's Negotiated Revolution." *Foreign Affairs* 71 (2): 147–164.

———. 1995. "The Hybrid Regimes of Central America." *Journal of Democracy* 6 (3): 72–86.

Karol, David, and Edward Miguel. 2007. "The Electoral Cost of War: Iraq Casualties and the 2004 U.S. Presidential Election." *Journal of Politics* 69 (3): 633–648.

Kasara, Kimuli. 2016. "Electoral Geography and Conflict: Examining the Redistricting through Violence in Kenya." Columbia University.

Kayser, Mark Andreas, and Christopher Wlezien. 2011. "Performance Pressure: Patterns of Partisanship and the Economic Vote." *European Journal of Political Research* 50 (3): 365–394.

Keesing's Record of World Events. 1987. London: Longman. http://keesings.com.

Kertzer, Joshua D., and Thomas Zeitzoff. 2017. "A Bottom-Up Theory of Public Opinion about Foreign Policy." *American Journal of Political Science* 61 (3): 543–558.

Key, Valdimer Orlando, Jr. 1966. *The Responsible Electorate: Rationality in Presidential Voting, 1936–1960*. New York: Vintage.

Kibris, Arzu. 2011. "Funerals and Elections: The Effects of Terrorism on Voting Behavior in Turkey." *Journal of Conflict Resolution* 55 (2): 220–247.

Kinder, Donald R., and D. Roderick Kiewiet. 1979. "Economic Discontent and Political Behavior: The Role of Personal Grievances and Collective Economic Judgements in Congressional Voting." *American Journal of Political Science* 23 (3): 495–527.

Kinzer, Stephen. 2008. *A Thousand Hills: Rwanda's Rebirth and the Man Who Dreamed It*. Hoboken, NJ: John Wiley.

Kitschelt, Herbert, and Steven I. Wilkinson. 2007. "Citizen-Politician Linkages: An Introduction." In *Patrons, Clients and Policies: Patterns of Democratic Accountability and Political Competition*, edited by Herbert Kitschelt and Steven I. Wilkinson, 1–49. New York: Cambridge University Press.

Kobrak, Paul. 2013. "The Long War in Colotenango: Guerrillas, Army, and Civil Patrols." In *War by Other Means: Aftermath in Post-Genocide Guatemala*, edited by Carlota McAllister and Diane M. Nelson, 218–240. Durham, NC: Duke University Press.

Koch, Michael T. 2011. "Casualties and Incumbents: Do the Casualties from Interstate Conflicts Affect Incumbent Party Vote Share?" *British Journal of Political Science* 41 (4): 795–817.

Kocher, Matthew A., Thomas B. Pepinsky, and Stathis N. Kalyvas. 2011. "Aerial Bombing and Counterinsurgency in the Vietnam War." *American Journal of Political Science* 55 (2): 201–218.

Kondracke, Morton. 1987. "Can the U.S. Put the Pieces Together? The Contra Crack-Up." Central Intelligence Agency.

Köszegi, Botond, and Matthew Rabin. 2009. "Reference-Dependent Consumption Plans." *American Economic Review* 99 (3): 909–936.

Kramer, Gerald H. 1983. "The Ecological Fallacy Revisited: Aggregate- versus Individual-Level Findings on Economics and Elections, and Sociotropic Voting." *American Political Science Review* 77 (1): 92–111.

Krasa, Stefan, and Mattias Polborn. 2010. "Competition between Specialized Candidates." *American Political Science Review* 104 (4): 745–765.

Krasner, Stephen D. 2005. "Building Democracy after Conflict: The Case for Shared Sovereignty." *Journal of Democracy* 16 (1): 69–83.

Kreutz, Joakim. 2010. "How and When Armed Conflicts End: Introducing the UCDP Conflict Termination Dataset." *Journal of Peace Research* 47 (2): 243–250.

Krosnick, Jon A., and Donald R. Kinder. 1990. "Altering the Foundations of Support for the President through Priming." *American Political Science Review* 84 (2): 497–512.

Kuant, Elia María, and Trish O'Kane. 1990. *Nicaragua: Political Parties and Elections 1990*. Managua: Coordinara Regional de Investigaciones Económicas y Sociales.

Kuchuj Voz Ciudadana. 1999. "Información cívica. Elecciones 1999."

Kupatadze, Alexander, and Thomas Zeitzoff. 2021. "In the Shadow of Conflict: How Emotions, Threat Perceptions and Victimization Influence Foreign Policy Attitudes." *British Journal of Political Science* 51 (1): 181–202.

Kuran, Timur. 1991. "Now Out of Never: The Element of Surprise in the East European Revolution of 1989." *World Politics* 44 (1): 7–48.

Kydd, Andrew, and Barbara F. Walter. 2002. "Sabotaging the Peace: The Politics of Extremist Violence." *International Organization* 56 (2): 263–296.

Kyle, Brett, J. 2016. *Recycling Dictators in Latin American Elections: Legacies of Military Rule.* Boulder, CO: Lynne Rienner.

La Botz, Dan. 2016. *What Went Wrong? The Nicaraguan Revolution. A Marxist Analysis.* Leiden: Brill.

La Comisión para el Escalarecimiento Histórico CEH. 1999. *Guatemala: Memoria del Silencio.* 12 vols. Guatemala City: UNOPS.

Ladd, Jonathan McDonald. 2007. "Predispositions and Public Support for the President during the War on Terrorism." *Public Opinion Quarterly* 71 (4): 511–538.

Lake, David A., and Donald Rothchild. 1996. "Containing Fear: The Origins and Management of Ethnic Conflict." *International Security* 21 (2): 41–75.

Langer, Lawrence L. 1982. *Versions of Survival: The Holocaust and the Human Spirit.* Albany: State University of New York Press.

LAPOP. 2006–2010. "AmericasBarometer." www.vanderbilt.edu/lapop.

La Prensa Gráfica. 1982. "D'Aubuisson no puede desmentirlo." March 24.

Lasswell, Harold D. 1938. *Propaganda Technique in the World War.* New York: P. Smith.

"Latin American Election Statistics." https://library.ucsd.edu/research-and-collections/collections/notable-collections/latin-american-elections-statistics/index.html.

Latin American Public Opinion Project (LAPOP). Various years. www.vanderbilt.edu/lapop/.

Latin American Studies Association. 1984. "Electoral Process in Nicaragua: Domestic and International Influences: Report of the Latin American Studies Association Delegation to Observe the Nicaraguan General Election of November 4, 1984." Austin, TX: LASA.

———. 1990. "Electoral Democracy under International Pressure: The Report of the Latin American Studies Association Commission to Observe the 1990 Nicaraguan Election." Pittsburgh, PA: LASA.

Laver, Michael J., and Ian Budge. 1992. "Measuring Policy Distances and Modelling Coalition Formation." In *Party Policy and Government Coalitions,* edited by Michael J. Laver and Ian Budge, 15–40. London: Palgrave Macmillan.

Lawson, Chappell, and James A. McCann. 2005. "Television News, Mexico's 2000 Elections and Media Effects in Emerging Democracies." *British Journal of Political Science* 35 (1): 1–30.

LeBas, Adrienne. 2011. *From Protest to Parties: Party-Building and Democratization in Africa.* Oxford: Oxford University Press.

Lee, David S. 2008. "Randomized Experiments from Non-Random Selection in US House Elections." *Journal of Econometrics* 142 (2): 675–697.

Lehoucq, Fabrice. 2002. "The 1999 Elections in Guatemala." *Electoral Studies* 21 (1): 107–114.

Lenz, Gabriel S. 2009. "Learning and Opinion Change, Not Priming: Reconsidering the Priming Hypothesis." *American Journal of Political Science* 53 (4): 821–837.

LeoGrande, William M. 1998. *Our Own Backyard: The United States in Central America, 1977–1992.* Chapel Hill: University of North Carolina Press.

Lessing, Benjamin. 2017. *Making Peace in Drug Wars: Crackdowns and Cartels in Latin America.* New York: Cambridge University Press.

Levitsky, Steven R., and Lucan A. Way. 2012. "Beyond Patronage: Violent Struggle, Ruling Party Cohesion, and Authoritarian Durability." *Perspectives on Politics* 10 (4): 869–889.

Levy, Gabriella. 2022. "Evaluations of Violence at the Polls: Civilian Victimization and Support for Perpetrators after War." *Journal of Politics* 84 (2): 783–797.

Lewin, Juan Esteban. 2017. "¿Qué dice de Uribe que su candidato sea Duque?" *La Silla Vacia*, December 13.

Lewis-Beck, Michael S., and Martin Paldam. 2000. "Economic Voting: An Introduction." *Electoral Studies* 19 (2–3): 113–121.

Lewis-Beck, Michael S., and María Celeste Ratto. 2013. "Economic Voting in Latin America: A General Model." *Electoral Studies* 32 (3): 489–493.

"Lexis-Nexis Academic." http://www.lexisnexis.com/hottopics/lnacademic/.

Ley, Sandra. 2017. "Electoral Accountability in the Midst of Criminal Violence: Evidence from Mexico." *Latin American Politics and Society* 59 (1): 3–27.

"Library of Congress Country Reports." https://www.loc.gov/rr/frd/cs/profiles.html.

Lijphart, Arend. 1977. *Democracy in Plural Societies: A Comparative Exploration.* New Haven, CT: Yale University Press.

Lindbeck, Assar, and Jörgen W. Weibull. 1987. "Balanced-Budget Redistribution as the Outcome of Political Competition." *Public Choice* 52 (3): 273–297.

Lindberg, Staffan I., Michael Coppedge, John Gerring, and Jan Teorell. 2014. "V-Dem: A New Way to Measure Democracy." *Journal of Democracy* 25 (3): 159–169.

Lindsey, Summer E. 2019. "Women's Security after War: Protection and Punishment in Eastern Democratic Republic of Congo." PhD diss., Columbia University.

Lipset, Seymour M., and Stein Rokkan. 1967. "Cleavage Structures, Party Systems, and Voter Alignments: An Introduction." In *Party Systems and Voter Alignments: Cross-National Perspectives*, edited by Seymour M. Lipset and Stein Rokkan. New York: New Press.

Locke, John. 1824. *The Works of John Locke in Nine Volumes.* Vol. 2. London: Rivington.

Loeb, David. 1999. "Bringing Back the General: Party of Rios Montt Wins General Elections." *Report on Guatemala*, Winter.

Londoño, Ernesto, and Manuela Andreoni. 2018. "Brazil Election: Jair Bolsonaro Heads to Runoff after Missing Outright Win." *New York Times*, October 7.

Londoño, Rodrigo. 2018. "Rodrigo Londoño: La justiciar para la paz busca que no haya impunidad." In *Conclusiones*. CNN.

Long, Tom. 2015. "Peace in Colombia? Lessons from the Failed 1999–2002 Talks." *Global Americans*, December 16. https://theglobalamericans.org/2015/12/peace-in-colombia-lessons-from-the-failed-1999-2002-talks/.

Lopez-Alves, Fernando. 2000. *State Formation and Democracy in Latin America, 1810–1900.* Durham, NC: Duke University Press.

Loxton, James Ivor. 2014. "Authoritarian Inheritance and Conservative Party-Building in Latin America." PhD diss., Harvard University.

Loxton, James, and Scott Mainwaring. 2018. *Life after Dictatorship: Authoritarian Successor Parties Worldwide.* New York: Cambridge University Press.

Loyle, Cyanne E., Christopher Sullivan, and Christian Davenport. 2014. "The Northern Ireland Research Initiative: Data on the Troubles from 1968 to 1998." *Conflict Management and Peace Science* 31 (1): 94–106.

Luciak, Ilja A. 2001. *After the Revolution: Gender and Democracy in El Salvador, Nicaragua, and Guatemala.* Baltimore, MD: Johns Hopkins University Press.

Lupu, Noam. 2016. *Party Brands in Crisis: Partisanship, Brand Dilution, and the Breakdown of Political Parties in Latin America.* New York: Cambridge University Press.

Lupu, Noam, and Leonid Peisakhin. 2017. "The Legacy of Political Violence across Generations." *American Journal of Political Science* 61 (4): 836–851.

Lupu, Yonathan, and Geoffrey P. R. Wallace. 2019. "Violence, Nonviolence, and the Effects of International Human Rights Law." *American Journal of Political Science* 63 (2): 411–426.

Lyall, Jason, Graeme Blair, and Kosuke Imai. 2013. "Explaining Support for Combatants during Wartime: A Survey Experiment in Afghanistan." *American Political Science Review* 107 (4): 679–705.

Lyall, Jason, and Isaiah Wilson III. 2009. "Rage Against the Machines: Explaining Outcomes in Counterinsurgency Wars." *International Organization* 63 (1): 67–106.

Lyons, Terrence. 1998. "Liberia's Path from Anarchy to Elections." *Current History* 97 (619): 229–233.

———. 2005. *Demilitarizing Politics: Elections on the Uncertain Road to Peace.* Boulder, CO: Lynne Rienner.

———. 2016. "The Importance of Winning: Victorious Insurgent Groups and Authoritarian Politics." *Comparative Politics* 48 (2): 167–184.

Macías, Javier Alexander. 2018. "Delitos electorales bajaron 73% en esta segunda vuelta: MOE." *El Colombiano,* June 18.

MacKuen, Michael B., Robert S. Erikson, and James A. Stimson. 1996. "Comment on 'Presidents and the Prospective Voter.'" *Journal of Politics* 58 (3): 793–801.

Madison, James. 2008. "The Federalist 51." In *The Federalist Papers,* edited by Alexander Hamilton, James Madison, and John Jay. Oxford: Oxford University Press.

Madrid, Raúl L. 2012. *The Rise of Ethnic Politics in Latin America.* New York: Cambridge University Press.

Magaloni, Beatriz. 2006. *Voting for Autocracy: Hegemonic Party Survival and Its Demise in Mexico.* New York: Cambridge University Press.

Mainwaring, Scott, and Timothy R. Scully, eds. 1995. *Building Democratic Institutions: Party Systems in Latin America.* Stanford, CA: Stanford University Press.

Mainwaring, Scott, and Matthew S. Shugart. 1997. "Presidentialism and Democracy in Latin America: Rethinking the Terms of the Debate." In *Presidentialism and Democracy in Latin America,* edited by Scott Mainwaring and Matthew S. Shugart, 12–54. New York: Cambridge University Press.

Malone, Mary Fran T. 2010. "Does Dirty Harry Have the Answer?" *Public Integrity* 13 (1): 59–80.

Mampilly, Zachariah Cherian. 2011. *Rebel Rulers: Insurgent Governance and Civilian Life During War.* Ithaca, NY: Cornell University Press.

Manning, Carrie. 2008. *The Making of Democrats: Elections and Party Development in Postwar Bosnia, El Salvador, and Mozambique.* New York: Palgrave Macmillan.

Manning, Carrie, and Ian Smith. 2016. "Political Party Formation by Former Armed Opposition Groups after Civil War." *Democratization* 23 (6): 972–989.

———. 2019. "Electoral Performance by Post-Rebel Parties." *Government and Opposition* 54 (3): 415–453.

Mansfield, Edward D., and Jack L. Snyder. 2007. "Exchange: The Sequencing 'Fallacy.'" *Journal of Democracy* 18(3): 5–9.

March, James G., and Johan P. Olsen. 1989. *Rediscovering Institutions: The Organizational Basis of Politics.* New York: Free Press.

Marcos, Ana. 2015. "Santos pide perdón a las víctimas de la toma del Palacio de Justicia." *El País*, November 6.

Mares, Isabela, and Lauren Young. 2016. "Buying, Stealing and Expropriating Votes." *Annual Review of Political Science* 19 (1): 267–288.

Markus, Gregory B. 1988. "The Impact of Personal and National Economic Conditions on the Presidential Vote: A Pooled Cross-Sectional Analysis." *American Journal of Political Science* 32 (1): 137–154.

Marshall, John. 2018. "Political Information Cycles: When Do Voters Sanction Incumbent Parties for High Homicide Rates?" Columbia University.

Marshall, Michael Christopher, and John Ishiyama. 2016. "Does Political Inclusion of Rebel Parties Promote Peace after Civil Conflict?" *Democratization* 23 (6): 1009–1025.

Marten, Kimberly. 2007. "Warlordism in Comparative Perspective." *International Security* 31 (3): 41–73.

Martí i Puig, Salvador. 2010. "The Adaptation of the FSLN: Daniel Ortega's Leadership and Democracy in Nicaragua." *Latin American Politics and Society* 52 (4): 79–106.

Mason, T. David, and Dale A. Krane. 1989. "The Political Economy of Death Squads: Toward a Theory of the Impact of State-Sanctioned Terror." *International Studies Quarterly* 33 (2): 175–198.

Matanock, Aila M. 2017. *Electing Peace: From Civil Conflict to Political Participation*. New York: Cambridge University Press.

Matanock, Aila M., and Miguel García-Sánchez. 2018. "Does Counterinsurgent Success Match Social Support? Evidence from a Survey Experiment in Colombia." *Journal of Politics* 80 (3): 800–814.

McCarthy, Julie. 2021. "Clan Politics Reign but a Family Is Divided in the Race to Rule the Philippines." *NPR*, November 29.

McCleary, Rachel M. 1997. "Guatemala's Postwar Prospects." *Journal of Democracy* 8 (2): 129–143.

McClendon, Gwyneth H., and Rachel Beatty Riedl. 2019. *From Pews to Politics: Religious Sermons and Political Participation in Africa*. New York: Cambridge University Press.

McClintock, Cynthia. 1998. *Revolutionary Movements in Latin America: El Salvador's FMLN and Peru's Shining Path*. Washington, DC: United States Institute of Peace Press.

McClintock, Michael. 1985. *The American Connection: State Terror and Popular Resistance in El Salvador*. London: Zed Books.

McCrary, Justin. 2008. "Manipulation of the Running Variable in the Regression Discontinuity Design: A Density Test." *Journal of Econometrics* 142 (2): 698–714.

McCullum, Hugh. 1992. "Ballots Replace Bullets in Angola." *Globe*, September 29.

McDermott, Monika L., and Costas Panagopoulos. 2015. "Be All That You Can Be: The Electoral Impact of Military Service as an Information Cue." *Political Research Quarterly* 68 (2): 293–305.

McDowell, Robin. 2009. "Indonesia Gets Ready for Parliamentary Elections." Associated Press International, April 8.

McElhinny, Vincent J. 2006. "Inequality and Empowerment: The Political Foundations of Post-War Decentralization and Development in El Salvador, 1992–2000." PhD diss., University of Pittsburgh.

Mearsheimer, John J. 2013. *Why Leaders Lie: The Truth about Lying in International Politics.* Oxford: Oxford University Press.

Meierhenrich, Jens. 2006. "Presidential and Parliamentary Elections in Rwanda, 2003." *Electoral Studies* 25 (3): 627–634.

Merolla, Jennifer L., and Elizabeth J. Zechmeister. 2009. *Democracy at Risk: How Terrorist Threats Affect the Public.* Chicago: University of Chicago Press.

Miller, Arthur H., and Martin P. Wattenberg. 1985. "Throwing the Rascals Out: Policy and Performance Evaluations of Presidential Candidates, 1952–1980." *American Political Science Review* 79 (2): 359–372.

Millett, Richard. 1977. *Guardians of the Dynasty: A History of the U.S. Created Guardia Nacional de Nicaragua and the Somoza.* Maryknoll, NY: Orbis Books.

Milner, Helen V., and Dustin H. Tingley. 2013. "Public Opinion and Foreign Aid: A Review Essay." *International Interactions* 39 (3): 389–401.

Mintz, Alex. 1989. "Guns versus Butter: A Disaggregated Analysis." *American Political Science Review* 83 (4): 1285–1293.

Misión de Observación Electoral (MOE). 2018. "Mapas y Factores de Riesgo Electoral: Elecciones Nacionales Colombia 2018." MOE.

Mockus, Antanas. 2010. "Propuesta de Gobierno: Mockus-Fajardo 2010–2014, La unión hace la fuerza: Juntos por la legalidad democrática." Bogotá.

Molina Mejía, Raúl. 2000. "Uneasy Allies: The Far Right Comes to Power." *NACLA Report on the Americas* 33 (5): 11–12.

Moncada, Eduardo. 2013. "The Politics of Urban Violence: Challenges for Development in the Global South." *Studies in Comparative International Development* 48 (3): 217–239.

Montgomery, Tommie Sue. 1983a. "The Church in the Salvadoran Revolution." *Latin American Perspectives* 10 (1): 62–87.

———. 1982. *Revolution in El Salvador: Origins and Evolution.* Boulder, CO: Westview Press.

Moravcsik, Andrew. 2000. "The Origins of Human Rights Regimes: Democratic Delegation in Postwar Europe." *International Organization* 54 (2): 217–252.

Mueller, John E. 1973. *War, Presidents, and Public Opinion.* New York: John Wiley.

Muller, Edward N., and Mitchell A. Seligson. 1987. "Inequality and Insurgency." *American Political Science Review* 81 (2): 425–451.

Nalepa, Monika. 2010. *Skeletons in the Closet: Transitional Justice in Post-Communist Europe.* New York: Cambridge University Press.

Nast, Thomas. 1886. "Chicago, May 21, 1868." *Harper's Weekly*, 353.

Neumann, Peter R. 2005. "The Bullet and the Ballot Box: The Case of the IRA." *Journal of Strategic Studies* 28 (6): 941–975.

New York Times. 1979. "Nicaragua's Revolution." June 30.

———. 1984. "U.S. Role in Nicaragua Vote Disputed." October 21.

———. 1996. "A Democrat Wins in Guatemala." January 12.

———. 1999. "A Guatemala at Peace Casts Ballots for President." November 8, A8.

Nickelsburg, Michael, and Helmut Norpoth. 2000. "Commander-in-Chief or Chief Economist? The President in the Eye of the Public." *Electoral Studies* 19 (2–3): 313–332.

Nindorera, Willy. 2012. "The CNDD-FDD in Burundi: The Path from Armed to Political Struggle." Berghof Transitions Series 10.

Niyoyita, Aloys. 2005. "Polls Close in Parliamentary Elections in Burundi." Associated Press, July 4.

Nohlen, Dieter. 2005a. *Elections in the Americas: A Data Handbook.* Vol. 1: *North America, Central America, and the Caribbean.* Oxford: Oxford University Press.

———. 2005b. *Elections in the Americas: A Data Handbook.* Vol. 2: *South America.* Oxford: Oxford University Press.

Nohlen, Dieter, Michael Krennerich, and Bernard Thibaut. 1999. *Elections in Africa: A Data Handbook.* New York: Oxford University Press.

Nohlen, Dieter, and Philip Stöver. 2010. *Elections in Europe: A Data Handbook.* Baden-Baden, Germany: Nomos.

Novick, Peter. 1999. *The Holocaust in American Life.* Boston: Houghton Mifflin.

Nuñez de Escorcia, Vilma. 2014. "Would a Truth Commission Be Possible Here?" *Revista Envío* 34 (395).

O'Donnell, Guillermo, and Philippe C. Schmitter. 1986. *Transitions from Authoritarian Rule: Tentative Conclusions about Uncertain Democracies.* Baltimore, MD: Johns Hopkins University Press.

Oglesby, Elizabeth. 2004. "Historical Memory and the Limits of Peace Education: Examining Guatemala's 'Memory of Silence' and the Politics of Curriculum Design." Carnegie Council on Ethics and International Affairs Fellows Program, History and the Politics of Reconciliation.

Oquist, Paul. 1992. "Sociopolitical Dynamics of the 1990 Nicaraguan Elections." In *The 1990 Elections in Nicaragua and Their Aftermath,* edited by Vanessa Castro and Gary Prevost. Lanham, MD: Rowman & Littlefield.

Organization of American States. 2000. "Report of the Electoral Observation Mission to Guatemala 1999 Elections."

Ottmann, Martin, and Johannes Vüllers. 2015. "The Power-Sharing Event Dataset (PSED): A New Dataset on the Occurrence of Power-Sharing in Post-Conflict Countries." *Conflict Management and Peace Science* 32 (3): 327–350.

Paige, Jeffery M. 1997. *Coffee and Power: Revolution and the Rise of Democracy in Central America.* Cambridge, MA: Harvard University Press.

Palfrey, Thomas R. 1984. "Spatial Equilibrium with Entry." *Review of Economic Studies* 51 (1): 139–156.

Palma Lau, Pedro Pablo. 2010. *Sierra madre: Pasajes y perfiles de la guerra revolucionaria.* Guatemala: F&G Editores.

Panamá, David Ernesto. 2005. *Los guerreros de la libertad.* Andover, MA: Versal Books.

Panebianco, Angelo. 1988. *Political Parties: Organization and Power.* New York: Cambridge University Press.

Paris, Roland. 2004. *At War's End: Building Peace after Civil Conflict.* New York: Cambridge University Press.

Partido Conservador Demócrata de Nicaragua. 1984. *Programa político.* Managua.

Partido de Avanzada Nacional. 1999. "Propuesta de acción gubernamental para el período 2000–2004: Una Guatemala que nos incluye a todos, una Guatemala en la que progresemos todos." Guatemala: INCEP.

Partido Demócrata Cristiano. n.d. "Por un gobierno de solidaridad, concertación y modernización: Plataforma electoral." San Salvador.

Partido Liberal Independiente. 1984. "Programa de acción: Democracia, libertad y justicia social." Managua: Junta Directiva Departamental y Junta Consultiva.

Pastor, Robert A. 2018. *Exiting the Whirlpool: U.S. Foreign Policy toward Latin America and the Caribbean*. New York: Routledge.

Paul, Christopher, Colin P. Clarke, and Beth Grill. 2010. *Victory Has a Thousand Fathers: Detailed Counterinsurgency Case Studies*. Arlington, VA: RAND.

Payne, Douglas W. 1985. *The Democratic Mask: The Consolidation of the Sandinista Revolution*. New York: Freedom House.

PCdeN. 1984. "Plataforma de Gobierno 1984." Managua.

Pearce, Jenny. 1986. *Promised Land: Peasant Rebellion in Chalatenango El Salvador*. London: Latin American Bureau.

Pepinsky, Thomas. 2017. "Southeast Asia: Voting Against Disorder." *Journal of Democracy* 28 (2): 120–131.

Pérez, Orlando J. 2003. "Democratic Legitimacy and Public Insecurity: Crime and Democracy in El Salvador and Guatemala." *Political Science Quarterly* 118 (4): 627–644.

Peskin, Victor. 2008. *International Justice in Rwanda and the Balkans: Virtual Trials and the Struggle for State Cooperation*. New York: Cambridge University Press.

Petersen, Roger D. 2002. *Understanding Ethnic Violence: Fear, Hatred, and Resentment in Twentieth-Century Eastern Europe*. New York: Cambridge University Press.

Petersen, Roger, and Sarah Zukerman Daly. 2010a. "Anger, Violence, and Political Science." In *International Handbook of Anger: Constituent and Concomitant Biological, Psychological, and Social Processes*, edited by Michael Potegal, Gerhard Stemmler, and Charles Spielberger, 561–581. New York: Springer.

———. 2010b. "Revenge or Reconciliation: Theory and Method of Emotions in the Context of Colombia's Peace Process." In *Forum for International Justice and Conflict: Law in Peace Negotiations*, edited by Morten Bergsmo and Pablo Kalmanovitz. Oslo: PRIO.

Petrocik, John R. 1996. "Issue Ownership in Presidential Elections, with a 1980 Case Study." *American Journal of Political Science* 40 (3): 825–850.

Pettersson, Therése, Stina Högbladh, and Magnus Öberg. 2019. "Organized Violence, 1989–2018 and Peace Agreements." *Journal of Peace Research* 56 (4): 589–603.

Pettigrew, Thomas F. 1979. "The Ultimate Attribution Error: Extending Allport's Cognitive Analysis of Prejudice." *Personality and Social Psychology Bulletin* 5 (4): 461–476.

Phillips, Dom. 2019. "Fury as Bolsonaro Orders Brazil Army to mark 55th Anniversary of Military Coup." *Guardian*, March 27.

Pico, Juan Hernández. 1999a. "Seeking New Ground in the General's Shadow." *Revista Envío* 19 (218).

———. 1999b. "Why Was the Referendum Defeated?" *Revista Envío* 19 (216).

Pilyatskin, Boris. 1994. "South Africa: White Begin, Black Win." *Russian Press Digest*, April 30.

Pinker, Steven. 2011. *The Better Angels of Our Nature: Why Violence Has Declined*. New York: Viking.

Pizarro Leongómez, Eduardo. 2004. "Comienza el Frente Nacional: paz de dos partidos." *Revista Semana*, 188–190.

Pocasangre, Oscar. 2022. "The Political Consequences of Chronic Criminal Violence." PhD diss., Columbia University.

Polimétrica. 2017. "Cifras y conceptos, Noviembre 2017." Bogotá.

———. 2018a. "Cifras y conceptos, Abril 2018." Bogotá.

———. 2018b. "Cifras y conceptos, Junio 2018." Bogotá.

———. 2018c. "Cifras y conceptos, Marzo 2018." Bogotá.

———. 2018d. "Cifras y conceptos, Mayo 2018." Bogotá.

"Political Database of the Americas." http://pdba.georgetown.edu/Elecdata/elecdata.html.

Posner, Daniel N. 2004. "The Political Salience of Cultural Difference: Why Chewas and Tumbukas Are Allies in Zambia and Adversaries in Malawi." *American Political Science Review* 98 (4): 529–545.

Potegal, Michael, Gerhard Stemmler, and Charles Spielberger, eds. 2010. *International Handbook of Anger: Constituent and Concomitant Biological, Psychological, and Social Processes*. New York: Springer.

Powell, Robert. 1993. "Guns, Butter, and Anarchy." *American Political Science Review* 87 (1): 115–132.

———. 2006. "War as a Commitment Problem." *International Organization* 60 (1): 169–203.

Press, Daryl G., Scott D. Sagan, and Benjamin A. Valentino. 2013. "Atomic Aversion: Experimental Evidence on Taboos, Traditions, and the Non-Use of Nuclear Weapons." *American Political Science Review* 107 (1): 188–206.

Programa Paz y Reconciliación. 2006. "Representación social de la reinsercion en participantes, familia y comunidad, beneficiarios indirectos y contratistas del programa paz y reconciliación de la Alcaldía de Medellín." Medellín.

"Pro-Quest Historical Newspaper Databases." https://www.proquest.com/products-services/pq-hist-news.html.

Przeworski, Adam. 1991. *Democracy and the Market: Political and Economic Reforms in Eastern Europe and Latin America*. New York: Cambridge University Press.

Pyes, Craig. 1983. "Salvadoran Rightists: The Deadly Patriots." *Albuquerque Journal*.

Quintero, Daniela. 2019. "Darío Acevedo y obstinación por negar el conflicto armado." *Prensa Rural*, September 18.

Reding, Andrew A. 1991. "The Evolution of Governmental Institutions." In *Revolution & Counterrevolution in Nicaragua*, edited by Thomas W. Walker, 15–48. Boulder, CO: Westview.

Reiter, Dan. 2009. *How Wars End*. Princeton, NJ: Princeton University Press.

REMHI: Recovery of Historical Memory Project. 1999. *Guatemala: Never Again! Official Report of the Human Rights Office, Archdiocese of Guatemala*. Maryknoll, NY: Orbis Books.

Reno, William. 1998. *Warlord Politics and African States*. Boulder, CO: Lynne Rienner.

Revista Envío. 1984a. "4 de Noviembre: análisis de los resultados electorales." 4 (41).

———. 1984b. "The Final Stretch of the Electoral Process." 4 (41).

———. 1984c. "Los partidos políticos en Nicaragua en dos meses de campaña electoral." 4 (40).

Revista Semana. 2005. "El 'Pacificador:' muchas voces le atribuyen a Adolfo Paz gran parte de la mejoría en las cifras de seguridad en Medellín." April 23.

———. 2015. "Uribe gana el considerado bastión de las FARC." October 25.

———. 2016. "El Placer, otra masacre por la que Santos pide perdón." January 23.

Riker, William H. 1982. "The Two-Party System and Duverger's Law: An Essay on the History of Political Science." *American Political Science Review* 76 (4): 753–766.

———. 1986. *The Art of Political Manipulation*. New Haven, CT: Yale University Press.

———. 1996. *The Strategy of Rhetoric: Campaigning for the American Constitution*. New Haven, CT: Yale University Press.

Rivera, Mauricio, and Barbara Zarate-Tenorio. 2016. "Beyond Sticks and Stones: Human Capital Enhancement Efforts in Response to Violent Crime in Latin America." *European Journal of Political Research* 55 (3): 531–548.

Robayo, Ricardo. 2016. "Presidente pide perdón por genocidio de la UP." *Centro Nacional de Memoria Histórica*, September 16.

———. 2020. "268.807: Muertes en el marco del conflicto armado." https://micrositios .centrodememoriahistorica.gov.co/observatorio/.

Roberts, Kenneth M., and Erik Wibbels. 1999. "Party Systems and Electoral Volatility in Latin America: A Test of Economic, Institutional, and Structural Explanations." *American Political Science Review* 93 (3): 575–590.

Roberts, Margaret E., Brandon M. Stewart, and Dustin Tingley. 2019. "stm: An R Package for Structural Topic Models." *Journal of Statistical Software* 91 (2): 1–40.

Robinson, James A., and Ragnar Torvik. 2009. "The Real Swing Voters' Curse." *American Economic Review: Papers & Proceedings* 99 (2): 310–315.

Robinson, William I., and Kent Norsworthy. 1987. *David and Goliath: The U.S. War Against Nicaragua*. New York: Monthly Review Press.

Roddy, Dennis. 2019. "Trujillo's Ghost: The Effects of the Dictator's Bloody Reign Still Linger in the Dominican Republic." *Pittsburgh Post-Gazette*, February 24.

Roeder, Philip, and Donald Rothchild. 2005. *Sustainable Peace: Power and Democracy after Civil Wars*. Ithaca, NY: Cornell University Press.

Roemer, John E. 2009. *Political Competition: Theory and Application*. Cambridge, MA: Harvard University Press.

Rohter, Larry. 1996a. "Guatemala Election Becomes Vote on Former Dictator." *New York Times*, January 7.

———. 1996b. "Guatemalans Formally End 36-Year Civil War, Central America's Longest and Deadliest." *New York Times*, December 30, A1.

Rosenau, James N. 1965. *Public Opinion and Foreign Policy: An Operational Formulation*. New York: Random House.

Rosenberg, Shawn W., and Gary Wolfsfeld. 1977. "International Conflict and the Problem of Attribution." *Journal of Conflict Resolution* 21 (1): 75–103.

Rozenas, Arturas, Sebastian Schutte, and Yuri Zhukov. 2017. "The Political Legacy of Violence: The Long-Term Impact of Stalin's Repression in Ukraine." *Journal of Politics* 79 (4): 1147–1161.

Rudloff, Peter, and Michael G. Findley. 2016. "The Downstream Effects of Combatant Fragmentation on Civil War Recurrence." *Journal of Peace Research* 53 (1): 19–32.

Rueschemeyer, Dietrich, Evelyne Huber Stephens, and John D. Stephens. 1992. *Capitalist Development and Democracy*. Chicago: University of Chicago Press.

Ruhl, Mark J. 2004. "Curbing Central America's Militaries." *Journal of Democracy* 15 (3): 137–151.

Rustad, Siri Aas, and Helga Malmin Binningsbø. 2012. "A Price Worth Fighting For? Natural Resources and Conflict Recurrence." *Journal of Peace Research* 49 (4): 531–546.

Sáenz de Tejada, Ricardo. 2004. *Victimas o vencedores? Una aproximación al movimiento de los ex PAC*. Guatemala: FLASCO.

Sagan, Scott D., and Benjamin A. Valentino. 2017. "Revisiting Hiroshima in Iran: What Americans Really Think about Using Nuclear Weapons and Killing Noncombatants." *International Security* 42 (1): 41–79.

Samii, Cyrus. 2013a. "Perils or Promise of Ethnic Integration? Evidence from a Hard Case in Burundi." *American Political Science Review* 107 (3): 558–573.

———. 2013b. "Who Wants to Forgive and Forget? Transitional Justice Preferences in Postwar Burundi." *Journal of Peace Research* 50 (2): 219–233.

Samuels, David J. 2003. *Ambition, Federalism, and Legislative Politics in Brazil*. Cambridge: Cambridge University Press.

Samuels, David J., and Matthew S. Shugart. 2010. *Presidents, Parties, and Prime Ministers: How the Separation of Powers Affects Party Organization and Behavior*. New York: Cambridge University Press.

Samuels, David J., and Cesar Zucco, Jr. 2014. "The Power of Partisanship in Brazil: Evidence from Survey Experiments." *American Journal of Political Science* 58 (1): 212–225.

Sánchez, María Camila. 2018. "Iván Duque, el presidente más joven en la historia de Colombia." *Radio Nacional de Colombia*, June 17.

Sanchez, Omar. 2008. "Guatemala's Party Universe: A Case Study in Underinstitutionalization." *Latin American Politics and Society* 50 (1): 123–151.

Sanford, Victoria. 2003. *Buried Secrets: Truth and Human Rights in Guatemala*. New York: Palgrave Macmillan.

Santos Calderón, Juan Manuel. 2010. "Plan nacional de desarrollo 2010–2014: Prosperidad para todos, más empleo, menos pobreza y más seguridad." Bogotá: Departamento Nacional de Planeación.

———. 2022. "From Hawk to Dove." George W. Ball Lecture, Columbia University, April 13.

Sartori, Giovanni. 2005. *Parties and Party Systems: A Framework for Analysis*. Colchester, UK: ECPR.

Saunders, Elizabeth N. 2015. "War and the Inner Circle: Democratic Elites and the Politics of Using Force." *Security Studies* 24 (3): 466–501.

Sawyer, Katherine, Kathleen Gallagher Cunningham, and William Reed. 2017. "The Role of External Support in Civil War Termination." *Journal of Conflict Resolution* 61 (6): 1174–1202.

Schirmer, Jennifer. 1998. *The Guatemalan Military Project: A Violence Called Democracy*. Philadelphia: University of Pennsylvania Press.

Schuman, Howard, Vered Vinitzky-Seroussi, and Amiram D. Vinokur. 2003. "Keeping the Past Alive: Memories of Israeli Jews at the Turn of the Millennium." *Sociological Forum* 18 (1): 103–136.

Schumpeter, Joseph A. 1976. *Capitalism, Socialism, and Democracy*. London: Allen & Unwin.

Schwartz, Rachel A., and Scott Straus. 2018. "What Drives Violence against Civilians in Civil War? Evidence from Guatemala's Conflict Archives." *Journal of Peace Research* 55 (2): 222–235.

Seawright, Jason. 2016. *Multi-Method Social Science: Combining Qualitative and Quantitative Tools*. New York: Cambridge University Press.

Seligson, Mitchell A., and John A. Booth, eds. 1995. *Elections and Democracy in Central America, Revisited*. Chapel Hill: University of North Carolina Press.

Seligson, Mitchell A., and Vincent J. McElhinny. 1996. "Low-Intensity Warfare, High-Intensity Death: The Demographic Impact of the Wars in El Salvador and Nicaragua." *Canadian Journal of Latin American and Caribbean Studies* 21 (42): 211–241.

Serra, Luis Hector. 1991. "The Grass-Roots Organizations." In *Revolution & Counterrevolution in Nicaragua*, edited by Thomas W. Walker, 49–76. Boulder, CO: Westview.

Sexton, Renard, Rachel L. Wellhausen, and Michael G. Findley. 2019. "How Government Reactions to Violence Worsen Social Welfare: Evidence from Peru." *American Journal of Political Science* 63 (2): 353–367.

Shah, Aditi, and Shihar Aneez. 2019. "Many Sri Lankans Want a Strongman Leader, and That Favours Gotabaya Rajapaksa." Reuters, August 10.

Shifter, Michael. 2012. "Plan Colombia: A Retrospective." *Americas Quarterly* 6 (3): 36.

Shugart, Matthew Soberg. 1987. "States, Revolutionary Conflict and Democracy: El Salvador and Nicaragua in Comparative Perspective." *Government and Opposition* 22 (1): 13–32.

———. 1992. "Guerrillas and Elections: An Institutionalist Perspective on the Costs of Conflict and Competition." *International Studies Quarterly* 36 (2): 121–151.

Sides, John. 2006. "The Origins of Campaign Agendas." *British Journal of Political Science* 36 (3): 407–436.

Sikkink, Kathryn. 2011. *The Justice Cascade: How Human Rights Prosecutions Are Changing World Politics*. New York: Norton.

Simmons, Beth A. 2009. *Mobilizing for Human Rights: International Law in Domestic Politics*. New York: Cambridge University Press.

Slater, Dan, and Nicholas Rush Smith. 2016. "The Power of Counterrevolution: Elitist Origins of Political Order in Postcolonial Asia and Africa." *American Journal of Sociology* 121 (5): 1472–1516.

Smith, Amy Erica. 2018. "'Law and Order' Politics Often Undermines the Rule of Law." *Vox*, July 9.

Smith, David. 2015. "Muhammadu Buhari: Reformed Dictator Returns to Power in Democratic Nigeria." *Guardian*, March 31.

Smithies, Arthur. 1941. "Optimum Location in Spatial Competition." *Journal of Political Economy* 49 (3): 423–439.

Snyder, Jack, and Karen Ballentine. 1996. "Nationalism and the Marketplace of Ideas." *International Security* 21 (2): 5–40.

Snyder, Jack, and Erica D. Borghard. 2011. "The Cost of Empty Threats: A Penny, Not a Pound." *American Political Science Review* 105 (3): 437–456.

Snyder, Jack, and Leslie Vinjamuri. 2003. "Trials and Errors: Principle and Pragmatism in Strategies of International Justice." *International Security* 28 (3): 5–44.

Söderberg Kovacs, Mimmi. 2007. "From Rebellion to Politics: The Transformation of Rebel Groups to Political Parties in Civil War Peace Processes." PhD diss., Uppsala University.

Söderberg Kovacs, Mimmi, and Sophia Hatz. 2016. "Rebel-to-Party Transformations in Civil War Peace Processes 1975–2011." *Democratization* 23 (6): 990–1008.

Somers, Margaret R. 1994. "The Narrative Constitution of Identity: A Relational and Network Approach." *Theory and Society* 23 (5): 605–649.

Soubeyran, Raphaël. 2006. "Valence Advantages and Public Goods Consumption: Does a Disadvantaged Candidate Choose an Extremist Position?" *Public Economics: Publicly Provided Goods eJournal* 2006.

Spear, Joanna. 1999. "The Disarmament and Demobilisation of Warring Factions in the Aftermath of Civil Wars: Key Implementation Issues." *Civil Wars* 2 (2): 1–22.

Spears, Ian S. 2010. *Civil War in African States: The Search for Security*. Boulder, CO: Lynne Rienner.

Spence, Jack, David R. Dye, Paul Worby, Carmen Rosa de León-Escribano, George Vickers, and Mike Lanchin. 1998. *Promise and Reality: Implementation of the Guatemalan Peace Accords*. Cambridge, MA: Hemisphere Initiatives.

Sprenkels, Ralph. 2011. "Roberto d'Aubuisson vs Schafik Handal: Militancy, Memory Work and Human Rights." *European Review of Latin American and Caribbean Studies* 91 (1): 15–30.

———. 2019. "Ambivalent Moderation: The FMLN's Ideological Accommodation to Post-War Politics in El Salvador." *Government and Opposition* 54 (3): 536–558.

Stahler-Sholk, Richard. 1994. "El Salvador's Negotiated Transition: From Low-Intensity Conflict to Low-Intensity Democracy." *Journal of Interamerican Studies and World Affairs* 36 (4): 1–59.

Staniland, Paul. 2012. "Organizing Insurgency: Networks, Resources, and Rebellion in South Asia." *International Security* 37 (1): 142–177.

Stanley, William D. 1996. *The Protection Racket State: Elite Politics, Military Extortion, and Civil War in El Salvador*. Philadelphia: Temple University Press.

———. 2006. "El Salvador: State-Building Before and After Democratisation, 1980–95." *Third World Quarterly* 27 (1): 101–114.

Stanton, Jessica A. 2016. *Violence and Restraint in Civil War: Civilian Targeting in the Shadow of International Law*. New York: Cambridge University Press.

Stedman, Stephen John. 1997. "Spoiler Problems in Peace Processes." *International Security* 22 (2): 5–53.

Steele, Abbey. 2011. "Electing Displacement: Political Cleansing in Apartadó, Colombia." *Journal of Conflict Resolution* 55 (3): 423–445.

———. 2017. *Democracy and Displacement in Colombia's Civil War*. Ithaca, NY: Cornell University Press.

Steimer, Thierry. 2002. "The Biology of Fear- and Anxiety-Related Behaviors." *Dialogues in Clinical Neuroscience* 4 (3): 231–249.

Steinberg, Michael K., Carrie Height, Rosemary Mosher, and Mathew Bampton. 2006. "Mapping Massacres: GIS and State Terror in Guatemala." *Geoforum* 37 (1): 62–68.

Stepan, Alfred C. 1988. *Rethinking Military Politics: Brazil and the Southern Cone*. Princeton, NJ: Princeton University Press.

Stewart, Megan A. 2018. "Civil War as State-Making: Strategic Governance in Civil War." *International Organization* 72 (1): 205–226.

Stokes, Donald E. 1963. "Spatial Models of Party Competition." *American Political Science Review* 57 (2): 368–377.

Stokes, Susan C., Thad Dunning, Marcelo Nazareno, and Valeria Brusco. 2013. *Brokers, Voters, and Clientelism. The Puzzle of Distributive Politics*. New York: Cambridge University Press.

Stoll, David. 1990. "Guatemala: Why They Like Ríos Montt." *NACLA Report on the Americas* 24 (4): 4–7.

———. 1993. *Between Two Armies in the Ixil Towns of Guatemala*. New York: Columbia University Press.

Stone, Walter J. 2017. *Candidates and Voters: Ideology, Valence, and Representation in U.S. Elections.* New York: Cambridge University Press.

Stover, Eric, and Harvey M. Weinstein. 2004. *My Neighbor, My Enemy: Justice and Community in the Aftermath of Mass Atrocity.* New York: Cambridge University Press.

Swain, Jon. 1995. "Exultant Croatia Heads for Murderous Election." *Sunday Times,* October 22.

Tavits, Margit, and Joshua D. Potter. 2015. "The Effect of Inequality and Social Identity on Party Strategies." *American Journal of Political Science* 59 (3): 744–758.

Teigen, Jeremy M. 2013. "Military Experience in Elections and Perceptions of Issue Competence: An Experimental Study with Television Ads." *Armed Forces & Society* 39 (3): 415–433.

Tellez, Juan Fernando. 2019. "Worlds Apart: Conflict Exposure and Preferences for Peace." *Journal of Conflict Resolution* 63 (4): 1053–1076.

Teten, Ryan Lee. 2004. "Reconstruction-Era Elections: 1868–1892." In *Public Opinion and Polling Around the World: A Historical Encyclopedia,* edited by John Gray Geer, 87–92. Santa Barbara, CA: ABC-CLIO.

Thaler, Kai M. 2017. "Nicaragua: A Return to Caudillismo." *Journal of Democracy* 28 (2): 157–169.

Themner, Anders, ed. 2017. *Warlord Democrats in Africa: Ex-Military Leaders and Electoral Politics.* Chicago: University of Chicago Press.

Thomas, Ward. 2001. *The Ethics of Destruction: Norms and Force in International Relations.* Ithaca, NY: Cornell University Press.

Tilly, Charles. 2003. *The Politics of Collective Violence.* New York: Cambridge University Press.

Toft, Monica Duffy. 2010. *Securing the Peace: The Durable Settlement of Civil Wars.* Princeton, NJ: Princeton University Press.

Tomz, Michael, Jessica Weeks, and Keren Yarhi-Milo. 2020. "Public Opinion and Decisions about Military Force in Democracies." *International Organization* 74 (1): 119–143.

Trainor, Bernard E. 1987. "Main Contra Faction Unveils Strategy for War." *New York Times,* January 22.

Trejo, Guillermo, Juan Albarracín, and Lucía Tiscornia. 2015. "Breaking State Impunity in Post-Authoritarian Regimes: Why Transitional Justice Processes Deter Criminal Violence in New Democracies." *Journal of Peace Research* 55 (6): 787–809.

Trudeau, Robert H. 1992. "Guatemala." In *Political Parties of the Americas, 1980s to 1990s: Canada, Latin America, and the West Indies,* edited by Charles D. Ameringer, 333–348. Westport, CT: Greenwood.

———. 1993. *Guatemalan Politics: The Popular Struggle for Democracy.* Boulder, CO: Lynne Rienner.

TVM Television Maputo. 1994. "The Election Campaigns, BBC Summary of the World Broadcasts."

United Nations Commission on the Truth for El Salvador. 1993. "From Madness to Hope: The 12-Year War in El Salvador." Report of the Commission on the Truth for El Salvador. S/25500. https://www.usip.org/sites/default/files/file/ElSalvador-Report.pdf.

United Nations Peacebuilding Commission. 2009. "Report of the Secretary-General on Peacebuilding in the Immediate Aftermath of Conflict: Report of the Peacebuilding Commission."

United States Information Agency (USIA). 1991. "USIA Poll # 1991-I91049: Guatemala Opinion, 1991." Roper #31084451, Version 2. Consultoría Interdisciplinaria en Desarrollo S.A.-CID/ Gallup. Cornell University, Ithaca, NY: Roper Center for Public Opinion Research.

———. 2000. "Government/Political Leaders Poll."

URNG. 1995. "Guatemala, propuesta a la sociedad. Cuatro objetivos, nueve cambios, cuatro prioridades." *Mimeo*, April.

U.S. Congress, Subcommittees on International Organizations of the Committee on International Relations. 1977. "Religious Persecution in El Salvador, 95th Congress, 1st session." July 21 and 29.

U.S. Department of Defense. 1991. "URNG-Government Dialog Is the Number One Concern of Guatemalan Officers." Declassified Cable.

———. 1994. "URNG Strength as of October 1994." DOI: 941028. Item no. 10250. Digital National Security Archive.

U.S. Department of State. 1990. "Guatemala: Presidential Election." Confidential Cable from U.S. Embassy, Guatemala, October 4. C-ALO-15805, State 333790.

U.S. Department of State. 1984. "Sandinista Elections in Nicaragua." October 30. Digital National Security Archive.

U.S. Department of State, Bureau of International Narcotics and Law Enforcement Affairs Narcotics Reward Program. 2001–2009. "WANTED: Luis Antonio Lozada."

U.S. Department of State, Guatemala Embassy. 1983. "Guatemala to Secretary of State: Analysis of Rios Montt Government after Eleven Months, February 1983." Declassified cable no. 82GUATEM01353.

———. 1997. "Big Rios Rally: More Fun Than a Pocket-Picking Monkey on a Sunday Afternoon." December 16. Doc. no. 90GUATEM12016.

U.S. Department of State, Nicaragua Embassy. 1984. "Nicaraguan Elections: All Over but the Shouting." Confidential cable, November 2. Digital National Security Archive.

———. 1990. "Text of the Speech Delivered by the President of Nicaragua, Daniel Ortega Saavedra to the People of Nicaragua on February 26, 1990." Digital National Security Archive.

U.S. Embassy Managua. 1984. "The Electoral Process in Nicaragua." Declassified cable.

"US State Department Reports." https://www.state.gov/j/drl/rls/hrrpt/.

Vaishnav, Milan. 2017. *When Crime Pays: Money and Muscle in Indian Politics*. New Haven, CT: Yale University Press.

Van Dyck, Brandon. 2014. "Why Party Organization Still Matters: The Workers' Party in Northeastern Brazil." *Latin American Politics and Society* 56 (2): 1–26.

Verdad Abierta. 2019. "Rutas del conflicto, cinco años de memoria y innovación."

Vicente, Pedro C. 2014. "Is Vote Buying Effective? Evidence from a Field Experiment in West Africa." *Economic Journal* 124 (574): 356–387.

Vickers, George R. 1990. "A Spider's Web." *NACLA Report on the Americas* 24 (1): 19–27.

Vickers, George, Jack Spence, and Melrose Huff. 1994. "Elections: The Right Consolidates Power." *NACLA Report on the Americas* 28 (1): 6–11.

Vigdor, Neil. 2020. "Conway Says the More Violence Erupts, 'the Better It Is' for Trump's Re-election Prospects." *New York Times*, August 27.

Villalobos, Joaquín Hueso. 1984. "Why Is the FMLN Fighting?" *Radio Venceremos*.

———. 1999. *Sin vencedores ni vencidos: Pacificación y reconciliación en El Salvador*. San Salvador: Instituto para un Nuevo El Salvador.

Villamizar, Daniel Mera. 2019. "La 'alerta roja' de Semana como llamado a la seguridad democrática." *El Espectador*, April 20.

Vinjamuri, Leslie, and Jack Snyder. 2015. "Law and Politics in Transitional Justice." *Annual Review of Political Science* 18 (1): 303–327.

Visconti, Giancarlo. 2020. "Policy Preferences after Crime Victimization: Panel and Survey Evidence from Latin America." *British Journal of Political Science* 50 (4): 1481–1495.

Vollhardt, Johanna Ray, Lucas B. Mazur, and Magali Lemahieu. 2014. "Acknowledgement after Mass Violence: Effects on Psychological Well-Being and Intergroup Relations." *Group Processes & Intergroup Relations* 17 (3): 306–323.

Wade, Christine J. 2008. "El Salvador: Contradictions of Neoliberalism and Building Sustainable Peace." *International Journal of Peace Studies* 13 (2): 15–32.

Walker, Thomas W. 1982. *Nicaragua in Revolution*. New York: Praeger.

———, ed. 1985. *Nicaragua: The First Five Years*. New York: Praeger.

———. 1991. "Introduction." In *Revolution & Counterrevolution in Nicaragua*, edited by Thomas W. Walker. Boulder, CO: Westview.

Walter, Barbara F. 1999. "Designing Transitions from Civil War: Demobilization, Democratization, and Commitments to Peace." *International Security* 24 (1): 127–155.

———. 2002. *Committing to Peace: The Successful Settlement of Civil Wars*. Princeton, NJ: Princeton University Press.

———. 2004. "Does Conflict Beget Conflict? Explaining Recurring Civil War." *Journal of Peace Research* 41 (3): 371–388.

———. 2017. "The Extremist's Advantage in Civil Wars." *International Security* 42 (2): 7–39.

Wantchekon, Leonard. 1999a. "On the Nature of First Democratic Elections." *Journal of Conflict Resolution* 43 (2): 245–258.

———. 1999b. "Strategic Voting in Conditions of Political Instability: The 1994 Elections in El Salvador." *Comparative Political Studies* 32 (7): 810–834.

———. 2004. "The Paradox of 'Warlord' Democracy: A Theoretical Investigation." *American Political Science Review* 98 (1): 17–33.

Wasow, Omar. 2020. "Agenda Seeding: How 1960s Black Protests Moved Elites, Public Opinion and Voting." *American Political Science Review* 114 (3): 638–659.

Watt, Nigel. 2008. *Burundi: Biography of a Small African Country*. London: Hurst.

Weaver, Eric, and William A. Barnes. 1991. "Opposition Parties and Coalitions." In *Revolution and Counterrevolution in Nicaragua*, edited by Thomas W. Walker, 117–142. Boulder, CO: Westview.

Weber, Max. 1946. "Politics as a Vocation." In *From Max Weber: Essays in Sociology*, edited by H. H. Gerth and C. Wright Mills. New York: Oxford University Press.

Webre, Stephen Andrew. 1979. *José Napoleón Duarte and the Christian Democratic Party in San Salvadoran Politics, 1960–72*. Baton Rouge: Louisiana State University Press.

Weghorst, Keith R., and Staffan I. Lindberg. 2013. "What Drives the Swing Voter in Africa?" *American Journal of Political Science* 57 (3): 717–734.

Weingast, Barry R. 1997. "The Political Foundations of Democracy and the Rule of the Law." *American Political Science Review* 91 (2): 245–263.

Weinstein, Jeremy. 2007. *Inside Rebellion: The Politics of Insurgent Violence*. New York: Cambridge University Press.

Weld, Kirsten. 2014. *Paper Cadavers: The Archives of Dictatorship in Guatemala*. Durham, NC: Duke University Press.

Werner, Suzanne. 1999. "The Precarious Nature of Peace: Resolving the Issues, Enforcing the Settlement and Renegotiating the Terms." *American Journal of Political Science* 43 (3): 912–934.

Weyland, Kurt. 1999. "Neoliberal Populism in Latin America and Eastern Europe." *Comparative Politics* 31 (4): 379–401.

———. 2000. "A Paradox of Success? Determinants of Political Support for President Fujimori." *International Studies Quarterly* 44 (3): 481–502.

White, Alastair. 1973. *El Salvador*. Boulder, CO: Westview.

White, Peter B. 2020. "The Perils of Peace: Civil War Peace Agreements and Military Coups." *Journal of Politics* 82 (1): 104–118.

"Who's Who in the 1995 Elections." 1995. Guatemala News and Information Bureau Archive. https://dpul.princeton.edu/catalog/a45603b044eec7cfc05acb96d7d66b79.

Wilkinson, Daniel. 2002. *Silence on the Mountain: Stories of Terror, Betrayal, and Forgetting in Guatemala*. Durham, NC: Duke University Press.

Wilkinson, Steven. 2004. *Votes and Violence: Electoral Competition and Ethnic Riots in India*. Cambridge: Cambridge University Press.

Williams, Laron K., Michael T. Koch, and Jason M. Smith. 2013. "The Political Consequences of Terrorism: Terror Events, Casualties, and Government Duration." *International Studies Perspectives* 14 (3): 343–361.

Williams, Philip J., and Guillermina Seri. 2003. "The Limits of Reformism: The Rise and Fall of Christian Democracy in El Salvador and Guatemala." In *Christian Democracy in Latin America: Electoral Competition and Regime Conflicts*, edited by Scott Mainwaring and Timothy R. Scully, 301–329. Stanford, CA: Stanford University Press.

Williams, Philip J., and Knut Walter. 1997. *Militarization and Demilitarization in El Salvador's Transition to Democracy*. Pittsburgh, PA: University of Pittsburgh Press.

Wittman, Donald. 1977. "Candidates with Policy Preferences: A Dynamic Model." *Journal of Economic Theory* 14 (1): 180–189.

Wolf, Sonja. 2009. "Subverting Democracy: Elite Rule and the Limits to Political Participation in Post-War El Salvador." *Journal of Latin American Studies* 41 (3): 429–465.

Wood, Elisabeth Jean. 2000a. "Civil War and the Transformation of Elite Representation in El Salvador." In *Conservative Parties, the Right, and Democracy in Latin America*, edited by Kevin J. Middlebrook, 223–254. Baltimore, MD: Johns Hopkins University Press.

———. 2000b. *Forging Democracy from Below: Insurgent Transitions in South Africa and El Salvador*. New York: Cambridge University Press.

———. 2003. *Insurgent Collective Action and Civil War in El Salvador*. Cambridge: Cambridge University Press.

Wood, Reed. 2014. "Opportunities to Kill or Incentives for Restraint? Rebel Capabilities, the Origins of Support, and Civilian Victimization in Civil War." *Conflict Management and Peace Science* 31 (5): 461–480.

Yanhaas. 2018a. "La Gran Encuesta: Elecciones 2018, Enero 2018." Bogotá.

———. 2018b. "La Gran Encuesta: Elecciones 2018, Mayo 2018." Bogotá.

Yarce, Elizabeth. 2002. "Medellín: 20 años de llanto en las calles." *El Colombiano*, April 30.

———. 2003. "Accionar de Auc se extiende en Medellín." *El Colombiano*, February 28.

Yashar, Deborah J. 1997. *Demanding Democracy: Reform and Reaction in Costa Rica and Guatemala, 1870s–1950s*. Stanford, CA: Stanford University Press.

———. 2018. *Homicidal Ecologies: Illicit Economies and Complicit States in Latin America*. New York: Cambridge University Press.

Youkee, Mat. 2018. "Five Takeaways from Colombia's May 27 Presidential Election." *Americas Quarterly*, May 28.

Zaller, John R. 1992. *The Nature and Origins of Mass Public Opinion*. Cambridge: Cambridge University Press.

Zamora, Rúben. 1998. *Heridas que no cierran: Los partidos políticos en la post-guerra*. San Salvador: FLACSO.

Zarate, Andrea, and Nicholas Casey. 2016. "Keiko Fujimori, Ex-President's Daughter, Heads to Runoff in Peru." *New York Times*, April 10.

Ziblatt, Daniel. 1998. "The Adaptation of Ex-Communist Parties to Post-Communist East Central Europe: A Comparative Study of the East German and Hungarian Ex-Communist Parties." *Communist and Post-Communist Studies* 31 (2): 119–137.

INDEX

Page numbers in *italics* indicate figures and tables.

ABC News, 200

advertising campaign, 289n115

Agencia Nacional de Seguridad Salvadoreña, 115

agenda manipulation, 54

Alape, Pastor, on mitigation of violence by FARC, 97, 98

Alejos, Sebastián, FMLN campaign manager, 121, 137, 141

Allison, Michael, 309n225

amnesty, 160, 191, 244, 245, 246, 293n6

anarchy, 17, 33; civil war and, 285n46; Colombian campaign and, 95, 96; end of, 261; Guatemalan campaign and, 173; strongman justification and, 258

anger, 294n22

Angola: subnational wartime victimization, 227, 228; violence, war outcomes and postwar elections, 271

ANN. *See* New Nation Alliance (ANN)

Anti-Sandinistas Popular Militia, 197

Árbenz, Jacobo, reforms in Guatemala, 159

Arévalo, Juan José, reforms in Guatemala, 159

ARENA party, 1, 115, 277n8; advertisements, 124, 125, 126, 133, 133, 134, 136; campaign plan, 129; campaign strategy, 122–35; candidates, 130–31; determinants of vote choice (1999), 150; internal groupings, 305n117; issue priming, 129; maps of FMLN violence, 135; messaging objectives, 123; partisan ownership of security,

149–50, 153; popular support, 148; positional strategy, 127; presidential slogans, 130; programmatic strategy, 122; security as valence strategy, 122–27; signing of peace accords, 124, 126; slogan, 122, 307n171; targeting moderate voters, 128–29; undermining FMLN's ownership of security valence issue, 131–35; winning security, swing and victimized vote, 145–47; winning some victims votes, 147–48

armed conflicts, threat of violence in, 11

attribution error theory, 288n100

Baldizón Méndez, Manuel Antonio, 192

ballot, secret versus open, 104, 105

Bangladesh, 227, 230, 271

Baum, Matthew, on public opinion toward use of force, 10

Believers, unconditional party loyalty and mobilization, 38

belligerent parties: burnishing their security credentials, 33–34; civil war and, 285n46; claim of Restrained Leviathan, 28–37; definition of, 18, 213; example of offsetting the violent past, 31–32; laundering their reputations, 28–33; leadership selection, 39; model of reference-dependent preferences on past atrocity, 29–30; political persuasion and communication, 44–45; predictors of performance, 13;

belligerent parties (*continued*)
programs and positional politics, 37–38;
propaganda of, 285n45; signaling
restraint from future victimization,
34–36; successors, over time, 52–54;
successor parties and, 13–14; valence
advantages, 36–37

belligerent-tied politicians, influence on
public safety and social services, 246–51

Berger, Óscar: PAN's candidate, 167; on
security issue, 166

Berinsky, Adam, on public opinion toward
use of force, 10

Berlin Wall, 117

Bianchi, Francisco, 313n41

Bicesse Accords, 241

Black Lives Matter, 329n22

bloodstained parties: elections of, 14;
electoral successes of, 1–3

Boix, Carles, on electoral institutions, 20

Bolsonaro, Jair, Brazil, 257

Brancati, Dawn, on belligerents accepting
election results, 5

Brazil, Bolsonaro of, 257

Buhari, Muhammadu, Nigeria, 257

Burundi, ethnic war, 234–35

Bush, Sarah, on election violence, 278n41

Bustamante, Enrique Borgo, 130

Bustillo, Juan Rafael, war criminal, 154

Cabal, María Fernanda, Uribista senator, 95

Calderón Sol, Armando, 130

campaign information, TV coverage,
295n49

Carpio, Ramiro de León, 175

Castro, Vanessa, on mixed middle voters in
Nicaragua, 199

Catholics, 182

CDN. *See* Democratic Coordinating
Committee (CDN)

CEH. *See* Comisión para el Escalarecimiento Histórico (CEH)

Central America: party strategy in, 110–14;
war outcomes in, 12–13

Centro Democrático (CD), 100; as electoral
vehicle, 94; fear of war recurrence and
votes for, 106; Uribista party, 94–96

Chamorro, Violeta, UNO leader, 200

Chapultepec Accords, 117

Christian Democratic Party (PDC),
Duarte, 116, 119–20

Christian Democrats, 156, 174, 175

Civil Self-Defense Patrols (PACs), Ríos
Montt and, 160

Civil War, General Grant and US, 34

Civil War Successor Party (CWSP), 13, 14,
16, 61, 212; correlates of, success around
the world, 219, 220–21, 269; cross-national
cases, 229; dataset, 237–39; frequency of
war outcomes in dataset, 217; postwar
elections, 242; summary statistics of
dataset, 268

clientelism: ARENA and FMLN and, 153;
voting determinant, 101, 102, 103; war
outcome and, 237, 238

Close, David, on Sandinistas' victor
advantage, 202

coercion: Colombia, 103–6; El Salvador,
150–51; Guatemala, 187–88; Nicaragua, 197

Cohen, Herman, on UNITA, 242

Cold War, 114, 117, 281n5

Colom, Álvaro, 191; on URNG party, 177, 178

Colombia, 49, 59; determinants of vote
choice, 101–3; elections (2018), 12;
experimental design of rebel and government belligerent party strategies, 79–80;
fieldwork in, 12; governance records of
paramilitary mayors, 247–48, 249, 250–51;
hypotheses of government armed forces
in experiment as winning belligerent, 82;
manifesto of nonbelligerent party in, 27;
mitigation experiment, 70–74; narratives
experiment, 74–78; National Planning
Department, 66; peace process in, 59;
probability of being elected for government belligerent candidate, 87; probability of being preferred on security for
government belligerent candidates, 84, 85;

sampling strategy, 67; subnational wartime victimization, 226, 227; survey, 64, 65–67; survey experiments, 68–70; survey of victims and nonvictims, 12, 68; victim status, 293n7; violence, war outcomes and postwar elections, 271

Colombia Humana, 91; Petro of, 98–99; voting determinants, 102

Colombian Center for Historical Memory, 107

Colombian Federation of Victims of the FARC (FEVCOL), 89

Colombian National Comptroller's Victim Survey, 67

Colombian Supreme Court, 246, 328n18

Colombia's 2018 elections, 90–100; coercion in, 103–6; equilibrium versus nonequilibrium party strategies and performance in, 99–100; Fajardo as Rule Abider, 91; FARC strategy of abuse-mitigating Radicalism, 91, 92, 97–98; ignorance and fog of war, 106–8; information and judgments about atrocities, 108; parties' strategies and electoral implications, 92; party system, 91, 108–9; Petro as Tactical Immoderate, 91, 92, 98–99; Santismo and Juan Manuel Santos, 90–91; Santismo strategy of Rule Abider, 91, 92, 92–94; Uribismo and Álvaro Uribe, 90–91; Uribismo strategy of Restrained Leviathan, 91, 92, 94–96; voting determinants, 101, 102, 103

Comisión para el Escalarecimiento Histórico (CEH), 160

Common Alternative Revolutionary Force (FARC), 98. See FARC (Revolutionary Armed Forces of Colombia)

communication, political persuasion and, 44–45

Communist Party, 115; Cuban Revolution and, 114

conflict: affected populations, 66; justifications for, 74, 75; understandings of, 88–89

Consultoría Interdisciplinaria en Desarrollo S.A., 121, 164, 302n10

Contra War, 197, 198, 205–6, 207, 208

core voter model, 287n81

Corstange, Daniel, Syria, 300n146

Couto, Mia, terror and democratic elections, 103

COVID-19 global pandemic, 70

crimes against humanity, 298n109

Cristiani, Alfredo: ARENA candidate, 305n122, 306n137; ARENA president, 124, 128, 131, 134; ARENA party, 153; on peace, 143, 144; on power balance, 310n235; on security, 145–47

Croatia: ethnic war, 235–36; HDZ (Croatian Democratic Union) party, 236, 327n80; Homeland War, 236, 327n82

Cuadra, Joaquín, Sandinista network, 204

Cuba, 115; Communist Party, 114

CWSP. See Civil War Successor Party (CWSP)

Dada, Héctor, on ARENA and FMLN platforms, 138

D'Aubuisson, Roberto: ARENA's founder, 120–21, 127, 154–55; party leadership, 130; U.S. Embassy on, 124

death squad, 115, 116; alliance, 115; FMLN referring to ARENA as members of, 141; networks of, 1, 120

de la Calle, Humberto: campaign of, 99–100; security plan of, 93–94; voting determinants for, 102

democracy: characterization of, 19; democratic transitions, 279n53; founding election influencing postwar, 6–7, 61, 244–45, 246

Democratic Convergence, 120

Democratic Coordinating Committee (CDN), election fairness, 198

democratic elections, 19–20

Democratic Republic of Congo (DRC), 286n51

Democratic Revolutionary Alliance, 197

demonstration elections, wartime, 20

Dix, Robert, on civil conflict in Colombia, 233

Domínguez-Trujillo, Ramfis, dictator's grandson, 257

dominance principle, 172, 314n86

Dominican Republic, Trujillo of, 257

Downes, Alexander, on public reaction to civilian targeting in war, 10

Duarte, José Napoleón, Christian Democratic Party (PDC), 116, 119–20

Duque, Iván: appointments of conflict-deniers by, 297n77; election win (2018), 70; on security, 95; in 2018, untouched by scandal, 96; voting determinants, 102

Duterte, Rodrigo, Philippines, 257

economic: voting and, 10; voting determinants, 101, 102, 103

education: non-paramilitary and paramilitary politicians and, 248; paramilitary politician win on, 251; public goods outcomes and spending, 249

Eguia, Jon: on disadvantaged party, 41; on tactical extremism, 42

Eichenberg, Richard, on public opinion toward use of force, 10

El Diario de Hoy (newspaper), 121, 133, 135

election(s): advancing justice, 260–61; democratic, 19–20; founding results influencing postwar justice and democracy, 244–45, 246; fundamentals of, 10; helping keep the peace, 259–60; postwar, 271–72; wars and, 24; World Values Survey, 273. See also Colombia's 2018 elections; El Salvador; Guatemala; Nicaragua

electoral incumbency, controlling state apparatus and media, 44–45

electoral institutions, 20–21

Electoral Law of 1984, Nicaragua, 198

electoral outcomes: alternative explanations for, 48–51; in cleaner and less clean elections, 224; correlates of success, 269;

following ethnic vs. nonethnic conflicts, 232; intimidation of voters, 49; organizational strength, 51; parties playing the wrong hand, 46–48; peace or war recurrence and, 52; political preferences and, 50; postwar, 55–56; power upsets, and remilitarization, 242–43; subnational data on, 271–72; with clientelistic and programmatic linkages, 238; war outcomes and, 15, 26, 55–56, 258

electoral success, 22; of bloodstained parties, 1–3; of violent victors, 5

electoral system: actors designing, 20; analysis of, 219; in El Salvador, 118, 121–22, 132, 146–48, 156; Guatemala, 158, 162–64, 183, 188, 193; Latin America, 56; median voter theorem and, 286n68; Nicaragua, 195, 197, 199–201; political power sharing and, 215; two-round, 323n13

electoral targeting, prioritizing swing voters, 38–39

ELN. See National Liberation Army (ELN)

El Nuevo Diario (newspaper), 200

El Salvador, 57, 155–57; alternative explanations, 148–51; ARENA's strategy to campaign, 122–35; balance of atrocities, 116–17; characterizing the voters, 118; Christian Democratic Party (PDC), 119–20; civil war belligerent successor parties, 120–21; civil war of, 114–21; credit for peace, 143–44; data sources, 121; determinants of vote choice (1994), 150; FMLN's strategy to campaign, 135–41; justice, crime and security brand, 152–53; mass violence in, 155–56; media and persuasion, 142–43; military draw, 13, 110; National Conciliation Party (PCN), 115, 154–55; nonbelligerent party, 119–20; party system, 153; peace, 151–52; popular support, 148; postwar democratic elections, 118; subnational war outcome, 228; subnational wartime victimization, 226, 227; violence, war outcomes and postwar elections, 271; voters, 143–48;

voters' understanding of war outcome, 117; wartime violence, 144–45; winning security, swing and victimized vote, 145–47; winning some victims votes, 147–48

endogeneity, 218–19; endogeneity problem, 24; spuriousness and, 218–19

Escobar, Roberto, PCN party, 154

ethnic wars, 231–37; Burundi, 234–35; Croatia, 235–36; East Timor, 236, Iraq, 235; Kosovo, 327n83; Namibia, 236–37; Rwanda, 233–34; Sri Lanka, 236; war outcomes and vote shares, 232

Fajardo, Sergio: Colombian election, 91, 100; strategy of abuse-punishing Rule Abider, 91

false positives, 64, 88, 292n4

Farabundo Martí National Liberation Front (FMLN), 115, 117, 213; ARENA undermining FMLN's security issue ownership, 131–35; campaign strategy, 135–41; candidates, 140–41; cartoon campaign ads, 138; constituent organizations of, 306n161; determinants of vote choice (1994), 150; factionalization of, 307n175, 307–8n180; owning the security valence issue, 136–37, 153; partisan ownership of security, 149–50; popular support of, 148; positional strategy, 137–39; slogan "First, the People", 139, 140; targeting the moderate voter, 139–40; valence strategy, 136; winning security, swing and victimized vote, 146–47; winning some victims votes, 147

FARC (Revolutionary Armed Forces of Colombia), 68–69; Colombian Federation of Victims of the FARC (FEVCOL), 89; combat boots, 81; Common Alternative Revolutionary Force (FARC) party, 65, 293n6; experimental design of rebel belligerent party strategies, 80; hypotheses of experiment as losing belligerent, 82; mitigation and contrition narratives, 77; peace process with, 65, 293,n5; political campaign, 88; probability of being elected, 87; rebels, 1, 24, 59; security improvements, 294n24; strategy as abuse-mitigating Radicalism, 91, 92, 97–98; war violence 107–8; war outcome between Colombian government and, 68–69

Farjardo, Sergio, voting determinants, 102

Fearon, James, on bargaining and war recurrence, 279n47

Feaver, Peter, on public opinion toward use of force, 10

Federalist No. 51 (Madison), 28, 169, 278n26

FEVCOL. See Colombian Federation of Victims of the FARC (FEVCOL)

Finnemore, Martha, on logic of appropriateness and justice, 7

Flores, Thomas, on democratic elections after conflict, 7

FMLN. See Farabundo Martí National Liberation Front (FMLN)

fog of war, 2–3; ignorance about atrocities and, 106–8

Fortna, Virginia Page, on postwar democratization, 6

founding elections, 22

FRELETIN (Revolutionary Front for an Independent East Timor), 236, 327n84

FRG. See Guatemalan Republican Front (FRG)

FRUD (Front for the Restoration of Unity and Democracy), 323n11; Djibouti, 213

FSLN. See Sandinista National Liberation Front (FSLN)

Fujimori, Alberto, legacy of, 257, 292n174

Fujimori, Keiko, Peru, 257

Galindo, David Escobar, Salvadoran government peace negotiator, 117

García-Sánchez, Miguel, attitudes about military, 105

Garrard-Burnett, Virginia: on URNG threat in 1982, 159; on victimized vote, 179

Gelpi, Christopher, on public opinion toward use of force, 10

genocide, Rwanda 1994, 233–34

Giovannoni, Francesco: on disadvantaged party, 41; tactical extremism, 42

Godoy, Virgilio, PLI candidate, 204, 320n41

Goebertus, Juanita: on arrogance of FARC, 97; on postwar party and voter strategies, 64

González, Remigio Ángel, media and FRG, 178

Gordillo Martínez, Luís, 313n41

governance, impact of elections on, 8–9, 61–62

government belligerent successor party, definition of, 18, 213

government victory, 23

Granados, Héctor Rosada, peace negotiator, 181

Grant, Ulysses S.: Civil War and presidential candidate, 34; Harper's Weekly ad, 35; military service of, 286n57

Greene, Kenneth, on birth defects of party's origins, 47

Green Party, manifesto of, in Colombia, 27

Groeling, Tim, on public opinion toward use of force, 10

Grzymala-Busse, Anna, on successor parties and contrition, 289n10

Guardado, Facundo: on peace, 143; rewriting of history of war, 124

Guatemala, 13, 57, 156, 157; balance of atrocities, 160–61; blame for wartime violence, 180; characterizing the voters, 162–63; civil war belligerent successor parties, 163–64; coercion, 187–88; credit for peace, 179–80; data sources, 164; determinants of vote choice, 189; FRG (Guatemalan Republican Front), 163–64; FRG postwar vote share and voter ideology, 184; FRG's party strategy, 167–76; government violence and FRG vote share, 183; government relative victory, 110, 158–59; ideology and economic voting, 188–90; incumbency, 186–87; media and persuasion, 178–79; National Advancement Party (PAN),

163; organizational assets, 187; PAN's party strategy, 165–67; partisan issue ownership, 186; party system, 192; popular support, 185; postwar democratic elections, 161–62; preference for belligerent's security, 180–81; security issue and, 149; subnational wartime victimization, 226, 227; URNG's party strategy, 176–78; violence, war outcomes and postwar elections, 271; voters, 179–85; war outcomes, 161; war setting the stage, 159–64; wartime government atrocities, 184; winning security, swing and victimized votes, 181–83; winning some victims' votes, 183–85. See also Guatemalan Republican Front (FRG); Guatemalan National Revolutionary Unity (URNG)

Guatemalan National Revolutionary Unit (URNG), 159; candidates, 178; positional strategy, 176–77; targeting immoderate voter, 177–78; valence strategy, 176–77; war outcomes, 161. See also Guatemala

Guatemalan News and Information Bureau Archive, 164

Guatemalan Republican Front (FRG), 1; candidates, 174–76; claiming competence on security, 168–69; determinants of vote choice, 189; FRG vs. PAN's security programs, 170–72; hand coding of security platforms, 172; issue ownership, 186; issue priming, 172–73; logo, 168; positional strategy, 173; public preference for strong-arm government, 317n168; targeting moderate voter, 174; valence strategy, 167–68; war violence as "the situation", 315n125

Guatemalan Tribunal Supremo Electoral, 183

Guatemalism, FRG's version of nationalism, 174

Guerrilla Army of the Poor (EGP) rebels, 175

guerrilla violence: terrorism, 282n9. See also FARC (Revolutionary Armed Forces of Colombia)

Guido, Clemente, PCDN candidate, 204
Gustavo, Petro, strategy as Tactical
    Immoderation, 91, 92, 98–99

Hammond, Thomas, on campaign
    positioning, 54
Handál, Shafik, on FMLN campaign,
    139
Harper's Weekly (magazine), 34, 35
Hartzell, Caroline, on quality of postwar
    democracy, 7, 244
heresthetic, 26; definition, 284n7
Hoddie, Matthew, on quality of postwar
    democracy, 7, 244
Holland, Alisha, on partisan issue
    ownership in El Salvador, 149
Homeland War, Croatia, 236, 327n82
Honduras, Somoza National Guard
    members in, 197
Howell, William, on use of international
    force, 9
Huang, Reyko: on postwar democracy, 6;
    rebel public goods and financing
    variables, 218–19
Human Rights Watch, 277n15, 292n4
Humes, Brian, on campaign positioning, 54
Humphreys, Macartan, on wartime
    violence, 324n27
Huntington, Samuel: on principle of legal
    accountability in democracy, 27; on
    strong parties born of war, 52; on
    torturer problem, 8
Hutu genocide, Rwanda, 233–34
Hyde, Susan, on election monitors, 283n30

ideology: as vote determinant, 50, 317n194;
    voting determinants, 101, *102*, 103
immoderation, explanations for, 288n103
India, 258; subnational wartime victimiza-
    tion, 226, 227; violence, war outcomes
    and postwar elections, 271
Indonesia, 231, 326n53; subnational wartime
    victimization, 227; violence, war
    outcomes and postwar elections, 271

information and communications
    technology (ICT), 289n120
Instituto de Historia de Nicaragua y
    Centroamérica, 200
Instituto Doxa, 200
Instituto Universitario de Opinión Pública
    (IUDOP), 121, 145, 302n10
Integral System for Truth, Justice,
    Reparation, and no Repetition, 93
International Criminal Court, 259
International Foundation for Electoral
    Systems, 118
International Organization for Migration
    (IOM), 277n17
IRA, 24
Iraq, ethnic war, 235
issue priming, 54

jail time for perpetrators, mitigation
    experiment, 74, 75
Junta de Gobierno, 198
Junta of National Reconstruction, 200
justice: advancing, 260–61; El Salvador,
    152–53; founding elections influencing
    postwar, 7–8, 244–45, 246; Guatemala,
    191–92; impact of elections on, 61;
    Nicaragua 196; transitional, 289n109
Justice Cascade, 252
Just War Doctrine principle, 328n3

Kagame, Paul, Rwandan Patriotic Front
    (RPF), 234
Kertzer, Joshua, on security and political
    behavior, 9
Kuchuj Voz Ciudadana, Guatemala, 175,
    315n123

La Prensa (newspaper), 200, 205
La Prensa Gráfica (newspaper), 121, 133
Latin America, 49, case selection of, 56–57
Latin American Public Opinion Project
    (LAPOP), 100, 121, 144, 147, 151, 164, 181,
    184, 188, 302n10
Latin American Studies Association, 319n31

Lau, Pedro Palma, guerrilla commander, 175

law and order, 257, 258, 329n21; ARENA's, 123, 124, 146; FRG's, 168, 172, 174, 180; Uribismo's, 96, 266

leadership, party elite and candidates, 39–40

leadership valence, definition, 288n91

LeBas, Adrienne, on us-them distinctions in conflict, 38

lemmings, view of public as, 106

Leviathan: Hobbes's term, 33, 35; strategy, 53

Levitsky, Steven, on successor party cohesion, 39

liberal democracy, 245

liberation theory, 114

Liberation Tigers of Tamil Eelam (LTTE), 213, 236

Liberia, 241; subnational wartime victimization, 227; violence, war outcomes and postwar elections, 272

Lipset, Seymour, on electoral institutions, 20

logic of consequences, justice, 8, 255

logic of appropriateness, justice, 7–8

Loxton, James, on El Salvador, 120–21, 154, on Guatemala, 165

Lucas García, Benedicto, 179, 313n41; political platform, 185; repression under, 175; scorched earth strategy, 168

Lucas García, Romeo, Guatemala, 159, 165

Lupu, Noam, on definition of electoral success, 22

Lyons, Terrence, on Rwandan Patriotic Front (RPF), 234

Mainwaring, Scott, on successor parties, 329n1

Magaloni, Beatriz, on electoral coercion, 278n22

McCrary Test, regression discontinuity design, 276

McDermott, Monika L., on impact of military backgrounds on voters, 34

Madison, James: on design of government, 28, 278n26; on party's credibility, 34

managerial competency, belligerent party claiming, 36–37

Marcos, Ferdinand, Philippines, 257

Martí, Farabundo, communist peasant uprising by, 114

Matanock, Aila: attitudes about military, 105; on postwar democratic elections, 7

Mayan holocaust, 160

media, El Salvador, 142–43

Medrano, José Alberto, "grandfather of the death squads", 120

Meléndez, Manuel: ARENA's campaign strategist, 121, 132; on Zamora as FMLN candidate, 141

Menchú, Rigoberta, on Guatemalan elections, 162

military balance of power, war and, 14

military draw, 21, 23; ARENA and FMLN, 135, 141, 142; in campaigns following, 45; FARC and, 68, 81, 86; El Salvador, 13, 110. *See also* El Salvador

military outcomes: continuum of, 23; public reactions, 10; terms, 23

Misión Observatorio Electoral, 104, 300n143

mitigation experiment: average treatment effects (ATEs), 72, 73, 74; heterogenous treatment effects, 74, 75; experimental set-up, 71–72

model(s): core voter, 287n81; reference-dependent preferences on past atrocity, 29–30; spatial voting, 286n68; swing voter, 287n81

Monsanto, Pablo, on Guatemalan elections, 162

Movimiento de Acción Popular Marxista Leninista, 200, 321n69

Mozambique, 287n78; subnational war outcome, 228; violence, war outcomes and postwar elections, 272

Multinomial Naive Bayes, 113; algorithm, 301n7

multipartyism, 21

Nalepa, Monika, on logic of consequences and justice, 8
Namibia, 323n13; ethnic war, 236–37
narratives experiment, 74–78; military contrition, 76, 77; military mitigation, 76, 77; order effects of narratives, 77; rebel contrition, 76, 77; rebel mitigation, 76, 77
Nast, Thomas, cartoon by, 286n57
National Advancement Party (PAN), 161; determinants of vote choice, 189; FRG vs. PAN's security platforms, 170–72; Guatemala, 163; hand coding of security platforms, 172; party strategy, 165–67; positional strategy, 166; security issue, 165–66, 186; tangible policy proposals, 313n60; targeting moderate voter, 166–67; war outcomes, 161
National Center for Historical Memory, 75, 94
National Conciliation Party (PCN), 115, 128, 154–55
National Conservative party, Somoza dynasty and, 195
National Fund for Peace, 178
National Liberation Army (ELN), 69
National Revolutionary Movement, 120
National Security Council, 200
negative peace, 6, 252, 279n45
Nepal: subnational war outcome, 228; subnational wartime victimization, 226; violence, war outcomes and postwar elections, 272
New Nation Alliance (ANN), 164, 178
Nicaragua, 13, 57, 156; backdrop of war and peace, 195–200; balance of atrocities, 195–96; belligerent successor and nonbelligerent parties, 199–200; campaigning to secure the future, 201–5; candidates, 204–5; characterizing voters, 199; data sources, 200; Electoral Law of 1984, 198; electoral targeting, 203–4; peace in, 207–9, 323n109; persuasion, 205; positional strategies, 203; postwar democratic elections, 196–99; rebel victory, 110, 194, 206–9; security issue and, 149; valence strategies, 201–2; voters, 205–6; war outcome, 196
niche parties, 48, 290n132
Nigeria, Buhari of, 257
nonbelligerent parties, 282n19; claim as rule abider, 27–28; definition of, 213; description of, 19; El Salvador, 119–20; forgive and forget strategy, 290n131; leadership selection, 39–40; National Advancement Party (PAN), 163; political persuasion and communication, 44–45; programs and positional politics, 37–38; rule of law and, 260
Nooruddin, Irfan, on democratic elections after conflict, 7

observational survey data, 88–90
Organization of American States, 162, 187–88
Ortega, Daniel: depiction as "man of peace", 321n77; FSLN candidate, 204; Sandinista commander, 201

PACs. See Civil Self-Defense Patrols (PACs)
PAN. See National Advancement Party (PAN)
Panagopoulos, Costas, on impact of military backgrounds on voters, 34
Panebianco, Angelo, on believers, 38
paramilitaries: atrocities of, 2; governance records of mayors, 247–48, 250–51; offsetting violent past of, 31–32; scandal of politics and, 298n92
Partido Comunista de Nicaragua, 200
Partido Conservador Demócrata de Nicaragua (PCDN), 199–200, 202
Partido Liberal Independiente (PLI), 321n58; Nicaragua, 199–200, 202
Partido Liberal Nacionalista (PLN), Somoza's, 199
Partido Popular Social Cristiano, Nicaragua, 199–200
Partido Republicano Institucional (PRI), 318n210

Partido Socialista Nicaragüense, 200

parties: combinations of strategy on perceived competence on security, 265; issue ownership, 26; niche, 48; Party Manifesto Project variables, 267; playing the wrong hand, 46–48; political persuasion and communication, 44–45; reputation of, 26; strategies in Central America, 110–14; strategies of, 56–58; war influencing, 11–12

Party Manifesto Project (PMP), 113, 139, 173, 177, 203, 301n6; variables, 267

party system, 21; definition, 279n52

PCDN. See Partido Conservador Demócrata de Nicaragua (PCDN)

PCN. See National Conciliation Party (PCN)

PDC. See Christian Democratic Party (PDC)

peace: assessing risk of war recurrence, 243–44; cases of postconflict war and, 244; El Salvador, 151–52; Guatemala, 190–91; helping elections keep, 259–60; Nicaragua, 207–9; process in Colombia, 59

Peace Accords, 312n24

Peace Agreement Dataset, shagov variable, 214

peace and prosperity, fundamental drivers of elections, 10

peace-versus-justice debate, voters on, 7–8

Pedraz, Santiago, 191

Pérez Molina, Otto, 191, 192

Peru, 257; subnational wartime victimization, 227; violence, war outcomes and postwar elections, 272

Peters, Johanna: on Fajardo and Duque, 297n73; on Uribe, 298n92

Petro, Gustavo: Colombia Humana movement, 91; strategy and electoral implications, 92; as successful Tactical Immoderate, 92, 98–99

Pevehouse, Jon, on use of international force, 9

Philippines: Duterte of, 257; Marcos of, 257; subnational wartime victimization, 227; violence, war outcomes and postwar elections, 272

piloting of survey, 300n147

Plan Colombia, President Uribe and, 68–69

PLI. See Partido Liberal Independiente (PLI)

PLN. See Partido Liberal Nacionalista (PLN)

political behavior, security and, 9–10, 14, 255–56

political life after war: belligerent successor and nonbelligerent parties, 213; correlates of CWSP success around the world, 219, 220–21; cross-national data, 222–25; electoral coercion, 217–18, 224–25; electoral performance in cleaner and less clean elections, 224; ethnic wars, 231–37; global tracing of, 212–25; government belligerent vote shares, 223; patronage politics, 237; postwar election results, 214; rebel vote shares, 222; security voting, 229, 230, 231; selection and bias, 214–15; subnational data around the world, 225–28; war outcomes, 215–16, 217, 222, 223, 224; wartime violence, 216–17, 225

Political Parties of the Americas, 146

political party, definition of, 18

political persuasion, communication and, 44–45

politics, valence, 25–27

popular support, definition of, 24

Popular Social Christian Movement, 120

Portillo, Alfonso, 175; security credentials, 315n113

positional strategies, Nicaragua, 203

positional strategy: ARENA party, 127; FMLN, 137–39; FRG, 173; FSLN, 203; PCDN, 203; PAN, 166; URNG, 176–77

positive peace, 279n45

postwar concerns, voters, 16–18

postwar elections: correlates of remilitarization after, 274–75; sources of selection, 21–22; subnational data on, 271–72

postwar political order, founding of, 283n30

postwar politics: electoral success, 22; founding elections, 22 power balance, 291n148, 291n151; peace or war recurrence, 52

power of media, persuading voters, 4

Power-Sharing Event Dataset, 215

Prada, Alfonso, Santos's campaign, 99–100

Prather, Lauren, on election violence, 278n41

Press, Daryl, on public opinion toward use of force, 10

Prevost, Gary, on mixed middle voters in Nicaragua, 199

Princeton University archives, 164

programmatic versus clientelistic politics, 237, 238

proportional representation (PR), 21

Protestants, 182

Proyecto Interdiocesano de Recuperatión de la Memória Histórica (REMHI), 160

public goods, outcomes and spending, 249

public safety, elections of belligerent-tied politicians on, 246–51

Radicalism, FARC strategy, 91, 92, 97–98

Rajapaksa, Gotabaya, Sri Lanka, 257

Ramírez, Sandra: on success of belligerent party, 63; on violence of FARC, 97

Ramírez Mercado, Sergio, Ortega's running mate, 205

rebel: definition, 18; movements, 282n19; violence, 107, 108

rebel successor party, formation of, 18–19

rebel victory, 23

regression discontinuity (RD): design, 62, 246; McCrary Test, 276; public goods outcomes and spending, 249; security outcomes, 249; validating the design, 276

Reifler, Jason, on public opinion toward use of force, 10

relative government victory, 23

REMHI. See Proyecto Interdiocesano de Recuperación de la Memória Histórica (REMHI)

research design: democracy impact, 61; equilibrium party strategies after large-scale violence in war, 57; governance impact,
61–62; justice impact, 61; party strategies, 56–58; voter strategies, 58–60; war and peace impact, 60; war outcomes and postwar election results, 55–56. See also 54–62

Restrained Leviathan, 4, 12, 44, 47, 62, 261; attracting votes for military winner, 63; belligerent party as, 35; belligerent party's claim to security, 28–37, 90; strategy of, 40, 56, 57, 59, 60; Uribismo's strategy in Colombia, 91, 92, 94–96; violent victors running as, 254; voters and, 45–46

Restrained Leviathan vs. Tactical Immoderate experiment, 78–88; average marginal component effect (AMCE), 82–83; experimental design of government belligerent party strategies, 79; experimental design of rebel belligerent party strategies, 80; probability candidate considered competent on security, 85; probability of assigning credit for ending conflict, 86; probability of being elected (government belligerent candidates), 87; probability of being perceived competent on security, 83; winning belligerent (government armed forces), 82

Revolutionary Armed Forces of Colombia, 98. See also FARC and Common Alternative Revolutionary Force

Revolutionary Governing Junta, 115

riding the wave logic, 172, 314n87

Riker, William: heresthetic, 284n7; rhetoric of political persuasion, 44

Ríos Montt, Efraín, 160; credit for peace, 179–80; FRG on security, 168–69, 180–81; FRG's manifesto, 168; FRG's strongman, 174–76, 314n80; Guatemalan Republican Front (FRG), 1, 163–64; guilty of genocide, 312n16

robberies, security outcomes, 249

robustness checks, correlates of CWSP success, 269

Rokkan, Stein, on electoral institutions, 20

Rueschemeyer, Dietrich, on support for democracy, 7

Rule Abider(s), 44, 47, 62; nonbelligerent party's claim, 27–28; nonbelligerent party strategy, 45, 46; PAN in Guatemala, 167; PDC in El Salvador, 119–20; Santismo strategy in Colombia, 91, 92, 92–94; strategy, 56, 57, 59

rule of law, 240, 242, 257, 327n8

Russia: subnational wartime victimization, 227; violence, war outcomes and postwar elections, 272

Rwanda, ethnic war in, 233–34

Sagan, Scott, on public opinion toward use of force, 10

Salvadoran National Museum of Anthropology, 121

Sandinista National Liberation Front (FSLN): election fairness and, 198; electoral targeting of, 203–4; undermining legacy of Somoza on security, 321n59; party manifesto, 320n56; valence strategy, 201–2; positional strategy, 203; rebels and Somoza regime, 194; Sandino, Augusto and, 195; tendencies within, 321n61; valence strategy, 201–2; victory of, 199; "War of Liberation", 196; war outcome, 196

Sandinista-Somoza war, 201

Sandino, Augusto, murder of, 195

Sandoval, Mauricio, on ARENA party, 304n85

Santismo: claim to mantle of belligerent party, 103; Rule of Law, 266; Santos, Juan Manuel, 90–91; strategy of contrite Rule Abider, 91, 92, 92–94; voting determinants, 102

Santos, Juan Manuel, 90–91; de la Calle and Vargas Lleras, 296–97n67; media advantage, 299n125

Saunders, Elizabeth, on elite cues and public opinion toward use of force, 10

Savimbi, Jonas, UNITA rebel leader, 241, 242

security: ARENA undermining FMLN's ownership of valence issue, 131–35;

attribution of blame and, 280n66; belligerent-tied politicians influence public safety, 246–51; combinations of party strategy on perceived competence, 265; Democratic Republic of Congo (DRC), 286n51; FMLN owning valence issue, 136–37; governance records of paramilitary mayors, 247–48, 250–51; Guatemala's FRG vs. PAN programs, 170–72; hand coding of platforms, 266; non-paramilitary and paramilitary politicians, 248; paramilitary politician win and theft, 250; political behavior and, 9–10, 14, 255–56; in positional politics, 37–38; proportion of voters around the world, 230; as valence issue, 25–26; voting, 10–11

security voters, respondents as, 295n38

security voting, 229, 231; marginal effect of, 230; proportion of, around world, 230; World Values Survey (WVS), 229

Sikkink, Kathryn, on logic of appropriateness and justice, 7

Snyder, Jack: on belligerents accepting election results, 5; on logic of consequences and justice, 8

social desirability bias, 88

social services, effect of elections of belligerent-tied politicians on, 246–51

Somers, Margaret, on social narratives, 261

Somoza, Anastasio: dictatorship, 201; dynasty of, 195; overthrow of dictatorship, 196; Partido Liberal Nacionalista (PLN), 199; Somoza regime and Sandinista rebels, 194; sons Luis and Anastasio, 195

Somoza National Guard, 197

South Africa: subnational wartime victimization, 226, 227; violence, war outcomes and postwar elections, 272

Soviet Union, 114, 115

spatial voting models, 286n68

Sri Lanka, 272, 323n13; ethnic war, 236; Rajapaksa of, 257; subnational wartime victimization, 226, 227

Stephens, Evelyne Huber, on support for democracy, 7

Stephens, John, on support for democracy, 7

Stoll, David, 179; on Guatemala, 179, 180

strategic entry, party system, 21

strategic voting, party system, 21

subnational data: from around the world, 225–28; violence, war outcomes and voting, 13–14; war outcomes and belligerent successor party vote share, 228; wartime victimization by government and postwar government successor party, 227; wartime victimization by rebels and postwar rebel successor party, 226

subnational paramilitary war outcomes, 285n41

subnational violence, war outcomes, and elections, data sources, 271–72

subnational war outcomes, 225–28

successor parties, belligerents and atrocities, 13–14

survey experiments: assessments of security competence, 89–90; Colombia, 68–70; descriptive statistics of sample, 263–64; mitigation experiment, 70–74; narratives experiment, 74–78; Restrained Leviathan vs. Tactical Immoderate experiment, 78–88. See also Restrained Leviathan vs. Tactical Immoderate experiment

SWAPO (South West Africa People's Organisation), 236, 327n84

swing voter: concept of, 295n37; electoral targeting, 38–39; model, 287n81

Syria, Corstange's methodology of sensitive questioning and, 300n146

Tactical Immoderate, 12, 44, 47, 62; attracting votes for military loser, 63; elite and candidate selection, 43–44; losing belligerent (FARC rebels), 82; probability of being elected (rebel belligerent candidates), 87; rationale of, 42; strategy, 56, 57, 59, 60, 90; strategy of Gustavo Petro in Colombia, 91, 92, 98–99; URNG party, 183; valence and position of platform, 41–43; war-loser party, 40–44; See also Restrained Leviathan vs. Tactical Immoderate experiment

Tactical Immoderation, strategy of contrition, 97

Tamil National Alliance (TNA), 213, 236

Taylor, Charles, NPFL warlord, 241

Teigen, Jeremy M., on evaluating candidates with military backgrounds, 34

terrorism, guerrilla, 282n9

thefts: non-paramilitary and paramilitary politicians' governance record on, 248; paramilitary politician win and, 250; security outcomes, 249

Tilly, Charles, on uncommitted middle, 17

Tomz, Mike, on security and political behavior, 9

torturer problem, 8, 259

Trujillo, Rafael, Dominican Republic, 257

Trump, Donald, 329n22

Truth Commission, on wartime violence, 144, 145

Tutsi violence, Rwanda, 233–34

Ubico, Jorge, 159; Guatemala's administration, 159

UCDP. See Uppsala Conflict Data Program (UCDP)

UN Commission on the Truth, El Salvador, 116, 147

United Kingdom, 226, 227, 272

United People's Freedom Alliance, 236

United States, 114; support of National Conservative party, 195

United States Information Agency (USIA), 121

University of North Texas, 309n225

UNO: composition of, 322n97; U.S.-backed opposition party, 208–9

Uppsala Conflict Data Program (UCDP), 15; Armed Conflicts Database, 15; estimates of violence, 325n46; Conflict Encyclopedia, 212; Conflict Termination Dataset, 16, 212; definitions, 281n1; Georeferenced Event Database Global version 18.1, 225; One-Sided Violence Dataset, 324n25

Urcuyo Maliaños, Francisco, 196

Uribe, Álvaro, 90–91; investigations of, 2; Plan Colombia and, 68–69

Uribismo: claiming mantle of belligerent party, 103; Law and Order, 266; strategy of Restrained Leviathan, 94–96; Uribe, Álvaro and, 90–91; voting determinants for, 101, 102

URNG. See Guatemalan National Revolutionary Unity (URNG)

U.S. Digital National Security Archives, 121, 200

U.S. embassy cables, on electoral contests, 13

valence: definition, 284n5; leadership, 288n91; politics, 25–27; security and economic issues, 84

Valentino, Benjamin, on public opinion toward use of force, 10

Vannini, Margarita: on election fairness, 197; on Casa de Chema Castillo raid, 318n3; on Somoza National Guard reorganization, 197; on UNO, 322n97

Vargas Lleras, Germán: campaign of, 99–100; on patronage, 93; voting determinants, 102

Varieties of Democracy, 215, 217, 237, 245; electoral performance in cleaner and less clean elections, 224

Vélez, Juan Carlos, 95

Victimization, heterogenous treatment effects, 74, 75

victor's justice, 43

Vinjamuri, Leslie, on logic of consequences and justice, 8

violence: attributing blame, 284n19, 285n19; Colombia, 64; El Salvador, 116–17;

Guatemala, 160–61, 191–92; mitigation experiment, 74, 75; Nicaragua, 195–96 phenomenon of violent actors, 13; Truth Commission on wartime, 144, 145; understandings of, 88–89; violent belligerents and voters, 4–5

violent victors: governance and, 8–9; theory, 63

voter(s): coding, 295nn38–39; craving security, 4; democracy, 6–7; emerging from war, 16–18; Guatemalan, 162–63; justice, 7–8; model of reference-dependent preferences on past atrocity, 29–30; Nicaraguan, 199, 205–6; parties prioritizing swing, 38–39; party and, 11; reference point of violence-affected, 30; Salvadoran, 118, 143–48; security and political behavior, 9–10; security voting, 10–11; single-issue, 282n14; war and peace, 5–6; war influencing, 11–12; war outcome and party strategies, 45–46

Voter Turnout Database, 324n39

voting: determinants in Colombia's 2018 election, 101, 102, 103; determinants in El Salvador's 1994 election, 150; determinants in Guatemala's 1999 election, 188, 189; economic, 280–81n81; strategic, 283nn35–36

Wantchekon, Leonard, on postwar democratic elections, 7

war: assessing risk of recurrence, 243–44; cases of postconflict peace and, 244; credit for termination of, 253–54; ethnic wars, 231–37; influencing parties and voters, 11–12. See also political life after war

war and peace, elections' impact on, 5–6, 60, 241–44

war-loser party: elite and candidate selection, 43–44; rationale of tactical immoderation, 42; Tactical Immoderate, 40–44; valence and position of platform, 41–43 war outcomes: belligerent successor party vote share and, 228; continuum of, 23, 215–16; correlates of CWSP success around world and, 220; explanations and endogeneity, 270; factors influencing, 23–24; frequency in CWSP dataset, 217; government belligerent vote shares in founding elections and, 223; influencing electoral success, 22–24; rebel vote shares in founding elections and, 222; subnational data on, 225, 228, municipal-level paramilitary, 285n41

wartime victimization, subnational: government and postwar government successor party vote share, 227; rebels and post rebel successor party vote share, 226

wartime violence: credit for ceasing, 3–5; cross-national analysis, 225; variables for, 216–17

war-to-peace transition, 291n152

Washington Post (newspaper), 200

Way, Lucan, on successor party cohesion, 39

Weeks, Jessica, on security and political behavior, 9

Weinstein, Jeremy, on wartime violence, 324n27

Wood, Elisabeth Jean, 6; on democracy after war, 6; on Salvadoran elite, 154

Wood, Reed, on popular support, 218

World Politics (journal), 303n49

World Values Survey (WVS), 211; founding election dates, 273; security voting, 229

Yarhi-Milo, Keren, on security and political behavior, 9

Yashar, Deborah, on reform and homicide rates, 152, 191

Zaller, John, on political framing, 10

Zamora, Rubén: choice of, 307n177; FMLN candidate, 117, 118, 141; FMLN slogan, 140; on media, 143

Zeitzoff, Thomas, on security and political behavior, 9

A NOTE ON THE TYPE

This book has been composed in Arno, an Old-style serif typeface in the classic Venetian tradition, designed by Robert Slimbach at Adobe.

GPSR Authorized Representative: Easy Access System Europe - Mustamäe tee
50, 10621 Tallinn, Estonia, gpsr.requests@easproject.com

www.ingramcontent.com/pod-product-compliance
Lightning Source LLC
Chambersburg PA
CBHW022256280326
41932CB00010B/886